Heather Martin was born in West Australia and grew up in Aix-en-Provence, Paris and Perth. She read languages at Cambridge, where she also did a PhD in Comparative Literature, and has held teaching and research positions at Cambridge, Hull, King's College London, and most recently, the Graduate Center, City University, New York. She now lives in London.

The Reacher Guy

The Authorised Biography of Lee Child

Heather Martin

CONSTABLE

CONSTABLE

First published in Great Britain in 2020 by Constable
This paperback edition published in Great Britain in 2021 by Constable

A CIP catalogue record for this book is available from the British Library.

ISBN: 978-1-47213-423-3

Typeset in Bembo Std by SX Composing DTP, Rayleigh, Essex
Printed and bound in Great Britain by Clays Ltd, Elcograf S.p.A.

Papers used by Constable are from well-managed forests
and other responsible sources.

Constable
An imprint of
Little, Brown Book Group
Carmelite House
50 Victoria Embankment
London EC4Y 0DZ

An Hachette UK Company
www.hachette.co.uk

www.littlebrown.co.uk

For Rosemary, my mother
In memory of Pat Parslew and Paul Glover

Contents

So as always he just told the story and answered the awkward questions and let her think whatever she wanted.

Lee Child, *Echo Burning*, 2001

1

The Library

His whole life was a visit.
The Midnight Line, 2017

He passed it every time they went to the library on Boroughgate, which during the holidays when he was dumped with his grandparents in Otley was about once a week. It was his grandmother who took him there first. She was a great reader, he told me. 'She only had about nine books, but she used the library, as was typical.'

She held his hand as they turned left out of the house and walked downhill past the biscuit factory and the tannery towards Kirkgate, a continuation of Queens Terrace and Station Road across busy Burras Lane. When he was older he ran ahead with his brothers, the middle one of three in those days, impatient to duck on to the cobbled lane to press his face up against the cast-iron railings of the churchyard. His parents had been married there in All Saints Parish Church, built in Norman times on Anglo-Saxon foundations, on 5 March 1949.

Later he would become famous for being tall. Other things too, but being tall was a big part of it. Tall and fair-haired and blue-eyed. Hair that was dirty blond. Eyes that could blink and come back different, like changing the channel, from a happy show to some bleak documentary about prehistorical survival a million years ago. Even back then he had a reputation – everyone could see he was bigger and stronger than his brothers. But he was only a child, and big as he was, the object of his attention – at six feet – towered over him. Literally, since it had four diagonally symmetrical towers, one on each corner, castellated and crenellated and embattled, connected by parapets and surrounded by eroded headstones buried deep in the emerald grass, like something out of a picture-book edition of *King Arthur* or *Robin Hood* or the *Canterbury Tales*. It was the kind of thing a boy might dream of having in his back garden, if he had a back garden, rather than a paved yard just big enough to string a washing line from one side fence to the other.

He hardly needed to go to the library. There were stories right there on his path, and all sorts of questions to be answered. Life was full of suspense.

Did he wonder what 'burras' meant, or whether the Queen had once visited the terrace that was named for her? Did he know about the Vikings who had been there before him, who said 'kirk' and 'gate' instead of 'church' and 'street'? He was never a trainspotter, nor a stamp collector, but had he always collected words?

Certainly by then he could read. He'd taught himself, eager to catch up with his older brother who was two years ahead of him and already at school, so had eavesdropped jealously on his mother as she helped her firstborn learn his letters and later practised by reading the back of his father's newspaper at the breakfast table. The first whole sentence he decoded was: 'Manchester closes down.' He'd taught himself to write, too. His signature touch was to add extra crossbars to the uppercase 'E' so it looked like a millipede bisected lengthwise. It wasn't vanity. He just thought the number was optional. It wasn't as though it was maths.

With a little effort, he would have been able to decipher the words carved in slate on the south side of this graveyard gothic monument:

IN MEMORY
OF THE UNFORTUNATE MEN
WHO LOST THEIR LIVES WHILE ENGAGED
IN THE CONSTRUCTION OF THE
BRAMHOPE TUNNEL OF
THE LEEDS AND THIRSK RAILWAY
FROM 1845 TO 1849.
THIS TOMB IS ERECTED AS A MEMORIAL
AT THE EXPENSE OF JAMES BRAY ESQ.,
THE CONTRACTOR, AND OF THE
AGENTS, SUB-CONTRACTORS
AND WORKMEN EMPLOYED THEREON.

It had come as a shock. To discover that the fairy-tale castle was a scaled-down replica of a railway tunnel, and was actually a tomb. Where dead people lived. If that wasn't a contradiction. A grisly place, inhabited by ghosts. Not that he was scared or anything. He wasn't the type to be scared.

But who were these *unfortunate men* and how had they lost their lives? Was it all at once, as the result of a single spectacular catastrophe, or one by one, at the hands of some sinister evil force? Was this the very same line that ran past the top of his grandparents' road, where he and his brothers would go to play, hanging out in the dank underpass and listening to the deafening roar of the steam trains or watching them thunder by like fire-breathing dragons from the footbridge overhead?

Then beneath this factual introduction and harder to read, in a cursive font rather than block capitals:

> I am a Stranger and a Sojourner with you: give me a possession of a Burying-Place with you, that I may bury my Dead out of my sight.

> [Genesis 23:4] Or those Eighteen upon whom the Tower in Siloam fell and slew them: think ye that they were sinners above all the men in Jerusalem? I tell you, Nay: but except ye repent, ye shall all likewise perish. [Luke 13:4]

This raised a whole new set of questions. Who was this mysterious Stranger newly arrived in town, and what was a Sojourner, and who was it that he needed to bury, and why was he so appealing? Had the unnamed Eighteen been building the tower when it fell and slew them, and was this how the railway workers too had died? Was Siloam connected to Bramhope? Where did sin come into it, and what was sin anyway, and was that the promise of retribution in the final resounding phrase, and if so who was going to deliver it and make right all the wrongs?

He would have to wait for the answers but he was hardwired to want to know. Maybe he would find out at the library. If he ever got there. There was so much to see on the way.

No doubt it was here his love of history was born. There was an intimation of fate in the coincidental connections between these everyday heroes of the Industrial Revolution and this early Christian church and his parents and the railway, leading out of town over the Wharfedale Viaduct to Harrogate and Leeds and the Wild West and beyond. The record-breaking tunnel, the longest on the historic North Eastern Railway system, was an architectural folly whose form (he felt inexplicably betrayed by this) belied its function. It was rumoured to have been made longer than necessary for the amenity of landowner William Rhodes, who conceived of the tallest tower on its north portal as a belvedere that would afford him a view of his expansive estate.

Some of this history was documented on the churchyard railings:

> The greatest challenge was to cut the Bramhope Tunnel 25ft high through 2 miles 243 yards of rock at depths of up to 290ft. Some

> 2,300 men and 400 horses were involved in this work, all being
> subject to sudden rock falls, subsidence, flooding and accidental death.

Even as a boy he would have lingered over the phrase *accidental death* and its self-absolving abnegation of responsibility, and intuited that vengeance was called for.

It would have bothered him that the Bramhope Memorial lists the names of twenty-three casualties, whereas other sources cite twenty-four. He had a thing about numbers and liked them to be exact, for their own sake. Numbers were either right or wrong. But this time there were lives at stake. If one man had been missed, then how many more? Twenty-three was a neat percentage of 2300 and therefore compelling, but what if it was fiction, what if it was wrong?

Years later, in 2017, when I went to see Lee speak at the Old Peculier Crime Festival in Harrogate, I told him of my plan to take a bus to Otley for the day.

'Make sure you visit the library,' he said. 'I read a lot of books there.'

So I did. While he was being fêted by fans and fawned over by billionaire sponsors, I sat and read *This Little Town of Otley*, spanning the mid-nineteenth century to the Second World War. Harold Walker, the author, was a retired printer who as a boy would happily forgo an iced bun to save the penny it cost to buy the latest 'blood and thunder' (the adventures of Buffalo Bill or Sexton Blake, detective). Otley was a market town that traded in stories.

> I have always been fascinated by the Friday Market, and the various
> characters who attended. I well remember such wags as 'Pot Bob'
> Morrison from Knaresborough, who could juggle with half a dozen
> dinner plates better than many a music hall artiste, and whose quick
> repartee always kept the crowds amused; Harry Sharp, the 'Oilcloth

King', from Bradford; and 'Cudball' Cooper, the cattle 'doctor' from Yeadon. There were vendors of patent medicines that were claimed to cure all ills, from corns to stones in the kidney, and whose rheumatism pills, if taken regularly, would land sufferers halfway up the centre of Chevin, before they even knew they had started; also 'Eye Lickers' who, for free, licked incipient cataracts from the eyes of anyone so afflicted, were frequent visitors and always drew a crowd of sightseers.

It sounded like the Macondo of *One Hundred Years of Solitude* – the heavy gypsy with the untamed beard and sparrow hands who so flamboyantly exhibited the magnet and magnifying glass in a clearing in the Colombian jungle would not have been out of place in this West Yorkshire plaza. In a contest between the magic of ice and the miracle of the Eye Lickers it wasn't clear who would win. But like Aureliano Buendía, the boy who would one day become Lee Child had breathed in stories like he breathed in air, or maybe – since the area was famed for its spa towns – it was something in the water. It was as though the storytelling gene had been passed directly to him, across the oceans and down through the ages.

The library was an airy structure of brick and glass, with data sockets and charging points embedded in the carpeted floor. I went back to the desk and asked if they had any pictures of how it used to be in the 1950s. Oh, said the librarian, who had grown up in a house on Station Road, facing Queens Terrace, it was on a different site then. She pointed me in the direction of Boroughgate. No. 4 was now a hardware store with a brash blue frontage and a colourful assortment of brooms and buckets arrayed on the pavement outside. The owners sent me out the back to take photographs, explaining that the library had encompassed both floors of a terraced house of the same soot-blackened sandstone as Queens Terrace, but older and more austere, without the assertive extravagance of the bay window. It must have felt like reading in the comfort of home, the dimensions so much more intimate and grandmotherly than the upgraded institutional splendour of its modern-day replacement.

By this point Lee had lived in (North) America for twenty years. He lamented the disappearance of libraries and feared the demise of bookshops, and stockpiled books against a rainy day like others hoarded cans of beans. (He hoarded those as well, along with tins of sardines and chicken noodle soup.) On two occasions I saw him leave a bookstore not with a bag but a cardboard box. I didn't offer to carry it for him, but once I opened the door of the cab and then stood on the 42nd Street sidewalk and watched as he sped away from the Grand Hyatt towards Central Park.

There were upwards of four thousand books in his Manhattan apartment alone. I'm not sure they included a bible (he'd read the major religious texts at school, and never again since). But if in pensive scholarly mood he had been moved to consult a gloss of Genesis 23:4 it might have felt weirdly like looking in a mirror.

I am a Stranger and a Sojourner, he might have read aloud to himself: 'one living out of his own country, dwelling in a land in which he is not naturalised; one whose origin is foreign, and whose period of residence is uncertain'.

2

The Wharfedale

He was multiplying big numbers in his head.
Die Trying, 1998

In 2016, the undisputed king of thriller writers, courted by the establish-ment and giving lectures at Oxford and Cambridge (which had rejected him forty years before), Lee would argue that storytelling was vital to our survival. The ability to make things up helped us outwit our enemies and inspired us with the courage to stand up to them. He made a persuasive intellectual case for the human importance of his chosen profession.

But however good the stories, man shall not live by words alone. Even Lee Child needs unlimited coffee and a bowl of sugar snaps, and was once (that time was vivid in his memory) motivated by the need to put food on the table. Yet for approximately one hundred years the little town of Otley came close. Perhaps they'd caught sight of the future in a crystal ball, or it was down to enterprise and ingenuity, but somehow the town's joiners and metalworkers seemed to sense what was coming.

Otley had always traded in cattle, even before this was sanctioned by Henry III in 1222, and was deemed by Walker to be 'excellently supplied with the common necessaries of life', among them some very tall tales. But it was only towards the end of the Industrial Revolution, with the tanning trade in decline, that the town made its indelible mark on the world.

The fifteenth-century invention of the Gutenberg Press was a turning point in history, heralding the advent of the Modern Age and the founding of the global village. By enabling mechanical reproduction of the Bible it led directly to the Reformation and the proliferation of Protestantism. The next significant advance in print technology, according to historian Paul Wood (*Otley and the Wharfedale Printing Machine*), was 'conceived in an 1830s joiner's shop of a small Yorkshire market town with a population of only 3,000 souls'.

The man credited with the cast-iron, steam-powered Wharfedale Press is machine-maker David Payne, recruited by cabinetmaker and founding father of the industry William Dawson to develop a flat-bed printing press. Payne was a visionary and a dreamer, a true son of Otley. He had previously devised a machine to drain land, which he demonstrated to one of the village farmers. The farmer was so astonished, writes Walker, that he swore young Payne 'was in league with the Devil, otherwise he could not have made a contraption like that!'

If the Gutenberg Press was responsible for the democratisation of knowledge, it is the nostalgically named Wharfedale (as local lore has it; there are rival claims) – harking back to the pastoral and hinting at the oral tradition – that we have to thank for the rise of modern publishing, the handing down of the story of the Eye Lickers, and the all-conquering dominance of the bestseller.

By definition the bestseller is about statistics. Lee's trajectory is ablaze with them, each eclipsing the last. 'In its first six days on sale in the UK,' said Transworld's Larry Finlay in November 2016, celebrating Reacher's twenty-first outing at the Haymarket Hotel in Piccadilly, '*Night School* sold one copy every ten seconds, *that's one copy every ten seconds*, six copies every minute, three hundred and thirty-three every hour or eighteen thousand copies a day, that's over forty-eight thousand copies in six days.' (Its closest competitors that week had managed fifty thousand in the entire year.) He rounded off this Reacheresque riff on big numbers with a heavily italicised prediction sublime in its confidence: 'It *will* be the *biggest-selling* adult hardback novel of 2016, *bar none.*' (And so it was.) All that was missing was a hat-tip to the Wharfedale, which by allowing continuous sheet printing and multi-plying the output of the Gutenberg tenfold (from two hundred to two thousand pages per hour), set the whole euphoric process in train.

'The sun never sets on Reacher,' said agent Darley Anderson in 2013, blithely deploying the rhetoric of imperialism when *Killing Floor* was published in Mongolia. It was a delicate moral balancing act for Lee, wanting to annihilate the opposition statistically speaking, wanting to crush them underfoot as he once put it, to hold rock steady at no. 1 without sacrificing the principles that made him who he was. He was a juggernaut, but a juggernaut with a conscience. And it could be argued – he'd done so cogently – that like William Dawson, by generating a profitable market for the industry he was keeping a community afloat.

Everywhere in Otley I saw connections with Lee. But strictly speak-ing he'd never been there. 'Yorkshire's my place,' I heard him say to a television interviewer in Harrogate. But that wasn't Lee Child speaking. His place was New York. Otley belonged to James D. Grant, middle name Dover, after his maternal grandfather. Commonly known as Jim.

Jim's parents had met and married in Otley, but not so his grand-parents. Harry Dover Scrafton and Audrey Leider Scott were natives of South Shields in County Durham (now Tyne and Wear), where Jim's mother was born in 1926. Harry had trained as a naval draughtsman and landed his dream job in a shipyard weeks before the Wall Street Crash. He was 'the only real human among my immediate ancestors', Lee wrote to me. 'Drank a little, gambled a little, smoked a lot.' That was what had first attracted him to smoking, the smell he remembered from the time and place he felt most loved as a child. He wasn't put off by an anecdote recounted by his grandmother, an early memory from before the First World War, when an enlightened health worker had visited her school, stood on the stage, whipped out a cigarette and lit it, holding a pristine white handkerchief in front of the burning tip. Brandishing the stained cloth before the chastened assembly of young girls, with an informed diligence ahead of his time, he had warned of the devastation they would wreak upon their lungs should they succumb to this self-destructive habit. Audrey didn't smoke. But Otley had been active in the manufacture of tobacco.

Harry Dover Scrafton was bowed but not broken when faced with redundancy from the bankrupt shipyard in 1932. He was offered a job in the Post Office Telephones drawing office on the understanding that there wasn't a vacancy and he would have to wait, while digging ditches. The digging dragged on for five years. He moved to Otley in 1938 when the opening finally came up, producing a small telecoms mast in the 1950s before becoming a teacher at the Post Office design school in the suburb of Kineholme, where he remained until retirement in 1965. The young Audrey Grant, Jim's mother, was bitter about being yanked out of her South Shields high school and sent to an inferior school in Otley. She never got over it.

Lee's methodology is distinctively organic: he feels, as much as thinks, his books into being. Like a glassblower or metalworker he has to get it right first time while the material is still hot. Yet his pragmatic approach to getting the job done is supremely mechanical. He starts each new book on 1 September *without fail*, and prides himself on delivering a reliable product in good working order precisely on schedule. 'They know I'll deliver,' he said, referring to both publishers and readers; 'I'm always on time' (a punctuality that carried over into his personal life too). 'I'm never late.' It wasn't just timing but content too. The people demand Reacher books and, like clockwork, that's what he gives them: Lee is to book production what the Wharfedale was to continuous sheet printing, a magisterial machine spitting out bestsellers like the press spat out pages.

Even his terms of praise, his images of beauty, draw on the metaphoric radiance of the machine. Something that marries form to function and does the job it's intended to do as well as it can be done. *Something that works.* Which renders the axiomatic adverb 'well' entirely superfluous. This example is from 2013 novella *High Heat*:

> At nearly seventeen Reacher was like a brand new machine, still gleaming and dewy with oil, flexible, supple, perfectly coordinated, like something developed by NASA and IBM on behalf of the Pentagon.

He emphasises the importance of the 'narrative engine', aspires to a 'propulsive prose', and if you're lucky he'll describe your writing as 'solid'.

Lee had more in common with Harry Scrafton than his middle name and a taste for tobacco. Both had been laid off due to 'economic restructuring' and forced to start afresh. We were sitting in the lobby of New York's Grand Hyatt in July 2017 taking a breather from the annual jamboree that is ThrillerFest when out of nowhere he said, looking down at his manicured hands, 'I keep my fingernails long to show I've got out of manual labour.' Not for him a five-year sentence with a spade. In conquering the New World through the well-oiled machine of his literary avatar, James Dover Grant was avenging the misfortune inflicted on his beloved maternal grandfather, doing battle on his behalf with the soulless spectre of Wall Street.

Traces endure in the handwritten first draft of *Killing Floor*, donated in 2018 to the British Archive for Contemporary Writing at the University of East Anglia in Norwich. 'I remember at the time hearing about this crash on Wall Street that took away all the folks' money,' muses the old barber in chapter nine. But this detail has been erased from the published version, along with the barber's misreading of the event as a train crash.

Paul Wood estimates that the Wharfedale had a functional lifetime of a hundred years. The same was true of the Otley railway, a casualty of the Beeching Cuts in 1965. Lee would accept the round hundred when it came to longevity. He didn't expect or even want to be remembered. So many others had been forgotten – why should he be any different? For a while in Kirkby Lonsdale his mortgage had been so catastrophically large that the only books he could afford were from the 10p section of the used bookstore: 1950s books, popular in their day and widely distributed through book clubs – 'all obscure, all forgotten now, all great'. He doubted his books would attain the status of enduring classics, once the massive machinery of publicity had ground to a halt. Success was fleeting. 'Mickey Spillane was gigantic, but who reads him now?' He was content to be absorbed in the spirit of literature.

Yet there was no denying he *worked*, as a writer, in both senses of the verb.

Through the rise and fall of empire the transcendent natural beauty of Otley remained surprisingly intact. In the early eighteenth century the landscape inspired J. M. W. Turner, whose patron Walter Fawkes (a descendant of his seditious namesake) lived across the valley from the Chevin, a mountainous ridge that stands sentinel over the town.

A much photographed view of the Chevin looks south up the gentle incline of Station Road, favouring the stone houses of Queens Terrace on the right, with the distant white dot of Jenny's Cottage (named for the shepherd's wife who fed and watered visitors) glinting against the rising green backdrop. No. 29, where Jim's grandparents lived, is one of the last houses in the row, on the last street before the railway line, and Jim and his brothers would frequently cut across Birdcage Walk, over or under the track (now the Leeds bypass), to climb up the hill. 'It was an easy climb,' Lee said, 'for a boy.' He didn't mention the Roman Road along the top, only the spectacular Frying-pan Rock and a massive bomb crater.

Sometimes on their way down the brothers would linger by the end house on the terrace, where the neighbour kept chickens in her fenced-off garden: forty-nine of them, not a single chicken more, since if you had fifty they were requisitioned for rations.

Jim's grandparents moved to West Busk Lane after Harry retired. It was a simple end-of-terrace house on the edge of town with sweeping views of the valley beyond. Jim went back to Otley in 1994 to bury his grandmother – Harry had died a decade earlier. So she never knew Lee Child then, I said, when he told me this, and he said no, which was sad, because she would have been 'very happy about it'.

He'd inherited three of her books. It wasn't until two years after my visit that I discovered one of these was *This Little Town of Otley*. The second was *A Century of Thrillers: From Poe to Arlen*, with a foreword by James Agate; the name SCRAFTON was written in pencil on the first page and the pen and ink frontispiece showed 'the foul fiend, in his ain shape, sitting on the laird's coffin'. The third was his own mother's *Collected Shakespeare* from her schooldays.

David Payne died in 1888. His headstone reads: 'Inventor of the Wharfedale Machine'. But it fell to Paul Wood a century later to write the epitaph for 'the simple mechanical device which had sustained a community for so long'. 'What better than to print Dawson, Payne & Elliott's own description at the end: "The Wharfedale; Simplicity, durability and long life."'

Reacher fans might feel their hero is better encapsulated by the more lyrical promotional eulogy afforded the '*Patented Improved* Wharfedale Printing Machine':

> Unequalled for Strength and Efficiency, Simplicity, Finish and Durability.

3

A Tale of Three Grandfathers

Reacher remembered his grandfather pretty well.
Second Son, 2011

There is a black-and-white photograph of the infant James Grant sitting on a wooden bench between his two grandfathers. Lee isn't sure where it was taken. He's around two years old, but it wasn't Coventry: 'the brickwork looks wrong' (he'd once read a book about geometric patterns in medieval English brickwork). The backdrop is a plain brick wall, like something drawn by the painstaking hand of a child, without a single straight line. It must have been a special occasion to bring both sides of the family together, for Audrey to dress her second son so prettily in soft, white Peter Pan collar and pristine white ankle socks in the manner of a cosseted prince. A christening? But no: 'None of us was christened or baptised – we're all heathens in that regard.' Maybe that's how all middle-class mothers dressed their boys, back in the day.

'I remember stories about a joint vacation on the east coast of Yorkshire,' Lee wrote.

His hair is combed in the same style as today, flopping to one side over his forehead, but his legs are chubby and too short to reach the ground.

From what he's told me it's easy to guess which grandfather is which. On the left Harry Scrafton exudes warmth, his thick hair brushed in glossy waves. He is dapper, in dark-framed spectacles, a lightweight, light-coloured suit with wide lapels and turn-ups, and a monochrome tie featuring a jolly geometric pattern. He is upright and alert, eyes to the camera, body turned protectively towards his grandson. He is holding the little boy's right hand in his own, resting lightly in his lap, perhaps encouraging him to sit still. James is solemn. On the right is John Grant. Even seated he is an imposing man, straight hair swept severely back off his brow, wearing a sweater and tie under his suit and a complex expression: the beginnings of a smile cut short by a frown or grimace, as though he were looking into the sun. On the bench is an old bellows camera of the type that folds flat when not in use. There are two pens smartly aligned in his breast pocket, clips facing outwards with regulation precision. His long pen-like legs are stiff and angled oddly to the side. His left leg, furthest from James, looks thinner and stiffer and straighter than the other.

If he looks ill at ease, it's because he was. He'd spent twenty years of his life in pain. Then things got better. The next twenty years had been merely uncomfortable.

James felt safe with Grandma and Grandad Scrafton. He liked that they were 'exclusively ours' and thought it weird that his Granpop (John) and Granny (Winnie) could be grandparents to two separate sets of children. But the earliest memory he can pinpoint takes him back to Northern Ireland.

It was 28 October 1957. His first time in an airplane. The day before his third birthday, when it was still free for him to fly. They were going to Belfast to visit John and Winnie, who lived in Cherryvalley at 13 Kingsway Avenue. The surplus DC-3 aircraft took off from Elmdon airport in Birmingham. It wasn't pressurised so flew at low altitude, but 'travelling on a warplane felt like heaven'. Plus he got boiled sweets on a silver platter when they were still scarce (even more so in the sober Grant household). James was paralysed with joy. *All this, and free sweets too?* It was a taste of the high life he would never forget.

Sixty years and countless airplanes later (peaking at seventy in 2006 alone), over lunch on East 22nd Street near his old place opposite the Flatiron, he would tell me how ironic it was that the richer he became the less often he had to pay for things. Tickets for the new Broadway hit *Hamilton* were almost impossible to come by and theatregoers were shelling out $2000 a pop for the privilege. Lee had been the night before; it hadn't cost him a cent. That very day, during a meeting to discuss a deal with iTunes, Apple had pressed a gleaming new-issue iPhone into his hands because they were mock-horrified by the obsolescence of his old one (considerably newer than mine). 'It's good to be king,' he smiled, polishing off the last of his croque-monsieur and looking around for the white-jacketed stewards and sweets.

The Grants had a double-fronted detached house with a door in the middle at the top of a rise, across the Gilnahirk Road from the more salubrious Cherryvalley Park and with a view of the surrounding hills. The approach took you over a modest stretch of the River Lagan that runs from Slieve Croob in County Down to the Irish Sea, and past a red-brick mansion called Elsinore. There was a row of low-rise single-storey shops with a cracked tarmac forecourt that appeared to have changed little since the 1950s. A butcher, a barber, a pharmacy, a greengrocer, a dry cleaner: the only adornments a bright red pillar box and a pocked and rusted cast-iron bollard dated 1918 marking the 'parliamentary and municipal boundary of Belfast'. Kingsway Avenue was the next turn on the left, after the petrol station on the corner.

John (*No Middle Name*) Grant was born in 1890 in segregated East Belfast, 'a puritanical self-denying Northern Irish Protestant', the seventh and youngest child of Sam and Jane Grant, whose eldest son was the first (known) James Grant, Lee's namesake. There were three further sons, all of whom emigrated to Canada. All three volunteered in the First World War and all three died at Ypres. Little is known of their two sisters.

Sam, Lee's great-grandfather, was a miller. He was able to recognise and sign his own name but could otherwise neither read nor write. Jane could read, but had little chance to do so. Her job was to separate the grain from the chaff. She needed the chaff to feed the hens. She needed the hens to feed her seven children, and any surplus eggs she sold to raise money, if not for books then at least for book learning. Eventually she saved enough to send her youngest son to school. Thus John Grant, Lee's grandfather, became the first in his family to receive a formal education.

I like to think of this strong, determined, literate woman as a pioneer, beating a metaphorical path to the library for her future great-grandson.

When the United Kingdom declared war against Germany on 4 August 1914, John was twenty-four years old. His schooling had won him a white-collar job with the Irish railroad company but he was ready to fight. There was no conscription. It was before partition. The situation was politically sensitive. John volunteered, as Lee himself would have done in similar historical circumstances. But 'like the ANZACs, the Irish were not entirely trusted' and were trained 'indefinitely'. Then one day John was sent to Gallipoli.

Lee knew I was Australian. 'I know Gallipoli is central to the Australian origin myth,' he observed dispassionately, 'but data-wise the casualty rate was one-tenth that of the Western Front.' Gallipoli was a 'clusterfuck' (a word he used mostly to describe his own schedule), but the Western Front was 'quantitatively worse – the numbers don't lie'.

Corporal John Grant landed at Suvla Bay as part of the 10th (Irish) Division of Kitchener's New Army. But the enemy held the high ground. The bay had strong natural defences. John didn't make it across the four miles of graveyard to the firing line. He didn't even make it across the exposed coastal plain and the dried-up salt lake to the knee-high prickly underbrush beyond. He barely had time to discern the puffs of smoke on the hills. Some time on the night of 6 August 1915 he stepped out of a dinghy into the surf and within seconds was machine-gunned in the leg. His war was over. He was triaged on the beach, but his wound was assumed to be fatal. He was left lying where he'd been treated. He wasn't alone. But forty-eight hours later, when the burial parties came out, John was one of the few to be found still alive. He was a hard guy to kill.

From Gallipoli he was evacuated to a hospital in Manchester with the other legless wounded. They were taught to sew. Their first job was to darn the bullet holes in their own uniforms so these could be redistributed to active troops. They were still serving soldiers. There was no room for self-pity.

A year later John Grant was discharged on medical grounds. The abscess on his stump had failed to heal. It went on failing to heal for another twenty years. From 1915 through to 1935 he changed his own dressings, daily.

He didn't complain about it. Literally millions of men were in the same situation. He wasn't – and didn't consider himself to be – in any way exceptional. It wasn't a thing you could complain about.

John was a big man, at least six foot, and in his youth had been strong, too. By the time he became a grandfather he was hunched with pain and physically distorted. He was given an articulated wooden leg as a government benefit but as he became less mobile and grew heavier the leg kept breaking at the joint. Finally he threw it away in disgust and made his own replacement out of a solid table leg, with no fragile joint to let him down, and then 'he would stump around on that'. It was the kind of thing a child would notice.

When asked to name his favourite of his own fictional villains at the New York launch of Reacher no. 22 in November 2017, Lee cited Hook Hobie from *Tripwire*, published in 1999. This came as no surprise to his readers; they tended to agree. What did surprise them was that in writing this character he was thinking of his own grandfather.

'My grandfather wasn't quite that bad,' he said. But like John Grant, Hook Hobie was forced to deal with that clumsy prosthetic twice a day every day for the rest of his life. Which made him 'sad and pathetic', yet was also 'his humanity, his redeeming feature'. There the resemblance ended, for while the cartoonish hook hand is the objective correlative of evil, the wooden leg was an accident of fate. 'My grandfather had to live sixty-two years with that disability,' Lee said. 'We care at the time, but we soon forget.'

The grandson never forgot. The forbidding patriarchal figure who loomed so large in his childhood was never far from his mind. Two of his novels are dedicated to soldiers and *The Midnight Line* illuminates the harsh realities of extreme disfigurement to such devastating effect that *New York Times* critic Janet Maslin summed it up as 'the one that breaks your heart'. In 2011's novella *Second Son* (an explicitly autobiographical title) Lee recycles the elements of John Grant's story, filtered through the heightened sensibility of thirteen-year-old Jack. Like John, Laurent Moutier 'volunteered immediately'. On returning to Paris 'with a chestful of medals and no scars longer than his middle finger, which was statistically the same thing as completely unscathed', he finds that his furniture-repair business has been commandeered to make wooden legs for 'an army of cripples'. Which he does, 'out of parts of tables bought up cheap from bankrupt restaurants'. 'It was entirely possible that there were veterans in Paris stumping around on the same furniture they had once dined off.'

Was this what James once imagined to have happened? Did he wonder if the hungry Grant family had come home one day to the house on Kingsway Avenue to find a three-legged table listing in the kitchen like some kind of Allied vessel that had taken a life-threatening hit?

Harry Scrafton was twelve years younger than John Grant, and died younger too (John went on stomping around until the grand old age of eighty-eight). His was a shorter life, but a sweeter one. He smoked. He didn't have to contend with a recalcitrant table leg, he wasn't haunted by the grim failure of Gallipoli, the sounds and smells of Suvla Bay weren't seared and scorched on his brain. It was always going to be easier for a little boy to snuggle up to the grandfather with two good legs and a twinkle in his eye, with his cosy, tobacco-warmed clothes, and it's no coincidence that Harry was seated on his right on that sunlit bench and John on his left, ever so slightly separate, no more than a couple of millimetres if you were to measure it with a ruler, but far enough that he might as well be sitting on his own.

That barely converted DC-3 warplane was more than Lee's earliest date-stamped memory. It was the cornerstone of his personal origin myth, and a symbol of the most startling change from his generation to the next. 'For us, the war was still so present and coloured every aspect of life. For them it means nothing. It's entirely absent.' I knew he was thinking then, like the stoic Moutier on his deathbed, of his own 'beautiful mop-haired' daughter.

In 2014, on the one-hundredth anniversary of the declaration of war, Lee contributed to the online project 'Letter to an Unknown Soldier', inspired by the statue of a soldier reading a letter that stands on Platform 1 of London's Paddington Station (just along from Paddington Bear). Lee's letter was one of 21,439. This is what he wrote:

> You don't know me yet, but I have things to tell you. You're about to go back, and I'm sorry to say it's going to be worse than ever this time. You're going to be wounded, I'm afraid. Very badly. But

you'll survive. You'll make it home. You have to, you see. Forty years from now you'll become my grandfather.

Not that home will be a bed of roses. Wages will be down, and three men will fight for every job. At times you'll be cold, and at times you'll be hungry. And if you say anything, they'll come at you with truncheons.

And then it will get worse. There are some lean years coming. And I'm sorry, but along the way you'll realise: the war didn't end. It was just a lull. You'll have to do it all again. This time your son will have to go, not you. You don't know him yet, but you will. But don't worry. He'll get back too. He has to. You're my grandfather, remember?

And I'll be born in a different world. There will be jobs for everyone. They'll be building houses. You'll go to the doctor whenever you want. I'll go to school. I'll get free orange juice. You'll get free walking sticks. But most of all we'll get peace. Finally, year after year. I will never go to war, you know. I will never have to. The first time I go to France will be a trip with my school.

So go back now, and play your tiny part in the great drama, and sustain yourself by knowing: it comes out well in the end. I promise.

Lee Child

His autobiography in 277 words.

Where there was pathos, humour was never far behind. John and Winnie Grant had an old Ford Anglia, like the Harry Potter car. John removed the front passenger seat and sat in the back with his wooden leg stretched out. Winnie drove, but she was a small woman and her legs couldn't reach the pedals. So her husband added a couple of wooden blocks, no doubt chopping up some redundant item of furniture to achieve his ever-practical end. They were an eccentric pair and made a funny sight driving around Cherryvalley.

When asked by the *New Statesman* in June 2017 for the best piece of advice he'd ever received, Lee said: 'My Irish granddad used to say: *Spend your money before it runs out.* I'm sure he was joking, but it's advice I have followed.'

Over the years there would be many more photographs of similar composition: Lee at the centre of a triad, dressed in black rather than white, no Peter Pan collar and no laces in his shoes, framed by a couple of adoring fans. But so far as I know there are none, apart from this, where he is the shortest of the three and his legs don't reach the ground.

4

Coventry

I didn't foresee any major difficulties.
Killing Floor, 1997

James Dover Grant was born in Coventry on 29 October 1954. But he doesn't self-identify as a Coventrian, however strenuously the city might claim him as one of its own.

'I'm from Birmingham,' he'd say, with the regularity of a stock refrain in an ancient epic.

Still, it was where his education began.

'I had gone through a lot of unpleasant education,' Reacher says in *Killing Floor*. 'Not just in the army. Stretching right back into childhood.'

When I asked what he remembered about Coventry, Lee told me a story.

He was outside in the street with his older brother Richard. Which was where they usually were, as kids. Which was normal, since their parents always did what was normal, since normal was all they cared about. The boys were completely untended. They would have breakfast, leave the house, find some bombsite to play on and maybe unearth an old gun or a grenade or two, and not come back till nightfall. 'This from the time I could walk.'

That unfettered freedom to go where he wanted when he wanted, the obverse of a 1950s brand of neglect, was something he had never forgotten.

On this particular day Nicky from the next street was tormenting Richard. Which was also normal. Richard was no lionheart. He was a dork, a geek, extremely bright, weedy, reedy, a little skinny guy with sticky-out ears who rejected food, a nuclear scientist from the moment he popped out of the womb. Nicky was calling him names. 'Say that again,' says Richard, aged five, 'and I'll smash you.' Which made his younger brother, a three-year-old Goliath placidly minding his own business on the sidelines, perk up and take notice. *Good*, James thought. Because he knew what would happen next. Sure as night follows day. Spoiling for a fight and true to the bully's code, Nicky said it again. Upon which Richard turned around and said imperiously: 'James, go smash Nicky.'

In those days, everyone called him James.

I had seen one photograph of the two boys with their parents. It was taken at the old Belfast mill where Sam and Jane Grant had once laboured, and on the reverse John Grant had written in a shaky hand, 'Apr 57, Jas, 2 1/2'. You could make out a grainy building, an overgrown dry-stone wall and the still powerful-looking wooden mill wheel. Audrey, on the left, is wearing a beret, set jauntily on her short brown curls. Front and centre is four-year-old Richard in a shirt and tie and belted overcoat and cap, with an alarmed expression, exactly as Lee had described him.

Lee had the long fingers of a musician, like he could cover a lot of keys on the piano. His hands weren't as big as they looked in photographs, where against that stark inky backdrop of black T-shirt, black jacket and black jeans they drew the eye like a full moon in a starless night sky, but they were strong; those carefully manicured fingernails too, which grew so fast, especially on the index finger: he had to trim that one every day so he could carry on typing with it, and it doubled as a screwdriver when the need arose. His father told a story of how the young James, sitting on his lap, had once turned in a random movement and hit him in the mouth with his fist: 'it was like being hit with a half-brick'. Another time, now an adult, Lee had been in a mountaineering shop and tested out a pair of hand-strengtheners displayed on the counter: he closed them instantly, something that should have taken months of rigorous training. He couldn't understand the mentality of free-form climbers. 'If I wanted to be at the top of a mountain I'd rent a helicopter.' But he always won at the game of human handcuffs (which so far as I know he only ever played with his daughter Ruth).

'I have unbelievably strong hands,' Lee said.

It was a grey day when I first visited Coventry, catching an early train out of Euston. The long walk south from the station into thoroughly middle-class Stivichall took me past the landscaped gardens and spreading cedar trees of War Memorial Park, opened in name of the 2587 citizens lost in the First World War and studded with barrage balloons and anti-aircraft guns during the Second, past the Open Arms Public House and the Church of St James. It was April, and impossibly unblemished pom-poms of pink and white cherry blossom made up for the lack of sun. At the end of Ridgeway Avenue was another place of worship, the United Reformed Church, opposite a row of sleepy shops: an Indian takeaway, then a butcher, pharmacy, post office, beauty salon and convenience store. Much like Cherryvalley.

No. 20, on an upward-sloping bend, looked neglected. By rights there should have been a blue plaque above the white-painted front door, but instead there was only a blue-and-white 'For Sale' sign tamped down into the weed-strewn lawn alongside the weeping cherry and a red camellia. The neighbours had beds filled with flowering heather. The five-bedroom red-brick semi-detached house (extended since the 1950s) was on sale for £375,000, but I couldn't help wondering how much more the owners might ask if only they knew. Maybe it wasn't yet like visiting 125 Hyndford Street in East Belfast, where Van Morrison was born, or 251 Menlove Avenue in Liverpool, where John Lennon spent most of his childhood, but for his millions of readers it was surely close. I was tempted to knock on the door and say, *did you know?*

With certain notable exceptions Lee was unsentimental about family. The first thing he does in *Killing Floor* is kill them all off.

> 'Have you got family?' [Hubble] asked me.
> 'No,' I said. [. . .] My parents were both dead. I had a brother somewhere who I never saw.

Reacher next sees his brother on a slab in the morgue.

> The truth was I never knew for sure if I loved him or not. And he never knew for sure if he loved me or not, either. [. . .] Most of those sixteen years, we didn't know if we loved each other or hated each other.

But they had the thing that army families have: unconditional loyalty.

> So time to time you might hate your brother, but you didn't let anybody mess with him. That was what we had, Joe and I.

Early drafts of *Killing Floor* were even closer to autobiographical experience, until Lee's first editor at American publisher G. P. Putnam's Sons asked him to tone it down a bit: 'Should Reacher hate Joe so much?' Was his hate 'too strident'?

> The truth was I didn't love him very much at all. And he didn't love me very much at all, either. [. . .] Most of those sixteen years, we hated each other.

'I'm toning down the stridency,' Lee replied, 'but only a little – because I want the relationship to be very confused and ambiguous. I think it's something a lot of siblings will understand. It's like that in my family, that's for sure.'

When asked about the tour de force choreography of his fight scenes, Lee replied it was 'mostly just muscle memory', as though rerunning past conflicts on autopilot. 'It's all autobiographical. I just toned down the sex and violence to make it more plausible.' It's true that stories he tells about his life can be found word for word in his novels. But equally that in its translation into fiction, reality has undergone a rectification as gratifying to the reader as it is to the writer.

In the books you can go years without seeing a winter. You can be a soldier and a beach bum too. Your older brother would be your leader and mentor, but also your comrade-in-arms: Little John to your Robin Hood, Lancelot to your King Arthur, Athos to your d'Artagnan. In the books, neighbourhood bully Nicky was 'a dead man'. The brothers would 'hunt him down and rip him apart'. They would 'hunt him down and smile at him as he died'. Well Reacher would, anyway.

So when Roscoe asks Reacher what he's going to do about Joe, his answer 'came very easily':

> I was going to stand up for him. I was going to finish his business. Whatever it was. Whatever it took.

But Roscoe is a police officer. She and Finlay, the displaced Harvard lawyer, were *sworn to uphold all kinds of laws,* and laws, like family, were designed to get in his way.

> Finlay couldn't understand the simple truth I'd learned at the age of four: you don't mess with my brother. So this was my business. It was between me and Joe. It was duty.

Lee was unsentimental about Coventry too. He hadn't been back since he was four. 'Weird,' he said, when I told him I'd taken a train and hiked a couple of hours to see the place where he was born. 'I was last there August 1959.' When it was still officially part of historic Warwickshire, since the 'West Midlands' was not invented until 1974, following the Local Government Act of 1972.

James was born fourteen years after the Blitz of November 1940, codenamed *Mondscheinsonate* ('Moonlight Sonata') (Goebbels would subsequently use the term *coventriert* – 'coventried' – as shorthand for wholesale destruction). When he was around three years old his mother would wheel his old-fashioned perambulator to Priory Street to watch the new cathedral (designed by Basil Spence, and the stimulus for Benjamin Britten's *War Requiem*) being built alongside the skeletal fire-bombed ruins of the old. It was what you did on Saturday afternoons, while Londoners paraded in Hyde Park.

Coventrians suspected (as some historians speculated) that Churchill had 'let Coventry burn' so as not to reveal to the Germans that the Enigma code had been cracked. They went to their graves believing that in the eyes of their southern lords and masters they were disposable. Lee thought it plausible that the capital might sacrifice the provinces, noting that only a few hundred were killed as opposed to 35,000 in Hamburg in 1943: at a geopolitical level, in light of the barrage of 'horrendously distasteful decisions' the wartime government faced on a daily basis and executed with 'astonishing brutality', the sacrifice was 'trivial'.

Though a poor second to Birmingham in his genealogical hierarchy, Coventry had left its imprint. For one thing, William Shakespeare had hung out there watching plays as a teenager, and the city features prominently in *Henry IV, Part 1*. For another, it was home to the eleventh-century Countess of Mercia, Lady Godiva, herself rectified in thirteenth-century legend as a spectacular advocate for the poor and oppressed, standing up – or rather riding through the streets naked – against the big guy, who happens also to be her husband, in the name of the little guy, his harshly taxed peasants. It was one of those stories handed down through generations, which was the kind of story Lee liked best.

A statue to Lady Godiva had been unveiled in Broadgate five years before James Grant was born.

Coventry was once the major weaving and dyeing town in England, attracting traders from all over Europe, among them John Shakespeare, glover and father of William, from neighbouring Stratford-upon-Avon. 'Coventry blue' – a lost recipe of pigment from the woad plant, chemicals and water from the River Sherbourne – was famed for 'staying true', hence the demotic association with loyalty. The 'mystery' plays (from 'ministerium', meaning 'occupation') really were performed by Bottom the Weaver and his Rude Mechanicals: guilds of craftsmen engaged in fabric and leather work from tanning to capping and ribbon-making.

In the second half of the nineteenth century the city became renowned for the manufacture of watches; then, more recently, cars. James had been born in a nursing home a few minutes' walk from the Browns Lane plant, built as a Second World War shadow factory but taken over in 1951 by Jaguar. The 1950s and 1960s were the golden age of the British motor industry and even though Coventry had lost much of its historic medieval centre to the Luftwaffe, this was the period of the city's greatest wealth.

In a small, significant way, Lee collected cars and watches (no ticking, no batteries). He 'normally' wore a Patek Philippe, but also had a Breguet and a Fabergé Agathon, the one he liked best, number 6 of a limited edition, which he bought in 2006 in Venice and which 'cost about the same as a family car'. It was gold, with Arabic numerals and a brown leather strap and a sapphire stud in the winder, and had a transparent back that revealed the exquisite mysteries of the mechanism. 'I love small intricate machines. But to be honest they're fragile and don't keep very good time. Cheap watches are better.'

The stable of cars kept changing, from the red VW Beetle through a couple of Mazdas to a red Jaguar X6 and a silver X8, then a special order black F-Type to replace the red. In Wyoming he had owned a black Toyota Land Cruiser, licence plate WSTERN, and in New York a secondhand Land Rover, bronze, LIC PL8 chosen by his daughter, both since traded in. He'd briefly kept a Jag with REA★CHR on the plate, but let it go because he 'started getting pestered'.

But, he wrote, 'the Bentley is the nicest'. It was a 1977 model he'd bought in 2014, a gorgeous dark green, lovingly polished to a deep gloss, about as distinctive as the most distinctive thing you could think of, a sentimental nod to Hubble's Bentley in *Killing Floor*, which as well as getting the whole bestseller game off to a flyer and transporting Reacher and Roscoe from one climax to the next had been weaponised in the final showdown and had literally saved lives.

> That old Bentley must have weighed two tons and it tore the metal door right off its mountings with no trouble at all. There was a tremendous crashing and tearing of metal and I heard the rear lights smash and the clang of the fender as it fell off and bounced on the concrete.

'Call me nuts,' Lee said, with a rare, verging on shy, sentimentality, unfazed by this orgy of destruction, 'but I love the way the C pillar resolves into the roofline. Metal pressing at its finest.' Then after a beat, almost apologetic: 'Hey, I'm from Birmingham.'

As it happens, James didn't smash Nicky. Not that day at least. He didn't need to. And it was his father John Grant, aka Rex, an unseen witness from the Ridgeway Avenue front garden, who described how the scene played out, how the compliant yet merciless James advanced towards Nicky with fists clenched and wearing a menacing look, and how Nicky turned tail and fled.

5

Humans v. Aliens

When he was grown, he was going to be unstoppable.
Second Son, 2011

Lee had a phenomenal memory, but mythifying stories about three-year-olds owe a lot to the fond reminiscences of doting parents. The stories about the half-brick fist and the menacing look, sufficient to defeat the foe and save a brother two years older than him, nuanced his claim that 'no one read to us or told us stories'.

Thanks to his father, James was already a legend on the mean streets of Coventry.

'He must have been proud of you,' I said.

'In a deep-down human way he probably was,' Lee conceded, 'but it was so buried under that superstructure of repressed respectability.'

No doubt James suffered from second-son syndrome. Not without just cause, since Richard enjoyed first-son privileges and was mean and patronising with it. At the age of sixty-three, his parents both recently deceased, Lee had inherited five photographs of himself as a kid. There were hundreds of Richard, he said. It was Richard who got to go places with his father. It was Richard who learned to read and write with his mother. One day Rex and Audrey gave Richard a watch. The three-year-old James wanted one too. Rex and Audrey told him: *Sorry son, you can have one when you learn to tell the time.* Which he did, within days, spurred on by the promise of a fair reward. *Sorry son, you'll have to wait until you're six.* 'That was a betrayal right there,' Lee said. 'I never forgave them.' Like Reacher (*Nothing to Lose*), he was a 'painfully literal child'. In his punctilious way he thought they should have said what they meant: *when you can tell the time or when you turn six, whichever is later.* It was a matter of trust.

He still had the watch, kept it in a drawer neatly laid out alongside the Fabergé and the Breguet and the Patek Philippe. It was a Westclox made in Scotland, with a small round silver face and a narrow brown strap, now faintly frayed with age. It still worked. It was one of only a handful of treasured objects to have been salvaged from his childhood.

Now he treasured the photographs too. Each had been lovingly framed and added to the collection of family snaps in his Manhattan dining room, on a long low shelf beneath his wife's collection of Shelley china. In 2018 he was interviewed by *New York Magazine* on things he couldn't live without and along with the coffee, slipping in a plug for his newly launched Jack Reacher brand ('robust, full-bodied, battle-tested') and the essential Wrangler jeans (30-inch waist, 38-inch leg – 'virtually no chance of getting that size in the store'), of which he had twelve pairs, six in each of two different shades ('I'm not really a fashionista, but I like the slim ones in the dark wash they call Root Beer or the lighter one called Storm Blue'), he mentions the need for a fuss-free, functional photo frame.

It's a matter of precision.

> Of course, photos are never exactly the four-by-six or whatever you need for the frames, which means you have to go cut them and head to the store and laboriously tell the guy what size you need. I found Matboard as an online alternative to all that — they do custom mats for photos — and now they just arrive perfectly sized without the hassle. It's so easy.

Now, I can display my photos with mats and with nice frames.

You could have given him a job in advertising. Lee was a sucker for internet shopping. It saved him from having to talk to anyone, even on the phone.

Given more space he could (and would) have given chapter and verse on the coffee mug too. It had to be taller than it was wide and made of white bone china so the heat stayed in the coffee rather than being absorbed by the mug. 'Proper bone china is almost translucent.' Now Wedgwood had moved to Indonesia and their china was 'that little bit heavier and denser'. But it wasn't all about heat retention. It was the feel against your lip. 'You don't want to be putting ironstone or stoneware in your mouth – it's like sucking on a rubber tyre.' He had six Cuisinart coffee makers distributed among his different homes, so there was always a back-up if one broke down.

All five photographs date from his pre-school years. There's the one with his two grandfathers. Another is a beaming chubby-cheeked portrait, his face as clear and round as a Westclox wristwatch. In the earliest he is propped up against a pillow in a romper suit with puffed sleeves and a band of smocking across the yoke, with a smile so wide he was probably laughing, like someone had tickled his feet. In the fourth, still sunny, he is sitting up unaided in a *Mary Poppins*-style Silver Cross pram, appreciating the joys of a good set of wheels and fabulous suspension. In the last he is riding a beast of a tricycle with wheels only slightly smaller than those of the pram, his hands holding tight to the cruiser handlebars and a frown of intense concentration on his face – you might even call it a menacing look. He was off and running – nothing and no one was going to stand in his way.

'I look at that happy little boy and wonder what became of him,' Lee said.

He let me study each in turn then restored each to its place on the polished white shelves. One, I put back myself: I knew exactly where it had come from. But Lee, saying nothing, with infinite patience and the meticulous care of an horologist, stepped in, and adjusted the angle and position by a crucial couple of millimetres.

Like all connoisseurs he was fastidious. But the array of delicate, silver-framed photographs, spreading with the profusion of wild blue-bells in an English woodland in May time, showed that he could be sentimental too.

Just like his father.

In *Second Son* US Marine Stan Reacher dwells thoughtfully on the respective attributes of his two boys. The second is a conundrum.

> He was going to be an eighth of a ton of muscle. Which was a frightening prospect. The kid had come home bruised and bloodied plenty of times, but as far as Stan knew he hadn't actually lost a fight since he was about five years old. Maybe he had never lost a fight. [. . .] When he was grown, he was going to be unstoppable. A force of nature. A nightmare for somebody. [. . .]
>
> He wasn't academic like Joe, but he was practical. His IQ was probably about the same, but it was a get-the-job-done type of street-smart IQ, not any kind of for-the-sake-of-it cerebral indulgence. Reacher liked facts, for sure, and information too, but not theory. He was a real-world character.

A degree of awe is built into parenthood. So it's only natural that in creating Reacher in his own enhanced image the author should make doubly sure he was awesome. What proud father wouldn't be given pause by a son who weighed in at one-sixteenth of a Bentley and was brainy to boot?

His father said, 'Stay calm, son. Don't do too much damage.'

Secretly rejoicing in the fact that he could, and almost certainly would.

In his no-nonsense way Stan shows Reacher the love that was lacking in Lee's childhood. 'My father was a cold, disapproving man, all about denial and self-denial.' Lee could not recall his father saying he loved him, not once in a whole lifetime. Neither Rex nor Audrey was demonstrative, there were no tender displays of emotion: no warmth, no affection. He couldn't recall a single occasion on which he'd had fun with his father, not one moment he would like to relive. 'Not a single bloody afternoon. Not an hour. Blank. He was like a Martian.'

But at least he was a Martian who could read. Who liked to read. Which was a great redeeming feature. Perhaps the greatest. When asked by the *Boston Globe* in 2015 who influenced him as a reader, Lee answered simply: 'My father.'

> He was always trying to get an encyclopedia for the family bookshelf. He ended up getting a magazine that came out every week and you'd put it in a binder to make an encyclopedia. If he didn't think something was accurate he would cross it out and write in neatly what he thought was correct. That knocked me out. You don't have to believe what is written — you can question it.

It's a big debt, and a big acknowledgement too. He might as well be saying: *I owe it all to you, Dad.* The love of books, the escape from 'boring' Britain, his salvation from the dole, his first book and his first bestseller, his home in America, the Jaguars, Bentleys and Fabergés, the views over the Empire State Building and Central Park, the Renoir on the wall and the entrée to Hollywood, the millions in the bank and the hundreds of millions of faithful fans. *Thanks, Dad.*

More than ten years earlier, in a 2003 interview for *January* magazine, Lee likewise links his father with books.

> I would say I'm from a worn-but-discreetly-darned-white-collar
> background. My dad was a civil servant on a fixed salary in a time of
> variable inflation in a city where the car workers' unions were very
> strong. So he was white-collar, but poorer than the blue-collar guys.
> He went to work in a tie, carrying an umbrella, but he went on the
> bus. We had books but no bikes. We always had three squares a day
> and wore leather shoes, but if there was a pound left over at the end
> of the month, it was a miracle.

But his answer as to who cultivated his passion for reading was
more evasive. 'It was just there, like the air. You have to imagine two
channels of TV, both of which took long breaks during the day. The
local library was all there was.'

Rex liked to play sergeant major to his troop of boys. He would
give them their marching orders: dispatch them upstairs to wash their
hands observing certain rituals on the way up and down or have them
stand to attention at the table. He wasn't a control freak. It wasn't a
power trip. But it wasn't playing either. 'He had no concept of play.'
Other than wordplay, that is. Rex loved the language of the parade
ground in the same way he delighted in legalese. When announcing a
win on the Premium Bonds and enforcing his rule that all winnings
should be divided equally, he would be scrupulous in formally
invoking 'The Lotteries' Sharing of Proceeds Act'.

But Rex was no storyteller. He lacked the imagination to be a
writer. 'And the empathy too.'

I couldn't recall seeing an encyclopaedia on the Vitsœ shelves in
Lee's back office ('the perfect office shelves', even though, being
designed by Dieter Rams back in low-fi 1959, 'they're not totally

practical'). But there was one in his head. He was often asked how he knew the things he knew, about fighting and weapons and the US Army. Did he do a lot of research? Not really. But he was alive. He'd been alive for a decent stretch of time. His eyes and ears were open. He talked to people and listened. He travelled. Like Reacher, he was only ever passing through. He didn't want to know too much, would simply file away his first impressions for future reference.

Mostly, he read. He read anything and everything, indiscriminately, voraciously, indefatigably, not excluding histories of air conditioning or the war against rust, choosing books at random or because he liked the look of the cover. He read his grandmother's back issues of the *Reader's Digest*. He read fast and all the time, tearing through books like a locust through crops in the Texas panhandle. His parents took out additional library cards for transient friends and relatives and even the family dog – a black poodle named Timmy, for the *Famous Five* – in a vain attempt to cater for that impossible, insatiable mythic appetite. He claimed to read an average of three hundred books a year and to have read more books by the age of ten than most people read in a lifetime. He liked saying this, and the gasps of admiration it provoked, but still he worried about the rate at which books were being produced and fretted about the ones he hadn't read and never could and all the things he didn't know and never would.

'I like to know things,' he said. 'Three hundred books a year for sixty years equals eighteen thousand books, approximately one tenth the number of ISBN titles published in a single year' (and the same as the number of copies of *Night School* sold per day in the first week of release). 'Statistically, it's amazing that any of us have ever read any books in common.'

Like the great explorers and the big nineteenth-century novelists, Lee wanted to encompass it all. But like Reacher, he plays it cool.

'Research and I have a distant and cordial relationship,' he said at ThrillerFest 2017, not long before picking up his ThrillerMaster award. And in a 2013 email to a friend: 'I like to pepper my manuscripts with the illusion of knowledge.'

He didn't often, as a boy, receive books as presents. The best was the *Wonder Book of the RAF*, given to him by his parents when he was about ten years old, when Richard got the companion book on the Navy. The front cover shows a sleekly sinister Vampire Night Fighter taking off against an indigo sky, with the letters R.A.F. picked out in triumphant red like a blazing sunset. The book still sits on a shelf in his Manhattan library. He knew exactly where to find it.

The way Lee put it, he had 'an extremely trivial mind'. The only problem he might face on *Mastermind* would be what to choose as his specialist subject: Aston Villa, Les Paul guitars, the books of John D. MacDonald, Led Zeppelin, the Toyota Land Cruiser 1957–2017, the New York Yankees, the construction of the Chrysler Building – all were contenders. Whichever way he went, he would expect to win.

'I've never lost a game of Trivial Pursuit,' he told me. As though challenging me to some sort of one-on-one, which I would have lost as surely as a game of human handcuffs. But there was substance to his boast. I'd been present when more foolhardy types had tried to best him. Take James Naughtie, the BBC radio presenter, who interviewed Lee in Harrogate that same July (when he was the recipient of yet another lifetime achievement award) and fancied himself on the subject of Georges Simenon. Which was risky, given this was right in Lee's ballpark.

Simenon, Naughtie chose to assert, had written forty-eight Maigrets to Lee's twenty-odd Reachers.

Lee stopped him.

'Not forty-eight,' he said. 'Seventy-five.'

He didn't mean to be rude. It was a reflex action. He couldn't help himself.

Naughtie was a confident man three years Lee's senior. He wasn't used to being corrected on air. Which is why he let the words 'forty' and 'eight' slip past his lips a second time before he collected himself.

'Let's not argue,' Naughtie said, all 'best-voice-to-wake-up-to' BBC balance and listen-with-mother wisdom. You could virtually see him smoothing the ruffled feathers.

But Lee couldn't let it go. Not the Birmingham scuffler. Not when it had to do with Simenon. And books. And above all, numbers.

'I'm the king of trivia,' he said loftily, willing the audience to contradict him, ready to take on all five hundred if need be. 'He wrote seventy-five Maigrets out of two hundred books.'

There was a steely say-that-again-and-I'll-smash-you glint in his eye.

Naughtie segued suavely on.

As he got older Rex loosened up a bit. One day, in the spirit of clearing the decks before it was too late, he told James what he felt most guilty about. Back in East Belfast he used to mow the lawn for his dad. He got sixpence for doing it. One day the lady opposite asks him not to, so as not to disturb her sick husband. I know your dad gives you pocket money for it, she says – how much do you get? Sixpence, replies the young Rex, innocently. I don't want you to be out of pocket, the kind lady says, so here – I'll give you sixpence. Later his dad asks, why haven't you mown the lawn? Rex explains. Well done, son, says his dad approvingly. Then adds, I don't want you to be out of pocket – here, have the sixpence anyway. Well into his eighties, Rex still felt bad about it.

'Typical bad timing,' Lee wrote when his father died. He'd just flown back to New York after the publication of *Night School*. 'No issues,' he said. 'Complicated relationship. Not upset at all.' But he could see how his mother might be. So he turned himself round and got back on a plane to be by her side.

'He read all of my books, and always had something to say about them,' Lee said when I asked. He remembered his father liking 'the oblique narrative way' it was established that Reacher was on the wrong prison floor in Margrave, how it arose out of incidental conversation.

On 4 April 1997, looking forward to the UK publication of *Killing Floor*, Rex wrote a neat, copperplate letter to his son. It begins 'Dear Jimbo', and ends 'your affectionate father, John Child', and includes a list of local bookstores, with contact details.

> As 5th Jun draws nearer we get more and more excited. The reviews are increasingly encouraging and on their strength I have decided to Read It. The reviews suggest that it is a novel properly so called in which the effect of the events on the hero is studied and we see why he reacts and not just how he reacts. This should widen the appeal of the book and draw in people such as myself who left off reading Alistair Maclean because they got sick of the endless "I did this. Then I did that" style leaving one no wiser at the end of the book as to why the hero ticked as he did. Such characterisation as there was was inevitably stereotyped.
>
> Mum and I are highly impressed at how you have carried this whole thing through. Apart from the actual writing you have obviously put great thought into every stage of the mechanics. The only two points I will take it upon myself to make are: (1) Don't forget the taxman cometh, shovel in hand and (2) Put the last penny you are allowed into a Pension Scheme (highly tax efficient), but as schemes vary widely take advice.
>
> It is good to hear that you are already at work on Book Three. Have you reached the stage of wondering where Jack Reacher is going to take you next? Is he real flesh and blood to you?

Turns out there was a little of the human in Lee's father, just as there is a little of the Martian in Lee. In a 2016 essay for the *New Yorker* he writes about Rex with ruthless compassion.

> The other day I saw my father, who is ninety-two years old, and in very poor health. Physically, he's a wreck, and mentally he's not much better. At his peak, he was a capable and intelligent man, by nature rational to the point of coldness. But the other day he was full of childlike fear of the darkness that lay ahead. He's religious, in an austere way. So I knew what he meant. 'Don't be afraid,' I said. 'You're a good man, and you lived a good life.' In fact, neither thing was true. But what else could I say?

The description of his dying father as 'a purse-mouthed bigot whose instinct was to prohibit, not encourage' had been cut from the original copy.

His father was his father, even if he did come from another planet. Probably he too was 'a trivia geek of enormous proportions'.

I could picture Rex and his DIY encyclopaedia, assembled with all the painstaking care of someone mounting photographs on custom mat boards in millimetre-perfect frames.

6

The Finest Hour

'Free country,' Reacher said.
'That's what you're working for, right?'
High Heat, 2013

John Grant senior met and married Winifred Crookes after the war. A lot had happened since 1918, what with the Irish War of Independence and Partition and the Anglo-Irish Treaty and the creation of the Irish Free State. But John was doing well. He had landed another white-collar job through the Protestant freemasonry and was working for some government department in means-tested benefits. A job in the civil service brought with it two types of comfort: a much-coveted middle-class respectability, and the financial security that later shielded the family from the worst effects of the Great Depression.

Winnie was a literate woman like her miller's-wife mother-in-law, Jane, and had attended Queen's University in Belfast. She hadn't graduated, since this privilege was not afforded to women no matter how fairly earned. Still, she was a university girl and rightly proud of it, and it was felt in her family that she had married down. She had also married in a hurry, with John Reginald Grant making his appearance on 22 May 1924 not nine months into the union. His sister Margaret showed up five years later, his mother having simply dropped out of circulation and returned with a baby. The unheralded acquisition of a sibling proved difficult, depriving John of affection, colouring his relationships with his family and shaping the formation of his character. Margaret was seen as a 'bad' girl. Which meant she grew up lively, outspoken and prone to sarcasm, a rebel who could hold her own. Lee said she was 'spirited', the epithet he chose for Roscoe in *Killing Floor*, the first in a long line of Reacher's spirited female allies.

Rex was born in the vicinity of Cyprus Avenue, in what would later become known as Van Morrison land. When he was around six years old the family moved across the railway line to Hyndford Street. The singer-songwriter famously idealises both locations. 'On Hyndford Street' (1991) is a nostalgic hymn to 'feeling wondrous and lit up inside with a sense of everlasting life', and invokes Debussy and Kerouac and Radio Luxembourg, but soon drifts away from the treeless terraces to dreamy summer walks up 'Cherry Valley' and apples that spill over from gardens brimming with fruit, flowers and fourteen-year-old girls who all 'rhyme with something' and make his heart beat faster and his insides shake like a leaf on a tree. 'Cyprus Avenue', recorded at Century Sounds studio in New York when Lee himself was fourteen, is pure mythification, with its lonesome engine drivers pining down at the rumbling station and the tormented young teenager being driven crazy in a car seat while longing for his 'lady' to come from 'yonder' in a carriage drawn by six white horses with rainbow ribbons in her hair.

Rex had long since left Belfast when these songs were written. Van Morrison was born in 1945, the working-class son of a shipyard electrician in a city of shipbuilders, where the *Titanic* was built, and grew up at 125 Hyndford Street. Which now has a blue plaque on the door and the occasional pilgrim outside taking photographs. His parents had bought the house from a couple with two children who were moving down the road to Kingsway Avenue in Cherryvalley. Their names were John and Winnie Grant, and they were moving up in the world.

I couldn't help thinking of the sixteen-year-old Reacher in *High Heat*, who passes through the died-and-gone-to-heaven enchanted kingdom of Manhattan on his way to see his older brother at West Point, and is likewise 'conquered in a car seat', but by the elfin Chrissie, a coed from Sarah Lawrence in Yonkers, hitting *the highest possible note in the whole history of high notes* in ways the young Van Morrison could only dream of.

Rex graduated from Belfast Royal Academy in 1942. Like his mother before him, he got a place at Queen's, and like her, he didn't graduate. In his case he didn't even attend. Instead, he volunteered for the army and thanks to his grammar-school education was commissioned as an officer, rising through the ranks from second lieutenant through lieutenant to captain. Queen's had pledged to defer places for soldiers but Rex never went back. Nor did he ever contact them, so technically he had a place open to him until the day he died.

Instead he took a boat to Glasgow and was put straight on a train heading south. He remembered waking up in Giggleswick and thinking, *Where the hell am I?* In fact he was between Lancaster and Leeds, on the fringes of the Dales, not far from Harrogate and Otley where he would eventually end up. But he must have felt like he'd fallen down a rabbit hole into some strange new world, which in a way he had, since from then on nothing would ever be the same again.

After completing his military training he served in the European campaign, from immediately after D-Day on 6 June 1944, when Operation Overlord was launched with the long-planned Normandy landings, codenamed Operation Neptune, the largest seaborne invasion in history, right up until VE (Victory in Europe) Day on 8 May 1945, which marked the unconditional surrender of the German armed forces to the Allies, when everyone said the war was over.

Unlike his father, Rex saw plenty of active service. The army had trained him in radiophysics but he was deployed as a combat engineer whose job it was to come in behind the tanks, troubleshooting, repairing and retrieving broken-down machinery. It was dangerous work. He followed the usual itinerary through the Western Front, from Normandy through northern France and Belgium into Holland, where he participated in the abortive campaign to capture the 'bridge too far' at Arnhem in September 1944 before ending up in Germany.

Rex was among the first to enter the Nazi concentration camp at Belsen, just south-west of the town of Bergen, with the 11th Armoured Division. He left no written record and like many veterans was not inclined to reminiscence. He did not regale his four boys with tales of heroism and derring-do.

But others have spoken for him. The website of London's Imperial War Museum states that:

> British forces liberated Bergen–Belsen on 15 April 1945. Thousands of bodies lay unburied around the camp and some 60,000 starving and mortally ill people were packed together without food, water or basic sanitation.

It's a stark introduction to an archive of harrowing audio-visual testimony.

They were used to terrible wounds, said medical assistant William Arthur Wood (IWM SR 15427).

> But [. . .] we hadn't been trained for this, and it was so, so different to, well to anything. I can't explain it, it was so terrible and so different from anything we'd seen in our move up from D-Day onward.

Major Dick Williams (IWM SR 15437), a staff captain in Supplies and Transport, had been sent ahead to assess conditions.

We went further on into the camp, and saw these corpses lying everywhere. You didn't know whether they were living or dead. [. . .] Some were trying to walk, some were stumbling, some on hands and knees, but in the lagers, the barbed wire around the huts, you could see that the doors were open. The stench coming out of them was fearsome. [. . .] It was just this oppressive haze over the camp, the smell, the dullness of the bare earth, the scattered bodies and these very dull, striped grey uniforms – it was just so dull. The sun, yes the sun was shining, but it didn't seem to make any life at all in that camp. Everything seemed to be dead.

I don't know if Rex was known to William or Dick. It is certainly possible. But I do know their experience was also his experience, that their horror was his horror too. They did their best for the wraith-like survivors. Treated the sick, made broth for the starving and buried the dead. But at least fourteen thousand more died, even after liberation.

You could say that unlike his father, Rex emerged from the Second World War without a scratch. Physically, it would be true. He hadn't lost any limbs. Hadn't been wounded at all. But it would be like saying the war was over on VE Day.

James and his brothers played fighting games out on the street. All the boys did, though it was as likely to be 'Cowboys and Indians' as a re-enactment of D-Day. One day their father said to them, without preamble and without elaboration: 'You wouldn't be doing that if you knew what death smelled like.' It was as though that ghostly alien greyness had touched his soul, even when the sun was shining.

Between May and August 1945 the army changed from a combat force to one of occupation. But the job wasn't yet fully done. Rex was given six weeks leave before he was due to be redeployed to the Far East in the Japan War. It was anticipated that there would be up to one million casualties. He was told by his commanding officer to go home and say his goodbyes, because he was not expected to return. Then the bombs were dropped, on Hiroshima on 6 August, on Nagasaki on 9 August, and the war really was over. To his dying day Rex was a fan of the nuclear bomb. You couldn't really blame him. It had almost certainly saved his life.

Somehow it was too late to go back to Belfast, too late to enrol at Queen's. Not for his generation the dreamy verdant idealism of Van Morrison. But Rex was no fool. He was all too conscious that he had graduated with a high-school education only. So after demobilisation he signed up for three years in India, where he stayed until independence was declared on 15 August 1947, when he was shipped back to England with a whole new vernacular.

It was the wind-down phase of the war and a ruinously severe winter. Supplies were cut off and vegetables froze in the ground. When the snow melted, the floods affected more than one hundred thousand properties. The country had run out of coal because of the extreme conditions, but as the industry had only recently been nationalised blame was laid at the Labour Party's door. Rex was assigned to clear the central communications systems. Once he was sent to Dent in Cumbria, on the western slopes of the Pennines, just eight miles north of Kirkby Lonsdale, where Lee would live when he worked at Granada. At more than 1100 feet above sea level Dent was the highest operational mainline station in England. The snow was so deep that Rex and his crew couldn't see the station or the line. Until they bumped into some chimney pots poking up from the ground under their feet, when they got out their shovels and set about digging.

'Nineteen forty-seven was the end of many things,' Lee said. Like the Lancaster bomber, which had carried the heaviest loads of the war, including the Grand Slam bomb, and would live on through the legendary stories of the victorious Dam Busters. Over seven thousand Lancasters were built, some at the Yeadon shadow factory bombed in

1940, leaving the crater on the Chevin that James and his brothers would play in as boys.

But 1947 was the start of something too. Rex was sent to clear the railway line in Otley. One evening he went to a dance at the Mechanics' Institute on Cross Green. He had gone to play cards, but never made it through the main hall to the game. Instead, he got waylaid by Audrey, who two years later would marry him in Otley Parish Church.

Lee's father died aged ninety-two in December 2016; his mother, aged ninety, in September 2017. There was no moment of epiphany or liberation. Perhaps had they died when he was younger, then it would have been *Wow, I'm free*. But 'they went on so long' it felt almost as if they'd been dead for five years before they died. So there wasn't a moment. Nothing changed. But now he was able to look back on their lives as whole completed stories and understand them a little better. 'They had hard lives, and they did the best they could, probably. They did pretty well in difficult circumstances.'

In 2016 he wrote for the *New York Times* about the day his publisher called him up and he heard for the first time those magic words: 'You're no. 1 in America.' It was a 'lovely, gilded, charmed' moment, beyond Van Morrison, right up there with the Beatles. Moments don't get much better than that. Especially for a boy from Birmingham.

It was all the more golden for being set against the backdrop of war.

> We had no bombs falling on our houses, and no knocks on our doors in the middle of the night. [. . .] We were very lucky.
>
> But it was very boring. Britain was gray, exhausted, physically ruined and financially crippled. The factories were humming, but everything went for export. We needed foreign currency to pay down monstrous war debt. Domestic life was pinched and austere.
>
> Not that we knew. We didn't miss what we'd never had. Worse for us was a kind of mental and emotional deadness that we felt all around.

There was nothing left for us. There was nothing in the future. It was all in the past. History was over. Britain's finest hour had been 1940, and now the clock was slowly winding down.

James and his contemporaries knew they had nothing to complain of, that boredom didn't register on the scale. But still they resented that feeling of being trapped and held down, that suffocating dullness, the civilian legacy of that oppressive murderous haze. Just as their parents – having gone into battle to save the world – resented their own missed opportunities and the insolent capacity of their offspring. Not only had they given it all up for their children, but their children were rubbing their noses in it by dint of being alive. Then there was the guilt, which was all-pervasive. Because compared to Belsen life in post-war Britain was a bed of sweetly scented sun-drenched roses.

Lee pictures his parents in June 1940. Though one is in Belfast and the other in Otley he brings them together in a single potent image that has the rich, fixed patina of an historic oil painting. It is as though their fate is predetermined, their young lives over before they have even met.

My father was then 16, listening to Churchill on the radio, heading inexorably for the army, sitting across the room from my one-legged grandfather, from the first war. My mother was 14, a schoolgirl near an industrial city, told to listen for planes and get under the table.

Rex and Audrey were lucky too. They had escaped death. The axe had not fallen. They were invulnerable, immortal, untouchable. By rights they should have been whooping and dancing in the street. For a brief while, at least for that one night at the Mechanics' Institute, they clearly were. But it didn't last.

They survived, with millions of others, young and free, but the sustained six-year emotional thunderclap they had endured left them weary and exhausted. The war and its winning (with a little help here and there, they would sometimes grudgingly admit) were both a horror and an achievement unlikely ever to be paralleled, ever again, and therefore anything that came by afterward was necessarily an anti-climax.

For Rex the worst was over but so too the best. Yet somehow he had to get through his threescore and ten, earn a living and bring up a family, drag himself through the increasingly ungrateful twentieth century and into the oblivious twenty-first. That terminal greyness had leached out of Belsen and seeped through to his bones.

When James was a boy the Grants made regular trips to Northern Ireland. They rarely flew. Mostly it was a long trek to Birmingham Snow Hill by taxi (an exceptional experience), then a train ride to Liverpool and a ferry across the Irish Sea. They would visit Rex's parents in Cherryvalley and his bad sister Margaret, who had fled to Londonderry. There was only one bridge across the River Foyle, and on one occasion the family paused in the middle to admire the view.

No sooner had they stopped the car than armed soldiers rushed them from both sides, anticipating a bomb or some other aggression. Which made this, in 1970, the family's last visit to Belfast. Audrey feared for the safety of her boys, especially the two older ones. They were so obviously English, and already big enough to be mistaken for soldiers. James was the kind of guy you'd think twice about giving a lift to at the side of the road, though he was only sixteen – the age Reacher was in the very same decade, the night he found himself beating up gangsters and tracking serial killers, from Washington Square to the Bowery to Bleecker and Carmine, on his second solo visit to New York, when all he'd set out to do was visit his brother Joe. Even his journey from Pohang in South Korea was analogous, in its ramped-up supercharged extra-muscular way: 'Bus to Seoul, plane to Tokyo, plane to Hawaii, plane to LA, plane to JFK, bus to the Port Authority. Then I walked.' Like James, Reacher was still a high-school kid and only just legal, which was all Chrissie needed to know, he hoped, but nobody was going to believe it.

So far as is recorded in the annals of his adventures, Reacher has never been to Belfast. James Grant returned only once, as Lee Child in March 2010, on tour for his fourteenth book, *61 Hours*. But he did set a story there, published in *Belfast Noir* in 2014. 'Wet with Rain' (alluding to Van Morrison) is about a couple of undercover con artists from America who invent a novelist no one has ever heard of. *Is he famous?* Mrs Healy asks. Not exactly: 'Writers don't really get famous.' But he was born in her house and they want to buy it and turn it into a research centre. *Do people do that? Research writers in the houses where they were born?* 'All the time.'

It was probably true that for the last five years of his life Rex was physically and mentally impoverished to the point of decrepitude, that he might as well have been dead as alive. But it had gone on far longer than that. Something inside him had died when the stench of Belsen got into his mouth and nostrils, and stuck to his lungs like asbestos and then, like the incurable cancer it was, started eating him up from within. Even further back, way back on Hyndford Street in 1940, it was the voice of death he heard on the radio, and it was death he had looked in the face.

Around the same time as the story of the lawnmower and the sixpences, Rex confided in his son that he had volunteered for the army out of a desire to avenge his own crippled war-hero father.

Objectively, in Lee's words for the *New York Times*, James Dover Grant 'was one of the luckiest humans ever born'.

In 1954, Britain was a stable postwar liberal democracy, at peace, with a cradle-to-grave welfare system that worked efficiently, with all dread diseases conquered, with full employment for our parents, with free and excellent education from the age of 5 for just as long as we merited it.

There was no war for him to fight. But if there had been – if they'd had to *do it all again* – he too would have signed up, just like his father. Not least for this reason, Lee Child created Jack Reacher and made him ex-military.

7

Grievous

A headbutt is always unexpected.
Killing Floor, 1997

A sense of narrative helped to redeem Rex and Audrey. But Lee was never going to go all soft about them. Showing their children 'zero affection, physical or verbal' was partly down to period, fashion and the type of people they were, but also because 'they were bad parents'. Unusually, he called on the support of his (ever absent) older brother. Emotionally, Richard was 'as hard as nails' but – Lee had checked, specifically – even he allowed that their parents had been cold and unloving.

On the other hand, if you subscribed to the mantra of benign neglect, they hadn't been all that bad. Let's face it, he'd turned out OK. Hadn't he? Had done all right for himself. 'I mean I'm not scarred or traumatised or broken. Not at all.' Then again, perhaps he had as many quirks as the next guy but didn't know it. Like Reacher, who was 'full of weirdness, eccentricities and oddness, but without all the tedious navel-gazing'.

He'd heard a radio programme once, a psychologist saying that the measure of good parenting was the self-confidence of the child. 'Well I'm one hundred and one per cent self-confident, so by that measure they were good parents. But that's not how it felt.'

It was rare to hear him invoke feelings. Normally he claimed not to have any.

There was no denying it. He was self-confident to the point of arrogance. 'That's my handicap,' he said, as if daring me to disagree. 'I've gotta win. If some guy is saying he's gotta be top dog in the schoolyard then I've gotta be top dog in the schoolyard.'

And that was exactly what he'd been.

The first paragraph of his punchy (auto)biography on IMDb reads:

> Lee Child was born in the exact geographic centre of England, in the heart of the industrial badlands. Never saw a tree until he was 12. It was the sort of place where if you fell in the river, you had to go to the hospital for a mandatory stomach pump. The sort of place where minor disputes were settled with box cutters and bicycle chains. He's got the scars to prove it.

He still didn't much like trees (but tolerated them eleven floors down in Central Park), if the 2014 novella *Not a Drill* was anything to go by. 'Lots of parkland and flowers,' he complained of Welwyn Garden City in his blog of 5 April 2007. 'The only expanses of green I want to see are what comes out of an ATM.'

Asked about the origins of Reacher's aptitude for crunching hand-to-hand – foot-to-knee, forehead-to-nose – combat, he said: 'A lot of it is me when I was nine.' So far as I know he never had to go for a stomach pump. But he had a scar above his left eye: 'from being hit with a brick when I was eight in Birmingham – a hard, hard city'. It went back to a game of marbles he had fixed in the schoolyard, positioning himself by an iron grille on the tarmac and thereby ensuring all the marbles flowed sweetly in his direction. His opponent took exception to his methods, picked up a handy half-brick and threw it straight at his face. No stitches. No one had bothered to patch him up or provide any comfort.

Which was nothing out of the ordinary. He'd come home bruised and bloodied plenty of times, but as far as he could recall he hadn't lost a fight since he was five years old. If a tooth came loose he shoved it back in with his thumb.

'I was a fighter,' Lee told Janet Maslin at ThrillerFest, 'which I had to be at elementary school, which was pretty rough.'

He'd got stuck in on day one. They'd left Nicky behind in Ridgeway Avenue but it was like he'd been cloned and was lying in wait all over again, along with a gang of his mates. Richard was still a dork and a geek and still had the sticky-out ears. Rex and Audrey had anticipated that their eldest son would still need someone to do the smashing for him. So the first thing they did when James was about to start school was take him aside for a quiet word. 'They were extremely normal, repressed people. It was mortifying to have to ask me to look after him.'

'That was my duty every recess,' said Lee. 'Go out to the playground, haul off the bullies, then go and play ball with my friends.' In exchange for biscuits he would extend his protection to other children, seeing off any number of monsters with cheery enjoyment. 'I operated it as a mutual benefit society.' Like Reacher, except Reacher acted first and only afterwards accepted the old-fashioned offer of a 'woman-cooked' meal.

It was in Birmingham that James discovered the headbutt, which Reacher so reliably made use of 'to help with the decision-making process' (*The Enemy*). It was in Birmingham he learned you never really fight five guys, because two always run away. One day his great aunt was visiting from London. Harriet (Hettie) Scott was his Otley grandma's sister and the senior matriarch of the family. Audrey had given him clean clothes so he knew it was a big deal. He had strict instructions to meet at Elmwood Library after school. To get there he had to go down a steep alleyway. Which was where they were waiting for him. The lead guy of five was named Douglas Cooper. Somehow that had stuck in his mind. He remembered thinking: *Oh no, I've got clean clothes AND I'm going to be late.* 'I took out the main guy, then two ran away, and I was left with two.' He had no problem with that kind of odds. Still, Lee couldn't help wondering if he'd lost a couple of potential readers that day.

Like the Reacher of *Second Son*, he was 'permanently jammed wide open on full auto'.

'I put that in *One Shot*,' he told BBC *Inside Out West Midlands* in 2017, as he walked down a leafy lane with reporter Mary Rhodes, 'literally word-for-word all from me being nine years old. It made it into the first movie in that famous scene with Tom Cruise outside the sports bar fighting five guys – that was written from life right here.' (*What, you were expecting someone bigger?* was an improvised one-liner from Cruise that sadly ended up on the cutting-room floor.)

'I always had a knife in my pocket,' Lee told me. First a wooden-handled fishing knife he'd been given by his grandfather, then a flick knife. 'All the boys did.' There were no gangs, 'but it was very tribal'. The key thing was to behave in such a way that you never had to use it. His thing was to threaten to break the arm of anyone who tried, and one day when someone did, James broke his arm and that was that. He would always stand by his word. Even in 2019, when he spotted a rope-style chainsaw in a hardware store in Wyoming, all he could think of was how cool it would have been to have one of *those* in his pocket back when he was nine years old.

Lee reiterates the physicality of Birmingham with the same conviction he asserts the class-consciousness of his parents and grandparents. Birmingham was 'functionally like Detroit'. Violence was 'the natural language', 'the only way to express yourself'. He was smart, which was like having a target on your back. 'Worst was that I won a scholarship to a fancy school on the other side of town, and I had to fight my way out of the neighbourhood each day and then fight my way back in. I loved every minute of it.'

Charles Spicer, who lived a few blocks away in Grestone Avenue and also went to the fancy secondary school, remembered getting trouble from other boys for being in uniform on Saturday mornings. But he didn't remember the knives, or the double-edged Gillette razor blades sewn under the lapels of the blue blazer (paired snappily with a purple and yellow tie).

King Edward's was bigger and better than the rough, tough state primary. It was why the Grants had moved to Birmingham in the first place. Both Richard and James were smart as paint and they were jolly well going to get a good education if it was the last thing their parents did. Which in Lee's view it was. 'Once they'd got us into good schools their job was done.'

If King Edward's was bigger and better it would be so in every way, thought the literal-minded James. It had been drummed into him: *You've got to take this seriously, son.* It was hard to get into, so the fighting would be harder too, right? Again it went down on day one. There was a guy called John Gregory who didn't like dorky Richard and took it out on James, shoving him against a locker. 'So I kicked the shit out of him, broke some bones, and sent him to hospital.' Then, taking stock, it dawned on James that the school wasn't like that, that it was very 'genteel'.

It was this incident that briefly earned him the nickname 'Grievous', from 'grievous bodily harm' (an offence he explained to his American audience as akin to 'wounding with intent').

He didn't get shoved against any lockers again.

He felt no compunction in using force. 'I won't see anyone bullied,' he told me, though he systematically stuck the verbal boot into his (bullying) older brother. In his own view he lacked 'the prejudice gene', which was debatable, but I was prepared to believe he lacked the inhibition one.

Once he showed me a selfie from August 2013. His right eye was swollen and purple, and there was bruising just above his eyebrow, in the shape of a gecko, with little padded toes branching out from it and a virulent crimson gash like the flick of its tail. It was taken the morning after a fistfight on Broadway, when he had intervened between a drunken frat boy and a small Sikh cabdriver. It was a comprehensive victory, at the cost of some minor damage. 'That never happens to the real Reacher,' he commented, like I needed proof there was a difference. And like he himself was the fictional character.

'The other guy [the frat boy] was a mess, because I got annoyed when he hit me. Broken nose for sure, and ribs too, without doubt, but I don't know for certain because I just left him there and went home to bed. You can still see faint bloodstains on my pillowcase. They never quite came out.'

The guy could think, too. He wasn't an academic like Richard, but he was practical. He was no rocket scientist, was never going to find the cure for cancer, as he took pains to point out, but he was street smart, a real-world character, and when fists wouldn't do the job he could always fall back on his brains. Oh, and that healthy dose of arrogance.

'I'll always win,' he said on Central Park West in November 2017. He'd just won a fight with the taxman, who he believed now owed him half a million dollars. 'I call that a result,' he said, mildly. 'I told them two things: one, you're going to lose, you're already losing, it might be slow, but in the end you'll lose; and two, I'm very vindictive, so you're going to lose your boss a lot of money as well.' The dispute centred on issues of 'creative product' and 'unincorporated business tax' and whether or not Lee should be taxed on profits from books not written, or only partially written, in New York. Hitherto he had split the income in their favour. Then they started asking awkward questions, so he'd taken to calculating it by the word and the dollar.

59

From now on he would keep a meticulous record of where everything was written, right down to the minute.

I said nothing. Like Lee remarked of Reacher at the Random House 'Big Ideas Night' for the launch of *Night School*: 'He's a geek and a nerd in a lot of ways. But are you going to tell him that?'

I knew I shouldn't make assumptions about the writer based on my reading of his novels. To do so would be foolish, facile, naive. I'd learned my literary criticism at Cambridge, where the author was dead and there was nothing beyond the text. But this author was sprawling on an XXL leather sofa right in front of my eyes, occasionally sitting up in the lotus position or flicking one improbably long leg over the other like some kind of indolent cat deity or filleted Scheherazade. Maybe there was a stitch or two of embroidery, a touch of self-mythification, some subtle adjustment after the fact. Maybe he was a blagger and a bluffer in some ways. But was I going to tell him that?

When I opened a copy of *Killing Floor* and looked at the words on the page, there it was, all laid out before me in Reacher's name. What was I supposed to do? Pretend I hadn't noticed?

> The first day at each new school, I was a new boy. With no status. Lots of first days. I quickly learned how to get status.

Then later he'd been trained by experts.

> They taught me that inhibitions would kill me. Hit early, hit hard. Kill with the first blow. Get your retaliation in first.

His brutality, as he nicely expresses it, had thereby been refined.
Looking out for his big brother became second nature.

Plenty of times I would run out into some new schoolyard and see a bunch of kids trying it on with the tall skinny newcomer. I'd trot over there and haul them off and bust a few heads. Then I'd go back to my own buddies and play ball or whatever we were doing. Duty done, like a routine.

In *Killing Floor* he can tell Roscoe thinks he's overstepped the mark, just as Chrissie and Hemingway do in *High Heat*.

I'd killed one guy and blinded another. Now I'd have to confront my feelings. But I didn't feel much at all. Nothing, in fact. No guilt, no remorse. None at all. I felt like I'd chased two roaches around that bathroom and stomped on them. But at least a roach is a rational, reasonable, evolved sort of a creature.

And on that 101 per cent-proof self-belief he owed to the *you're-on-your-own-now-son* indifference of his parents: 'The books are all about the contest between the bad guy's arrogance and Reacher's arrogance.' Arrogance was an unattractive characteristic, but it helped keep Reacher on the right side of caricature.

Reacher has more unsightly scar tissue and a few more bullet holes, and yes, maybe Rapid City's Jimmy Rat can call on six thugs to Douglas Cooper's four, and it's a military base instead of a schoolyard, or Vietnam rather than Birmingham, or even Birmingham, Alabama, but these were incidental details. At heart, they were the same guy.

'By some genetic accident, I was enormous,' Lee said. 'I really have not grown very much since I was ten or eleven; I was a giant, a freak.' Reacher doesn't stand around shooting the breeze when what is called for is a knee to the groin. Infamously, he doesn't even hold good on a promise to count to three. 'He lies, he cheats, he shoots people in the back.' Which kept him real and made him human. There is darkness and light in all of us.

You could trace a direct line from Margrave, Georgia, all the way back to a school playground in a north-west suburb of 1960s Birmingham and even a single side street in 1950s Coventry. Maybe it was a matter of genes, and evolution. Every little thing had turned him into what he was. But for better or worse you could lay most of the responsibility at his parents' immaculately polished front door. It was his parents who had instilled in him that survival-of-the-fittest mentality, if only to improve the survival odds of his slightly-less-fit older brother. He had them to blame or thank for the never-say-die kill-or-be-killed winner-takes-all attitude to life that had made him unstoppable, *a nightmare for somebody*. He'd got status all right, that's for damn sure.

Lee didn't go to his mother's funeral. He was on the wrong side of the world again, for one thing. Funerals were about comforting the bereaved, and since his father was gone and the sons had moved beyond grief that wasn't really an issue. Anyway, he had something else planned for that day. Something he'd been looking forward to more than anything he'd looked forward to in a long time. There were other people involved and he didn't want to disappoint them: 'We'd all been looking forward to it. Why should I put them off, for a dead woman I didn't even like?' And more poignantly, he might have added, who didn't like him.

There was no scar above his right eye, where he'd been slugged defending the little guy on a Broadway sidewalk at the age of fifty-eight, because of a thousand dollars' worth of stitches. 'I wasn't going to bother, but Ruth [his daughter] made me.' He liked to be mothered from time to time, if only for the novelty of it, the unaccustomed, almost alien humanity. It was never a given. Was Ruth's insistence behind that obscure, much-debated title, *Make Me*? When Reacher got hit on the head and had dizzy spells, was this why Chang made him see a doctor? You could tell Reacher/Lee remembered it fondly, this small measure of affection, an unsolicited token of tenderness, because he refers back to it at the start of *The Midnight Line*:

> Fortunately I no longer have a headache. I got hit in the head, but that's all better now. A doctor said. A friend made me go. Two times. She was worried about me.

'I was totally unwanted,' Lee said, with startling and unrefined brutality, when he was shadowed during the writing of *Make Me*. 'And disliked. My mother said I was dog shit brought into the house on someone's shoe. Obviously I'm writing with an idea of getting people to love me.'

Writing. Fighting. Pure linguistic coincidence. Euphony. No more than that. But still it was funny how they rhymed so exactly.

8

Cherry Orchard

'We have to piss all over their stupid test.'
Second Son, 2011

Mairi Wilson and Alison Yeomans were best friends, in the same primary-school class as James. They didn't believe his stories about fighting, especially not the knives. Unless they were penknives. Alison carried a penknife in her purse for peeling oranges. But girls played at the back and boys at the front, so maybe they were sheltered. They laughed at the idea Lee had grown up in a rough area (which they assumed had been put about by his publicists). 'He lived in Handsworth *Wood*, for goodness sake!'

Rod Cooper owned all the Reacher books. He was an Old Edwardian from Northfield near the former Longbridge plant, where his grandfather had worked on the track and his mother, father and aunt in the offices. In 1961, when Rod was at primary school, Longbridge employed more than twenty-four thousand people in the car-manufacturing industry; now it was a gigantic retail park. 'If you lived in Handsworth Wood life was comfortable.'

'Cherry Orchard was a lovely school with gently enforced discipline,' Mairi wrote. 'It had an excellent academic reputation,' said Alison. The cane was in use but somehow would never be found, or if it was, would simply be cracked over the table to make everyone sit up.

A class photograph from 1962 against a background of trees shows an eight-year-old James top right of the back row, in pullover and shirt and tie, with a long fringe, smiling straight at the camera. Tall, but not taller than a couple of his peers. Not freakish. Not a giant. The pupils are all white. Lee could remember playing with two West Indian boys in infants' class, but by junior school they were gone.

The boys did woodwork and the girls needlework, but all mucked in together for drama and pottery and maypole dancing. After two years Mairi and James were promoted straight to Mr Grisedale's class, where at first they sat in the front row with the other 'Babies' (around ten precocious high-achievers in a class of forty-five), then at adjacent desks at the back for their final year, until they were separated for talking. In the monthly progress tests of fifty questions the Babies would aim for full marks while others rarely got beyond twenty; there was no stigma attached either way.

'Cherry Orchard taught me reading, writing and arithmetic,' Lee said. 'I have no complaints about King Edward's, but if I'd never had another day's schooling in my life I would have gotten on just as well.'

The headmistress was Maisie Lyster, who wrote a memoir entitled *Keep Your Sunny Side Up*. Miss Lyster was the first headmistress of Cherry Orchard Primary, which opened in 1947, the first new school to be built in the Midlands after the Second World War. She had watched it go up from her former temporary school, housed in a disused pavilion in the park next door. She was the aunt of Carolyn Lyster, who played a young female lead in the ITV soap opera *Crossroads*, and Lee surmised that this accounted for her (and therefore his) obsession with show business. She insisted on two big productions a year, high-intensity musicals jam-packed with action and emotion. Miss Lyster was a 'battle-axe', whereas Miss Flavell from Austria was young and pretty, objectified by the eight-year-old James as 'the archetypal fräulein' (though most likely she was married).

Mike Buckland, another of Mr Grisedale's Babies who went on to King Edward's, described Miss Flavell as a humourless disciplinarian who rapped inattentive pupils on the knuckles with a ruler and loved to yodel. But at least she allowed them to join in with BBC radio's *Singing Together* and anyway, he was used to being smacked by his mother. Lee thought it unfair to single out Miss Flavell. Use of the ruler was routine, especially in Miss Dawson's class. Miss Dawson taught him in the first year of junior school. Her job was to instil the school motto – *Aim high* – from day one, and the ruler proved helpful in ensuring they knew how to spell tricky words such as 'autumn' correctly.

Mike didn't recall much fighting, just football and marbles, with the odd game of cricket led by a caretaker who liked to show the boys how to bowl. But the girls' playground was another world. 'The only similarity was the tarmac.'

> They played 'The Big Ship Sails', singing a well-known street song and running through the arch made by the ever-increasing number of joined hands. I have to confess I took part in dive-bombing attacks to sabotage their games on the rare occasions we shared their playground.

Only Lee likened the grounds to a 'superfund site' (a US government designation for contaminated land) and spoke of 'black oily pollution bubbling up in one corner of the yard'. Admittedly he was on stage at the time, performing for a large American audience at the aptly named Rancho Mirage Writers Festival. It was 2016. By now he had to keep himself entertained, as well as his public.

At Rancho Mirage he also told (again) the (embellished) story of his first fight. Richard the nuclear scientist was riding his third-hand tricycle down the ruined street. James the giant was following behind on foot. Normal-sized Nicky shoved Richard off his tricycle; Richard said *I'll smash you*; James thought *Great, I'm gonna see a fight*; Richard said *Go smash Nicky*. James didn't really know how to smash somebody but his mother's instructions had been clear: *Do what Richard tells you.* So he thought: *I'll give it a try. How hard could it be?* But he was wobbly in the legs and the sidewalk was broken up from the wartime bombing, so 'to be absolutely, totally frank I tripped. My momentum smashed Nicky. I totally laid the guy out.' His hand was hurting. When he looked down he saw 'there were two little white things stuck in it', which he 'realised were Nicky's teeth'.

It was a happy ending. Richard got his tricycle back. James got a reputation as 'some kind of psychopath'. It was the most elaborate version I heard, but it was a long keynote and Lee was the master of pacing.

Mike Buckland recalled the eight-year-old James coming round for a party and wriggling through the serving hatch from the dining room to the kitchen and stuffing a cushion up his jumper to trick his parents into thinking he'd eaten too much. But only Mairi could remember going to James's house, and Mrs Grant flirting with her doctor father when he came to pick her up. Mairi knew Richard well enough to say hello to, but he 'wasn't the hello-saying kind of person'. 'Richard was polite,' Alison said, 'like his father. He just didn't notice other people the way James did.'

Later they would go to senior school by bus. Richard went on the early bus and played bridge on the lower level with his bridge-playing friends. Mairi went on the early bus too ('we self-organised into cool and non-cool groups'), but not late-rising James (now Jim) or Alison. When they were eleven or twelve Alison was Jim's date for the Scout Barn Dance. She wore an off-white wool dress with a boat neck and bracelet sleeves and zigzag detailing around the waist, with tights and heels, and in getting ready had burned two fingers through an electric shock from a hairdryer plugged into the bulb socket of a lampshade.

Jim wore a shirt and tie. He was polite too. 'He would never get on the bus ahead of me.' Jim's father picked her up in the car then went on to fetch Richard's date as well.

One day when Alison was sixteen years old and five foot nine-and-a-half inches tall but still wearing long socks and a boater and they were waiting at the bus stop, Jim told her she was 'the typical erotic schoolgirl'. He was tall and slim with a narrow waist but they were never boyfriend and girlfriend. Her father was a butcher, safe from the attentions of Jim's social-climbing mother.

Rex was demobilised in 1948. His priority was to avoid working with his hands, so he had little hesitation in joining first Her Majesty's Customs and Excise and then the Inland Revenue. He was obsessed with Britishness. His ambition was to sport the uniform of striped trousers and a briefcase embossed with the letters O.H.M.S. (*On Her Majesty's Service*), which James joked stood for 'Only Holds My Sandwiches'. He started out as a basic grade inspector but for years declined promotion, or accepted it only if the move wouldn't compromise the boys' schooling. After a series of long, selfless stints in Coventry, Birmingham, Walsall and Wolverhampton he at last found himself free to graduate to the role of Principal Inspector, which brought with it not only a furled umbrella but also the prized bowler hat. It couldn't, for Rex, get better than that. It was the cherry on the cake, his own secret gold standard for the absolute upper limit of you-have-arrived. It also entailed a move to Harpenden, closer to the capital, but by then it didn't matter because Richard and James had left for university. The two younger boys, David and Andrew, would have to cope.

They did the best they could, probably. Rex and Audrey belonged to a generation that revered the education they themselves had been prevented from getting and did 'the whole middle-class thing of moving to the right area so we could go to the right primary school, and then the right secondary school'.

'We realise now that we were privileged,' said Alison. 'Not that we came from privileged backgrounds. But our parents worked incredibly hard to make things better for us.'

It made sense to John Claughton, an Old Edwardian a few years younger than Jim. In their day King Edward's had been the direct grant school with the highest number of government-allocated free places (80 to 90 per cent) and was perceived as the beating heart of the community. It was normal for a bright Cherry Orchard boy to aspire to go there. 'It had an incredible density of bright kids because nearly everybody was there for free. Every junior school in Birmingham and beyond wanted to send their boys to King Edward's and every boy wanted to go there.'

Cherry Orchard Primary School was built to serve a 1930s housing estate on the former Cherry Orchard Farm, sold at auction in the early 1800s. In 1876 the Hamstead Colliery Company sank a mine shaft by the Tame, thereby ensuring that the farm's 'fine stream of water' would soon degrade into Lee's toxic river. The estate had been the brainchild of former schoolmaster Francis Daniels, who dreamed of improving living conditions for ordinary working people and in 1893 established the Ideal Benefit Society to pay members a pension on retirement at sixty-five. When the first state pension scheme was introduced in 1908 Daniels began building his 'Ideal Village' in Bordesley Green, designed by the same architects as the 'terrifyingly verdant' (Lee's words) Letchworth and Welwyn Garden Cities in Hertfordshire.

Lee traced this social conscience back to the Mechanics' Institute, where his parents first met. Originally called the Otley Useful Instruction Society, it had been founded in the early nineteenth century by local industrialists to provide working men with an alternative to playing cards or knocking back the week's wages at the pub. People still believed in the value of education because the benefits were immediate and tangible: you could go to evening classes and get a qualification leading directly to a job or promotion. No matter what they did to earn a living, the citizens of Otley had energy for self-improvement.

I wondered if this cultivation of simple virtues was a response to the horrors of war. After six years of sacrifice the country had voted in a Labour government, demanding nationalisation of key industries, building a National Health Service and putting their trust in public servants to allocate resources. But Lee thought it went beyond shell-shocked solidarity to a core of fundamental human decency. People understood that caring about each other's welfare 'was what belonging to a union meant' and 'basic honour and loyalty still prevailed'. These were not gentlemanly qualities, as commonly held, but belonged to the skilled working class. He'd seen this first-hand growing up in Birmingham, where old-fashioned work practices held good and employees were paid in cash on a Friday and no boss earned dispro-portionately more than the lowest-paid worker. This, in his view, was why his home city had been the last of the great industrial centres to falter. He cherished the memory of that lost world order, a system where 'education guaranteed advancement', which even at fifteen he sensed was already 'nearly over'.

For all it was 'the heart of the industrial badlands' and a prison he dreamed of escaping, Birmingham was also, in some other compartment of his brain, a lost socialist paradise. 'People might be uncomfortable about being labelled socialists but in their hearts they are,' Lee told the *Express* in 2011. He believed in the humanity of the average human being, and saw the rise in gang culture as a consequence of the disappearance of an industrial workforce and the decline in trade unionism, similarly hierarchical in structure and governed by a sense of shared purpose and comparable codes of loyalty.

Cherry Orchard was in hilly Handsworth Wood, which once belonged to Handsworth Manor and was the 'woodland half a league long and the same wide' referred to in the Domesday Book, with archaeological digs dating back to the Stone Age. Little is left of the wood. But immediately north is Sandwell Valley, with a lake and nature reserve and at its highest point, Hill Top, the remains of a Second World War gun emplacement. Charles Spicer, whose parents were publicans, played at Hill Top Farm as a boy, but not Jim. He'd never messed about on the pedal boats at Perry Hall Playing Fields either. Having fun was something other families did.

The Grants lived at 6 Underwood Road near the junction with Vernon Avenue, which the brothers would walk down on their way to school. It was a broad treelined street that I reached via a roundabout route from Hamstead Station, crossing the lacklustre River Tame and passing yet again an Indian takeout, laundrette, off-licence, convenience store and beauty salon. No. 6 was a two-storey red-brick semi-detached house with steeply sloping tiled roof and leaded windows and a white-painted built-in garage, a couple of blocks from the golf course. No blue plaque. A wafting pampas grass dominated the small raised flower bed set into a stubby tarmac driveway. At first James shared the room over the garage with Richard. When he was about twelve and they got central heating he moved to a room of his own, also looking out on the street. Later the family extended the house and he bagged a loft room at the back. But by then he was partying hard: 'I barely spent a night in my own bed beyond the age of fourteen.'

Handsworth Wood was seen as posh by residents of adjoining Handsworth (without the wood) and was designated an official evacuation zone during the Second World War. It no longer corresponded to Lee's idea of affluence, if it ever had, but as a boy he had been acutely conscious of the fine distinctions of class between one street and the next. Greenridge Road was a turning off Underwood, a short walk from the Grants' front door, but was a definite step up, because it was a cul de sac. Vernon Avenue too, a through road but more established, with bigger, greener, leafier trees, and bigger, greener, leafier detached houses, with fences and gates and hedges, and sweeping, semi-circular in-and-out driveways.

It had been the same in Otley. The sense of class was more four-dimensional than three, with a definite hierarchy between towns just a few miles apart on the map. Ilkley was a spa town and better than Otley, a factory town, which was better than Guiseley, likewise a factory town (where Silver Cross prams were made and the Brontë parents married and John Claughton was born), and as for the grand old spa town of Harrogate, 'it felt like you needed a passport to go there'. Grandma Scrafton would take the boys on the bus, but the idea of going to the world-famous Betty's Tea Rooms was greeted with derision. 'We used to go for the toffee,' Lee said. 'It's amazing I have as many teeth left as I do.' No doubt there were similar subtleties at street level too. Certainly there were competitions among Otley housewives for who had the cleanest doorstep.

When Lee went back to Cherry Orchard with *Inside Out* it seemed to him that little had changed. The mix of children was the same: the same ratio of 'thugs' to 'weaklings' and 'smart' kids to 'dumb' ones. But the system around them had changed, and it was hard to see how even the smart ones would escape. It wasn't enough any more to sit an exam: since the termination of the direct grant scheme in the mid-seventies you now had to afford the fees as well.

To get into King Edward's James had only to pass tests in intelligence, general knowledge and creativity. He'd known all along that he'd 'aced' the tests. Had walked in to the examination hall confident and strolled out again the same. It was a simple matter of logic. General knowledge was 'a walk in the park' and 'the IQ test was easy'. But the tests were 'such a big deal' for his parents that he felt he had to play along with their psychodrama. So when he came out to find them waiting he pretended to be nervous and uncertain: *They were really, really hard. I think I did OK, fingers crossed.*

There were probably celebrations in Underwood Road the day the results dropped through the letterbox. Of an austere, emotionless and withholding type. But Rex and Audrey's ambitions for their boys remained depressingly modest. 'Big dreams were discouraged,' Lee wrote in the *New York Times*.

> My parents' ambition [. . .] was for me to live in a two-family house instead of a rowhouse, and to drive a two-year-old car instead of a five-year-old.
> Couldn't argue. Still can't. What felt cautious and limited to us must have felt entirely sigh-of-relief natural to them. But it was frustrating. At the age of 8, I was gloomy. I remember wondering if it would ever change. If any of us would ever escape.

Lee didn't set out to be a writer, never dreamed of it. He was dogged on this point, not least because it would have been derided as madness. 'Ten thousand to one against,' his father said of his prospects of success when in 1994 he told Rex and Audrey of his post-redundancy plan. It would take years to free himself entirely of those parental shackles.

When Reacher rolls into town at the start of *Killing Floor* chief detective Finlay wants an address. Reacher doesn't have one. Reacher is from nowhere.

Finlay is patient and stubborn.

But Reacher is stubborn too. A geek and a nerd in a lot of ways. He resists for a full four pages before things come to a head and Finlay spells it out:

> 'What I mean is, where were you born, or where have you lived for that majority period of your life which you instinctively regard as predominant in a social or cultural context?'

What he got in reply was one of Reacher's short, imperious speeches, a potted history of life in an allegorical land called Military: 'Show me a list of US bases all round the world and that's a list of where I lived.'

For Lee the answer was always going to be simple.

'I'm from Birmingham,' he'd say.

The name 'Lee Child' tended to open doors. But when in 2017 the Head of Cherry Orchard saw him loitering outside on the street and invited him in, it wasn't because of who, or what, he was. They weren't looking for tips on how to write dialogue or create suspense or how to stage a *mano a mano* fight against seven bikers and be sure of coming out victorious, or even for a motivational speech on winning at the one-off game of life.

She led him into the classroom and stood him in front of the assembled thugs and weaklings and dumb kids and smart kids like an exhibit she'd brought in for show-and-tell. 'He used to be you,' she said. And maybe one day, she might have added, you could be him. Especially if you start out by reading every book in the library.

Her Year 4 pupils were doing a history project and struggling with the concept of time. Lee had turned up right on cue to step in as a handy, still-living example of what it meant to be old.

9

Elmwood

'So are there many irrational phobic
landscape gardeners at Quantico?'
The Visitor, 2000

'It was a nice little oasis in the town environment,' wrote Mairi,
who at the age of three was exiled south from Inverclyde Road to
Beaudesert Road in Handsworth proper. 'There was a formal garden,
and a field called the Paddock.'

'All I had to do was walk out the gate of my back garden,' wrote
Alison. 'There was a wooded path that ran behind our house, and on
the other side was a wildflower meadow.'

Until I found Mairi and Alison it felt like trying to track down the
hanging gardens of Babylon. Only a few people had heard of Elmwood,
and no one knew where it was. It didn't appear on the map, like
'Handsworth Wood' or 'Holly Wood'.

But once I found the Cherry Orchard gang I knew it was more
than just a poetic creation or one of the many wonders of Lee's fertile
imagination.

Elmwood had 'a wonderful children's library', said Mairi. 'It was
small, but crammed with books,' said Alison. Charles Spicer used to
go there on Saturday mornings, choosing books for the week to come:
The Hobbit and *Farmer Giles of Ham* and *The Chronicles of Narnia* or

ripping adventure yarns such as *Jennings Goes to School* and *Jennings Follows a Clue*.

'They were on the library shelf, so I read them,' said Charles, sounding like Lee. 'I would read anything. After washing the kitchen floor my mother laid down newspapers to help dry it. My sister relates that she often saw me on all fours reading the papers.'

James started with *Janet and John*, then moved on to Enid Blyton – his first real books, without pictures. 'Not so much the *Famous Five* but the *Secret Seven*, with that guy Fatty – a kind of mystery/crime fiction primer.' He read a book about explorers in the jungle who would tap their boots upside down to make sure there were no scorpions inside them, and, though the chances of there being scorpions in Birmingham or Manhattan were small, had turned his own boots upside down ever since. He read the story of David and Goliath ('the ultimate conflict paradigm'), rewriting it in his head so that just one time the big guy might turn out to be the good guy too. He read *The Cruel Sea* by Nicholas Monsarrat and then *The White Rajah*, a good brother/bad brother story that stuck in his mind for its gasp-out-loud plot moment and spoke straight to his second-son soul. The two 'ever-fighting brothers' were 'so different, so long-divided': one older and shorter, 'already set in the ways of self-importance', the other with a look of 'careless pride' about him, exhibiting a certain wildness 'as if he were life itself'. He read *Biggles* and *Gimlet* by W. E. Johns. Gimlet was another aristocratic officer type, but Copper was a London policeman seconded to the Royal Marine Commandos and Trapper was a Canadian trapper, and 'between them they were lethal'. He read all of Conan Doyle.

He loved series.

It seemed to James that Elmwood held a cornucopia of books. But he'd read all fifty volumes in the children's section by the age of four and the few hundred in the adult section by the time he was eight. He never thought about where they came from. Books were just there like the air. They seemed far more natural than cherries on trees. He had no concept of the writer. Not until he was about thirty-five years old.

Along with disused coal mines and bombsites, the library was all there was. Reading was what qualified you to get into King Edward's, like it was the only thing that might one day qualify you to become a writer, but the odds of picking up a book or crouching on the floor to scour the papers were greater then than now.

Elmwood Library was named for Elmwood House, the last of four large Victorian houses collectively known as the Colony, sold to the United Reformed Church in 1946 to save it from being demolished (the council had wanted the site for the new Cherry Orchard School). The congregation met there until their new church was completed in 1969. Which was when the library, like the hanging gardens, disappeared almost without trace.

The Grade B (locally) listed house had a pitched slate roof and was double-fronted but asymmetrical, with a double-height bay on the left and three flat-fronted storeys on the right. Above the arched and gabled double door with its swirling decorative metalwork rose a tall tower, with an arrow slit beneath two porthole windows, like two startled eyes and a surprised mouth, a mansard roof perched on top like a hat. It was a fanciful, free-spirited house straight out of a story book.

'The library was in the house,' Mairi said. 'The library and Sunday School were in the old stable block,' said Alison. 'It had blue criss-cross bricks in the courtyard to prevent horses from slipping.' 'The library was in an old Nissen hut on a bombsite,' said Lee. 'It could have been a Nissen hut,' said Charles. 'I can't remember.'

'There were no Nissen huts on the grounds,' said Alison. But the site had been commandeered by the military during the war, so maybe Lee was right.

Elmwood had a large church hall (built in 1953) where the girls did ballet and the boys went to Cubs. James belonged to the Cub Pack, like Mairi's brother and Martin Brown, who lived in Rocky Lane and went to King Edward's and Sheffield University and would one day act as best man at Jim's wedding. Their neckerchief was black with yellow edging. During 'bob-a-job week' (introduced in 1949 to foster community spirit and discontinued in 1992 on account of health and safety) the Cubs would knock on doors to offer their services for a 'bob' (a shilling, roughly five pence): shining shoes, walking dogs, mowing lawns, pulling weeds and washing cars. When the task was complete they would give compliant homeowners a yellow-and-black JOB DONE sticker to display in the window, like a shield to ward off further enthusiastic appeals for employment.

'Bob-a-job was OK,' said Lee, 'but I didn't get to keep the money.'

He could earn a penny per kill from his father, who would poke rats out from under the house using a broom handle pushed through the air bricks while his sons stood ready to bash them with sticks. But snow days were more lucrative. In the cold winter of 1963 James and his mates would charge a shilling for pushing cars uphill around the tight left corner onto the main road into town. 'They were all light vehicles with rear-wheel drive and crossply tyres,' Lee said. 'Useless in the snow.'

Reacher preferred to keep gardens at arm's length. Few things distressed him more than the property he inherited from Colonel Garber at the end of *Tripwire*.

> It was a physical weight, exactly like the suitcase in his hand. The bills, the property taxes, the insurance, the warranties, the repairs, the maintenance, the decisions, new roof or new stove, carpeting or rugs, the budgets. [. . .] Yardwork summed up the whole futile procedure. First you spend a lot of time and money making the grass grow, just so you can spend a lot of time and money cutting it down again a little while later.

Fields and meadows only rarely connoted some kind of pastoral idyll. At worst they were the locus of evil and exposure to the enemy, as in the hideously agricultural *Worth Dying For*. In his post-Reacher monograph *The Hero* Lee blames the advent of farming for 'a whole mess of issues', beginning with the ownership of land.

But Lee had read the old stories. It was inconceivable that there should not be a special place in his heart for woods and gardens, even if for the most part he kept it hidden under lock and key. Maybe he was more attuned to *Hansel and Gretel* and *Little Red Riding Hood*, where bad things happened and bad people (and wolves) needed sorting out, and later the adventures of Robin Hood and King Arthur and the dangers of the Black Forest. But how could he not be moved by Oscar Wilde's lonesome giant, whose selfishness causes his garden to fall into perpetual winter until both it and the reclusive, misanthropic Goliath himself are redeemed by innocence and trust and love; or by the orphaned Mary Lennox and crippled, motherless Colin Craven, who gain in health, strength and humanity as they become friends and cease to obsess over themselves and learn to tend the plants and animals of Frances Hodgson Burnett's secret garden?

Lee had said it plainly. He felt unloved as a child. The books he sought out were all about the same two things: being an orphan, and escaping. Books saved him. Books healed his failing heart. Books made him strong.

At some point the once again abandoned Elmwood House became a mosque. A tarmac road was built off Hamstead Hill opposite Vernon Avenue – a dead end called the Grange – the freshly minted address of a string of dull detached houses. Back in the Cherry Orchard days Elmwood was a secret, tucked-away place. 'I had to walk down a cinder path to get there,' Lee said, like he was following a trail of crumbs. Only he was never just walking. He was piloting a jet fighter, or driving to Checkpoint Charlie in Berlin to liberate a spy. All libraries were a haven and a refuge, but Elmwood was a hideaway too. If you could find your way in, then who knows? Maybe you would get to climb the beanstalk or scale the heights of *The Faraway Tree*.

I went back to the map and took another look at the street names. *Underwood, Elmbank, Earlswood, Woodend, Croftway, Greenway, Greenridge, Beechglade, Park Hill, The Spinney* . . . If I were to believe the words on the page I would think he had grown up in an enchanted forest.

'All that stuff his publicists come out with about how he never saw a tree? That's complete cobblers,' Martin Brown volunteered unprompted when I met him in London in 2019. Martin could remember walking up the drive to the door of Jim's house but never quite crossing the threshold. Jim's father was stiff and straight and reserved, he said, like his older brother Richard.

Once upon a time at Elmwood, James read the book that changed his life. It was the most well loved of the Lee Child origin stories. He remembered it very precisely, or at least the story he had told of it hundreds and thousands of times (more often even than the story of his first fight).

My Home in America was a twelve-page picture book he discovered when he was four years old. In his mind's eye, the eye of a four-year-old, the book is large format. On each page is a single captioned image of a different type of American home, lovingly painted in mimetic detail in creamy translucent watercolour: a California bungalow, a New England salt box, a Pennsylvania log cabin, a prairie farmhouse with windmill and water pumps. One page was captioned 'New York skyscraper'. It was the only one to include a human figure. Specifically, a small boy: a fair-haired blue-eyed boy of around five years old, sitting on the window ledge gazing out at the Empire State Building, with the city lit up like Christmas around it. 'I realise now,' said Lee, 'that he was there to emphasise the perspective, so the reader would follow his diagonal eye-line downwards. It was a very fifties New

York. The buildings were mostly lower, square and solid, and the light in the windows was yellow, not blue and glassy like it would be today.'

In that apple-cheeked boy James Grant recognised himself. It was a curious, out-of-body experience, like he was seeing himself for the first time, more clearly than in a mirror. 'That was me,' Lee said, to everyone who ever interviewed him who ever wanted to know who he was. 'It was there that I belonged. It was there that I was supposed to be living. Not in Birmingham. That was my city. That was my home.'

From then on his course was set. One day, the power of his words would conjure that alternative reality out of empty fictional space.

Logically, *My Home in America* presented as part of an educational series. But it stood alone on the shelf at Elmwood. Mairi hadn't read it. Nor had Alison or Charles. No one had ever been able to find it. No library had it in their back catalogue, no online search ever revealed it. It was Lee's and Lee's alone: the perfect mystical magical match between book and reader.

It was the same with Elmwood. There would be many more libraries – next up the purpose-built Tower Hill Library in Perry Barr, which he got to by crossing a high footbridge over the Tame Valley Canal. But only Elmwood (so far as I knew) had been founded in the year of his birth.

Lee accepted more invitations to libraries than anywhere else. He routinely topped the annual most-borrowed lists (one reader complained of being 297th on the list for the newly released *Blue Moon*). Thanks to him the King Edward's library was no longer merely 'worthy' but had a popular fiction annexe too (the teenage Jim had trekked over to Birmingham Central to feed his love of Alistair MacLean), presided over by his image and featuring well-thumbed copies of his books. When I visited, the librarian's face lit up at the mention of his name. His £20,000 donation in 2008 had funded not only a writing journal but a reading group, where pupils got to choose the book they read and each had their own copy, plus drinks and biscuits too.

When asked what he would do when he retired, Lee said: *Read*. When asked for his definition of happiness, he said: *Reading in a deckchair in the sunshine*. When asked for the downside of being a multi-millionaire bestselling author, he said: *Not having enough time to read*.

He could still remember how annoyed he'd been one Christmas Day when his daughter came home from her shift as Assistant Manager at the Angelika Cinema on West Houston Street and he'd had to put down Val McDermid's *A Place of Execution*.

Birmingham was no Garden of Eden. Nor was childhood a lost paradise.

But Elmwood was touched by those myths. Reading was 'just there, in the air'.

10

Maman

She was a mother, but that wasn't all she was.
The Enemy, 2004

His mother was 'mean' and 'malicious'. He had not a single happy memory of her. She was 'a monster of martyrdom' who resented her children and especially James, because he was the bad boy: the smoker, the football hooligan, the trade unionist, the Labour supporter, she didn't know which was worst. One thing she did know: he was of no use to her. 'I was the one who most disappointed her expectations,' Lee said, although she never made clear what these were. But this much was clear: it was all about her.

For a while Audrey perceived a certain seductive symmetry between her own brood of boys and the high-flying Denning brothers, entertaining fantasies of how they might likewise rub shoulders with the great and the good as Master of the Rolls or Lieutenant General or Deputy Chief of Defence. Perhaps that was what the Christmas Wonder Books were about. Maybe one of them could get killed or die during a war like Alfred (Lord) Denning's oldest sibling, and his youngest too. James, perhaps. Chief Troublemaker. Rex was employed On Her Majesty's Service, which had to be a notch up from draper. The Dennings had started life at a school run by the National Society of Education for the Poor, no less. And then won scholarships to

Andover Grammar and in the case of Lord Denning, a good conservative Christian, to Magdalen College, Oxford. Her boys had brains, and surely King Edward's, founded in 1552, was the equal of Andover, not founded until 1571. Hadn't William Shakespeare gone to King Edward's, or as good as? And wasn't he venerated by educated folk as the greatest of all Englishmen? Not that she wanted her sons to be writers or go on the stage. The neighbours might frown. Chief Justice or Chief Medical Officer would be acceptable. Anything the Dennings could do, the Grants could do better.

In the meantime, Audrey would focus on scrubbing the front doorstep. Cleanliness was next to godliness. She and Rex were not churchgoers, but adherents of a religious cult of respectability. They wanted to win first prize in the competition of the cleanest.

Lee had brushed up pretty well in the end. You could say he sparkled. But it wasn't until she was into her seventies and had moved to Wales that his mother was able to take pleasure in his success, when she heard someone talking about one of his books at the hairdresser's. She had waited long enough. Now at last that troublesome second son had given her some return on her emotional investment.

Which had been tremendous. After all, he had nearly died, when he was still her little boy. Not unlike Lord Denning, born two months early and so small and weak he was nicknamed 'Tom Thumb'. James wasn't like that. He had always been big. But being big didn't make him invulnerable, and for a while it had been touch and go. And who was it who looked after him? Her, of course. His mother. Devoted, as a mother should be. Not that this had been appreciated, except by the ladies at the hairdresser's.

James didn't die, though he did metamorphose into someone else, out of Audrey's reach. It was some kind of a heart thing, Lee said, brought on by a bout of rheumatic fever after a day spent heading the new leather football given to him by his Otley grandma ('an old-fashioned two-panel design, with a pink rubber inflation nipple nestled in an opening that did up with a square-sectioned leather lace'), which explained why 'heart things' featured so regularly in his writing. He spent four weeks in Birmingham Children's Hospital at the age of seven ('a vital month of re-education') and for a while was expected to drop dead at any moment. Everyone agreed that his life expectancy was limited. But it was fine, because being an invalid (like so many characters in fiction) gave him a lot of scope for reading. The flip side was it gave his mother a lot of scope for drama, too. There was a legitimate basis for her protective anxiety, but she stretched it as far as it was possible to go. Audrey didn't really want him to recover, not totally. Being the mother of a boy who was flirting with death had a romance all of its own, second only to flirting with the doctors that came with it ('like phoning Clark Gable or Omar Sharif, and having them show up at your house forty minutes later'). Come to think of it, that was another way he had let her down, by not actually dying. She could spare one son in the interests of a really good story. There was no getting away from it. He had been a disappointment.

James didn't die. But he never fully recovered. Even now, doctors checking out the messed-up state of his valves and ventricles would marvel at his continued existence. Not that he had much time for doctors. The smoking probably didn't help, either. Although if he gave it up he reckoned his heart might give up too. As it was it stopped beating a couple of times a week, sometimes while he was just sitting at his desk in front of the screen, the next Reacher story unfurling beneath his two index fingers, a thin string of cigarette smoke spiralling up from the glass ashtray to his left, and he would urge it to get going again: *Come on, come on*, he would say, underlining the point by a vigorous winding action of his right hand.

There was no doubt it had affected his outlook. But in a good way. Made him feel immortal. Death had missed its chance where he was concerned. He felt liberated. What fear could death hold for him, when his death had been so thoroughly rehearsed in his own – and his mother's – mind? 'I'm not afraid of death,' Reacher-Lee says in *Persuader*. 'Death's afraid of me.'

You could see how the drama was re-enacted in his writing. Maybe he owed to his mother Reacher's loneliness and alienation.

Audrey had inherited her father's skill with a pencil. When she and Rex wanted to enclose the front porch at Underwood Road she gave the builder a picture to work from, a blend of architectural drawing and artistic sketch. Another time, on a visit to Otley, Harry Scrafton had dug out her old school sketchbook and shown Jim her winning entry in a poster competition for a London Zoo advertisement to go on a double-decker bus. Audrey had included the bus for context, showing how her design would run the full length of it, with a monkey dangling sweetly from the lower bar of the 'Z'.

James wasn't great at art. But once when a new teacher joined Cherry Orchard he'd somehow fluked something halfway decent in the first lesson. Then again the week after that. Whereupon the teacher gave him responsibility for producing the class wall art and he spent the rest of that term living in fear of being found out. Impostor syndrome. It was an anxiety he would relive in writing each of his twenty-four novels – would he be revealed as a fraud, was this *a book too far*?

Was art something Audrey liked to talk about? I asked.

He didn't stop to think about it. 'It was impossible to explore any conversational subject with her.' Some uneducated people were auto-didacts, he said, and remain open to learning all their lives. Not so Audrey (though she was a competent academic Germanist, just as Rex could read and translate from Italian). At the time of the lunar landings there were lots of pictures of the moon's surface. The impact craters were due to the moon having no atmosphere, Jim explained. But

Audrey scorned this scientific fact. 'Every woman who's ever cooked porridge knows why the moon looks like that,' she said, banging her wooden spoon on the rim of the saucepan. 'She was claiming knowledge while revealing ignorance, at the same time making sure we knew that all she ever got to do was cook porridge for her ungrateful family. It was painful.'

As it was for Richard the time she lost her temper and whacked him with a handy plastic racquet from their beach tennis set. Rex was buttoned up, but Audrey was volatile.

The Grant family women had all suffered lifelong frustration: the miller's wife who could read but only afford to send the youngest of her seven children to school, the university student who left Queen's without the degree she deserved, and Audrey Scrafton, Lee's mother, dumped in the nowheresville of Otley and delivered into the suffocating hands of middle-class morality.

Josephine Reacher, in contrast, has no need to live out her fantasies through her sons.

Reacher's mother, not his Marine Corps father, is the rock on which the family is founded.

> The way she took charge spooled us all backward in time. Joe and I shrank back to skinny kids and she bloomed into the matriarch she had once been. A military wife and mother has a pretty hard time, and some handle it, and some don't. She always had. Wherever we had lived had been home. She had seen to that.

Only eighteen months before 'she had looked like a person with a lot of life left'. But this, in *The Enemy*, is their last meeting as a (now fatherless) family. Maman is too good to live forever. She has only days left. But she has put fresh flowers on the nightstands and made up the beds with crisp, clean linen. Next morning they had breakfast together:

'It was a civilized meal. Like we used to have, long ago. Like an old family ritual.'

Other than the sorry tale of the loveless porridge Lee had little to say about the meals Audrey presided over, except that if she ever found out he liked something she would strike it off the menu. Her attention was focused on first-born Richard, who had caused his helpless parents lifelong trauma by flat-out refusing to eat from the moment he was weaned. James was never fussy, but had grown up 'without learning that food had any value', and could still remember the specific taste sensation of the first meal he consciously enjoyed, at a Lebanese restaurant in Washington, DC. By which time it was 1976 and he was twenty-two years old. He had got into the habit of living off bowls of cereal. Home alone, cheese on toast was pushing the boat out.

Reacher's mother is warm, affectionate, demonstrative – everything that Audrey is not. She smiles at her boys, hugs them and kisses them and tells them she loves them. She calls them darling. But they're all grown-up now, and her job is done. They don't need her any more. 'That's natural, and that's good. That's life. So let me go.'

Like Reacher himself, his mother is a fatalist. Conceptually, death doesn't come as a surprise.

> 'It's something that's been happening since the dawn of time. It has to happen, don't you see? If people didn't die, the world would be an awfully crowded place by now.'

This, I knew, was Lee speaking. He was always spooling back to *the dawn of time*, to the point where the human story began, and had for a few years belonged to the Voluntary Human Extinction Movement. It was a commitment to having only one child, a way of pushing back against the population explosion.

When interviewers put it to him, he rejected the legacy question. He had no interest in living on through his grandchildren. He liked reading biographies of other people, but wasn't sure he wanted one of his own. (He would far rather dream up fictional versions: *After ten years as Aston Villa's top scorer and a brief marriage to Charlize Theron . . .*)

Reacher's big-picture perspective is established in *The Enemy*. Sidekick Summer puzzles over his calm containment in the face of imminent loss. Doesn't he like his mother? 'I like her fine. But, you know, nobody lives forever.' Whether you like them fine or not. Missing the dead was an integral part of life.

Lee gets us emotionally entangled with Reacher's mother only to immediately kill her off. So it's both a miracle and a mercy when he brings her back to life in *Second Son*, a prequel to a prequel, set before *The Enemy*, which is set before *Killing Floor*. The advance knowledge the author has of his main characters is what gives this novella its resonance. When Josie gets a phone call that her father is dying, she drops everything and heads for Paris in just the same way her sons will, sixteen years later.

The leave-taking at Okinawa airport prefigures that future farewell. It is Reacher who asks if his mother wants company. It is Reacher she takes aside (just as Rex and Audrey did when James was about to start school), because it's to him that she entrusts responsibility for the family in her absence (just as Richard was entrusted to James). Both brother and father get into trouble and it's Reacher who *steps up and does what is necessary*, not all of it pretty, but all of it 'what Mom told me to'.

Wondering at the moodiness of Stan and Joe, Reacher finds them 'silent and strained' to an 'excessive' degree.

No question that grandpa Moutier was a nice old guy, but any ninety-year-old was by definition limited in the life expectancy department. No big surprise. The guy had to croak sometime. No one lives forever.

Death. That's life. Or the obverse of it, at least.

Audrey Grant lacks Mme Reacher's sophisticated *savoir faire*. But like Audrey, Josie 'cared about our education. She taught us things, me and my brother Joe.' Like Latin. In a rare scene showing Reacher with both his parents – the first time we see all three together – they are discussing how he can't skive off to Paris to see his dying grandfather because he has an all-important entrance test to take.

His own mother didn't even teach James to read and write English. But it was thanks to her that he fell in love with Shakespeare. Audrey belonged to the Young Wives' Club and would occasionally get tickets for the Royal Shakespeare Company at Stratford-upon-Avon. One day Rex took his second son to see *Henry IV, Part 2*. James was nine years old and 'already a hater'. He knew he'd been dragged along because going to Shakespeare plays was what aspirational families did. But 'the two hours just vanished'. The experience was inexplicably intense and he was transfixed, from the first moment to the last.

After that he went back whenever he could, catching the bus to Stratford on his own. It was nice of his mother to get the tickets, I thought. But Lee was having none of that. 'She got them as part of her own class fantasies. My enthusiasm was a happy collateral consequence.' Had he asked for them, she would have artfully contrived to provide something else. It was all-out psychological warfare, with each of them trying to outwit the other.

Audrey was as much a disappointment to Jim as he was to her. At the Darien Library in 2010 he explained how Janet Salter got her name in *61 Hours*. Mark Salter had won a charity auction in aid of autism research and asked for his mother's name to be included in Lee's next book. Mark Salter was clearly a very nice man. 'Often,' Lee said, 'not always – *perhaps not in my case* – if there's a nice man, standing behind him somewhere is a nice mother.' The personal aside had been strictly unnecessary.

Reacher doesn't fight against his mother, not even when he is losing her.

You die when it's your time, Josie says.

> 'It's like walking out of a movie. Being made to walk out of a movie that you're really enjoying. That's what worried me about it. I would never know how it turned out. I would never know what happened to you boys in the end, with your lives. I hated that part. But then I realized, obviously I'll walk out of the movie sooner or later. I mean, nobody lives forever. I'll never know how it turns out for you. I'll never know what happens with your lives. Not in the end. Not even under the best of circumstances. I realized that. Then it didn't seem to matter so much. It will always be an arbitrary date. It will always leave me wanting more.'

This stands as Lee's take on John Donne ('For Whom the Bell Tolls'), or Dylan Thomas ('Do Not Go Gentle into that Good Night'), or Corinthians ('When I was a child, I spake as a child'). Maybe one day it would become equally canonical.

In the latter part of his career, New York's Mysterious Bookshop began to release leather-bound and marbled collectors' editions of the Reacher novels, lettered and numbered. Each includes an introduction by the author. Reflecting on *The Enemy*, Lee says:

> The 'walking out of the movie' speech the mother delivers, and the dialogue before and after it, is some of the writing I'm happiest with. There was something important I wanted to tell my daughter, but some things are hard to say, so I had Reacher's mother tell Reacher and his brother instead.

Readers took comfort in the down-to-earth no-nonsense way he cut the enemy down to size and rendered it human: the one thing we all share in common. 'People live, and then they die,' Reacher says in *Tripwire*. 'And as long as they do both things properly, there's nothing much to regret.' There's a caveat. But the basic message is *Hey, don't beat yourself up. You did the best you could, probably.*

'I'm with Kafka,' Lee says at the end of Andy Martin's *With Child: Lee Child and the Readers of Jack Reacher.* 'The meaning of life is that it ends.'

He didn't want a fuss.

Our period of residence was uncertain. Death was always going to come knocking in the middle of the movie.

11

An Armful of Air

Nobody knows what a fatal heart attack feels like.
The Enemy, 2004

The Enemy begins with a phone call at two minutes before midnight on 31 December 1989. A death, from natural causes. Heart attack. 'Happy New Year,' says Reacher, to the cop who calls it in.

There is a meditation on what a fatal heart attack might feel like (nobody knows):

> Medics talk about necrosis, and clots, and oxygen starvation, and occluded blood vessels. They predict rapid useless cardiac fluttering, or else nothing at all. They use words like infarction and fibrillation, but those terms mean nothing to us. You just drop dead, is what they should say.

I wondered how much of that vocabulary Lee had picked up when he was seven, dozing in a hospital bed while his mates were kicking a football around the park.

There is a disquisition on average death rates. In the absence of combat, soldiers 'don't die any faster or slower than regular people', and they die of the same things as regular people too, every single day of every single year: 'accidents, suicides, heart disease, cancer, stroke, lung disease, liver failure, kidney failure'. *People live, and then they die.*

Three minutes after midnight Reacher gets another call, from the duty sergeant. She's a mountain woman from north Georgia, all bone and sinew, as hard as woodpecker lips. But what matters is 'she had a baby son'. What matters is: she is a mother.

The sergeant brings Reacher his New Year cup of coffee. The Berlin Wall is halfway down. People are partying in Germany, complete with sledgehammers. But not in the army. In the army they're looking at their own dissolution. It's like that great edifice has already been half demolished.

'We won,' I said. 'Isn't that supposed to be a good thing?'
'Not if you depend on Uncle Sam's paycheck.'

The issues dig deep. What to do when we defeat the enemy. When there is no enemy any more. When our whole reason for living and dying is ripped out from under our feet. Do we have to invent one? Is peace the thing we fear most? Do we need someone to hate as much as we need somebody to love? Someone we can point to and say: *they are not us, but they define who we are*? What are we going to do with all those high-spec guns and 70-ton, $4-million tanks? I knew Herman Wouk's *The Winds of War* and *War and Remembrance* featured among the 180,000 books Lee had read, and that he considered them the most evocative account of what it was like to live through the Second World War: this was a 1990s remake, with the Armoured Divisions instead of the dinosaur-battleships bucking against the apocalyptic threat of redundancy.

Reacher's brother calls at the start of chapter two. Leaves no message. Some time between daybreak and nine in the morning he calls again. Leaves no message. Reacher figures Joe must have made a big effort to find him. The last time they'd met was at their father's funeral, three years before. He writes the name 'Joe' on a slip of paper and underlines it, twice. Chapter two ends with a dead woman on a hallway floor. Chapter three starts with a description of what she looks like.

Joe calls again in chapter four. Leaves a number. Reacher finally calls back. It's night-time on New Year's Day. Their mother is dying. By nightfall on 2 January the brothers are in Paris.

The 'heart thing' did more than expand the future writer's vocabulary. It made James grow up fast, and maybe a little morbid. Death was something he'd thought about more than the average guy, irrespective of age. It was like an apprenticeship.

The word 'nothing' appears 326 times in *The Enemy*. Its use is entirely natural. About half the time, slightly less, it arises when people find nothing. Like when Reacher, still a military policeman working homicide, uses 'traditional, time-honoured methods of investigation' to look for things.

Here, in chapter one, Reacher is searching Kramer's motel room.

> Nothing in the pockets. I checked the shoes. Nothing in them except the socks. I checked the hat. Nothing hidden underneath it.

Here, in chapter ten, he is searching a suspect's quarters.

> There was nothing else in Carbone's six-by-eight cell. Nothing significant, nothing out of the ordinary, nothing explanatory. Nothing that revealed his history, his nature, his passions, or his interests.

It's not hard to see how nothing adds up.

> 'What have you got?'
> 'Lots of nothing.'

About half the time, slightly more, it arises when people say nothing. 'I said nothing' appears eighty-three times. 'The books are cerebral,' Lee told *Playboy* magazine in 2012. Reacher says nothing because 'he's thinking. Given that the books emphasize the physical, there's a quietness that is reassuring. It's comforting that this giant is capable of rational thought. He's like a dancing bear.' But it isn't always Reacher. *I, we, she, he, they*, all 'said nothing'. Sometimes because they have nothing to say; sometimes because it's safer; sometimes when faced with a higher authority.

In Paris, Jack and Joe run up against the ultimate authority, and the ultimate enemy too. Josie opens the door to them. But she is and she isn't their mother. This woman is already inhabited by death. She is only sixty. Her bones and veins and tendons are standing out, and her skin is translucent. When they hug (of course they hug) she feels 'cold and frail and insubstantial'.

Reacher asks what happened. 'It's nothing.' Reacher says: 'Doesn't look like nothing.' Though that's exactly what it looks like, since she is fading before his eyes. Why didn't she tell them? She doesn't answer. They prompt her. 'She said nothing.' When she finally reveals she has cancer, 'nobody spoke for a long time'. She has known it for a year. 'Nobody spoke.'

Joe rages against the dying of the light. He doesn't want to let his mother go, not gently or in any other way. But Reacher 'said nothing'.

Josie harks back to the arrival of the Germans in Paris when she was ten. Her sons 'said nothing'. She says how everything after that has been a bonus. 'We said nothing.' She knows they will miss her. 'We said nothing.' She knows they might feel abandoned. 'We said nothing.' Because of them death will always find her 'wanting more'. Everyone 'sat quiet for a spell'. Joe asks how long. Not long. 'We said nothing.' They go out for dinner and all order the same thing. 'But my mother ate nothing and drank nothing.' There is no eating in the

Underworld. No need to feed the shades. They took a cab home 'in silence'.

The phrase 'said nothing' appears twelve times in chapter six of *The Enemy*, in some of the most moving prose Lee has written. If you include variations on the theme, references to silence number at least twice that.

The plot takes Reacher and Summer to Berlin, next stop California. But first, between the two, they go back to Paris. 'I have to see my mom,' Reacher says.

Reacher never does see Josie again. Not alive. He's waiting for Joe, flying in the next day. It wouldn't be right to go see her on his own. They were brothers. They belonged together. Deep down, there was always the faint echo of that old routine, that he would watch out for Joe like Joe was watching out for him. Their mother loved them equally. It wouldn't be right to suggest he loved her more by muscling in ahead. Reacher wasn't the type for showy self-righteousness. He was the second son. Didn't need to be number one.

On the night of her death he is lying in his hotel bed listening to the sounds drifting in from the street.

> Then the city went quiet and silence crowded in on me. It howled all around me, like a siren. I raised my wrist. Checked my watch. It was midnight. I dropped my wrist back down on the bed and was hit by a wave of loneliness so bad it left me breathless.

This pinpoints the 'moment', of epiphany or liberation, that was lacking when Lee's own parents died. Which compensates for the anti-climax of reality. Brilliantly, with that seamless integration so characteristic of his writing, it is also the moment in which the puzzle of the plot is finally solved. Like a small intricate machine embedded in the heart of the text, and making it tick. A heart thing, but 101 per cent healthy.

Reacher stands by his mother's coffin for five long minutes, 'eyes open, eyes dry'.

> 'Life,' Joe said. [. . .] 'A person lives sixty years, does all kinds of things, knows all kinds of things, feels all kinds of things, and then it's over. Like it never happened at all.'
>
> 'We'll always remember her.'
>
> 'No, we'll remember parts of her. The parts she chose to share. The tip of the iceberg. The rest, only she knew about. Therefore the rest already doesn't exist. As of now.'

It's the same for Josie's father in *Second Son*. Grandpa Moutier dies at ninety, taking with him like everyone does 'a lifetime of unknown private hopes and dreams and fears and experiences, and leaving behind him like most people do a thin trace of himself in his living descendants'.

Lee's mother was gone. Where she had been was nothing. There was no need to go to her funeral. The time for talking was over.

He wouldn't forget her. She was the only mother he had. She had left something of herself in him, if only the thinnest of thin traces. Every little thing had turned him into what he was.

'Kiss your baby for me,' Reacher tells his hard-as-woodpecker-lips sergeant.

> 'My mom just died. [. . .] One day your son will remember mornings like these.'
>
> She nodded once and walked to the door. A minute later we saw her in her pickup truck, a small figure all alone at the wheel. She drove off into the dawn mist. A rope of exhaust followed behind her and then drifted away.

Mist. Exhaust. Drifting away into nothing.

The comfort and consolation and joy Reacher finds with Summer are what most of us are looking for. But there's only one kind of love in this book that really matters: the love of a mother for her son. Of a parent for her – or his – child.

Three times the homeward-bound Odysseus tries to hold his mother in his arms when by chance he encounters her in Hades. Three times she sifts through his grasp like a shadow.

Nobody knows what a fatal heart attack feels like. Not even Lee, though in the ingenious 'Pierre, Lucien & Me' (*Alive in Shape and Color*) the first-person narrator pictures his body falling to the floor in the theatre 'like an empty raincoat slipping off an upturned seat'. But if pushed, the medics in *The Enemy* predict 'nothing at all'. So when their mother tells Jack and Joe that what is happening is 'nothing', we've been primed all along to know what it means. That hollow word has sounded dully throughout the book, 326 times, strangely comforting, almost soothing, like a slow heartbeat, the insistent tolling of a funeral bell.

Send not to know for whom the bell tolls, It tolls for thee.

'This case was like a wave on the beach,' says a JAG Corps guy in the final chapter. 'Like a big old roller that washes in and races up the sand, and pauses, and then washes back out and recedes, leaving nothing behind.'

When all is said and done, when the last word is written and read and we turn the last page and close the book, only one thing remains.

Nothing.

12

A Heart Thing

He enjoyed watching soccer, to an extent.
Die Trying, 1998

It has to have a beating heart. That was what he said, when would-be writers asked for advice. It was true for books in the same way it was true for human beings. The book was something more than a well-oiled machine. Which explained his attitude to editing.

Lee was famous for writing only one draft. He saw it as an intellectual challenge: an elegant, mathematical game. But it was also musical: a jazz-like improvisation or composition-in-performance. First sentences were his favourites. In the beginning the possibilities were infinite. Anything could happen. Then the possibilities were reduced by half, then by half again, and so it continued, with the constraints increasing and the possibilities decreasing until finally you reached the end: the last, inescapable, *necessary* word. The book followed its own inexorable evolutionary logic, almost as though it was writing itself. It's like a funnel shape, he said, that narrows with every decision the writer makes, and when you get far enough along there's only one way to go – which gave writing its high-stakes drama, like Reacher having only one way out of the underground tunnel in *Die Trying*. A Lee Child novel was the inverse of the never-ending text imagined by Jorge Luis Borges in 'The Garden of Forking Paths', an eight-page

First World War thriller and detective story first published in English in *Ellery Queen's Mystery Magazine* in 1948, in which all possible outcomes of an event occur simultaneously, with each then leading to further proliferations of possibilities.

But mostly his refusal to edit (aside from 'combing' and 'smoothing' and 'churning' his work for the first hour of every working day, which meant all of it was edited at least once) arose out of his commitment to authenticity. This is what he told ThrillerFest:

> When I've finished – even though I'm perfectly normal and sane and rational – there's this strange thing going on, where once it's written, that's what happened. It's as simple as that. You can't change the facts. You can't change history. My editor says: 'but wouldn't it be better if this happened before that?' 'Yeah, probably,' I say, 'but it didn't.' On an emotional level I would find it dishonest to change it. It would betray the organic nature of the narrative. If you pull on one thread on page 294 then the whole thing can fall apart. And the final product will feel over-tampered, artificial.

You can't mess with a beating heart. In the worst case it would be tantamount to murder.

But the heart goes about its business unseen and unnoticed. Its sole point is to get on with the job, without clamouring for attention.

Not so in the King Edward's school song, with its boastful opening lines:

> Where the iron heart of England throbs beneath its sombre robe,
> Stands a school whose sons have made her great and famous
>   round the globe,
> These have plucked the bays of battle, those have won the
>   scholar's crown;

Old Edwardians, young Edwardians, forward for the School's
renown.

Lee didn't like the song, had never liked it. Too pompous, too
grandiose, even allowing for the inflated idealism of the genre.
He thought the image was 'ridiculous'. It was also wrong in two vital
ways. The Birmingham legacy was all about getting the job done
properly without fuss or fanfare. It wasn't even a heavy industry town.
That was Sheffield, the city of steel, which once had more cooling
towers than trees. Furthermore, he argued, Coventry was at the
geographic centre of the country, not Birmingham. The metaphor
was completely off. The song had been written by an Old Boy (son of
the Town Clerk of Birmingham and an Oxford-educated poet) but
that was no guarantee of authenticity. The final product was over-
tampered and artificial.

What lay at the heart of Birmingham was not the belching monster
of the foundry but the *small intricate machine*. Birmingham was about
craftsmanship.

It was craftsmanship that led Jim to the Villa. By a roundabout
route, via David's dad's workshop.

Underwood Road was about equidistant between the Hawthorns
and Villa Park, the home grounds of West Bromwich Albion and
Aston Villa football teams. James could have gone either way. At first,
because of David Harris, the odds favoured West Brom. David was a
Handsworth Wood friend whose father had a season ticket to the
Albion. Sometimes Jim would wander over to David's place on
Saturday mornings to see if his dad was working overtime and there
was a ticket going spare. Mr Harris made beautiful things in metal. He
had a simple workshop with a bare earth floor. The work he under-
took was anything but simple. His skills were in high demand. Lee
remembered exquisite cruet sets in finely wrought silver, possibly

made for Cunard's original *Queen Mary*. He remembered fake coins commissioned by the Greek government for archaeologically inspired travellers to find on Knossos, home of the Minotaur, to facilitate a good tourist experience. Traces of both these memories recur in his life and his writing.

He would take technical drawing at King Edward's and liked to design things. But he had no special desire or ability to make them: 'I'm accurate plus or minus an eighth of an inch' – but that wasn't the precision he was after. Like storytelling, metalworking was in the blood. It came with the territory, for a boy from Birmingham.

The two seven-year-old mates would walk the two miles to the Hawthorns and back. They didn't have the patience to stick around the workshop and learn a trade. But James never became a Baggies fan. Ironically, treacherously, the thing he remembers most about the place is Aston Villa.

It was the last time he went there. Villa were playing away to West Brom and won 2–1. The scoreline was close but the gulf in style was unbridgeable. The Villa players were 'pirates', full of swagger, swash-buckling rock-and-rollers. In the end it came down to hair, and it was Derek 'the Doog' Dougan (a 'lippy', combative, streetwise maverick and fan of psychedelic rock who was thrown out of the club before becoming a leading light in the players' union) who sealed the deal. Or more specifically, his bald (shaved) head. Back then 'the only man in the world with a bald head' was Yul Brynner. Now Yul had company, in the most unlikely of places.

It was a *coup de foudre*. James said *au revoir* to David and set out to walk the two miles in the opposite direction, to Aston. There, on his very first visit, as if decreed by fate and written in the stars, he watched Villa thump Ipswich 8–3. Or possibly it was Leicester. He wasn't 101 per cent sure. Except about it being a thumping, executed with swagger and style. Simon Inglis (fellow Villan and Old Edwardian, author of *Villa Park: 100 Years* and *Sightlines – A Stadium Odyssey*), with a cooler head, remembers 'watching Villa trounce Leicester 8–3' on 21 April 1962, when he too was seven years old. He doesn't mention the hair. For James, it was as if cutting off Samson's locks had made the hero stronger. He on the other hand had gone weak at the knees. To this day he remains 'a helpless fan': for better for worse, for richer for poorer, in sickness and in health.

'The Aston Villa guys were so cute,' says Holly in *Die Trying*. 'I was in love with soccer from that night on. Still am.'

'It's a feeling you never get over,' Lee told club historian Rob Bishop in a 2011 interview ('Reach for a Villa thriller', for AVFC Official) on publication of *The Affair*. It was as passionate as Reacher's tumultuous relationship with Carter Crossing sheriff Elizabeth Deveraux, but Lee was entangled for life.

For Inglis too the victory against Leicester was his first time at Villa Park. But he was already committed. It didn't make sense when he lived a mile from St Andrew's, but the 'cheap and nasty' blue-and-white of Birmingham City left him cold, whereas Villa's claret-and-light-blue was 'Victorian, elegant, almost considered'. It was a conscious aesthetic choice. (I didn't dare mention the historical connection with Coventry.) When he was six years old his mother had taken him to Aston Park and he had written in his composition book about how the ground had 'fourty-two flud lights for at night when they play'. A year later he went back, learned his first swearword, and wrote that 8–3 'was a high football score'.

The route to Villa Park took you through Aston, past the old HP Sauce factory and the Alpha Television Studios. Coming back from a game you might see a small crowd gathering in hope of catching a glimpse of Cilla Black, who hung out with the Beatles and in the 1960s was the UK's bestselling female recording artist. 'I think there is something deep in the Birmingham psyche that is suspicious and intolerant of winners,' said Inglis. 'In London or Manchester you could be a pumped-up winner, but in Birmingham they'll say, *Oh yeah, why are you so special then*?'

Like Lee, Inglis no longer lived in Birmingham. Its charm was founded on past glories. His maternal grandfather had a workshop in Hockley and sold screws out of the back of his car, and Simon had travelled around with him visiting the old forges and metal-bashing workshops: 'the engine room of old Birmingham, which was on its way out'.

In his 2018 introduction to Bishop's *Euros & Villans* Lee singles out European nights as the high point, the climax, the equivalent of three days with Deveraux. 'The place went insane.'

> The crisp, cold evenings, the high stakes, the sense of importance, the big stage. And the butterflies in the stomach, the slight sense of unease, the slight sense of fear – often we were playing huge, famous clubs, packed with stars. Now the Premier League gets who it wants, but back then our only foreign buys were Scottish or Irish, and it was the Italians and the Spanish who had the international superstars. I remember watching the warm-ups with a sense of dread. How were we going to beat these guys?

Not that Reacher suffered from performance anxiety: he got on with the job like James Grant running his mutual benefit society from the playground. But the potential for ecstasy (and its bedfellow, agony) was roughly the same.

The experience of attending weekly soccer matches was akin to life on the road.

> [Most games] were random and often meaningless, home and away, some wins, some draws, some defeats, marked out as special for me by

the sheer fun of being with the people around me, most of whom I had never met before, and would never meet again, but for the couple of hours we were jammed together in the crowd, if the mood struck just right, there would be fast wit and blazing sarcasm, and laughs and jeers, and I couldn't imagine a better place to be.

These are the casual, glancing encounters that punctuate Reacher's solitary journey through the vast American interior. Take the opening of *The Midnight Line*, which reads like a compressed, toned-down riff on *The Odyssey*. First comes the strong confident farm woman with a dog the size of a pony who gives him a lift out of the small sad town and out of Wisconsin towards Minnesota in the general direction of South Dakota and Rapid City in her Honda pick-up truck, dark red metallic, 'lots of chrome and lots of shiny paint':

> An hour later she stopped and let him out at the I-90 cloverleaf. He thanked her and waved her away. She was a nice person. One of the random encounters that made his life what it was.

He lies, he cheats, he shoots people in the back. But he's a well-brought-up lad at heart. Will give thanks where they're due, thanks to Josie and Stan.

Then he sticks his thumb out again, turning sideways to the oncoming traffic to minimise his bulk, because there was nothing he could do about his height, because the less threatening the better, because he knew he was subject to snap decisions. Next up is a stainless-steel milk truck with a tanker shaped like a boat-tail bullet and a driver Reacher kept awake by telling stories, some true, some made up, like some kind of 'human amphetamine'. After a night in a motel he catches a third ride in a huge red truck pulling a white boxed-in trailer, driven by a canny old guy whose wife is a reader and thinks about things and would have pertinent theories about guilt and transference and Reacher maybe needing a girlfriend to talk things over with.

> As always the driver wanted to know where his temporary passenger was travelling to, and why. As if in payment. A long story, for a long distance. For some reason Reacher told him the truth. The pawn shop, the ring, his compulsion to find out what connected the two. Which he said he couldn't entirely explain.

Which at that point (chapter seven) was exactly the position the writer was in – he hadn't yet reached that fork in the path. There was still a choice. Which road would he take? Which offered the best odds of success? For Reacher, like Odysseus, like Lee, storytelling was a bus ticket to a final destination, and often enough a meal ticket too.

The rhythm was the same with women: a sequence of episodic affairs rolling up with the reliable regularity of rides in Wisconsin or waves on a beach, each of them sweet and each of them fleeting, when *the mood struck just right* and he *couldn't imagine a better place to be.*

When he eventually gained consciousness of James Grant's new identity, Lee came to realise how much he derived from such 'glancing contact with life': snatches of conversation overheard at random, chance encounters with strangers, unscripted intersections with other stories and lives. He gave a trivial example. He was in a boutique that sold leather goods when a smartly dressed woman came in asking for a Filofax binder. Lee still used a Filofax, so her request registered. But time had marched on into the digital age and the shop had only two, which the assistant laid out on the counter. Whereupon the woman pulled out a phone, made a call, and said without superfluous pleasantries: 'They've got a green one and a blue one.' Then after a short silence: 'No, I'm not being passive-aggressive.' Lee filed it away for future reference. One day he might subtly transmute it into Reacher gold. He said nothing. He was content to walk away from the passive-aggressive woman. 'I don't have to live with the fall-out. It just becomes inherently interesting.'

So it was at Villa Park. Ninety minutes of intense communion. The stadium pulsating to the beat of a single heart. The fans living and breathing as one, then splitting apart again into separate, unrelated individuals each going their separate, unrelated ways. Fusion. Followed always by fission.

I hadn't had Lee's opinion of the motley collection of Villa songs, which ranged from the obscene to the murderous. 'I remember loads of those chants,' wrote poet Benjamin Zephaniah for the *Guardian* in 2009, 'there's something really tribal about them.' Zephaniah was born four years after Lee. In his 2015 'Ode to Aston Villa' for the FA Cup quarter-final clash with West Brom he recalls a similar pivotal moment:

> I was born here on the Handsworth Aston border
> I had a choice
> I could go one way to West Brom or the other way to the
> Villa
> But the sound that I could hear loudest in my ears
> Was the sound of claret and blue

Zephaniah couldn't remember another black spectator as a kid, and only one black player on the pitch, Clyde Best, who played for West Ham: 'When he came to play at Villa it was a special occasion.' But he embraced the whole microcosm of fabulous, flawed humanity:

> When does a community of that size come together and sing like that? Even churches don't have those kind of numbers. And the joy

when your team scores is still unbelievable. I was at the Villa recently and we scored and this girl, a complete stranger, jumped up and hugged me.

Even Reacher is susceptible at one remove, out of empathy for kidnap victim Holly, who has a soft spot for Villa because they beat the Germans:

> He enjoyed watching soccer, to an extent. But you had to be exposed early and gradually. It looked very free-form, but it was a very technical game. Full of hidden attractions. But he could see how a young girl could be seduced by it, long ago in Europe. A frantic night under floodlights in Rotterdam. Resentful and unwilling at first, then hypnotized by the patterns made by the white ball on the green turf. Ending up in love with the game afterward.

Jim went to home games all the way through school, walking the two miles each way, standing on the terraces in the legendary Holte End around two-thirds of the way down and singing and swearing with the best of them. Perhaps this was the crucible for some of Reacher's choicer threats, such as the much-loved, often-cited 'Either you can walk out of here by yourself, or these other fat boys behind you are going to carry you out in a bucket' (*Killing Floor*). In the 1980s, when he had a job and an income, he bought a season ticket in the lower level of the more glamorous Trinity Road Stand. He had a seat on the end of a row 'which was great for standing up when they scored'. For away games he could watch the live feed at Granada Television, like he did for the 1994 League Cup final against Manchester United (when Villa won 3–1 at the old Wembley Stadium) and the European Cup final against Bayern Munich in 1982, where Holly was with her father (when Villa, then champions of England, won 1–0 in Rotterdam).

The stadium was built in the parkland of seventeenth-century Aston Hall and opened in 1897. Previously the site had been home to Aston Lower Grounds, a Victorian theme park with boating lakes, a theatre and gardens. For a while Villa's offices were housed in the former aquarium. It was the ambitious Fred Rinder, chairman from 1898 to 1925, who built the Trinity Road Stand with its architectural echoes of the hall: leaded windows, curved panelling on the balcony, gold-leaf mosaics and pavilion-style towers flanking a sweeping central stairway. 'After today,' wrote Inglis in an impassioned eulogy on the eve of demolition ('Last Rites for the Holy Trinity', 2000), 'Villa Park, and the landscape of English football, will never be the same again.'

Sceptical about the prospects for a replacement, doubting the new could rival the old in romance and beauty, Inglis drew on an analogy close to Lee's heart: 'I can't help feeling as if a solid old Bentley with leather seats and a walnut dashboard is being sacrificed for a new hatchback.'

Perhaps it was all to the good that by then Jim Grant had also gone, to be replaced by a new model, Lee Child. With the crucial difference that the hatchback was being traded in for a Bentley, the pumpkin for a carriage with six white horses, the frog for a future king.

The young James had once dreamed of starring as a shaven-headed centre-forward, though in reality the only football he played was at Cherry Orchard, and then mainly as a defender: 'a bit crap because we played on full-size pitches with a heavy ball'. There was a silver-framed photograph of him taken by Physical Education teacher Mr Weaver, half smiling, half frowning at the camera in white shorts and rolled-down socks and a pullover, his knees grubby, his right foot resting on a leather ball, his long arms dangling by his thighs. 'Having thought about it,' Lee told Bishop, 'I would have played in goal. Writers are very solitary, weird individuals and if you're going to find that sort of character in a football team, it's usually the goalkeeper.'

Lee was an outsider born and made, more Petr Čech than Peter Crouch, not for nothing dubbed the Camus of crime by the *New Statesman* in 2016. Camus played in goal for his university team in Algeria, and famously claimed that everything he ever learned about 'the morality of men' he had learned from football. Lee had learned plenty too, if mainly from the bench and the terraces.

Lee's obsessive attention to detail, at the origin of Reacher's situational awareness, reminded me of Funes the Memorious, in the short story of the same name by Borges. But he also shared the Argentine writer's power of suggestion. In his introduction to Bishop's club history he uses repetition to evoke the intrinsically ritualistic nature of fandom, communicating with Borgesian economy the essence of an experience that eludes the mere accumulation of detail. He isn't a full-on anorak, despite being a geek and a nerd, and his memory is not so perfect as to become the garbage heap under which Ireneo Funes is ultimately buried and asphyxiated, but without attempting to enumerate them exhaustively he is still able to suggest the unique singularity of each and every game in much the same way that Funes is able to recall every leaf on every tree in the forest and every grain of sand on the beach. 'I remember the visit from Santos of Brazil', 'I remember the slow-motion once-a-fortnight friendships', 'I remember watching the warm-ups', 'I remember them all'.

The slow-motion friendships were formed in a later, more established phase in his relationship with the club, but before Jim had become Lee, when he was an ordinary guy with a job and a mortgage.

> One guy worked in the Jewellery Quarter and made me two sets of earrings at cost, from scrap material, one with chips of rubies, one with emeralds, that I gave my wife for Christmas. Major brownie points for me, for not much more than a Bovril and a meat pie.

In the early 1900s about thirty thousand people worked in Hockley's Jewellery Quarter, a couple of miles from Villa Park. It still lays claim to being one of Europe's largest communities of manufacturing jewellers, producing 40 per cent of jewellery made in the United Kingdom and boasting the world's largest Assay Office, which hallmarks about 12 million items a year.

'They had this great tradition of making stuff,' Lee said. 'The small old-time artisans were really good at it.' Then he told me a story, like I was driving him some place he needed to go and he was paying for the ride.

> One day we had this bed in a box. Probably the box had a hole in it. Anyway, we were missing a bolt by the end of it. No bolt, no bed. We had the matching bolt. But it was metric at a time when everything else in England was the old imperial measurement. You couldn't walk into a shop and buy a metric one. So I go to one of these old-timers under the railway arches. One-man band. Rough-and-ready work-shop. And I say to him can you make me another one of these? He has a good look at it and says, sure, come back in half an hour. So I go back in half an hour and he had these two identical bolts in his hand and I say, 'But I only wanted one!' Thinking oh no that's going to be twice the cost and we're broke. The guy grins at me. Turns out one of them is the original bolt. The second one is the one he has made. A perfect copy. They really knew how to make stuff back then.

This was a Filofax moment, recycled in chapter seventeen of *The Enemy* – where the bed becomes a table – as a simile for Reacher wrestling with an intractable problem.

Now Lee was a Villan in exile. Mostly he watched his team from the comfort of his Manhattan library, slouched back on the sofa with his feet up on an ottoman, lighter and ashtray within reach of his hovering right hand. But he could always catch a plane. One Friday night he and brother Andrew took in a game at the Yankee Stadium then flew to England and drove from London to Birmingham in the red Jaguar to watch Villa play the next afternoon. 'We did it to see if it was possible,' Lee told the *Express* in 2011. 'It was a mental health break. It was fabulous.' He owed it to his Irish grandfather to spend his money before it ran out.

His loyalty hadn't worked wonders for his physical health. One Saturday in 1984 Lee made a bargain with himself. Villa were playing away to Leicester. Leicester had rallied from the 1960s trouncing and thumping with an attack led by England centre-forward Gary Lineker. Lee vowed he would give up smoking if only Villa might be granted a victory. He was testing his team and his atheism in one fell swoop. Villa lost 5–0. They were massacred. There was no God and more importantly, no reason to give up smoking. On the contrary, he would redouble his efforts. *Never go back, never give up*, like the movie poster said, featuring images of non-smoking, fast-running Tom Cruise. Lee could never give up smoking. He saw that clearly now. It wouldn't be his life if he did. It would be someone else's life, not his.

When I met Rob Bishop it felt like meeting a character out of a real-life Villa thriller. But he was too affable to be CIA head of station at the Hamburg consulate (as Lee had cast him in *Night School*). He was proud to be worthy of inclusion but disappointed by his appearance. Not that he was pitching for 6 foot 5 inches and 250 pounds, let alone a 50-inch chest, that would be delusional, but he wouldn't have been averse to a touch of creative enhancement. Like Lee himself, who when asked which painter he would like for his portrait was quick to respond 'not a realist' and went on to propose Piet Mondrian. Rob, a former sports writer for the *Birmingham Post* and *Mail* (and closet West Brom supporter), introduced me to the head of matchday security. Keith Wiseman was a fan of Lee Child. I think everyone I met that day was, though I didn't get round to asking the bus driver who dropped me off at Witton Square. He wasn't as forthcoming as the friendly folk of western Wisconsin. 'You came by bus?' my hosts gasped incredulously, like I'd had to fight my way in and would likely have to fight my way back out again.

Keith was from Birmingham too. But he was in deeper than Lee, had been born there and grown up within a stone's throw of Villa Park, and despite a stint as police commander at Birmingham airport had never managed to quite get away. He loved everything about his job except the derbies with Birmingham City. He was a fan first and foremost. As a boy he would sit in his garden with his pocket radio held up to his ear and, like a supplicant before a religious icon, fix his eyes on the heavens. Actually he was looking at the letters 'AV' picked out in high-voltage lamps on the 108-foot pylons marking the four corners of the pitch, but the terror and awe were the same.

The pylons went up in 1958 but the lights were added in 1970 for a colour television broadcast of an FA Cup semi-final between Manchester United and Leeds. Like the DUNLOP TYRES sign on top of Fort Dunlop in Erdington (once the world's largest factory, where the first pneumatic tyre was made) they could be seen as you drove into town on the Aston Expressway via Spaghetti Junction. Two had been demolished before the old Trinity Road Stand. Two were still standing around awkwardly like a couple of old guys without a job to do.

Villa could boast an illustrious history. It was formed in 1874 by four members of the Villa Cross Wesleyan Chapel in Handsworth and was one of the oldest clubs in England. The founder of the Football League, teetotal Scottish draper William McGregor, lived in Aston and had served as the club's umpire, president, director and chairman. Villa Park had hosted more FA Cup semi-finals than any other ground. But all that vision and ambition seemed to Lee a thing of the past. 'They took the pylons down, but replaced them by nothing better.'

It was more than symbolic: despite their 2019 return to the top tier, Aston Villa no longer lit up the sky.

'Apart from home,' wrote Inglis, 'no other place in the world has ever felt so much like home.' Lee never really left the Villa, like Reacher never really left the military. The team was never far from his thoughts. He told Bishop how he turned to the club in search of character names. 'It started with Mayor [Shaun] Teale in my first book and went on from there.' [Paul 'Kumbaya'] McGrath and [Savo] Milosevic turn up in *Die Trying*, along with [Dwight] Yorke as an abandoned mining town in Montana. [Pete] Withe is a military base in *The Visitor*, which also includes [Riccardo] Scimeca, and there are parts for [Kenny] Swain in *Without Fail*, [Juan Pablo] Angel in *Persuader*, [Tommy] Docherty in *Bad Luck and Trouble*, [Gary] Shaw in *Nothing to Lose* and [Ashley] Westwood in *Make Me*. Not forgetting the infamous General [Darius] Vassell and the misunderstood [Benito] Carbone of *The Enemy*, in whose name Reacher accepts demotion in a first momentous step towards leaving the army. Hapless England manager Graham Taylor is a suspected kidnapper in *The Hard Way*, which also showcases [John] Gregory and the lesser known but 'industrious' midfielder [Mark] Burke from Solihull, which was virtually Birmingham, so it was no surprise to discover Lee considered him a true craftsman of the sport.

'Partly it saves me the effort of dreaming up names and partly it's homage,' Lee said. 'The only one I've not used is [Gordon] Cowans. He was my absolute favourite player and he's too precious for me to use.'

After the publication of his twentieth novel Lee got to interview his idol for the Villa v. Leicester City matchday programme of 16 January 2016 ('Give me Cowans over Cruise'), when the home team succeeded in snatching a draw against their old foe as they spiralled towards end-of-season relegation precisely three months later.

I have a great job and it has brought me many opportunities. I have met President Clinton, and President Obama. Tom Cruise flew me in his helicopter. I have had dinner with kings, lords, sirs, and Oscar-winning actresses. I have watched the Boston Red Sox with Stephen King. I have thrown out the ceremonial first pitch at Yankee Stadium.

But best of all was an invitation to meet Gordon Cowans at Villa Park. He gave me a stadium tour and we talked all afternoon. He was funny and modest and a really nice guy. I treasure the memory, because I think he was the best player we have ever had – a truly world-class talent – and no Villan gave me more pleasure to watch. I was glad to get the chance to tell him that.

Lee saw relegation as part of the divine struggle. He had seen it coming the day he splashed out $4000 on a round trip to watch them get thumped 4–0 by Arsenal in the 2015 FA Cup final at Wembley. A thousand dollars per goal, like adding insult to injury. If he hadn't gone they would have won, he knew that.

When Reacher retired it would be time for Lee to buy another season ticket. He owed it to the guys who had helped make his fortune. He'd struck writing gold in part thanks to them, like winning the Premier League and the Champions League and the FA Cup all rolled into one. Not just once as a lucky fluke like a slot machine, but year after year, for twenty-two years in a row.

Now, like Ozzy Osbourne and Zephaniah and the Duke of Cambridge, Lee was a celebrity superfan, who could legitimately claim that David Beckham – a promising new signing from Leytonstone, east London – had once washed his Vauxhall Astra when it was parked up alongside a Jaguar and a Land Rover outside the Manchester United training ground. This was when a Granada Studios sticker was enough to get you into the private car park, and he was only there because of daughter Ruth and her teenage friends, but as a Villa man he was more interested in the cars. He didn't then grasp the full enormity of the moment, as he watched the blond-haired blue-eyed rookie set to with a bucket and sponge, just as Mr Harris was in no position to appreciate the significance of the occasion when he passed on his season ticket to the young James Grant back in his Handsworth Wood workshop. Lee liked to joke that his life had been downhill ever since, but only because he knew he now had more fans than the club he supported. Not even the Camp Nou would accommodate them all, assuming you could gather them together from across the globe. Villa fans were counted in thousands, Child fans in millions: it was a whole different order of magnitude.

The next time he went to Old Trafford was with Tom Cruise.

Like I told Keith and Rob as we shook hands, it was about time Villa got Lee's face (and Zephaniah's) up on the Witton Lane hoardings leading to the claret-and-blue wrought-iron gates of the *cathedral of football*. And while they were at it, maybe a blue plaque on his seat. Except that like him, it wasn't there any more.

13

Always Lucky

Part of his mind always said:
you've just been lucky. Always lucky.
Die Trying, 1998

Objectively, Jim Grant was one of the luckiest humans ever born. That's how Lee saw it, looking back on his life from the elevated vantage point of Central Park West. Certainly from day one he was luckier than his older brother Richard. He had the brains without the sticky-out ears. He could do the math, but also charm the birds out of the trees. He could read, and he could fight too.

He still thought Richard was pretty lucky though. Born in south London two years after the end of the country's worst polio epidemic and eleven months before the Great Smog of December 1952, Richard was lucky to be alive, let alone able-bodied. Rates of infant mortality were high when you couldn't see a metre in front of you as you shuffled down the pavement feeling your way along the walls, when not even staying inside was enough to protect you from the yellow-black vapours that seeped through the cracks in windows and doors. Only from the front row of the cinema could you actually see the movie and by the time you got home again you were covered in soot. 'It was as if I'd fallen into a puddle of mud,' said a participant in the 2002 witness seminar conducted by the

Centre for History in Public Health at London's School of Hygiene and Tropical Medicine.

Rex had recently started with the Inland Revenue, and he and Audrey were living in a cold-water flat on the top floor of great aunt Hettie's house in Balham, just down the road from the concrete towers of Battersea's 'brick cathedral' and within a ten-mile radius of at least four other coal power stations in the Greater London area, which between them pumped out thousands of tons of pollutants a day. The smoke particles and hydrochloric acid and fluorine compounds and sulphur dioxide mixed in with the emissions from domestic chimneys and the exhaust from cars and steam locomotives and diesel buses. The weather was windless, with a blanket of cold trapped under a heavy layer of warm air pressing down on the city like a cast-iron lid, or the steroidal Paulie squeezing the life out of his victims in *Persuader*. It was the worst air-pollution event in Britain's history. More than ten thousand people died, and ten times that number were affected by chronic long-term illness.

The risks were only marginally lower for James, born two years later. The Clean Air Act wasn't passed until 1956, by which time the family had moved to Leicester, where James was conceived, and then to Coventry, where he was born, and where they all somehow came unscathed through a local outbreak of polio in 1957 before mass vaccination was introduced in 1962 and the last of the dread diseases was finally conquered. By then they were living in Birmingham and he had also survived the heart thing. He was lucky all right. Lucky Jim. There were children who couldn't breathe without being strapped into the iron lung, and others who came back to school deformed. Some didn't come back at all.

For his parents, the capital was still the epicentre of the empire, if not the world. They were respectful of its institutions, its centrality and its importance. It was an old, old mindset. They kept placemats with London scenes printed on them, and if his mother had a Harrods carrier bag she would give it to one of her Birmingham friends to use as a handbag.

Lee can still remember the lucky day he was vaccinated at Cherry Orchard. It wasn't the Salk needle, but the Sabin sugar cube: the first time he'd ever seen one. It looked like a precision-tooled brick from a miniature igloo, but felt deliciously warm when it so yieldingly dissolved on his tongue. Perhaps it reminded him of that other gilded moment when they were handing out sweets on the plane to Belfast. Perhaps those sugar-steeped memories come flooding back every time he bites into a Snickers bar, a staple of his millionaire writer's diet.

But life was still just bad enough to be interesting. His parents took out a ration card in his name on the day he was born, though it turned out they didn't need it. 'In many ways World War II wasn't over yet,' he wrote in the *Wall Street Journal* in 2013.

> The economy still limped along, damaged infrastructure still hadn't been rebuilt, and austerity was absolutely ingrained. My earliest memories are playing in bombed-out houses, 12 years after V-E Day. We played soccer on fields made of crushed brick from ruined factories.

Then in a 2018 vignette for the *Guardian* captioned 'Made in Birmingham':

> Pollution was insane. Rivers would catch fire. We had a patch of mud with two sickly trees, which with yearning irony we called 'Bluebell Woods'. Except the mud was bubbling oil waste. If it got on your clothes they were ruined, and if it got on your skin you had to run home and clean it off with lighter fluid. I remember pea-soup fogs. I was a kid, and therefore short, but I couldn't see my feet. We put wet towels against windows and doors, but after three days the fog was as thick inside as outside.

Boyhood friend Charles Spicer read this and remembered the 'pea-soupers'.

> On a foggy day, before walking to Grestone Junior School I would wrap a scarf around my mouth, and by the time I arrived the outside of the scarf would be blackened. Hamstead Colliery was nearby, but I suspect it was coal fires in homes which were the main contributors to dirt in the air. I remember the hooter sounding to mark the beginning and ending of shifts.

The colliery closed in 1965 but in its heyday was the deepest in the world. Alison Yeomans remembered the nodding donkey – the overground drive for the borehole's submersible pump. Cedric Barker, a third-generation miner who contributed to the Voices of Birmingham Oral History Project in 2012, recalled how the Bull went off at half past six each morning, then again at ten to seven, clocking in time, and finally at seven, when the wheel of the shaft lift started winding. If after that it stopped, the office manager would want to know why. By Cedric's day they had a pithead bath so miners could change after work and a canteen, which – because it was used mostly by surface workers (engineers and bosses) – was 'very good'.

Life was grey, but in a vividly colourful way, like a child's drawing dashed off in bold felt-tip over pencil.

In benign imitation of the seeping smog, colour was beginning to wash back into bleached monochrome post-war Britain. In the elegiac memoir *A City Dreaming* about Derry, where Jim had holidayed with his bad Aunt Margaret, BBC broadcaster Gerry Anderson summarised the 1950s as 'different shades of grey, each one duller than the next' and claimed colour and sex were not invented until 1963. The Grants got their first black-and-white television in 1960. There were few programmes and even fewer were permitted, and it was off air for large parts of the day. But it was around this time that Jim first went to the Villa Cross Picture Palace in Handsworth and paid nine pence to watch his first film, the 1955 war epic *The Dam Busters*, with brother Richard, featuring second-in-command RAF bomber pilot Australian Micky Martin, a 'very brave hooligan'. They went back a year later to see *Reach for the Sky*, about the even more legendary Douglas Bader (a possible subliminal influence in the naming of Reacher). The cinema had an outsized rose window in brilliant stained glass and the auditorium was decorated with sculpted angels and signs which read: 'The World Before Your Eyes'. Rex 'had a thing about the American Civil War' and took his two older boys to see *Gone with the Wind* at the Gaumont in town. James – little imagining he would one day meet Scarlett O'Hara's real-life husband – thought it was silly, but there was no denying it was steeped in velvet-rich colour, and it had in fact won the 1939 Academy Award for Best Colour Cinematography. When he started dating around 1968, the Gaumont became Jim's regular but by then he only quarter saw any movie he went to.

In 1969 the Grants acquired a colour television. Two years before, Britain had become the first country in Europe to offer regular programming in colour, starting with four hours a week on BBC Two. The first broadcast was from Wimbledon. 'I remember the first time I realised the grass was green,' Lee said. 'Before that I thought Wimbledon was played on grey tarmac.' But sure enough it was in 1963 that colour first exploded into his world. It was like all the fireworks going off at once.

'Then we all escaped,' Lee wrote in the *New York Times*.

> A weird kind of pressure built up, between the luckiest generation in history and the survivors of its worst catastrophe, so that something had to happen. And it did, opposite in every way to the stakes and fears of 1940, full of joy and love and energy.

The Beatles happened. I was beyond passionate. Finally, something was going on. To us, for us, by us. Something was ours. I was depressed at 8, but I was fine by 9. Four guys had escaped, in the biggest possible way.

The kids had to battle their way out from under the blanket of smog.

For Jim grace descended on 23 August 1963 during a miserable vacation in Wales. The three boys – Richard, Jim and now also David – were stuck in a caravan with their parents. The rain was lashing down outside. To get away from his fractious family Jim went and sat in their thirdhand grey Rover 100 P4, sold and resold down the economic ladder, and switched on the radio. He tuned in to the Light Programme, which was all there was apart from the Home Service and the highbrow Third Programme, which later morphed into Radio 3. It was an old tube radio, but through the popping and crackling of the valves he could make out Brian Matthew's voice saying, 'and here's the new one from the Beatles'.

That was when life went Technicolor.

'She Loves You' was the first Beatles song Jim ever heard. It went on to become the group's all-time bestselling single, setting a record in the States as one of five Beatles songs to hold the top five places simultaneously in April 1964, peaking at no. 1 in March after 'I Want to Hold Your Hand' had launched the British invasion in January. The first eleven seconds of 'She Loves You' – Ringo's drums, the mad, crazy, exuberant chorus, the three-part vocal harmony setting up the first verse – changed, or saved, his life. At first I wasn't sure which verb I heard, but when I asked he answered simply: 'Both, really.' The song was short, but afterwards he was a different person. Then it was just 'one perfect song after another' – 'There's a Place', 'All My Loving', right up until 'Can't Buy Me Love'. It wasn't the guitars so much but the voices, the inventive harmonies, the way 'She Loves You' ended on a major sixth, the quasi-erotic attraction of those fresh boyish faces.

What mattered most about the Beatles, apart from their innate primordial swagger, was probably *to us, for us, by us*. It was the sentiment expressed by Graham Nash (the Hollies, then supergroup Crosby, Stills, Nash and Young) in recalling how in February 1957, aged fifteen, he saw Bill Haley and the Comets at the Manchester Odeon.

> The audience was made up of mostly kids my age, whose faces were lit with an eerie intensity. They bought right into the music. It was something new, something our own – not the crap they played on the BBC or fed us at school, not our parents' brand of postwar schmaltz [. . .] It was like a new religion, and Bill Haley was delivering the Word.

Nash was born twelve years before Jim but at times they sounded like twin souls. Growing up in Salford, Nash writes in *Wild Tales*, 'all of us stuck in that vast northern gulag, I used to think there was no escape'. You had to be 'pretty creative'. 'There wasn't much for kids to do except play soccer and explore the skeletons of bombed-out houses.' Like Jim, Nash was happy with his own company: 'I've always looked for places where I could shut out the world and just groove on the solitude that fuelled my dreams.' Like Jim – and Van Morrison over the Irish Sea – he would tune in to Radio Luxembourg at night on 208 medium wave: 'When the weather permitted, its signal came in like magic, [and] fired up all of my dreams.' It was 'our station', Lee told me, 'our secret, our music'.

Jim listened to all the Beatles songs on the wireless as they came out. He couldn't afford to buy records, and even if he could he wouldn't have been able to play them. The family had a record player, an upmarket one-piece PYE Black Box in a substantial wooden cabinet that was intended to be a tabletop, but his father had placed it proudly on legs and positioned it in a hallowed corner of the living room under the reproduction of the *Mona Lisa*. The boys weren't allowed to use it and their parents rarely did. Like everything else they bought, its overriding value was as a symbol of status.

But it didn't matter. On Sunday 10 November, 1963, just twelve days after his ninth birthday, James got to live the dream, when he went to see the Beatles at the Birmingham Hippodrome on Hurst Street courtesy of David Harris's mother. It was the first live gig he attended. The band had played there in March, when James was still plunged in the Dark Ages, but now they were returning as superstars and he had seen the light. It was a month into Beatlemania. John, Paul, George and Ringo were delivered in the back of a police van and smuggled in via the back door wearing policemen's helmets. They liked the look so much they posed for a photograph with the police. The set list was a hit parade in itself, from 'I Saw Her Standing There' to 'Twist and Shout' via 'From Me to You', 'All My Loving', 'You've Really Got a Hold on Me', 'Roll Over Beethoven', 'Boys', 'Till There Was You', 'She Loves You' and 'Money (That's What I Want)'.

'I'm a lucky man,' Reacher says to Brigadier General Eileen Hutton (named for his publisher at Brilliance Audio) in *One Shot*. 'Always have been, always will be.'

James already wanted to be a Beatle, but it was then he determined to buy a guitar of his own. He knew he would have to fund it himself, and to boost his pocket money agreed to have four teeth extracted from his supposedly overcrowded mouth so that he could extract a ten-shilling note from his father in exchange. Maybe it should have been four ten-shilling notes. It was a classic case of clumsy British dentistry, and he needed the consolation: 'I can still remember the smell of the gas.' The guitar was a steel-strung Spanish style with slotted headstock and a tailpiece, and he bought it in 1964 from Kay

Westworth's on Cannon Street, not far from Barnbys Children's Store. It cost him £7.

On a shelf in his Manhattan office he kept a small china plate with a monochrome portrait of the Beatles on it: like the Wonder Book and the Westclox, a rare memento of a now distant childhood. Just a cheap item of merchandise, but in pristine condition. Visitors loved to see it sitting there amid the framed covers of his own no. 1 hits. They loved to hear it had come from his mother. Not just social but personal history, a glimpse into a sweet, tender relationship, that unique bond between mother and son. He was quick to disabuse them. At best it was 'her high point'. It had to have been an impulse buy, no way was it lovingly planned. Perhaps it was a second, picked up at a jumble sale. Perhaps like his mother herself it wasn't the genuine article. 'It wasn't out of empathy,' he said, looking me straight in the eye.

'I met Paul McCartney once, at a charity gig,' Lee recalls in the *Wall Street Journal*, 'and I told him how he had rescued me. "Yeah," he said. "I've heard that before."' Like Nash said: 'When the Beatles opened that door, we all wanted to run screaming through it.'

It was in September 1965 that a still ten-year-old Jim Grant (probably the youngest as well as the biggest in his year group) became a pupil at King Edward's School. It was another life-changing experience that with its classical education threatened to refine the Brummie out of him altogether (but would also equip him to discuss Reacher in light of 'Virgil, Ovid, Plutarch, Cicero, Seneca and Dante' in Italy a lifetime later). The school had been ordained by royal charter in 1552:

> From henceforth there is and shalbe one grammer Schoole in Birmingham aforeseyd whiche shalbe callid the free Grammer Schole of King Edwarde the Sixte for the educacion and instruccion and institucion of children and younge men in Grammer forever to endure . . . (Anthony Trott, *No Place for Fop or Idler*)

It started life in a timber-framed wattle-and-daub structure, the former Gild Hall of the Holy Cross, and was open to all boys whose families could afford to lose a son's income, teaching Latin (with a touch of Greek) as the prerequisite of social advancement. In the early nineteenth century the governors leased some of their land to the London & Birmingham Railway Company, which according to the *Birmingham Post* in 2011 meant that 'smoke and steam would soon be enveloping its walls, and Latin verbs drowned out by the 9.15 from Euston'.

Sometimes, instead of taking the school bus, Jim would catch the number 16 from Handsworth Wood into town and then connect with the 61, 62 or 63 along the Bristol Road to Edgbaston, an affluent suburb to the south-west of the city that he once described to me as 'tony', where the school now sat comfortably on its new 50-acre site across the road from the University of Birmingham and the art deco Barber Institute of Fine Arts.

The King Edward's of the 1960s was a green and pleasant land of immaculate playing fields. No Satanic Mills, no bubbling oil waste. Which didn't feel right to young Jim. Deep beneath his desire to escape there remained an inviolate substratum of grey, a stubborn loyalty to the smog that he could never bring himself to betray. He felt a natural affinity with smoke, like it was part of his birthright or destiny. He wasn't expecting to be called up or go down the mines. But that wouldn't stop him from getting lung disease.

So it was an especially lucky day when, in the first term of his first year, he found an unopened pack of ten Rothman's King Size on the number 16 bus.

He told me in an email, 'Loved it from the first drag.'

Lee had a title for the autobiography he said he didn't plan to write: *Always Lucky.*

14

The Age of Aquarius

Maybe two pounds of grass a week,
with someone to share the hut.
Killing Floor, 1997

There was another thing Lee still kept from his boyhood days: the medal he won at the end of his fifth (O level) year. It was round and weighty, brass, but dull in colour, with the head of Edward VI on one side and, on the other, carved lettering in glinting block capitals reading: 'Awarded to J. D. Grant on election to a Foundation Scholarship 1970', with 'The Schools of King Edward VI in Birmingham' running around the circumference.

Jim joined King Edward's on academic merit, like Richard, 'hungry for intellectual fodder'. He recalled walking in with ninety-nine other boys and how 'the air itself was crackling and buzzing with intelligence and potential'. At last he had something to sink his teeth into and a whole new library to devour. He took piano lessons and learned to read music (Rex and Audrey harboured a fond vision of him playing the organ at Richard's wedding). He went to Granville on the Cherbourg Peninsula. He got at least one Distinction Prize every year, sometimes two, which meant he had qualified in the top three in at least three subjects. He won prizes across the board, including Art, except in Chemistry, which he was never any good at.

He boycotted O-level Chemistry so as to preserve his immaculate grade average ('Sorry he was ill in exams,' comments the Chief Master on his report). But he was the only kid to get full marks in Biology. In Fifths, Jim ranked second overall so they were 'forced' to give him a scholarship, albeit through gritted teeth.

Unusually for a guy who *had to win*, Jim was happy with second place. He had achieved his goal. 'I did it to spite them, because they hated me, because I was bad.'

He wanted to stay in control of the narrative. 'I had enough native wit to make sure I succeeded.' But he didn't care that his headmaster couldn't in good faith recommend him to Cambridge, where Richard had won yet another scholarship to study Engineering at Churchill College: he didn't want to go there anyway.

Jim was fourteen when his 'Age of Aquarius' kicked in. He felt a compulsion to show off and was quick to accept a dare. On a 1967 ski trip to Sölden in Austria a bunch of guys bet he wouldn't jump off the chairlift heading up the mountain. Their skis were waiting at the top. They were about 30 feet above the slope when he picked a spot where the snow looked deep and jumped. His mates paid up but his teachers made him return the money.

From that point on Jim treated school itself as a dare. 'I came to school high every day. My parents were so backward-looking, so far behind the curve they just feared I was drinking. It worked out the same as if they'd been totally permissive.' He'd be going out and they'd say, 'Don't drink!' 'I won't drink,' he would answer, the picture of filial innocence. Not only did he like weed better, he couldn't afford to do both. Was he going to buy a cider or score a joint? No contest. Once his mother found a tab of cannabis neatly wrapped in foil inside his blazer pocket. She left it there, had perhaps mistaken it for an OXO cube, even though her son was doing woodwork, not domestic science, at school.

'I remember the exact weekend,' Lee recalls in a 2017 interview for *High Times*:

> April 1969, in Birmingham, England. I was 14. A weekend party at a guy's house – it started Friday night and lasted until Monday morning. Had sex for the first time with two sisters in quick succession. Smoked my first joint. One of the greatest weekends of my life.

It was all about pleasure. 'Weed is the thing I really enjoy. It makes me feel really good.'

But it's also the only sane way to behave:

> The psychological roots are incredibly interesting. From when I was a tiny kid – and I saw the same thing in my daughter – I know that children love spinning around and around until they get dizzy and fall over. Seems to me there is a basic built-in instinct to alter your consciousness.

When he and wife Jane had 'the talk' with Ruth they kept things simple. Only three rules, they told her (in the style of a Lee Child novel): 'No unprotected sex. No intravenous drugs. No religious cults.' Ruth thought about it and said: 'Does that mean I can smoke weed?' She was a smart kid, a chip off the old block, and for a while, they would supply each other.

Lee didn't talk much about his sexual awakening. Only to say it ushered in five years of free love and his most successful pick-up line was *will you fuck me in the parking lot?* ('which usually worked') and he almost never slept in his own bed. But there was one myth-busting detail he chose to reveal. They weren't really sisters. At least not biological. One of them was adopted, or maybe both. He liked sisters though. Sisters made a better story. It was like he was wired to turn life into story in real time. And as soon as the story was told, it was 'a true story'. Which mattered more than the actual sex.

Not long after this conversation I met one of his closest friends, Robert Reeves, who had worked alongside him at Granada Television in the late 1970s and early 1980s. We talked about his Bob Dylan-like tendency towards fictionalisation, and Rob observed:

> The thing is, it didn't matter whether or not you believed his yarns. You held him in affection, and anyway, they were good stories. There are tall-story tellers I've met that you would instinctively mock. Never Jim. I think Jim's attitude was if I say something about myself it becomes true because I've said it. The actual truth is an afterthought.

It was a true story he'd made up from start to finish. I was reminded of Lee's respect for Reacher's irrefutable (fictional) reality: *I can't go back and change it because that's the way it happened.* Truth was not merely a matter of fact, but authenticity. It was the way you made sense of life, the way you held it together.

Back when Jim was fourteen 'everybody smoked'. Now smoking was enough to make you a wild child, however old you were. People who didn't smoke got 'a real vicarious kick out of it', which Lee found 'pretty pathetic'. But useful. It helped promote the idea he was 'a bit of rough' and even well into his sixth decade could still kick ass. 'I can light up the pipe if you like. Could probably find a needle somewhere.'

Directors and cameramen loved his addiction to cigarettes. To be given licence to shoot was thrilling. In summer 2017 he was the subject of a short film made by New York's 92Y as part of Xerox's *Set the Page Free* project, bringing together fourteen writers (including, among others, Joyce Carol Oates, Jonathan Safran Foer, Valeria Luiselli and Roxane Gay) to produce original material based on the theme of the workplace.

For much of it Lee was sitting at his riveted aluminium desk, writing. There were about a dozen people behind him and some hefty machinery rolling back and forth on wheels, but the atmosphere was hushed. It was like watching a programme by David Attenborough. A lot of zooms and close-ups. Long lean fingers hovering above the keys, then moving about slowly, questingly, like a crab picking over invisible crumbs of food. A pause. A cigarette in his left hand resting lightly on the rim of a heavy glass ashtray, the smoke curling lazily upwards. A thoughtful expression, right hand on his chin. Eyes focused on the screen. Silence. Stillness. Then the cigarette drifting back to his lips, a barely perceptible nod of the head, a small movement of his right index finger, a single comma deleted. It was compelling viewing. Light on special effects but heavy on ritual. How much of the magic was down to the smoke?

A guy asked if he was interested in acting in films, which of course he already had, in two, opposite Tom Cruise, which meant he was already a member of the Screen Actors Guild. Lee smiled and like he often did, said both yes and no: 'For a walk-on part where I can just turn up, do it, be out of there. Play a gorilla or an ageing rock star.'

'Somewhere inside Lee's head there's violent brutality,' the director said to his crew, helpfully, to get them on the right page.

Our culture placed too much importance on self-preservation, Lee thought. He knew smoking was bad for him. He had even given up for ten months in 1985. Nothing to do with fatherhood. He wanted to buy a Philips CD player and he (still) couldn't afford to do both. He'd also just bought his wife a horse. But once he'd achieved his short-term financial goals he started up again. Because he enjoyed smoking. He enjoyed it more than not smoking. He liked being a smoker. If he'd had a business card it could have read, *Jim Grant: Smoker.* Did any of us really want to live forever? He didn't think so.

The story he wrote for *Set the Page Free* – one of four he wrote over a four-day long weekend that summer ('I'd rather hang myself than spend four weeks on a short story') – was about smoking in the workplace. It was called 'My Rules'.

Lee was glad they'd taught him woodwork at school rather than cooking or typing. Not being able to touch-type was an advantage. He recalled an essay by Umberto Eco on the importance of handwriting. It encouraged you to think through each sentence before you started writing. Lee had used a computer since partway into *Die Trying* but still took the Eco approach. 'It makes for a cleaner first draft.' Computers, like digital film, bred a lazy extravagance, because you knew you could go back and fix it later. The speed of his typing was perfectly adapted to the speed of his creative brain, and if he went any faster his hands would trip up his head. It was slower, but more efficient. Disciples would often quote his dictum: 'Don't get it right, get it written.' But it was more *Get it right as it's written*. A waste-not want-not methodology in tune with his frugal upbringing.

Before sex and drugs there was rock and roll. Because of the sloping elevation, Jim's new loft bedroom at the back of 6 Underwood was very high up. His father had done the electrics to save money, having learned how in the army, and Jim had learned by watching him. He hung a circle of wire around the top of the room to improve his chances of picking up Radio Luxembourg and after that 'could get it pretty good'. It would come in and out for five minutes at a time, but that made it more desirable: 'it was your thing that you were secretly on'. He could also pick up the American Forces Network from Germany, which played whatever was in the US charts – country, rhythm and blues, and pop. When his Otley grandma acquired an iconic Bush transistor radio he inherited her table radio, standing two feet across in a polished walnut veneer casing, narrower at the top than the base, with a long glowing dial and a brown grille cloth with gold threads. It was a heavy thing, had a warm mid-range sound with very little treble or bass, and he had to ground it externally to his iron bed frame to stop it humming. He took it to university and rigged it up as an amplifier for the old turntable he picked up from a junk shop. At some point he got hold of a Dansette, a suitcase record player, that he would take round to friends' houses for listening to new records.

Piano lessons went out the window. Piano bashing became a spectator sport at the fair, as opponents competed to wreak total destruction with a sledgehammer. Jim upgraded his guitar to a solid body electric and joined a band called Dark Tower, more likely after old Edwardian J. R. R. Tolkien than Robert Browning and the Childe Roland of medieval legend. There were two other boys from school, the lead guitarist and vocalist, and two from outside who played drums and bass, but what brought them together was the recently established, community-funded Arts Centre in Cannon Hill Park, not far from King Edward's, a symbol of the revolutionary zeitgeist. Cannon Hill was conceived as a space for young people to come together and explore the creative arts. It was open round the clock, with free access, and young teenagers would typically book from 7 to 11 p.m., with older, cooler kids going for the overnight slot.

During one Dark Tower session a clean-shaven well-mannered softly spoken guy came in to check out the studio. Turned out the guy was a young Robert Plant, and the next night the two groups overlapped and helped move each other's gear. It was one of Led Zeppelin's earliest rehearsals, said Lee, the first having taken place in August 1968, when the former Yardbirds convened with their new members in a London basement.

Jim was a regular at Henry's Blueshouse on Hill Street and the newly opened Mothers club on Erdington High Street, converted from the Carlton Ballroom. Mothers only ran from August 1968 to January 1971 but DJ John Peel called it 'the best club in Britain'. All the big groups played there, many for the first time: Joe Cocker,

John Mayall, Pink Floyd, Deep Purple, Fleetwood Mac, Jethro Tull, the Who, Led Zeppelin, the Moody Blues, King Crimson, Yes, Black Sabbath – virtually the resident band, from just down the road in Aston – as well as the Edgar Broughton Band and Soft Machine, who took their name from a William Burroughs novel.

It cost five shillings (25 pence) to get in, twelve and six for the top bands. The stairs were creaky and the walls painted black. There were posters on the ceiling and the tang of beer in the air. Dress code was hair, plus bangles, beads and badges with battered jeans, patched and turned into flares by the addition of flowery, triangular vents, or stripy blazers and duffel coats, maybe the odd mod suit, bespoke, four-button. Curry and chips on the long walk home. No one was asking to see your ID, unless in reverse, when you were buying a child's ticket for the train.

Jim saw Pink Floyd at London's Roundhouse in October 1968, when he was thirteen, amid a fog of incense and dope and patchouli oil. Six months later he was at Mothers when they partly recorded the live disc of the double album *Ummagumma*. In June 1969 he saw Led Zeppelin at the Birmingham Town Hall, where the music was so loud his watch shattered. In July he was in the capital for the Stones in the Park, which he watched from up a tree. (Trains were cheap, or he would hitch, and the all-night gigs meant he didn't need a place to sleep, not that he was short of offers.) It was Mick Taylor's first performance with the Rolling Stones, just two days after the death of Brian Jones. Mick Jagger wore white and released a cloud of white butterflies into the air.

In 1969 he went to the Isle of Wight Festival and in 1970, with his then girlfriend Liz, to the Bath Festival in Somerset. The line-up was spectacular: Santana, Jefferson Airplane, the Byrds, Frank Zappa, Canned Heat, Steppenwolf, Pink Floyd, Fairport Convention, and John Mayall with Peter Green. Led Zeppelin headlined, playing to an audience of 200,000 for three hours, including five encores. Jimmy

Page played the guitar with a bow. Forty years later the band would set the mood and pace for *Gone Tomorrow* ('It got off to a great start and just kept on going') with 'Since I've Been Loving You' and 'Dazed and Confused', as featured in *The Song Remains the Same*, filmed at Madison Square Garden in 1973. Most of the film was reshot and re-recorded at London's Shepperton Studios, but still it conveyed the spirit of the 'gritty' New York Lee remembered from his early visits with Jane, and that he sought to evoke in his writing.

Jim listened to everything. He wasn't that into Sabbath and thought King Crimson and Genesis were 'too undergraduate'. He was 'a bit of a snob, always seeking out the obscure and the esoteric, especially new American imports or what nobody else had discovered yet, like the Ed Broughton Band and Bachdenkel'. He remembered how Birmingham band Bachdenkel gained notoriety for some *avant la lettre* guerrilla marketing, spraying advertising stencils on walls and pavements and then skipping the country and moving to Paris.

The members of Dark Tower were all self-taught. They didn't write their own music. They were in a band because everyone was, and like everyone else they put their own spin on all the great songs already bubbling in the hyper-creative ether. They did 'two really good paid gigs that gave you the flavour of what it might have been like', the second on New Year's Eve 1969 at Digbeth Civic Hall in the old industrial quarter, going out on a high supporting 'folk-rock hippie eccentric woo-woo band' Tea and Symphony. There might be some old three-inch reel-to-reel tape mouldering on a shelf, nothing Lee could lay his hands on. But 'it felt bloody huge'. He remembered setting up before the show and some older guy, a musician with another band, wandering over to take a look. The guy saw they were just kids and didn't have much kit, so he said: 'take some old tables from over there and cover them with black cloth, to look like a bank of speakers'. It was then Lee learned that faking it was part of the job.

He was proud of the lighting. They rigged it up themselves, including some improvised strobe lighting involving a single-blade electric engine and a vat of saltwater.

In the tradition of all great bands Dark Tower formed, swelled, peaked and crashed. The bass player had 'a real cute girlfriend', which brought kudos to the group, but he and the drummer were older and moved on to other things. Among the King Edward's contingent decadence set in early. The lead vocalist Alan, a 'dark-haired magnetic Adonis' from Jim's class, got tangled up with a girl at sixteen and had to leave to get a job, 'so kind of expelled himself'. Dumbo, the lead guitarist, and Handsworth Wood local Mike, who helped out with lighting, got expelled for real. Turned out they'd been stealing violins from the Music School and selling them to a shop in town to fund their rock-star lifestyle of clothes, gigs and substances. When they were caught they tried to blame the scam on Jim, which turned out unlucky for them since he'd been off sick with scarlet fever, or possibly acute tonsillitis, for those two or possibly three weeks, and also because he wasn't about to let the bad guys get away with it.

The friends 'fell out big time' and the whole band experience was tarnished. Jim never forgot. 'I put it in *Killing Floor*,' Lee said, 'at the end of the first chapter [he put everything in *Killing Floor*]. You can't prove something that didn't happen.'

> I was under arrest. In a town where I'd never been before. Apparently for murder. But I knew two things. First, they couldn't prove something had happened if it hadn't happened. And second, I hadn't killed anyone.

His old bandmates would never have got the grades anyway. Lee was certain of that.

Mike Holt lived at 70 Underwood Road and had gone to Grestone

Avenue with Charles Spicer. Jim had seen him at the entrance exam, but it wasn't until they got on the bus on the first day of senior school that they really hooked up. Jim liked going round to Mike's place because it was so wild in comparison to his own. Mike's mother was a frustrated actress and his father an alcoholic. He was one of four sons. The second-oldest died in a car accident aged fifteen. The third was an epileptic who wore a helmet to protect him when he fell, but he also died young. Toby, the youngest, was 'the only sane one'. Mike was a thin, wiry, scrappy kid, clever but unfocused. There was nowhere for him to do his homework and no expectation that he should. Lee remembered him as a 'mental drop-out who didn't care', but with hindsight could see it was the kind of 'home–school interface problem' 1960s King Edward's wasn't equipped to deal with, or even conscious of, which meant Mike fell by the wayside.

One day Lee Child was in Manchester and a portly, balding guy turned up in the signing queue and said: 'Remember me?' Lee didn't. Like Lee himself, Mike Holt was totally transformed and had become a Professor of Arabic. They agreed to meet up when Lee was next in England, which turned out to be November of that same year, just a few months later. Then Lee got a message from Toby that Mike had died in a bicycle accident while on holiday. His tyre had caught on a stone, he'd flipped over the handlebars, and hit his head on a rock.

Mike was a 'full-on Age of Aquarius' guy. He lacked Jim's instinct for self-preservation, his ability to pull back from the brink.

'I was the only one who survived into the Sixth Form.'

But he arrived there, as his English teacher recalls, with 'something of a reputation'.

15

Happy Days

Then they sliced his balls off.
Killing Floor, 1997

The boys had their blazers off so it must have been a hot day. 'Slack' (Jack) Hodges, French master and head of Jim's House, was writing on the blackboard.

'Sir,' said a boy suddenly, standing and twisting slightly so his back was turned towards the teacher. 'My shirt's got covered with ink.'

The boys were seated at individual desks with inkwells.

Immediately behind the ink-spattered Chris ('mini-Slack') Hodges was Jim Grant, and behind Jim, John Holder. Both boys were wielding pens. A ripple of sniggers ran round the room.

'Grant, did you do that?'

'No sir.'

'Holder, was it you?'

'No sir, it wasn't me sir.'

Slack Jack was grasping at straws, since Holder was too far back, and no kind of skill would make ink flicked from a fountain pen curve round the man in front to score that kind of goal.

'Grant, are you sure it wasn't you?'

'No sir. Couldn't have been me – ballpoint, sir.'

In the smooth-cheeked floppy-haired face of stout denial, Mr Hodges was left with nowhere to go in defence of his hapless son.

Could be Jim was bored in Middle School French. Not long after, he was playing about with a flick knife under his desk. Steve 'Jonse' Johnson was seated next to him, a self-avowed 'goody two shoes' who had never even seen a flick knife before and taunted Jim by saying he would never dare use it. Not just once (according to Lee), but twice, maybe three times. *Go on then, show me.* Whereupon Jim did, 'by cutting me across the cheek in the middle of the lesson. I was dumbfounded – as blood trickled down my face – but Jim continued as if nothing had happened.' Johnson's family were used to him coming home with scratches so there were no confessions and no repercussions, and he didn't want to overdramatise the cut. It hadn't left a scar. Not on his cheek, anyway. He expected neither apology nor remorse.

'He asked me to do it,' Lee said, fifty years later, matter-of-factly.

'Jim's side of the story,' Steve commented, wryly.

Johnson went on to become captain of the rugby team. He could still picture the way Jim would rock his head backwards and look you in the eye without blinking, so as to signal he wasn't frightened of you, however big and physical you were. 'Like an opposition player facing down the haka.'

Like Reacher, Jim didn't need to be liked. It was the smartest way (he believed) to increase your chances of being loved.

Already in adolescence he had a way of imposing his will. Once in Upper Middles (third year) a Shell (first year) accidentally bumped into him. Jim's response was to require the child to write a two-page essay on 'the importance of being earnest'. He carried authority, not least thanks to his height, and the next day a teacher approached the jumpy Shell to ask what the matter was. *I have to write an essay for Mr Grant and I don't know what to do.*

'Jim was a consummate liar,' Nigel told me, sitting in a pub in North Wales drinking black coffee. 'He could get away with murder just by putting on an angelic expression and saying he didn't do it.'

Once Nigel and Jim had been sent off with a Primus stove and a tent for an overnight hike and got lost on top of Ingleborough in the Yorkshire Dales. They could see the camp 1500 feet below but couldn't figure out how to get there, so had the bright idea of tossing their rucksacks down the rocky slope to lighten the load. The sacks burst open and the stove flew out and arrived at the bottom in pieces. When they got back to base the scoutmaster wasn't buying their story of an accidental fall and summoned them to sentencing at dawn. The punishment would have been worse than a lecture about how ungrateful the posh boys of King Edward's were and how the young lads from his part of town would have given their eye teeth to come on a camp like this had it not been for Jim Grant's quivering lip and perfectly judged sniffle. 'Silly twat,' muttered Jim, as they were dismissed with a warning.

'He could really lie,' Nigel said. 'I know. I saw him do it.'

Nigel Clay had won a Foundation Scholarship to King Edward's in the 13+ examination. He'd written a story on the theme of 'Plastic' about a plastic-hating old codger who'd woken up in hospital with a vertical scar down his chest and a shiny new plastic heart. In those days of Saturday school, Friday afternoons were for 'doing things' and like Jim, Nigel opted for the Scouts as the lesser evil over the CCF – the Combined Cadet Force. Neither of them was bothered about serving Queen and Country, but signing up for the Scouts was the best means of 'doing things' that were otherwise forbidden, like swigging Newcastle Brown after lights-out in your tent. Jim got Nigel smoking on his maiden trip on the train up to Scotland, citing the example of his Grandad Scrafton, who smoked one hundred Capstan Full Strength a day and had nicotine stains up to his elbow.

Nigel grew up in a four-bedroom semi in Harborne and like Jim was acutely conscious of class nuance. Unlike Jim he wasn't a fighter, so there were streets he avoided for fear of being beaten up in his uniform. King Edward's was a big step up: 'There were kids building rocket motors at home and studying astronomical spectroscopy as a hobby.' He skipped straight from Upper Middles to Fifths as part of the accelerated Science stream, came top in A-level Biology and went on to become an orthopaedic surgeon. It wasn't that he worked all that hard: opportunities arose by virtue of being there, so that in Sixth Form he was already doing work experience in the cancer research lab at Birmingham University. *We'll have you,* they said to him at interview at Dundee. *We don't care what A levels you get if you're doing that sort of stuff at that sort of school.*

The boys knew they were lucky compared to their parents and grandparents. But they hardly needed teaching, said fellow pupil David Collis (now a professor at Harvard Business School), and therefore the teaching was uneven, with the best of it reserved for the A streams. A typical History lesson consisted of copying and rote learning: 1.0 Causes of the English Civil War; 1.1 Relations Between the King and Parliament; 1.1(i) Religious Differences.

> The entire definition of success was getting into Oxbridge. Partly because half the masters had gone to King Edward's as pupils and then gone on to Oxbridge and then come back to teach – King Edward's and Oxbridge were the limits of their world. There was no sense of noblesse oblige or making a contribution to society or what you should do with your life. They were teaching you to pass exams but they didn't have to teach you anything because we were smart enough to teach ourselves.

There was rarely anything out of the ordinary. The only thing that had stuck in his mind that didn't come from a textbook was when a substitute Science teacher asked how many senses they had and the class said 'five' and he replied 'wrong!' and instructed them to close their eyes and move their arms around. 'You know where your hands are,' he pointed out. 'That is your sixth sense.'

There were some very dull teachers, Classics scholar John Claughton recalled. 'But we didn't mind.'

> The vast majority of boys were clever, but also biddable, obedient, conformist, virtuous. We were so proud of being there that the idea of being awkward or contrary was unimaginable. The worst we did was have long hair, wear army or RAF surplus greatcoats and carry *The Yes Album* or *Dark Side of the Moon* to school. However, there was a small minority of the awkward squad, more likely to be in the Scouts than the Combined Cadet Force, to go to the Union for a smoke at lunchtime, to be contrary and 'other'.

Jim was 'other'. 'He must have felt like a fish out of water at times.'

'I felt parallel to the place,' Lee told *Playboy*. 'I didn't understand it. What was the point? Give me a problem, and I'll solve it. Give me a task, and I'll do it. Tell me to study Virgil and Homer, and I'm asking why.'

'He was one who liked to make his presence felt,' said the ageless David Rigby, who fifty years before had given Jim a detention for persistent failure to hand in his Biology homework (and been upbraided for doing so by a 'dour' Mr Grant).

What saved the school for Collis, as for Jim, was the Dramatic Society. Collis worked backstage on *Twelfth Night*, graduating to principal stage manager for *As You Like It* and *The Tempest*. Drama was 'a collaborative coming together', 'a real and meaningful experience, the only thing that involved women and went beyond teaching yourself to pass an exam.' Only a select few would go on to join the National Theatre like Charles Spicer, who had wanted to act from the age of five, but the ambition and professionalism set standards for them all. Contemporary photographs show head of drama Mr Parslew *tête-à-tête* with individual members of his troupe or kneeling at the front of the performance area in rapt attention. After the show he would send handwritten letters of thanks for what each had brought to the whole.

'I worshipped Michael Parslew,' said Andy Forbes, who played Touchstone in *As You Like It* and a soulful Caliban with full Hendrix afro and glasses and the hint of a moustache in *The Tempest*. 'I was just there to meet girls,' said his more sceptical mate Simon Inglis. It was no coincidence that 'the Jew and the black boy' should end up with the radicals and idealists. While Parslew was intent on the magic of theatre, the group as a whole was quite political. It was there Forbes met his first girlfriend Eileen, the daughter of a dinner lady and a clerk at the Longbridge plant, who in March 1973 picketed outside King Edward's High School for Girls in support of a campaign for higher student grants organised by the (short-lived) National Union of School Students.

The school was a meritocracy, but the community was still not as diverse as it might have been. One-third poor to two-thirds rich, Lee estimated, and if you were poor, even getting as far as the entrance exam depended on having a proactive teacher or an aspirational parent who was aware of the options or belonged to the freemasons or had some other kind of in. Some boys came to school on a complicated string of trains and buses, and others were chauffeured in Rolls-Royces and wore Rolexes on their wrists.

There was nothing like rubbing shoulders with boys who had more than they needed to rub your nose in what you lacked. Howard Williamson (now a highly decorated youth worker) sat next to Jim in A-level History ('no modern stuff at all') and had coined the phrase 'ethical theft' to describe the system they devised to take advantage of their wealthier peers' casual disregard for privilege. Once Jim lost his fountain pen and went to lost property to look for it. The porter dug out a tin (like the pawn-shop guy in *The Midnight Line*) and Jim poked around inside of it and came back empty-handed and said: 'My pen wasn't there but he had a fabulous blue Waterman.' Then when Howard suggested he might recently have lost a blue Waterman Jim said yes, but it might be some other kid's cherished Christmas present, so we should give it a month and go back and see, and if it's still there, then we'd be duty bound to take it, because of that other kid's spoiled indifference to a loving gift. At the same time as collecting the Waterman they could conduct further useful research.

'I stole things,' Lee admitted. 'Small amounts of cash, mostly.' Like Reacher, he wasn't above redressing the balance. Johnson recalled spotting Jim slipping paperbacks into a plastic bag in WHSmith on Corporation Street back when they were about thirteen years old, and Jim saying he'd take Jonse down with him if he was caught. It was true he'd nicked the odd book (he felt bad about that now), mostly technical manuals about how to build audio equipment (and at university a copy of Alex Haley's *Roots*), though he didn't recall this particular incident. He doubted it would have been Smith's, as they didn't have the kind of books he was interested in. 'More likely Hudsons.'

Six months later Jonse wrote to me again. 'It was Hudsons,' he said.

It was a vote in favour of Lee's memory. I knew he'd tried to tell it to me straight. But we both knew that his fact was someone else's fiction, as was mine, and it was precisely the precarious, personal nature of memory that most appealed to him about the biographical process.

Howard's grandfather made penknives, and when he was eleven his father had given him a bone-handled sheath knife for Scouts. He allowed that there might have been pockets of culture – in Aston, Small Heath, Lozells, Nechells (none far from Handsworth) – where they were perceived as weapons rather than tools.

Of course they had knives, said Martin Brown, like Collis a back-stage guy in the Dramatic Society, which he'd joined when he heard they would be touring to Berlin. They used them for 'Split the Kipper', which required a boy to throw a knife to the side of a mate standing opposite, who then had to move his near foot to that spot while keeping the other grounded and plucking the knife from the turf and challenging his opponent in return, until one of them either collapsed or conceded. So long as you had a knife, a pair of stout shoes and a streak of madness you were good to go. Flick knives were well adapted to the soft ground of the luscious King Edward's playing fields and coveted for their sharp points, which decreased the chances of a foul throw.

Nigel didn't much like Kak, or Cack, or Cack Face, as they called Chief Master Canon R. G. Lunt, who went about in a gown and dog collar 'like an alien', using his mortar board as a tray to carry his prayer book and bible. When Lunt accompanied the Scouts on an expedition in breeches and wide-brimmed hat it was like being led by founding father Baden-Powell himself. But he disliked him less than Slug, who took hymn practice on Tuesdays and had taught music at his previous school, where he would beat unfortunate miscreants with a slipper dubbed Excalibur. 'He would make you put your head underneath the table so that when he whacked you, you banged your head as well.' There were canes in Lunt's office, but such was the force of his per-sonality that their symbolic power proved potent enough.

Up until Fourths boys had to eat in the dining room, but beyond that they were free to leave school grounds. As an instance of privilege by association they could get membership of the Student Union at Birmingham University across Edgbaston Park Road, and frequented the tuck shop for cigarettes and hand-rolling tobacco, the coffee machine (they drank it black) and the Common Room, which had a snooker table. Back on site they found places to hide out when they were supposed to be in assembly, like the CCF short-wave radio room, tucked up in a turret, where they would smoke with the windows thrown open, or the Green Room, or the prefects' Cartland Club. Once they were caught and required by Lunt to learn and recite 'The Walrus and the Carpenter'.

Mostly they talked about music and girls and the regrettable revival of the midi skirt and compared different brands of cigarette, which they pinched off unsuspecting friends and relatives and brought into school and swapped like football cards. They'd debate the relative merits of Old Virginia v. Old Holborn and whether or not to use filters, or liquorice papers, or red v. blue, and then one day Jim came in touting Gauloises and Gitanes, which were simultaneously prized and reviled for their exoticism and foul smell. They learned how to use an open matchbox as a windshield when lighting up and revelled in the existential ironies of iconic brand names: Swan Vesta, featuring the goddess of health, and England's Glory, which carried the image of a battleship called HMS *Devastation*.

When many years later they met up at Hay-on-Wye, Nigel the medic had given up smoking but Grievous was still puffing like a chimney. He didn't want to live to be an old man, and recalled how as kids they had talked about driving a motorbike off the White Cliffs of Dover on the day they turned thirty, after which they might as well be dead anyway. Jim was one of only two boys Nigel knew who smoked other substances at school. Once at a party he said, 'I've got some Moroccan kief' and Nigel said, 'What's that?' and Jim said, 'I'm going outside, do you want to come?' and Nigel said, 'No'.

No physical barrier separated King Edward's from the neighbouring high school for girls, but each was out of bounds to the other and only the most reckless would risk covert operations in the woods on the edge of the grounds. Inglis would take the long way round on his BSA motorbike so as to cruise down the main drive, studiously ignoring the girls lined up at the windows, his Villa scarf streaming out behind him in all its elegantly considered claret and blue. 'It was like treading the catwalk,' he said. Mingling was sanctioned only on the last day of Summer Term, and it was in preparation for this hotly anticipated event that Nigel took up the guitar. He wanted to play on the lawn and went into training leading singalongs from the Scout songbook, where the Rolling Stones joined hands with Flanders and Swann and 'The Woad Ode', written by an Eton housemaster to memorialise the ancient British tradition of fighting naked, daubed only with the blue dye of the woad plant.

Howard Williamson first encountered the concept of 'airport fiction' when he stumbled across 'a bloody great wodge' of Lee Child at Cardiff airport in the early 2010s. Likewise David Collis in Reykjavik, where he came face to face with a display devoted entirely to Jim's books. One day the two backstage hands hooked up again at a fundraiser in New York – they couldn't forget how the government had paid for their education and wanted less fortunate boys to get it for free like they did – and Collis thought how, despite his metamorphosis, Jim was the least changed. He was the same guy to talk to and looked the same as well, boyish despite the lines, and with all his hair.

Nigel discovered Lee Child on a trip to Auckland when he picked up a book in a shop and recognised his old chum and was briefly amazed and then put the book down again, dismissing it as too expensive. On his return to England he'd sought out *Killing Floor* in a second-hand bookstore. 'I thought it was pure Jim, because Jim is quite cynical and I could see him writing a book that would get maximum sales rather than going after literary prizes – that didn't surprise me at all.' His next thought was, 'this is brilliant, and I'm going out to buy another one'.

Killing Floor took Nigel right back to the intimacy of the campfire.

> Jim used to have a fascination with gruesome things, and when I read his first book and someone had his balls cut off and shoved in someone

else's mouth I recognised it as a story he'd told me at school. He'd heard it from someone, or read it somewhere, that Russian women soldiers would capture their prisoners and then strip them off and dance naked in front of them, and then when they got an erection would chop off their dicks and force them down their throats.

I thought this must have given him nightmares, as an impressionable boy, and sympathised. 'No,' he said. 'We thought it was brilliant, really.'

Then he paused a beat.

'But you can see how it might have stuck in my mind.'

16

Blessed or Cursed

'You've got the strength of two normal boys,' she said.
The Enemy, 2004

When Andy Saunders read *Killing Floor* he couldn't stop laughing. Andy was Jim's best friend in Sixth Form, and when he discovered Lee Child at around the same time as Nigel Clay he found himself thinking, 'this is just Jim taking the piss'. It was the cynicism and humour, and the way Jim had taken on the American vernacular to reinvent himself.

'Only Jim could do that. He was the master of reinventing himself.'

Which was roughly how Lee saw Birmingham: 'a dirty-hands business city where things are made to be sold – and if something's in the way you tear it down and build something else.'

Andy's father was a dentist who had been appointed to a job as a consultant. Andy had been uprooted from his home in Leeds and thrust by his upper middle-class, 'very Jewish, neurotic, dysfunctional' family into the merciless spotlight of King Edward's, where he was picked on as a stroppy outsider with a funny accent. 'The Midlands is south when you come from up north,' he said, still feeling the pain. He was good at Chemistry and Physics and Maths, and his parents were lining him up to be a doctor, but all he was interested in was music. He was good at that too, had taught himself to play piano and guitar from the age of ten.

'I was an unsociable loner,' he said, 'but I covered it with attitude and aggro and told everyone to fuck off, which earned me the nickname Terry Tough.'

Andy first knew Jim only as a peripheral member of a gang of heavy-metal types headed up by Arthur Bates, a thick-set reprobate who lived with his aunt somewhere around Nechells (where it was common to share an outside toilet and a tin bath hung up in the alleyway) and was a skilled and vicious cartoonist. The group included Dave 'Gobbler' Bartlett, who wore a tasselled leather jacket and would become a Hells Angel, Dark Tower band members Alan and Dumbo, who managed to lose the moniker when he acquired a cool guitar, and hanger-on Mike Holt, a wild bunch who slouched around in greatcoats and were always skiving off school or in detention. Jim was with them but apart from them too, with his own look and demeanour: 'very tall and thin and pale, he kind of strutted along in a gangly, belligerent way'. They were more bark than bite, but Jim 'couldn't give a shit about authority. Part of me was impressed by that.'

'We all wore military greatcoats in those days,' recalled Williamson, 'and carried twelve-inch records under our arms as a status symbol, and as items of trade.'

There was an old Birmingham joke about a boy who goes for a haircut and halfway through the barber says, *I see you go to King Edward's*, and the boy says, *Oh, how do you know that?* and the barber says, *I've just found your cap*. But they were too cynical to be hippies, Collis remarked. 'The hippies were rebelling and you could appreciate that, but you could see it wasn't going anywhere.'

Andy had sent me some old photos and looked like the definition of a hippie to me. His thick dark hair was long and lustrous and parted in the middle and he was wearing blue jeans with contrasting inserts in the flares, and a long black velvet coat appliquéd with swirling celestial motifs in reds and golds and blues like he was cloaked in Van Gogh's *Starry Night*. In another he was wearing tan flares and a sleeveless white T-shirt with a pendant peace symbol and had his 1969 Rickenbacker (copy) 360 plugged into a Vox AC 30 amp like Rory Gallagher used to use, which Jim loved, because Gallagher (from Taste) was one of his favourite guitarists. Andy had left a lasting impression on Alison Yeomans. 'He was gorgeous,' she said dreamily. He had a 28-inch waist and 'looked like Marc Bolan'. Girls would come up to her and say: *Excuse me, you know Andy Saunders, don't you? Would you introduce me?*

Andy made friends with elfin-faced Rick Tudor, 'the only other serious guitarist in the year', who owned an original pink Fender Stratocaster that he later sprayed white. They used to go over to Cannon Hill and play with the amps turned up to full volume, and sometimes they would see Jim, jamming with his mates on Canned Heat's 'Goin' Up the Country' or rehearsing with Dark Tower. They discovered Hendrix and heard Jeff Beck soloing with the Yardbirds and then Black Sabbath came along and suddenly Birmingham felt like the place to be. Roy Wood of the Electric Light Orchestra, Robert Plant of Led Zeppelin – they were virtually neighbours.

If there was a prank, Jim would carry out the dirty work. Or maybe he didn't, but people thought he did, which amounted to the same thing. Like the time someone switched the wires in the wall clock to make it go backwards instead of forwards, so that every minute the clock jumped back the class would burst out laughing, tormenting Mr Crow for an entire lesson before he discovered what was up and issued a whole-class detention. *No sir, it wasn't me, sir.* Or when they pushed the Latin master's desk to within a millimetre of the edge of the plinth on which it was positioned, then acted up like hooligans until Crow banged both hands down on the desk and it went hurtling over the precipice, taking him down with it. A favourite form of psychological torture was to jump out the window then hurry straight back in through the door saying *Sorry I'm late, sir* – repeatedly, poker-faced, on a loop.

Not long before O levels Jim disappeared for several weeks and Arthur Bates and his gang were saying he was a kleptomaniac responsible for the theft of violins from the Music Department. When he came back, exonerated, 'Slack' Jack Hodges sat Jim next to Andy, who was perceived as a good influence. Andy was an innocent who didn't know what was going on, and he wasn't about to say: *Look, have you got a problem?* That wasn't how fifteen-year-old boys operated.

> We didn't talk about it. He just seemed like a really nice guy and we had loads in common musically and that was the thing that bonded our relationship. But he didn't talk to those guys any more. It was like he'd come back a different person, like he'd completely reinvented himself, and suddenly he was my best mate.

Increasingly there was genuine affection between them, but Lee freely admitted that part of the attraction was 'hanging out with a rich kid for a change'. For once his parents approved. 'They liked the fact he was now associated with me,' said Andy. In Sixth Form, wrote Paul 'Sweat' Glover, Jim 'rehabilitated himself by changing his mates to us lot'. 'I can't say he exactly reformed,' said Johnson.

The downside was that Andy became a target for the rejected Bates gang, who would follow him home and try to beat him up. 'Me and Jim would be going to my house and we'd meet them, and Jim – who's this skinny, weedy, pale guy – would just stand there and push out his chin. He had these enormously long arms and was kind of fearless.' The way Andy remembered it there were regular punch-ups, and when he read *Killing Floor* and Reacher got into his first fight, his first thought was 'this is Jim standing up to Arthur Bates'.

There was a sadness about Jim too. 'I saw it in his eyes,' Andy said. 'This guy's been damaged in his childhood and taken on the world.'

For once playing it down, Lee recalls only one fight with 'Arthur' Bates, whose real name, he said, was Paul. Which was when he caught him fiddling with the combination padlock on his locker. He knew Bates wasn't planning to steal anything because he didn't have anything worth stealing, only to cause mischief – trash his possessions or set them on fire – but Reacher-style he took pre-emptive action and punched him hard in the right side of his face. Which gave him the advantage, which he needed, because this was a big guy. He'd gone on punching and kicking Bates until he had him laid out on the floor, then walked away while some 'puny acolyte' went off to fetch the Head Porter. Bates left King Edward's at the end of that year.

The whole-school photograph of March 1971 shows Jim in the first year of Sixth Form (known as Divisions) in blazer and white shirt and tie in the back row, his hair parted on the right and swept long over his left eyebrow. The strong jaw is there and the moody expression, as though he is looking beyond the camera to somewhere far in the distance. He is tall and broad-shouldered by comparison to his peers. But not freakishly so. The others had caught up by then.

'What I remember about Jim,' said Andy in 2019, 'is that he was a very loyal friend who couldn't tolerate any kind of abuse. I lived in fear, and he would stand up for me.'

They spent their lives trying to get out of things. Andy had been forced into the CCF but hated the army. So he claimed to be a conscientious objector and started doing sculpture instead, at around the same time Jim swapped Scouts for drama and others took up social work. The electric guitar didn't count as music. Rugby was another bugbear, though Glover said 'Jim displayed a taste for low-level thuggery as a second row.' 'We spent hours in these naked showers and it was really weird,' Andy commented. When they discovered the school had a rowing boat the two friends made up a four with Rick Tudor and Fred Farmer, who had a motorbike with a sidecar, and once a week they would argue about who would ride pillion and drive the four miles to Rotton Park Reservoir and muck about on the water. Then the Master i/c Rowing enrolled his one-and-only crew in their one-and-only regatta, hiring an enormous articulated truck to transport them to Worcester where they duly came last. 'We weren't very physical,' said Andy. 'It was more of a Zen thing.' Jim once played in the House water-polo final but lost on penalties.

Andy was a pole-vaulter. He'd taken it up partly as a fantasy about escaping the concentration camps and partly because he was good at gymnastics. Then he became West Midlands champion ('I was competing against one other guy, and he only had one leg') and got front cover of the Birmingham sports magazine. On the back of this triumph he and Jim recruited the normally derisive pub-going rugby team to carry his Henry Moore-inspired sculpture from the art room to his back garden in Moseley. 'We'd shown them they weren't the only winners and harnessed their brute power to artistic ends, which felt good.' Turned out the Gun Barrels regulars had a soft spot for the 'hippie freak weeds' after all.

At some point (with a change to a bouffant hair style) Terry Tough became Perry Poof and Grievous became Half-Breed, a dig at Jim's Irish father, and cartoons of the two friends did the rounds of the school. Lee didn't recall the homophobia the way other old boys did – he'd always thought having gay men in the tribe was a welcome evolutionary advantage (less competition for girls) and anyway the whole mindset was incomprehensible to him – but he did remember the anti-Irish prejudice and persistent anti-Semitism. 'It always took me by surprise,' he said. 'Perhaps it shouldn't have, because of the war, but it was precisely because of the war that it did.' Hadn't we answered that question? Were we really going to revisit it every time some neo-Nazi poked their head above the parapet?

When it came to fascism, even schoolboys knew what was right. Perhaps especially schoolboys. The ethics are set out towards the end of *Night School*.

> Reacher said, 'It was a hardcore moral question. Some said no, because the guy has broken no laws. Not yet. But that was true of all of them once. If you would come back in a time machine to do it, why wouldn't you do it now? Some worried about degrees of certainty. What if you're only ninety per cent sure? Some said better safe than sorry. Which logically meant anything better than fifty per cent. But not really. Anything over one per cent might be worth it. A one-in-a-hundred chance of saving eighty million people from terror and misery? Do you have a view, Herr Dremmler?'
>
> Dremmler said nothing.
>
> Reacher said, 'We were undergraduates. West Point is a college. It's the kind of thing we talked about then. Were we serious? Didn't matter. There was no way to prove we would do what we said. Or not. But life's a bitch. Now I get to answer the question for real.'

It was a passage I knew Lee was glad to have written.

Jewish boys could choose to go to the 'Jew Room' during assembly. It meant they could do whatever they liked, which was definitely not warble hymns under the eye of Slug or endure another of Cack's sermons from the carved wooden throne of Sapientia. In the final gathering of the year Lunt would invite 'the boys of the Mosaic persuasion' to depart early, which meant you could steal a march on the summer holidays, which also meant there would always be two or three stowaways trailing along in their wake, ready to claim a sudden conversion.

Once Jim and Andy wrote a song about Bates and his gang that they recorded in a single take on the Tandberg reel-to-reel tape recorder owned by Andy's dad and played at House assembly, scarpering from the stage while the rest of the boys remained captive to the bitter, biting end. On a later, more edifying occasion, Jim led a Sixth Form assembly on the topic of racial harmony using Jimi Hendrix and Charlie Parker. It made a change from hymns, said Glover, 'and was pertinent in a largely white school at a time of increasing racial tension'.

The single non-white guy in their year group was Andy Forbes, who like his fictional counterpart in *The Rotters' Club* loved Shakespeare, but unlike him made it to Cambridge (and later became principal of London's City and Islington College). Jonathan Coe's 2001 novel was an inescapable point of reference for any Old Edwardian from the seventies onwards, cited in every interview – did I know the Carlton Club was really the Cartland and the *Bill Board* the *Chronicle*, that the school had once been on New Street, that part of the building designed by the dream team of Charles Barry and Augustus Pugin had been dismantled brick by brick and lovingly reconstructed as the chapel after the war? Did I know the original building had been replaced by an art deco office block, that the Tavern in the Town in its basement had been bombed by the IRA in November 1974, causing horrific casualties, and that this was also a pivotal plot point in the novel? Coe didn't join the school until 1972, but his characters 'could have been based on me and Jim', said Andy Saunders. 'He really captured that moment in the seventies.' Coe's book 'mirrors my life so exactly I asked Jonathan if he was stalking me' (Spicer). 'I cannot work out whether my life is imitating art or vice versa' (Claughton).

Forbes hadn't read it.

I've never got to the end of *The Rotters' Club*, perhaps because its rather accurate depiction of Birmingham in the 1970s brought back too many unpleasant memories. In the 1960s Black people were still a novelty – I remember middle-aged ladies asking my mother if they could touch my hair to see what it felt like, and racism was more to do with ignorance than aggression. But as the sixties turned into the seventies the mood darkened. It's perhaps difficult for people to remember the sheer scale and normality of routine everyday racism – the constant racial epithets – wog, coon, sambo, nig-nog – not necessarily said in anger, and the total absence of any positive narrative about Black communities. It wasn't just the Blacks and Asians, either. If someone was mean you'd call them a hook-nosed Jew without any sense that it was forbidden or wrong. There was no racial etiquette around language and tolerance.

Jim was thirteen when Birmingham-born Old Edwardian Enoch Powell delivered his inflammatory 'Rivers of Blood' speech at the Bristol Hotel in April 1968, warning of 'a nation busily engaged in heaping up its own funeral pyre'; together with the unrest spilling over from the university it had a profound impact on his developing political consciousness. Four years previously Conservative Member of Parliament Peter Griffiths had won his Smethwick seat in 'the most racist election campaign in British history', with the slogan 'if you want a n***** for a neighbour, vote Labour' – which tellingly, a national majority did. A 1996 BBC retrospective records how landlords refused to let houses to immigrants and barbers to cut their hair, how churches would close their doors to pious, well-dressed families.

Coe's budding writers hone their skills on the school newspaper and the Grunwick strike, the first black and migrant worker struggle to win widespread support from the labour movement, extolling the power of words. Jim Grant collaborated with Glover and another mate, John Burton, on a book that Glover described as 'an episodic soft porn tale of the implausible sexual adventures of a well-endowed but acne-ridden youth, entitled *10-inch Cyril*'. There are no surviving copies.

Forbes wrote a poem for the *Chronicle* called 'Canal-Side in Birmingham', inhabited by the ghosts of nineteenth-century industrial splendour and now also overlaid with flashes of twenty-first-century regeneration:

> The canal stretches, limp-limbed,
> Beside the mud frown of the towpath,
> Only the still wind tasting its ugly waters.
>
> Amongst the waters, houses, dust red,
> Gardens, fields of people, petrol,
> Shift, and leave reflections.
>
> In this nowhere place between a graveyard and a factory
> The dead rise with the evening's warning,
> And the living die at dawn.

Andy never went to Jim's house ('Jim was just too embarrassed'). No one did. But even so he formed an impression of the Grant household that was 'stark and grey and military and unloving and rejecting'. Jim, in contrast, spent most Saturday nights at 155 Russell Road. Sometimes his father would drop him off, and Andy retained a strong visual image of 'this huge guy in a black coat and a black hat and moustache' blotting out the light on the doorstep. Jim dressed like he'd walked out of Captain Beefheart and Andy had a taste for green stacked heels and orange leather. 'Neither of us fitted into boxes.' Andy thought Jim was trying to express that part of himself that was stomped on at home. 'He was troubled, but not neurotic or depressed – on the contrary, he was a real survivor. He may have been a poser and a bullshitter, but never a phoney.'

It was easier to talk to Andy about personal things, said Alison Yeomans. She thought the qualities Jim didn't like about his father and older brother – their cold self-containment and their inability to express emotion – were the very things he was fighting against in himself. 'He was fighting against that internally the whole time,' she said. It wasn't easy being a Grant male. The difference was that Jim was more aware – of others, and also himself.

Mostly Jim caught buses between Moseley and Handsworth Wood, but otherwise Mrs Saunders would give him a lift home. He reacted to the unaccustomed kindness of Andy's parents like a houseplant responding to water and sunlight, reinventing himself effortlessly as though that was the person he was secretly yearning to be.

> He used to have dinner with us. My mother loved him, my sister loved him, I think he felt this was like a new home, where there was warmth and welcome. All that Jewish emphasis on food and family, which I hated – for him it was like fodder, he was so deprived of it.

Lee didn't deny it.

But he reinvented himself all over again for the sister.

> She was three years older and used to come home with all her hippie friends from Keele and Jim would just go in there and take on this new persona. He just had this way. He was like a pig in shit with them, he'd have these joints and just really enjoy it.

The bad boy charm was firing on all cylinders. 'He can go from one extreme to the other,' Andy said. 'He was brilliant at that.' Andy was a 'very straight non-risk taker', so Jim was the brains as well as the brawn behind the ongoing pranks.

The telephone was their connection to the outside world, and half the fun was recording calls on the Tandberg and reliving them over playback. One Saturday they hatched an elaborate plot to torment the parents of Dave 'Ernie' Mudd, who was away for the weekend.

Jim corralled a string of accomplices to phone the house saying they'd heard there was to be a party that night and what time would it start. Last was Jim himself, pretending to be 'Mr Jones' enquiring after his sons and when were they going to get home. 'I guess you had to fill the time somehow,' said Glover, looking back ruefully on this event. 'I think we were all cruel,' said Andy. 'We tended to judge everyone by how bad their acne was.' 'Or by how fat they were,' Lee added.

With the adrenaline running high, Jim rounded off the night by assuming a broad Brummie accent and calling Cack Face himself, claiming to be from the British Rail lost property department at New Street Station and respectfully advising Canon Lunt that he had left his umbrella, his cheque book and a copy of *Playboy* magazine on the train, and would he like to come and pick them up.

Only Jim had the chutzpah to pull off such an audacious stunt, but the apprentice had learned from the master. The sixty-four-year-old Andy couldn't quite believe Jim hadn't done A-level Maths, because he couldn't quite believe that he, Andy Saunders, could have blown up his Maths teacher all by himself, without Jim egging him on or holding his hand, but the fact was Jim had done English, French and History at A level, like Glover, so devising that smoke bomb by mixing glycerine and potassium permanganate to create an exothermic reaction and placing it in the teacher's desk and when it exploded following the bicycle-chain-swinging Gobbler out of the open window and running away with the rest of the class – it was all down to him. Anyway, Jim had never liked Chemistry ('too smelly'), which was how Andy was found out and sent quaking to Cack's office, only to discover an unexpected ally who agreed that the young Maths teacher recently arrived from Cambridge was indeed 'problematic' and let him off with a standard detention.

Glover was present at Jim's last lesson, with a French master called Workman: 'forty minutes of anarchy that ended with Jim wearing a false beard impersonating Workman, threatening Workman with unspecified punishment for impersonating *him*.' 'It was feral,' Lee admitted, almost apologetically. 'We picked on the weakest, and the weakest was often the teacher.'

'We quite liked Canon Lunt,' said Andy, 'because he quite liked us.' They did General Studies with him for Cambridge Entrance, and one time he was talking about subliminal adverts and said surely they'd all read the recent book on the subject and what was it called and surely their fathers were all educated men and had this book in their libraries, upbraiding them until Jim's hand slowly went up and he said, '*Hidden Persuaders*, sir, by Packard.' 'Cack Face adored him for it,' said Andy. They were eighteen years old. It was almost the end of Jim's prolonged stay at King Edward's, and perhaps the first time he'd let on that there was this nerdy, erudite, bookish side to him that would later shape the complex character of his alter ego Jack Reacher. 'It wasn't even a recent book,' Lee said scornfully, looking back on this moment, and he was right, since it had been published when he was three years old. Which prompted him to recall how he liked to test the limits of his teachers' knowledge by embedding false references in his essays that more often than not would receive a tick of vainglorious approbation. It struck me as inevitable that – again like Borges – there should be times he was toying with his readers too.

For English they studied *Hamlet* and *Measure for Measure* and Webster's *The White Devil*, poetry of the thirties (Auden, MacNiece), poems of faith and doubt (Donne, Arnold, Hopkins), Pope, T. S. Eliot and *The Canterbury Tales*, Greene's *The Power and the Glory* and Golding's *The Spire*. In French they read Baudelaire and *Manon Lescaut* and Stendhal's *Le Rouge et le noir* and Albert Camus, anagrammatically known as Alec Ratsbum.

'I always thought Jim was an intelligent son-of-a-bitch and much smarter than me,' Steve Johnson wrote, 'so it doesn't surprise me that he has become a world-renowned novelist.' 'He would write incredible stories,' Andy said. 'We had to read them out in class and I had this envy at his ability with words. It was probably the same for him with me and music.'

'I actually learned to write in my Physics class,' said Lee. 'The teacher was an absolute tyrant, but he taught me how to be brief and concise.'

Yet no one was making a case for Jim being the outstanding English scholar in Upper Sixth. 'He was more peripheral,' Collis said, 'not one of those spouting new theories about the metaphysical poets.' Jim drove Andy and Collis down to Cambridge for their interviews in his mother's white Riley Elf (dubbed the Riley Dwarf), but no one was surprised when he was the one who didn't get in. Marks were routinely read out in class, so everyone knew the pecking order, but even so, and even though it was self-evident that not everyone who applied to Oxbridge could possibly get in, since that was the sole purpose of a King Edward's education not doing so still counted as failure.

As a Foundation Scholar Jim should have been a shoo-in, John Claughton said, but having done O levels in five rather than an accelerated four years he was already on the back foot. Claughton suspected Jim of having sabotaged his chances at interview, refusing to play the game as a dirty protest against pretension, but when I put this theory to Lee his recollection was more poignant. Two things sabotaged him, he said. One, he was certain of it – from inside information from a mate with a connection to the school secretary – was Lunt, who had warned Cambridge 'to stay away'.

The second was a rare – but devastating – loss of confidence. Cambridge was a quantum leap. Jim was unimpressed by the old buildings and the cold wind, but overwhelmed by the 'infinite range of intellectual enquiry'. Literally in the moment of interview, he experienced the demoralising realisation of being handicapped by his background. What, really, was the point of sitting those retakes? He lacked 'the last fifteen years of wide-ranging discourse at the dinner table'. He was 'stunted'. You have to understand, he said: 'I'd been isolated, raised inside a religious cult. It was like growing up a cripple.'

However metaphorical his words, the experience had made him feel small: it was 'the exact analogue' to having his nose rubbed in his inability to act and sing at Cherry Orchard, 'the same feeling all over again'.

Andy and Jim hung out at Gigi's in Moseley, a faux-leather-seated diner-coffee bar opposite the Bull's Head, both centres of Birmingham hippie culture, and sought out live music at the Hare and Hounds in King's Heath, the Bourne Brook Hotel in Selly Oak and the Tamworth Country Club. They went to discos at the convent school in Edgbaston, which guaranteed a high ratio of girls, and at Cannon Hill, which promised experimental music with long Hammond organ solos and wild psychedelic dancing late into the night. When they got their licences they would drive out to the Hollywood bypass to experience the thrill of driving over 60 miles per hour.

Jim had a sideline cobbling together HiFi for his mates, using speakers from old television sets, often delivering well over budget and beyond the agreed date. He had temporarily abandoned the guitar for the alto saxophone. He'd picked up a silver-coloured Selmer for £12 ('almost certainly stolen, because I didn't have £12') at the same little cave of a pawn shop where Andy and Rick had bought their guitars, and had polished it up and replaced the pads and played it for a while, wearing a sling round his neck as a badge of office, then sold it for twice as much when he needed the cash. Upstairs in the black-painted loft of the Saunders' vast Victorian house he and Andy were free to live out their dreams. They would dress up like rock stars and play loud, and sometimes Jim would add vocals in the style of Mick Abrahams, the original guitarist from Jethro Tull but by then of trendy

Blodwyn Pig. In the end they'd both made it big, but even as a bestselling author Lee would lie in bed fantasising about being lead guitarist in the band they used to fantasise about. Did Andy remember when they painted the poster for their first gig on the wall and the band was called Dark Tower?

Andy got a place to study medicine at Cambridge and promptly formed a band called Missing Morris with Richard Wolfson from outside of school (with Collis as roadie), leaving Jim behind to improve his grades. Richard was a bit like Jim and they bonded immediately, but he'd always felt bad about it, as though somehow without meaning to he'd jilted his old friend. Andy hated Cambridge. He and Wolfson reformed as experimental duo Towering Inferno and released their own-label Holocaust-inspired album *Kaddish* – fusing chanting rabbis with heavy-metal guitar and hypnotic systems music – described by Brian Eno as the most frightening record he had ever heard and later picked up by Island Records. In what seems an homage to their misspent youth, there's a track featuring a fax machine where he and Wolfson phoned random numbers in Germany and recorded the voices of strangers.

A while after *Kaddish* appeared (which he didn't know about), Lee came across a copy of *Rattlesnake Guitar*, a compilation CD of songs by Peter Green, founder of Fleetwood Mac (whose eventual vocalist Christine Perfect/McVie was the daughter of a teacher at King Edward's) and in Lee's view possibly the greatest, and most tormented, of British blues guitarists. He felt a special affection for Green, who though eight years older shared a birthday with him, not least because in 1970 he and Andy had seen him play live at the Cannon Hill outdoor amphitheatre. The track that seduced him was a version by Americana duo Naked Blue of 'Closing My Eyes', a song he had always loved but imagined would be impossible to cover. Despite himself, he thought it worked.

Some years later, around 2003, he received a letter from married couple Jen and Scott Smith in Baltimore, who said they loved the Reacher books and were due to visit New York and were keen to meet up. Oh and by the way, they were playing a gig at the Bitter End in the Village and would he like to come and their band was called Naked Blue. Fast forward to 2018 and the release of *Just the Clothes on My Back*, a Reacher-inspired album with lyrics by Lee Child, featuring the following chorus from track 8 ('Blessed or Cursed'):

> I was born on a Friday
> Either blessed or cursed
> Never knew which came first
> Yeah, I'm hoping for the best
> Planning for the worst

On the balmy November launch night at City Winery on Varick Street, Lee said he had no idea whether or not 29 October 1960 – Reacher's birth date (beyond a certain point deliberately fudged by his publishing team) – was actually a Friday (it wasn't), but that Wednesday and Saturday didn't scan, and Sunday was overdetermined with religious connotations, and Monday and Tuesday and Thursday were just too banal (the Mamas & the Papas might not agree), so it had to be Friday, and that, broadly speaking, was how literature worked.

What Lee did know but didn't say was that Friday was the day James Dover Grant was born in Coventry – on 29 October 1954, both hero and villain, both *blessed and cursed*.

In his first exchange of messages with Andy for forty-five years, Jim played down his professional career – 'Not much to report . . . 18 years at Granada TV, which was a fun job, but it all fell apart in the upheavals of the 1990s, and I became a writer as a desperation move, but fortunately it worked out OK' (his autobiography in forty words) – and chose to focus on music instead. 'Funnily enough I am making an album this year, with some musician friends. I wrote the lyrics, and might play a bass line or two, but probably not, because as much as I love music, I'm really bad at it.'

The truth was he'd been writing music for twenty years. It was the inverse of Andy telling the Holocaust story through heavy-metal guitar. This is how he explained it to the *New York Times* in 2009:

> For me, music is narrative – and not just music that has stories within lyrics but instrumental music too. Music has a time base, it unfolds, it has pace and rhythm, it has light and dark, it has key changes and movements that act like chapters. It starts somewhere and takes you somewhere else. When I listen to a jazz solo or a rock solo, I hear the guy telling me something, arguing, explaining, justifying, cajoling. I want my books to do the same thing, both in terms of the longer arc and the shorter sections or paragraphs or lines.

He always read his finished work aloud to check it sounded right. He couldn't have music on while he was writing – the book had its own pace and rhythm – and he didn't like to have it on while he was reading either. Music demanded attention. 'If I'm caught up in someone else's narrative, I can't be generating my own.' But away from his desk he used albums like Massive Attack's *Protection* to unwind plot problems, identify dynamics and see potential harmonies. 'If writing a novel is about getting from A to Z, then music helps me hop from B to C, and C to D, and so on, and see how P could carry an echo of F, and how H could prefigure an inevitable X.' He loved Pink Floyd's 'Money' for the time-signature change between saxophone and guitar solos: 'that's a feeling I try to replicate whenever I start a major set-piece scene. Like saying: You want action? Try this.'

'Someone knowing you from such an embryonic elemental stage leaves you exposed and vulnerable, stripped of image, myth and defences,' Andy wrote. He'd been nervous about the reunion. Perhaps Jim was too. It was precisely the situation Lee had envisaged for Reacher in *Bad Luck and Trouble*:

> After ten years of magnificent self-confidence I wanted Reacher to be in front of people that even he will compare himself with – his peers and his equals. They made a certain set of choices and he made a different set of choices. He looks at them and he thinks: am I the jerk or are they the jerks?

It worked out fine in the end, in both real life and fiction. 'There's two characters,' Andy said when I met him, a little awed, a little anxious.

> There's Jim Grant, and there's Lee Child, who I don't know at all. He was Jim Grant when I met him. He's got these two personas. I watched him on YouTube and I can see it's Jim Grant, but he's playing this character that's not him.
>
> He was always so brilliant at that.

But now 'all Jim talked about was betrayal'. Clearly this wasn't true. I knew that, because of all the other things Andy told me they'd talked about. But he was a sensitive, empathetic character. So even allowing for dramatic instinct and artistic licence, to which they were both prone, I took what he said seriously.

Lee tended to cite *Romeo and Juliet* as his favourite Shakespeare play and had a soft spot for *The Tempest* because he'd done it with Mr Parslew – perhaps it was Prospero who first gave him the idea of writing as revenge. But experience had poured poison in his ear and the darkness of *Hamlet* had wormed into his soul.

I've been betrayed massively twice in my life, Jim told Andy, who took it to refer to Bates and the band and his trade union colleagues at Granada. But what about his parents? What about the promise of the wristwatch? Which led us to agree that he had been betrayed massively three times, and that he'd never forgotten those betrayals, and that taken together they had massively defined his life.

'For him it was very extreme,' Andy said, 'and he was already an extreme character to begin with. He has no time for lack of loyalty, that's what I remember about him most of all. His dislike of his parents was so isolating. It made him build these incredible defences. And it created this ability to completely and endlessly reinvent himself. The betrayal has made him what he is.'

17

Gentleman Jim

His life was like that. It was a mosaic of fragments.
One Shot, 2005

'In Middle School you could drift, cover your own tracks. Not in Sixth Form.'

Mr Parslew was Jim's English teacher in Sixth Form. 'Jim is an example of how I work, my method of exasperated tolerance.'

When I met Michael Parslew he was in his early eighties, hair still thick but now snow-white, more jovial than he appeared from those brooding black-and-white Dramatic Society photographs, brimming with an infectious *joie de vivre* and with a mischievous, almost flirtatious gleam in his eye – what P. G. Wodehouse would call a dash of *espièglerie*. He had the inexhaustible reserves of energy you need to survive as a teacher.

Mr Parslew sat me down on the sofa in his comfortable living room, with a view out over the tranquil Worcestershire countryside, and asked me sternly what I was doing there. He laughed out loud when I told him I was writing Jim's biography. 'Jim would laugh out loud at the idea of a biography,' he said, once he'd managed to contain himself. 'He doesn't think of his books as literature, just a way of making money.' I was forced to concede that Lee had, it was true, thought the idea absurd, and that Mr Parslew clearly knew him well.

Jim was very self-deprecating, Michael said, he didn't take his books seriously. I wasn't so sure about that.

I told Mr Parslew that Lee had identified the compulsion to win as his greatest weakness. He disagreed. 'His greatest weakness was his capacity for idleness. It took great determination to drive him along. Jim was bright, but not one of those who projects himself, he hid it as much as he could, would sit there with a slightly cynical, enigmatic smile on his face.' He was regularly a day or so late handing in essays and with exasperated tolerance his teacher would anticipate his excuses: 'Yes, I know, Jim.' What he knew was that Jim had been to the Gaumont the night before, that he had 'other commitments'.

Michael was an Old Boy himself. He first left King Edward's in 1955, three years after the appointment of the Reverend Ronald Geoffrey Lunt as Chief Master. It was his own former English teacher, Tony Trott, who invited him back, ostensibly to celebrate the retirement of the Master i/c Cricket, and Michael formally rejoined the school a term after Jim. His arrival is recorded in the *Chronicle* of May 1966: 'Mr Parslew, O.E., joined the English Department in January, bringing the number of Old Boys in the Common Room to seven.'

Lee remembered Mr Parslew as old because teachers were old by definition. But he was rather a young Old Boy. 'It was very funny in the Common Room. I was one of a group of young'uns. The older staff were constantly scandalised by the boys. They couldn't grasp their new ways of thinking and doing things.'

Lee remembered the Chief Master as an intimidating but enlightened leader. He had been educated at Eton and done Greats at Oxford (as he thought everyone should, even the engineers). He was a Church of England canon. He had served as a chaplain in the army, attached to 7 Commando and Layforce and the Coldstream Guards and the Special Raiding Squadron of the 1st SAS Regiment. He held the rank of Captain and had won the Military Cross for actions in the Knightsbridge Box on the Gazala Line in the Western Desert Campaign in 1942. And on top of that, he had a much younger Norwegian wife and went skiing. There was an aura about him that commanded respect.

'We followed Birmingham industry hours,' Lee said. 'We weren't at school all that much.' There were Saturday-morning lessons but on Wednesday and Friday afternoons the boys could choose to stay on site and make use of the facilities or go home. The luxury of emptiness, of private time and space, was empowering. Lunt cracked the whip during timetabled hours but otherwise advocated 'total unsupervised freedom'. Nor did he engage in pointless battles against the length of your hair. It was this instinct for what mattered that (mostly) stopped the free spirits from lighting out for the open road.

The Chief Master's pragmatism was a legacy of his wartime experience. The following is from *Commando: Memoirs of a Fighting Commando in World War Two*, by Brigadier John Darnford-Slater:

> Allan Peile was the Intelligence Officer, and I took from Special Raiding Squadron a good padre called Ronnie Lunt. I put Ronnie in charge of all the ecclesiastical arrangements within the brigade. He was shrewd and capable, exactly what we wanted as a padre. He was also tactful. Late one night, after we had had a few drinks, I asked him to name a price against my entering heaven. I was expecting at least ten to one. To my great surprise he told me that I was a six to four on shot, as all my sins were of a healthy type.

Mr Parslew debunked the romantic notion that King Edward's had anything to do with Birmingham industry. Lunt was nostalgic; Saturday school was an 'aping of the public schools'. King Edward's was handsome and well endowed but no Eton or Rugby. But he agreed Lunt was a good headmaster. Despite his pre-war morality he was flexible. The young'uns banded together and advised him to drop Saturday school, which he duly did, as the *Chronicle* records in recounting his 1966 Speech Day address.

Lee in turn debunked the notion that King Edward's aspired to be like the public schools. 'We were nothing like them,' he said. 'We were better.'

In Sixth Form, Michael said, the Chief Master would 'bend around the edges', allowing more latitude to the boys and immense independence to his staff. The school was forgiving of radicalism and intellectual dissent on both sides. 'So long as you were doing the job, you could do whatever you liked.'

What Michael Parslew and Jim Grant liked was theatre. It was an out-of-hours thing, purely voluntary. Thanks to Cherry Orchard's Miss Lyster, Jim had always loved drama, but 'when the band imploded then theatre took over'. 'We felt like the theatre group was ours, something we owned, like it was real, a guerrilla group.' Jim was perceived as a loner, but in the Dramatic Society everyone was accepted on their own terms. They came together as 'a happy band of brothers and sisters', in Michael's words, then let go and went their separate ways. It was an intense shared experience that was guaranteed to be finite, like a football match or one of Reacher's short-lived affairs, the brief encounters that collectively formed the mosaic of his life.

Michael was master i/c and Jim was his sound engineer. He was never 'a one hundred and ten per cent committed thespian', Michael said, 'and I suspect he privately viewed the people who were as barmy. He was an efficient and reliable technician.' But at the very moment the sound engineer was wanted he would sometimes disappear. 'Is Jim Grant around?' Mr Parslew would ask. 'No sir, haven't seen him, sir.' Then: 'Right. Go and find him, and tell him to finish his cigarette and get straight back up here.'

Smoking was against the rules, but only a problem if you were caught red-handed. On one occasion, when his sound man had gone AWOL once too often, Mr Parslew went in search of him himself. It was the only time he could recall Jim looking embarrassed. 'Get up there and do the job,' he told him, exasperated, his tolerance wearing thin. Lee looked mystified at this account, like the equation 'Jim Grant + embarrassment' was one he found difficult to compute.

Mr Parslew was fond of Jim, and proud of him too. But he entertained no illusions. Jim was 'a sharp one' who knew how to play the system, and 'a lot of staff didn't like him'. They felt he lacked respect and literally looked down on them. He was a 'slippery, shadowy figure', a 'tall, languid, reticent person', who would 'slither and slide' his way around like someone either conducting covert surveillance or seeking to evade it. 'There was a sort of sideways movement in his walk.' He had evolved into 'a handsome man', but back then he was 'slightly scruffy and shifty'.

Michael, from the perspective of a smaller man, put this down to self-consciousness – intrinsic to adolescence but aggravated by extreme height. Jim's shoulders were hunched and he was 'gangling, with just that hint of lack of coordination'. Which was one reason he belonged backstage. Whenever he had the idea of stepping out in front of the curtain Mr Parslew would hasten to dispel his illusions: '"Jim! Don't try." To be an actor [he gave the two syllables equal stress] you've got to know what your limbs are doing.' Perhaps Lee was thinking of his old teacher when in *Make Me* he refers to Reacher's 'innate and inevitable slight clumsiness': 'He was no ballet dancer. Neat and deft and dexterous were adjectives that had never applied.'

'He creates an image because of his unsureness about himself, his sensitivity,' Michael said. In his view, Jim was unusually 'sensitive to his surroundings, to his situation, to the people in the room'. I was reminded of the great Shakespeare scholar Harold Bloom, who when shown a photograph I had taken of Lee reading Bloom's *Possessed by Memory* remarked: 'He looks a sensitive fellow.'

Jim did what he wanted on his own terms and kept himself to himself. The school was organised into Houses (each named after an old Chief Master), a hangover from boarding-school days. Jim was in Gifford (not Prince Lee, sadly), whose colour was purple. 'If he was forced to turn out he would,' Michael recalled. One year he turned out as basketball captain – 'I was tall, I was reasonable, we did middlingly well' – and wrote his end-of-season report in rhyming couplets. 'I was into Alexander Pope and wrote everything in rhyming couplets.' But my question about sport provoked another outburst of hilarity: 'Sport?! Jim?! I could never imagine him with a cricket bat in his hand. The very idea!' Like many boys he supported Aston Villa, but otherwise presented himself as 'a languid, laid-back character, a sophisticated loather of games'. He didn't do anything fast. He wasn't going to run if he could walk.

Perhaps he could be judged a good all-rounder. Mr Parslew thought about that for a moment. 'Well, if you mean cutting school when he could, smoking when he could, then yes – he was that kind of allrounder.' But that didn't make him stand out, not in the sixties and seventies. 'It was all about image, pose, persona.' If Jim Grant was a 'sharp one', his teacher was no less so.

Jim liked English, but not especially at A level. Lee recalled his frustration at the airy-fairy tone of discussion, when he wanted to pin things down to nuts and bolts and analytics. Others would leap to symbolic interpretation (he cited a poem by Blake), while he insisted on grappling with what a particular word actually meant. It was his idea that the class should first translate Shakespeare into contemporary language, so that when they returned to the original they would have a deeper appreciation of what the actors were saying.

Parslew admired this practical discipline. But both he and his pupil were hazy about lessons. It was the obverse of that glorious freedom.

No one really knew what they were doing. Lee thought his set texts were probably *Measure for Measure*, *Hamlet* and Matthew Arnold's *Culture and Anarchy*, but he wasn't sure. The only thing he was sure of was that the notion of set texts didn't come up until the examination room, which left even him floundering, except when the task was to write two verses of poetry in the style of Arnold, in which case his were the best, because he was 'an excellent parodist' (and wondered even now if his novels were not fundamentally parodic). But it wasn't as plain sailing as Fifths. He had the wit but not the study skills, the brain but not the *savoir faire*. The system was hit and miss. Luckily, Oxbridge was 'totally not his scene', said Michael, who read English at Selwyn College. 'It would be all the collegiate things he didn't like about King Edward's, writ large.'

Early in Sixth Form Jim took his French penfriend to London. He got on well with Jean Denis Moutier. They had overlapping tastes in books and music. Jean's accent made him a sensation with the girls. Something similar applied when Jim visited Chantilly and there were vague stories in the collective memory of a French girl in a French field, or possibly on a train. The Moutier family had a horse farm in Argentan, and when Mr and Mrs Jim Grant were passing through Normandy in the late 1990s they tried to look them up. They even went to the Mairie, like Reacher goes to the library to trace his father's origins in *Past Tense*, but twenty-five years had gone by and as in the book no one recognised the name. But Jim never forgot Jean, even if he didn't immortalise him until he wrote his eighth novel, *The Enemy*. Which was when he gave Reacher's French mother a back story and named her father Moutier.

Neither Michael nor Lee remembered Jim Grant's moment in the spotlight. But there it was, reviewed in the *Chronicle* of September 1973, an end-of-year production by the drama syndicate of T. S. Eliot's *Sweeney Agonistes*.

Eliot calls for perfect enunciation and careful attention to rhythm, and all the actors fulfilled these prerequisites perfectly. The second scene was particularly successful, containing as it did performances by Jim Grant and Chris Springall as the natives on either side of the stage.

When I told Lee I was due to visit his old teacher he chose to get his retaliation in first by telling me 'the worst he could say'. Drama was about mixing with girls. It was especially about mixing with Dot from the next door High School (where Michael's wife Pat worked as a special needs teacher). Dot's name appears often in reviews in the *Chronicle* and the praise is always fulsome. 'Tall,' wrote Michael, *'très gamine* [an epithet of which Lee was fond, notably in *Blue Moon*] – a lovely dancer and a good actor. She played Rosalind in my production of *As You Like It* and had the gentlemen of our Sixth Form in quite a tizzy! The last I heard she was married with children, living somewhere south of Birmingham. She could have made a career in the theatre if she had wanted, but opted to teach.' There is something poignant in that brilliant trajectory, flying so high so fast only to come back so soon to earth.

More than anything it is the difference in style that reflects the generational gap between pupil and teacher. But Lee's recollections of Dot are remarkably similar. She was popular, sexy, a figurehead, like a character out of Frederic Raphael's *The Glittering Prizes*. She could have gone anywhere, had anyone, done anything. Dot was beautiful and talented. She had short, dark hair in a classic seventies bob. There was about her 'a sense of boundless possibility in the future', you just knew she would end up at the Royal Shakespeare Company. Then out of nowhere 'she went on to do absolutely nothing, became a housewife and a schoolteacher'. Harsh words, but you could tell it hurt. 'It was such a Midlands thing, it was so hard to escape.' Harder still for women and girls.

'She was my girlfriend from July to December 1973,' Lee told me. Dot was from a posh part of town: 'a modest house, but in a much nicer spot'. Her parents were liberal and progressive, and he mostly saw her at her place. 'She was fabulous in bed, very exciting and adventurous.'

Dot used to babysit for Pat and Michael Parslew. One time Jim went to hang out with her and they had exciting, adventurous sex on the Parslews' sofa. Somehow Mr Parslew found out about it, and wrote Jim a letter that left him in no doubt about how badly he felt let down.

Perhaps Michael had decided discretion was the better part of valour or blanked this upsetting episode from his mind. Certainly he said nothing about it, not even when tested with leading questions. But it was a story Lee had told, and therefore *a true story*.

The other boys had always dismissed it as rumour: Dot had 'an aura about her, and came across as unattainable', like Cicely Boyd in *The Rotters' Club*. But they all believed Jim Grant and Sue Iles – also from the High School – had been caught naked in their living room by Sue's parents.

There is a photograph of seventeen-year-old Jim sitting at a table in Underwood Road, a luridly pink drink at his side and a spoon in his right hand suspended halfway between a bowl of cereal and his mouth, a copy of the *Chronicle* in his left. He is reading a letter from fellow Edwardian David Willetts – later Conservative Member of Parliament, member of the House of Lords and Chancellor of Leicester University – or possibly his own scathing response of January 1972:

Sir,

I'm writing about the article 'Youth and Age Can Never Agree' in the last issue of the 'Chronicle'. There is a danger that this may seem a personal attack on Willetts, which it isn't; if I said I didn't know who he is it might hurt his feelings, but there you go. This is directed at the attitude of pseudo-maturity which his article radiates.

Willetts, D. L., the blue book tells us, is fifteen. Well, I'm glad that this has given him enough maturity and experience to say 'Many adolescents are basically immature . . . I sympathise with our parents' generation . . . I respect their middle-class charm and appeal.' His article is full of such judgments which Willetts, as if possessed of total human experience and infinite wisdom, tosses casually down for us to grope gratefully for. No doubt many of these judgments are true, but they are surely not a fifteen-year-old's (nor a seventeen-year-old's, nor even a twenty-year-old's); they seem to come from people who are much older than us who know what life is about. Why Willetts assumes possession of these judgments and expounds them in so posturing a style I don't know. Perhaps it's part of '. . . the correct idea that adolescents regard themselves as grown-ups directly they enter their teens'.

Some of Willetts' article is ludicrously trite. 'How often do my generation really laugh?' he asks. Well, we can all chuckle over the breath-taking perception that '. . . not realising the great significance of the youth movement, they (the middle-aged) claim that patched jeans are no more serious than Oxford bags'.

I humbly venture that a lot of the article is true, but why bother to produce other people's ideas with an air of spurious maturity? Never mind, David, come back in fifty years.

Yours etc.,

JIM GRANT

Willetts – cited by Parslew as 'mad keen', in contradistinction to Jim – responded succinctly: 'Since when have deviations from norm or age been valid critical arguments?'

Two things stand out: Jim's command of genre and his dislike of pretension. He wasn't into European films because it felt 'phoney and pretentious'. There was no arthouse cinema where he grew up.

He remembered hearing a bunch of kids from another school talking about T. S. Eliot in the Kardomah 'like they were something special', mocking some other kids for not knowing it. 'I loved Eliot and still do, but I only read it in the first place because I was told to. Scoffing at someone else for not knowing it seemed to me like a double layer of self-delusion.'

The Kardomah, 'an alleged coffee house' on New Street near Rackhams department store, the closest thing in 1970s Birmingham to a diner and in Parslew's view a place of sin, was where King Edward's boys and girls would congregate out of school. Mainly on Saturday mornings, when most would be on site for sport but take civilian clothes in their kit bags and change in the cubicles at Rackhams afterwards. Unlike Reacher (or Lee Child himself), however, they didn't dump the old stuff in the trash on the way out.

Reacher wasn't into fashion. Nor was Jim. He couldn't afford to be. Lee was more pernickety. He would no longer put up with sleeves that were three inches too short ('I like Paul Smith but know none of it will fit me') and hated it when his black jeans faded after a few washes or his jackets got pilled, but even when he hit the red carpet with Tom Cruise in 2016 he hadn't gone overboard on the outfit: 'Clothes all mail order from Lands' End. Shoes Duckie Brown by Florsheim. Black suit, gray shirt, skinny black tie. Total cost about $300 for clothes and $400 for shoes.'

Michael Parslew left King Edward's in 1973, the same year as Jim Grant. He was headed for Bristol Cathedral School. He didn't want to become another Mr Chips. His departure is recorded in September's *Chronicle*:

> Michael Parslew left K.E.S. for the second time at the end of last term, his previous departure having been 18 years before.

The valedictory note pays tribute to his contribution in the class-room, where 'he combined the styles of spell-binder, cultural jeremiah, fastidious literary intellectual and *obergruppenführer*'. Which tells you more about King Edward's than any historian could do.

Best of all we learn that 'the Old Parse' owed it all to his strict regimen of coffee and Benson & Hedges, to living on 'nerves and nic'. Which eloquently explains that affectionate bond between master and pupil.

It was 'a theater impresario called Mike Parslew', Lee Child said in an interview (for Bestsellersworld.com) in August 2002, 'who taught me my first and last responsibility is to the audience'.

Lee had since become a benefactor of the school. He hadn't enjoyed his time there and thought it was the government's job to fund education. But he remembered how much it had meant to his parents, how they believed that if he went to King Edward's his future would be safe whatever he did with it. He didn't have to like his parents to feel able to honour them. But he wanted to honour his roots, too.

> I remember my gran coming down to visit from Yorkshire and she saw people in Birmingham using £5 notes – she'd never seen one before! Birmingham has always been about energy, talent and creativity and that hasn't changed even though the place feels very different now.

The assisted place Lee had endowed in the name of Rex and Audrey meant that from here to eternity there would be one boy going through school funded by the Grant family. His gran would have been impressed. It was a lot of £5 notes (at least sixty-five thousand of them, probably more).

In principle the school sought to match donor to pupil and when pressed, Lee had asked for the son of a civil servant, because he knew civil servants were still poorly paid and he wanted to respect the memory of his father and grandfather. But it hadn't worked out that way. The first recipient of the Grant family grant was the second son of an Afghan market trader. Which was fine by Lee. His parents weren't around any more to know.

'I'm not some kind of saint,' Lee hastened to assure me. 'I spend money on myself. I buy everything I want' (so far as I could see mostly audio equipment). But there were numerous instances of spontaneous gifts to friends and dependents in need, medical bills covered, houses bought and mortgages paid. Jim and Jane were repeat donors to the Raystede Centre for Animal Welfare in East Sussex – fittingly established by a former headmistress in 1952; they had paid for a new entrance hall to attract more visitors, and a new enclosure for rescued cockerels to be called 'Reacher's Pen'. 'I have to go to the bank,' Lee said once, after we'd met at the diner on Columbus. Turned out he was collecting $5000 in cash for his long-serving housekeeper, whose husband had fallen on hard times.

The day came in 2010 when Lee was invited back to school as guest of honour on Speech Day, hosted by John Claughton, now Chief Master and the first of the King Edward's establishment to fully appreciate his worth and stature. Jim wanted the Parslews to be there too. 'Leave it to me,' he said. 'A car will arrive for you and take you to the Hyatt Hilton.' He didn't want them to worry about being late. So they stayed the night in central Birmingham and went together.

The speech was as close as Lee had come to addressing his teenage self. He warned the boys against the heartbreak of being a Villa fan. He said their biggest problem in life would be their minority status: 'Nothing to do with ethnicity or religion, but a far more pernicious and frustrating minority – that of intelligent people required to live in a profoundly stupid world.' He begged them not to make the mistakes of his generation. First, he set the scene by summing up the twentieth century as a game of two halves.

'I look at that happy little boy and wonder what became of him,' Lee said. James, aged two, Coventry. *(family photo)*

He always did like a good set of wheels. Ridgeway Avenue, Stivichall, Coventry, 1955. *(family photo)*

Already plotting his escape. Ridgeway Avenue, on big brother Richard's tricycle. *(family photo)*

The six-year-old's coveted Westclox wristwatch, tainted by a never forgotten sense of betrayal. *(HM)*

James Dover Grant, aged two, with his grandfathers, Harry Dover Scrafton of South Shields and John 'No Middle Name' Grant of East Belfast. *(family photo)*

Two-and-a-half-year-old 'Jas', 1957, in Belfast with father Rex, mother Audrey and brother Richard, visiting the mill where Lee's great-grandparents worked. *(family photo)*

The Cherry Orchard gang, Birmingham, 1961. Seven-year-old James top right; barn-dance date Alison Yeomans four along from best friend Mairi Wilson, top left. Mike Buckland is a row down from James, far right. *(Cherry Orchard Primary School, courtesy of Mike Buckland)*

(above left) Nine years old and dreaming of joining the 'swashbuckling rock-and-rollers' at Aston Villa. Cherry Orchard playing fields, taken in 1964 by PE teacher Mr Weaver. *(family photo)*

(above middle) 1965: Ten-year-old Jim Grant joins King Edward's School, Birmingham, founded by royal charter in 1552: 'At first, I was hungry for intellectual fodder.' *(KES Archive)*

(above right) 1969: Fourteen, and soon to be elected a Foundation Scholar: 'After that I treated school itself as a dare.' *(KES Archive)*

(right) Mr Parslew, English teacher and head of drama at King Edward's. 'Jim is an example of how I work, my method of exasperated tolerance.' *(Courtesy of Andy Forbes)*

If it's not black, it's got to be pink. Seventeen, Underwood Road, reading the King Edward's *Chronicle*: 'I was in the middle of a big argument (by letter to the paper) with fellow pupil David Willetts, who later became a Tory minister.' *(family photo)*

Fifteen, with Richard and baby brother Andrew – 'a cute kid and a happy experience' – outside 6 Underwood Road, Handsworth Wood. *(family photo)*

Eighteen, with five-year-old Andrew, who would one day inherit the Reacher franchise, somewhere in Switzerland. *(family photo)*

1975, the Student Years: Somewhere in the Lake District. 'My emaciated drug addict look.' *(family photo)*

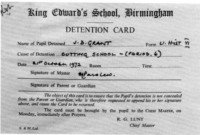

King Edward's School, Birmingham

DETENTION CARD

Name of Pupil Detained __J. D. GRANT__ Form __IVB__
Failure to report to Mr Whalley following
Cause of Detention __Expulsion from scouts for persistent unsatisfactory__
__behaviour__
Date __31/5/69__ Room _____ Time _____

Signature of Master __D. C. Rish.__

Signature of Parent or Guardian __John R Grant__

The object of this card is to ensure that the Pupil's detention is not concealed
from the Parent or Guardian, who is therefore requested to append his or her signature
above, and cause the Card to be returned.

The card must be brought by the Pupil to the Chief Master, on
Monday, immediately after Prayers.

R. G. LUNT
Chief Master

X.V.M. Ltd.

King Edward's School, Birmingham

DETENTION CARD

Name of Pupil Detained __J. D. GRANT__ Form __U. Hist VI__

Cause of Detention __CUTTING SCHOOL — (PERIOD. 6)__

Date __21st October 1972__ Room _____ Time _____

Signature of Master __M Pardew.__

Signature of Parent or Guardian _____

The object of this card is to ensure that the Pupil's detention is not concealed
from the Parent or Guardian, who is therefore requested to append his or her signature
above, and cause the Card to be returned.

The card must be brought by the pupil to the Chief Master, on
Monday, immediately after Prayers.

R. G. LUNT
Chief Master

S. & M. Ltd.

Detention cards 1969 and 1972. 'Has paddled his own canoe,' writes one of his teachers.
(British Archive for Contemporary Writing, University of East Anglia)

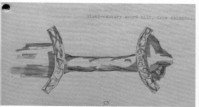

(right) 1972: Jim Grant wins the Medieval
History prize. 'Amazing to think there is only
one copy in existence,' said Lee, who had grown
accustomed to big print runs. *(BACW, UEA)*

(above) Ninth-century sword hilt, from
Abingdon. Illustration by Jim Grant.
(BACW, UEA)

1972, Sixth Form: Best
friend Andy Saunders
at home in Moseley,
Birmingham. 'We weren't
very physical, it was more of
a Zen thing.'
(Courtesy of Andy Saunders)

'All writers are wannabe rockstars.' *(Adrian Mudd, friend and wedding photographer)*

August 1975, Sheffield: Wedding day at Crookes Valley Park, with a view of the Arts Tower. Jane was 'invisible' to her future in-laws, and Jim a 'wastrel' with no obvious prospects. *(Adrian Mudd)*

1973, Sheffield University: Mike Gibbons of Thornsett Road, with Falcon pipe. 'We would talk over a cigarette or something less legal and endless coffees long into the night.' *(Courtesy of Mike Gibbons)*

1981, the Granada Years: New parents Jim and Jane at The Circuit, Alderley Edge, Manchester. 'Like he's having a day off from fronting the Eagles.' *(Robert Reeves)*

1974, Sheffield: Jane Shiren at 34 Wadbrough Road. 'She was unbelievably beautiful, unbelievably exotic. It was no hardship at all.' *(family photo)*

'Until she moved in with me, I moved in with her.' *(family photo)*

1975, Sheffield: Married life at 329 Crookesmoor Road. *(family photo)*

'It's programmed. I was brought up as a man to be the breadwinner.' *(family photo)*

1980, Manchester: At Janet Brown's house, with Jane and 'little Ruthie'. 'I'm very sentimental about my daughter.' *(Courtesy of Janet Brown)*

1948: Future Granada loggist Janet Brown, aged six, at Biddulph Grange in Staffordshire. Sister Burgess ruled with a rod of iron. *(Courtesy of Janet Brown)*

1984, USA: Father and daughter on holiday at Stillwater Lake, Millwood, the home of Jane's parents. *(Norman Shiren)*

22 May 1997, Harpenden: With proud father John Reginald Grant, after Lee's first official author photo was taken in London for Transworld. Rex writes: 'The reviews are increasingly encouraging and on their strength I have decided to Read It.' *(family photo)*

The first half contained four gigantic catastrophes – the First World War, a global flu pandemic, the Great Depression, and the Second World War. Between them those four catastrophes brought untold suffering to perhaps a billion people and killed perhaps two hundred million of them in circumstances of abject misery and terror. It was almost certainly the worst half-century in all of human history.

Then things changed dramatically, and while things were far from perfect for many people in many places, for people like us in a place like this, the second half of the 20th century became perhaps the best half-century in all of human history.

Among the 'basket of benefits' they enjoyed was an 'otherwise unremarkable Prime Minister' (Harold Wilson) who kept them out of Vietnam (and, he might have added, whose two Labour governments oversaw the introduction of race relations legislation by Roy Jenkins, the MP for Stechford in east Birmingham).

He finished by urging them not to chicken out. 'If you want to study law, go for it, but don't then become a solicitor in Erdington, doing divorces and conveyancing. Go to Texas or Mississippi and abolish the death penalty, or go to Africa and write a constitution.'

Yes he was a bestselling writer, one of those alumni who made England 'great and famous through the globe'. But he hadn't changed the world.

'Despite the advantages conferred on us we somehow rose to the level of mediocrity,' Howard Williamson agreed. 'Much as we hated the Chief Master telling us so, we should have been leaders of the nation.' '*Leaders of tomorrow*,' Inglis chimed in. 'We were told that on a daily basis.' Boys arrived at King Edward's with fire in their bellies, but once that Oxbridge line had been drawn in the sand they'd either made it or they hadn't, and either way it was over.

Lee's personal rite of passage was not becoming no. 1 in America (*New York Times*). 'That came later, from being tempted to look back and sum up. To assess. To confront the evidence. [. . .] Mine was a lucky generation and we did a lot of fun things, and some great things, too.'

> But did we do enough? Seven years of my free education were at a school 224 years older than the United States. It had all kinds of mottoes in Latin. One said: 'Much is expected of those to whom much is given.'
>
> And we were given a lot. Historians will say some of us were the luckiest in all of human evolution's seven million years. And we blew it, basically. We missed things, and eventually we settled for something short of what we could have had.
>
> Nothing to be done about it now. It's all in the past. Our history is over. That's the real rite of passage: knowing that you've written and spoken your lines, for better or worse, and now it's someone else's play.

More than an appetite for success, Lee thought, King Edward's had inculcated a fear of failure. Maybe 20 per cent of boys would turn out to be wastrels, but that still left 50 per cent who should have been taking the world by storm. 'It should have been a tsunami.' The school had been founded by four entrepreneurs, practical, plain-speaking sons of Birmingham, but with the passage of time had capitulated to the myth of southern superiority, revering Eton and Harrow and seeing mere acceptance by Oxford and Cambridge as the pinnacle of human achievement. In so doing it had betrayed the commercial common sense of its forefathers and the 'Birmingham mentality' had become defeatist, shot through with a sense of unworthiness.

Audrey wrote to congratulate Jim, thanking him for sending a copy of the *Gazette* with the text of his address:

Hasn't it all worked out remarkably well and I know it has given pleasure and interest to countless people. Not many could claim that! (No one seemed to appreciate my and then Dad's efforts in the Inland Revenue to the same extent.)

The last time Michael and Pat saw lucky Jim was in April 2016, after his appearance at the Cambridge Literary Festival, when he drove up to Stoulton to see them. 'He took us out to dinner at our favourite pub,' Michael recalled. 'Jim feels at home here, and we like to have his Jaguar parked outside in our drive.'

But the man they saw was no longer Jim Grant. He was Jim Grant plus Lee Child. And Lee Child struck Michael as 'a man of great honesty and self-awareness. But guarded.'

Jim was never in any serious trouble, 'not like those two boys who got caught stealing books from Hudsons'. But nor was he ever quite out of it. Mr Parslew eventually became a Housemaster involved in selecting the new School Captain. He was perfectly placed to assure me that Jim was never a contender. There was no beating about the bush. Jim was too much of a rogue, too often 'on the slippery side of events'. 'I can safely say,' Mr Parslew concluded with authority, fixing me with a schoolmasterly gaze, 'that on no occasion did Jim Grant's name come up.'

'He never walked openly through a door,' he said, as though seeing the scene in his mind's eye. 'The door would open halfway and he would sidle in. And I would say: "Ah, here's Gentleman Jim Grant."'

18

School Report

'Don't blame the kids,' Reacher said. 'Look at the families. Tell the truth, at our school there were a lot of parents who had killed people.'
The Midnight Line, 2017

Jim Grant's colourful career as a risk-taker is factually documented in his sixteen school reports, from Shell C in 1965 to History UVI in 1973.

At eleven years old he is a bright young thing with 'impressive all-round ability'. Comes top in History and Latin. Weakest subject English. He signs up for the Natural History Society, gymnastics and swimming.

At twelve he 'lacks patient application', is 'forgetful and dreamy', 'late and scruffy'. He joins the Aeronautical and Film societies and collects medals for life-saving and personal survival. Then he pulls his socks up to achieve the highest grade for Combined Sciences and English (the latter feat never to be repeated). He is 'a cheerful boy', 'lively and interesting', with 'plenty of imagination'.

At thirteen he is 'very good: imaginative' in English. He joins the Music Society. He gets a 1* in Physics, doing 'very good work when he exerts himself'. In other subjects he rarely exerts himself.

At fourteen he is sinking, except in Physics, where his 'ability far outstrips what is demanded'. He is a promising cross-country runner and has joined the Modern Languages and Junior Science societies.

He does Music on Friday afternoons – 'progressive stuff, I guess'. His form master writes: 'Tendency to be idle, apathetic. Needs prodding all the time.'

In March 1969 J. D. Grant is put on a Report Card. For the first week his card is marked mostly with As (Good), with a smattering of Bs (Adequate) and one C (Could do better). The second is mostly Bs, a handful of As, a C and an E (Unsatisfactory). On 31 May he is issued with a detention for 'failure to report to Mr Whalley following expulsion from Scouts for persistent unsatisfactory behaviour'. The task is to 'write an essay on aquatic respiration'. The card is countersigned by John R. Grant.

Jim's end-of-year report concludes: 'A bad term: mixed with a bad gang, has lowered his standards and done the minimum. This is unworthy of him and his potential. Must get thru' this stage quick.'

He gets through it quick at fifteen, his sights set on O levels. He joins the Debating and History societies. In English he is 'very good indeed: mature, evocative, accurate'. In Physics he is flying: 'Excellence without effort.' His form master writes: 'Reformed character: deliberately, almost ostentatiously, keeps away from old cronies. Very able, if not exactly endearing, boy.'

At sixteen, the immediate hurdle cleared and a scholarship under his belt, Jim reverts to inconsistency with patches of brilliance. He is stronger in discussion than on the page. He joins the Shakespeare Society. Chief Master: 'Evidence of better things. Has now to sustain effort and purpose and work dynamically to the maximum of his good ability.'

He is not dynamic. At seventeen, in what should be his final year, nerves are becoming frayed. Mr Parslew, now also his form master, puzzles plaintively over his contrary pupil: 'It's just that he seems incapable of consistency. If that comes he'll be very good indeed. A very likeable character.' Canon R. G. Lunt: 'James has still an imp on his shoulder, but if he can resist him, he should do well.'

The imp got him a detention 'for cutting school' on 21 October 1972.

Jim's predicted grades were B/C for English, A–C for History and C/D for French. Parslew: 'A good hand but still too dour for his own benefit.' Lunt: 'He shows the kind of mind likely to do well at Law.'

His next report – Christmas 1973 – is cursory: too little too late. 'Laziness resulted in A Level disaster 1972 [English B, History D, French E]. Repeating History and French 1973 [he would go up a grade in each]. Only his own efforts can ensure success.' Housemaster: 'Too indulgent and self-centred.' Lunt: 'Gifted, capable, clever but a potential wastrel.'

Jim Grant's final report has the school washing its hands of him. History: 'Has paddled his own canoe.' Form master: 'A rather late recovery from complete collapse of morale.' Housemaster: 'Very much a drop out.' Lunt: 'He has an able brain but is temperamental about its use.'

'Reacher sees school as an assault course,' Lee commented. 'If the pass mark is 60%, he'll get 61%. Why waste energy?' Either that or he'll go for full marks. 'I'm not interested in 75%.' He was unfazed by the slippage in personal pronoun.

But it wasn't all doom and gloom. In 1972, aged seventeen, J. D. Grant, Eng VI, submitted a collection of essays for the Medieval History Prize. He won the prize. It's possible that his was the only entry. Maybe it was a little like being crowned West Midlands Pole-vaulting Champion against a guy with one leg. But there was no doubt he'd put in the effort. 'Anglo-Saxon England: the Life of the People' was sixty-five double-spaced pages and approximately 20,000 words. I found it in the Lee Child Archive at Norwich, in a bottle-green ring-binder complete with desiccated spider. The title page was hand-drawn in bubble-writing, in red and blue ink, with an image showing three farmhands and a span of oxen pulling a plough set at right angles to the lettering.

Jim's spelling is not flawless (*dependant, privelege, specemin*), and he goes back to correct 'semisphere' to 'hemisphere' with a pencil. But his work is certainly scholarly. The introduction relies heavily on metaphors of enlightenment. A 'rush of interest' has 'lightened the darkness' of this 'twilight area', but 'a large number of inferior books [has] clouded the history of the period with over-complicated political narratives and a plethora of nearly identical names'. The young – and very earnest – J. D. aims to bring clarity, and put the popular image of the warrior hero in its proper social perspective.

Next is a hand-drawn map of 'Anglo-Saxon England c. 730' and list of contents. The text is illustrated by impressionistic line drawings, in tastefully themed red and yellow watercolour over pencil: Royal Hall in Cheddar; Hut with Sunken Floor, from Thetford, and Section; A Rich Man's Dress, from an 11th Century Manuscript; Early 11th Century Female Dress, from the Charter of the New Minster (B.M.); Ninth-Century Sword Hilt, from Abingdon; The Benty Grange Helmet (Derbyshire); Mail-Clad Warrior from the Bayeux Tapestry.

The bibliography lists fourteen principal sources. J. D. isn't afraid to express an opinion. His discourse is precociously aphoristic and he writes a pithy blurb. No bestsellers here. Stanton, Loyn and Maitland are 'invaluable'; Hodgkin 'is so complicated that it is hardly comprehensible'; Oman is 'interesting for little gems of character description', Brooke 'conceptually clear if lacking in detail', Whitlock 'valuable for its sensible, balanced, human approach', Green 'slight but descriptive', and the introduction to Bede by his translator 'sugary and pious'. Jim upbraids the *Observer Colour Supplement* for 'many breathtaking superficialities and inaccuracies' in its series 'The Making of the British'.

The essayist feels no need to translate his Latin quotations. He is well versed in the Laws of Ine, 'the first legal document of the West Saxon kingdom', and au fait with digs at Sutton Hoo and Sutton Courtenay, Sulgrave, Bifrons, Benty Grange, Cassington, Kingston,

Cheddar, Dorchester, Yeavering, Warendorf and Oberflacht. He is fearless in challenging the assumptions of established scholars and their glib parallels with Germanic and other Continental sources. He is sceptical of the reductive division of Anglo-Saxon society into four broad strata (king, noble, yeoman and slave), preferring the often elusive distinctions between king, thegn, eorl, ceorl, gebur, craftsman and serf. He notes that the entertainer or 'gleeman' belongs with the craftsman, just one step up from the bottom of the ladder.

He tracks the decline in kindred and rise in territorial lordship from the seventh to the eleventh centuries and how a theocratic element permeates the ruling classes following the Conversion. He knows the relative values of men according to the law of wergeld: 'a rather morbid way of evaluating a man's status – the amount of money which had to be paid in compensation by the murderer to his victim's household'.

Like his father, he delights in words. He elucidates the shifting meanings of 'thegn' by reference to the Latin 'minister'. The thegn was always 'somebody's thegn', therefore despite his elevated status still by definition a servant. The term 'eorl' won out over 'thegn' because of the pleasing rhyme with 'ceorl' (morphing eventually into 'earl and churl').

Jim argues that the structure of Anglo-Saxon society, far from being primitive, is 'rigidly compartmentalised and extremely intricate'. It was possible to change your status (especially downwards). Through service you might even aspire to become a Knight of the Realm. But fundamentally, a man's value depended on 'the stratum of society into which he had been born'.

He charts the diminishing status of the ordinary freeman as his land decreases in value. 'Many ceorls had to purchase protection and financial help in times of stress and disorder at the cost of relinquishing some of their rights.' The loss of rights of 'the small man' was one of 'the greatest abuses of the day'. As the little guy became tied to the land of others, so 'the big man' became bloated with power. But slaves could be freed, too; ceremonies took place at a crossroads, 'a symbol of the slave's new-found freedom to go whichever way he wanted'.

In *Persuader*, Dominique Kohl asks why Reacher became a cop. Cops look after people, he says: 'They make sure the little guy is OK.' Then when she pushes further: 'I don't really care about the little guy. I just hate the big guy. I hate big smug people who think they can get away with things.' It was the same compulsion to stand up for the downtrodden that drew Lee to John D. MacDonald's (far more sexist) Travis McGee.

There is particular enthusiasm in Jim's final essay: 'Weapons and Warfare'. Anglo-Saxon warriors were 'dominated by their pagan instincts' (paving the way for Reacher's 'lizard brain'). Scabbards and hilts and pommels and quillons are described in loving detail. The pattern-welded sword (we learn how it is made) is superior for its greater strength and flexibility, not to mention its marbled beauty. He distinguishes between the spatha (later improved by the addition of the 'fuller', a broad, shallow groove running the centre length of the blade), the scramasax (the single-edged long-knife) and the angon (a short barbed weapon used as a javelin, or in a 'vicious stabbing action'). He notes how spears evolved to be more easily withdrawn from the wound and therefore more efficiently redeployed. He celebrates the refinement of an iron haft on the battleaxe, making it possible to split a man from head to crotch as hymned in *The Song of Roland*. He records how this led to the iron helmet being topped by an ornamental feature to mitigate against this gruesome risk by distributing the force of the blow. He describes the composition and construction of shields (limewood covered in leather or painted) and how they might be used offensively as well as defensively, and what to do if your shield is chopped to bits in your grip (use the central iron hand-guard as a knuckleduster). He considers tactics at the Battle of Maldon:

> As usual the battle was fought on foot, and was a fairly solid affair – once the opposing forces had met, the fighting consisted of hand-to-hand hacking until one side was wiped out or fled.

And ever the boy from Birmingham, he opines on the quality of metalwork:

> Parts of a mail shirt were discovered at Sutton Hoo, but this was of inferior manufacture, in that the rings were not riveted, but merely butted together – a weak method which had no advantages to recommend it except ease of manufacture.

Lee said two things when I told him I had read his A-level essay. First, how amazing it was to think of there being only one copy in existence – his brain had adapted to big print runs. Second, that he hadn't chosen that topic out of any special interest in medieval history, but merely expediency, knowing no one else would and thereby maximising his chances of coming out a winner.

If that is to be believed, then this cynical exercise was a truly formative moment. Because he undoubtedly did develop a lifelong special interest in history, both modern and ancient – further fostered by a meeting of minds with archaeology student turned environmentalist Jane.

In 2019 Lee Child was commissioned by the *Times Literary Supplement* to write a 10,000-word essay. *The Hero* would be published as a slim volume, one of two that would launch their new imprint with William Collins. They would offer an honorarium, a sum so trivial (to him) that Lee couldn't recall what it was, or whether or not they had paid him. 'It's funny,' he said. 'I can remember when a million dollars

seemed like a lot of money.' It wasn't much of an earner, but it did feel
a bit like winning a prize.

> Most dreams are unattainable [Lee said for the press release] – Aston
> Villa never called, asking me to play centre forward on Saturday; the
> Yankees don't need a new right fielder; Massive Attack already have a
> bass player. But some compensation came when a 117-year-old literary
> institution I have read and admired all my life asked for a contribution.
> That's validation for you.

Two months later he would tell ITV News that only the opinion of
the people who bought his books mattered, and that he therefore had
upwards of '100 million reasons to ignore the snobbery towards crime
fiction writers'.

'Anglo-Saxon England: the Life of the People' is – of course – a less
assured piece of writing than *The Hero* (though no less didactic). But
from linguistic analysis through socio-historical consciousness to the
knowledge of how things work and the desire for justice, the essence
is all already there.

Including the embryonic Reacher: a variant of the thegn who
assumes responsibility for enacting local law and order. Reacher is also
a true 'freeman'. He is answerable only to himself. He has the right to
deal with his own property howsoever he chooses, and to head for the
crossroads and go whichever way he wants.

19

Lee Car

He didn't want anybody to try to keep him there.
Echo Burning, 2001

Lee felt more attuned to *Nice Work* (likewise set in the seventies) than *The Rotters' Club*. David Lodge's Rummidge – 'a monochrome landscape, grey under a low grey sky, its horizons blurred by a grey haze' – was recognisably Jim Grant's Birmingham, and Lee could relate to its central character, working man Vic Wilcox. When in 2017 I asked if he would stop after Reacher no. 24 (three more than originally intended), Lee replied:

> Without being sexist about it, it's programmed. I was brought up as a man to be the breadwinner, to earn the money, support my family, so it would seem very irresponsible to turn down that kind of money when it was available to me, almost like a betrayal of the species.

And another time, more dryly, 'it would be hard to turn down the GDP of Belgium'.

But he could relate to radical academic Robyn Penrose too. While he agreed with Vic that reading should be 'the opposite of work', 'what you do when you come home from work, to relax', he was equally seduced by Robyn's theory of reading as production, a cooperative contract between two people whereby he, the writer, made strange black marks on white paper and then months or years later the reader would expend her mental energy 'generating meaning'. 'Reading is not passive,' he would insist, 'it's active.' Or in the elegant words of Rebecca Solnit, from her essay 'Flight' in *The Faraway Nearby*:

> The object we call a book is not the real book, but its potential, like a musical score or seed. It exists fully only in the act of being read; and its real home is inside the head of the reader, where the symphony resounds, the seed germinates. A book is a heart that only beats in the chest of another.

Even so, it matters that the book is an object that sits solidly on the shelf, and Lee also appreciated Robyn's perception of the novelist as a capitalist of the imagination:

> [The novelist] invents a product which consumers didn't know they wanted until it was made available, manufactures it with the assistance of purveyors of risk capital known as publishers, and sells it in competition with makers of marginally differentiated products of the same kind. The first major English novelist, Daniel Defoe, was a merchant. The second, Samuel Richardson, was a printer. The novel was the first mass-produced cultural artefact.

Lee liked this. It made his books sound like something the Greek government might pay good money to buy. Which is why he described himself as a 'book writer' (rather than 'author'), to shift the emphasis to the book as product, like a fake coin or a watch or a car. Writing wasn't something to approach with kid gloves; you didn't have to dress up like you were giving a speech at a wedding. He had no truck with writer's block. 'You ever hear of truck-driver's block?' It was just 'a fancy name for not wanting to go to work that day'.

The book writer was 'the front end of a big machine'. He himself had sold a mere twenty-four books. The hundred million? That was down to his agent and publishers.

But what really tipped the balance in favour of *Nice Work* was a starring role for the British Motor Corporation, ushered in by Vic's paean to the Jaguar in chapter one.

Lee's first luxury car was the silver S-Type Jaguar he bought in 2005, when *One Shot* came out and Tom Cruise signed on, which was also the year Jaguar Land Rover closed its Browns Lane plant in Coventry. It was 'a watershed moment', like the day he bought the Renoir, and there was a degree of boyish excitement in his choice of licence plate, which read simply: REA*CHR. Since then, the Jaguar had become the automotive equivalent of *the irreducible minimum* in his life. When the lease expired on Transworld's Audi and they asked what he wanted for touring, Lee said: 'A Jag would be nice.' And a Jag was what they got, a black F-Pace to go with Chelsea-supporting driver-cum-bodyguard, Brad. Their 'road food tradition' was a pitstop at McDonald's.

The Grants' first car was a pre-war Morris of indeterminate species: 'a piece of crap'. The next was a six-cylinder Wolseley 6/80, a black saloon of a type mostly used by the police. James loved that car, with its leather bench seat up front, and its 'wicked-looking protruding knobs that I was allowed to pull and push'. Then came a sequence of P4 Rovers, including the one in which he discovered the Beatles. Rex was happy, because he had fulfilled his dream of owning a straight-6 engine, 'a sweet, smooth-running engine, the best-balanced engine you could make'. But also unhappy, because he couldn't afford new, which he felt bad about, and Audrey would rub salt in the wound by 'brutally' complaining they were 'businessmen's cast-offs'. 'Well,' he would retort, 'you shouldn't have married a civil servant.'

It was his mother who taught Jim to drive. It wasn't that she wanted to, it was just one of those things she couldn't in all conscience avoid. He didn't really need teaching. The first British motorcar was made in Coventry in 1897, where the industry peaked when James was born, so he was raised in company towns and had driving in his DNA. 'Everyone knew about cars, talked about cars, dreamed about cars.' He passed his test first time on 3 January 1972 in the Riley Elf, 'a gussied-up Mini with a small trunk at the back'. It still counted as one of the greatest days of his life. 'It opened up a world of freedom and possibility. It represented prestige and responsibility. It was a great girl magnet too.'

'She was looking forward to driving,' Lee writes in *Never Go Back* of Reacher's putative teenage daughter, teasingly crafted in the author's own image. 'Driving [. . .] would widen her scope.'

Jim was looking forward to driving far away from his parents. He was seventeen years old and burdened by a bitter sense of déjà vu. Rex and Audrey had promised their boys 'that if we forewent motorbikes they would buy us cars instead'. Jim didn't want a motorbike (nice machines but anti-social and cold), but his parents didn't buy them cars anyway, only handed down their old ones. 'For three out of the four, but not me.' It was another broken promise, the learn-to-tell-the-time-and-we'll-buy-you-a-watch story all over again, and Jim felt the same sense of betrayal. It reminded him of all those Enid Blyton books at Elmwood about yearning to be an orphan.

He had to wait four years to get a car of his own, when he'd moved out of 6 Underwood and was a student at Sheffield. Thereafter he had a string of them in quick succession.

I had no car until the 1969 red VW Beetle in 1976. Then the Ford Capri in 1978, which I bought from a friend at Granada – 3-litre, automatic, the fastest thing going but soon stolen and trashed. It was replaced with a yellow Renault 4, which I liked very much, but the timing chain broke, which compromised its lifetime economy. Then came the first car I bought new, in 1981, a blue Fiat Strada automatic. It rusted like crazy, so I part-exchanged it for a new red Renault 5 automatic in 1985. Meanwhile I had bought a new black Mini City in 1984. I traded that in 1989 for a black Peugeot 205 automatic, which ended up with 125k miles on it. I traded that in 1993 for a used silver Mitsubishi Colt automatic, which also ended up with 125k miles. Eventually I sold the Renault 5 for scrap in 1997 and bought a used green Vauxhall Astra, which Ruth learned to drive on. Then I sold both the Vauxhall and the Colt in 1998 when we emigrated.

The dates were right up there in his mind with his wedding anniversary.

'His cars were quite ordinary,' Granada mate Rob Reeves remarked unprompted, in his bubble-bursting way. 'I remember he drove a VW.' Then in 2015 Jim swept up to Rob's door in Coniston in a gleaming red Jaguar. Rob recalled a conversation in Soho almost twenty years earlier, after the publication of *Killing Floor*, when Jim had announced: '"Rob, I'm a millionaire, I'm never going to have to work again." And I said: "That's great, but the sex wasn't convincing."'

Cars were in Lee Child's DNA too, especially the humble Renault 5. The story went back to the VW days, when they were visiting Jane's parents in New York.

We were on the last train out of Grand Central and I was sat next to a stranger who started talking to me. Back then Renault was marketing their Renault 5 as Le Car, to give it Parisian chic. Hearing my English accent, he stated he had a European car – a 'Lee Car'. It became a family joke that everything thereafter was prefixed by 'Lee'. So, when our daughter Ruth was born, she was 'Lee Baby' and when she got older she was 'Lee Child'.

It was as much a sentimental as a strategic choice of alias. In 1994 when his research revealed that 'sixty-three per cent of bestselling authors' names began with 'C', Lee must have felt the gods were smiling on him. 'Child' would slot right in next to Chandler, Christie, Clancy, Coben, Cole, Connelly, Cornwell and Crais. If he was lucky – and wasn't he always? – some of that gold dust might rub off on him. 'People browse from the left, but they get bored very early.' Better to be Child than Crais.

When he told this story on his 2018 tour of New Zealand an eager publisher's analyst had hurried away to crunch the numbers, returning to confirm that twenty-four years later your book was still eight times more likely to be a bestseller if you had a name beginning with the letter 'C'.

People sometimes asked if, in writing *Killing Floor*, Lee had ever feared failure. No, he said. He had tricked his brain into believing he could do it. 'You're Jack Reacher, he had been told. You can do anything' (*Die Trying*).

Reacher doesn't much like driving. 'I don't even carry a driver's license,' he tells Jodie in *Tripwire*. It was a way of telling author and character apart, like the fact that Reacher used to smoke but didn't any more because 'smoking implied carrying at least a pack and a book of matches, and Reacher had long ago quit carrying things he didn't need'.

But sometimes the author invaded his character. Like in *Never Go Back* when Turner seeks Reacher's opinion in Cool Al's Rent-a-Wreck lot and he says, 'I'm the last guy to ask about cars,' but then when she chooses the Range Rover because she's never ridden in one before says approvingly, 'You'll love it.' It's Reacher's mouth moving, but his Coventry-born creator speaking.

Reacher doesn't object to cars. So long as he can move on from one to the next when it suits him, then cars – and vans and trucks and buses

– are highly desirable. He's more at home on the cloverleaf than in Jodie's all-white Manhattan loft, and if a car is on the highway then chances are he's ridden it. Audi, Bel-Air, Bentley, BMW, Bravada, Buick, Cadillac, Caprice, Charger, Chevy, Chrysler, Citroën, Civic, Corolla, Corvette, Datsun, DeVille, Dodge, Ferrari, Ford, Grand Marquis, Gran Torino, Honda, Humvee, Hyundai, Impala, Jaguar, Jeep, Kia, Land Rover, LeBaron, Lexus, Lincoln, Lotus, Malibu, Maxima, Mazda, Mercedes, Mercury, MG, Mini Cooper, Mustang, Nissan, Oldsmobile, Peugeot, Plymouth, Pontiac, Porsche, Prelude, Range Rover, Roadmaster, Rolls-Royce, Saab, Saturn, Seat, Silverado, Skoda, Subaru, Suburban, Tahoe, Taurus, Toyota, Vauxhall, VW, Yukon – it was like Jules Verne trying to name all the fish in the sea.

> The silver mirage was boiling and wobbling and a white shape pulled free of it and speared out toward them like a fish leaping out of water. The shape settled and steadied on the road, moving fast, crouching low. A white Mercedes sedan, wide tyres, dark windows. (*Echo Burning*)

If a car isn't spearing and leaping, it's bucking and wallowing, dipping and nosing, bouncing and belching, crouching and pouncing, snorting and sputtering, or '[settling] back on its haunches, like prey ready to flee' (*Nothing to Lose*). More hot than cold, more flesh and blood than lump of metal. A living, breathing, panting Wild West cowboy's ride.

In *Never Go Back* Reacher says his spatial awareness and reaction times are on a human not a highway scale, 'up close and personal', 'animal, not machine'. He uses this argument to excuse his bad driving. But the animistic imagery also explains his occasional prowess.

His senses are finely tuned to the poetic presence of motorised vehicles.

His engine was running rich. Reacher could smell unburned gasoline in the air, and he could hear the muffler popping with tiny explosions. Then the car accelerated into the distance and he could hear nothing at all except the grasshoppers clicking and chattering. (*Echo Burning*)

They felt it before they saw it. There was gradually a deep bass presence in the air, in the distance, like a shuddering, like a tense moment in a movie, as if huge volumes of air were being bludgeoned aside. Then it resolved into the hammer-heavy throb of a giant diesel engine, and the subsonic pulse of fat tires and tremendous weight. Then they saw it drive out of the trees. (*Past Tense*)

A twin-engine Cessna, that kind of thing, hopping and jumping, weightless on the wind. It came in low, and landed, and slowed immediately to a fussy, bustling land-bound scuffle, like a nervous bird, roaring with noise. (*Past Tense*)

It's like being on safari or exploring the primeval forest, but the animals have been replaced by machines.

And in the tradition of the Lone Ranger he can ride away when his work is done. Or walk a whole hot mile before hearing the shudder of diesel and catching the next eighteen-wheeler. Sticking around like the Pied Piper creates 'awkward gratitude issues'.

If Lee were to choose an extract it might be this from *The/Enemy* – all sound and fury, signifying the fearsome, ecstatic, cacophonous century of his birth:

What is the twentieth century's signature sound? You could have a debate about it. Some might say the slow drone of an aero engine. Maybe from a lone fighter crawling across an azure 1940s sky. Or the scream of a fast jet passing low overhead, shaking the ground. Or the whup whup

whup of a helicopter. Or the roar of a laden 747 lifting off. Or the crump of bombs falling on a city. All of those would qualify. They're all uniquely twentieth-century noises. They were never heard before. Never, in all of history. Some crazy optimists might lobby for a Beatles' song. A yeah, yeah, yeah chorus fading under the screams of their audience. I would have sympathy for that choice. But a song and screaming could never qualify. Music and desire have been around since the dawn of time. They weren't invented after 1900.

No, the twentieth century's signature sound is the squeal and clatter of tank tracks on a paved street. That sound was heard in Warsaw, and Rotterdam, and Stalingrad, and Berlin. Then it was heard again in Budapest and Prague, and Seoul and Saigon. It's a brutal sound. It's the sound of fear. It speaks of a massive overwhelming advantage in power. And it speaks of remote, impersonal indifference. Tank treads squeal and clatter and the very noise they make tells you they can't be stopped. It tells you you're weak and powerless against the machine. Then one track stops and the other keeps on going and the tank wheels around and lurches straight toward you, roaring and squealing. That's the real twentieth-century sound.

'Academia is a closed book to me,' Lee once remarked. But he could open it any time he chose.

Cars get Reacher from A to B. Though that notion is irksome to him, as he reflects in *The Visitor*, where he is grappling with the uncomfortable business of home ownership:

> He was new to the concept of driving a regular journey from A to B. He was new to even having an A to B. He felt like an alien in a settled landscape.

He didn't want to be a commuter.

Cars get Reacher from A to X. Into trouble and out of it again. In both phases, his Holmes-like observational skills are critical. He registers this information at the start of *The Hard Way* without any inkling that he might be called upon to provide it:

> Silver, four-door sedan, an S-420, New York vanity plates starting OSC, a lot of city miles on it. Dirty paint, scuffed tires, dinged rims, dents and scrapes on both bumpers.

In *Bad Luck and Trouble* Neagley encourages him to think like a guy who likes cars to figure out Calvin Franz's password, and in *Echo Burning* he deduces which motel Ellie is being held hostage in on the basis of the distribution of cars in the parking lot.

I could see it as a dissertation topic: 'Cars as a Vehicle of Characterisation in the Writing of Lee Child'. It would open with a snapshot of the author in 2010 looking out of his London hotel (from several floors up) and spotting an anomalous NYPD squad car. 'A movie prop, presumably,' he blogs, 'and subtly wrong in that the license plate and the light bar pre-date the car itself.'

The first car he bought as Lee Child was the Vauxhall Astra. The next was his first off-road vehicle, a red 1998 Jeep Cherokee that he purchased new when 'Lee Family' moved to the wide open spaces of upstate New York and that pops up in his fourth, roughly contemporaneous book, *The Visitor*. Soon after, he acquired a black Crown Victoria, which connected up with his past through the Wolseley, but also his present through *Echo Burning*:

> Ford builds Crown Victorias at its plant up in St Thomas, Canada, tens of thousands a year, and almost all of them without exception are sold to police departments, taxicab companies, or rental fleets. [. . .] Which makes private Crown Vics rarer than red Rolls-Royces.

'I specced it out to look like an FBI squad car,' Lee said. 'I bought three cellphone antennae, cut off the wires and mounted them on the trunk lid. For two years I never got a parking ticket.' Not that he paid the fines when he did: he was a law graduate and could spot a legal loophole. Still, he liked the idea of going undercover.

His cars are all in his books, like the Mini he had in Alderley Edge, which punches above its weight in the UK section of *The Hard Way*. 'I wouldn't have recommended anyone sitting behind me,' he said, 'though I often drove around four other friends.'

After the Jeep and the Crown Vic the luxury vehicles came thick and fast. The 2002 Ford Thunderbirds, eleventh generation retro-futuristic, red for him and pale blue for Ruth, the 2005 Jaguar, the 2011 Land Rover Defender, a second silver Jaguar, then the red one, the two Mazda MX5s, the Toyota Land Cruisers, the black F-Type with the growling exhaust and the yellow stitching on the seats. It was hard to stay on top of it. He kept most of them in a garage in Sussex, like other wealthy men might keep a stable of thoroughbred racehorses. But he had a weird and wonderful fantasy – inspired by a hotel lobby in Wellington containing an E-Type Jag – of building a private library in the English countryside big enough to house a Bentley R-Type Continental, the real-life version of his favourite Corgi car as a boy: 'black over grey with great suspension and a spare wheel and sparkling jewel headlights'. The car would set him back a million pounds from Frank Dale & Stepsons, 'London's Rolls-Royce and Bentley Specialists', but he might spend that much on a painting, so why not? It would look handsome set off against the books.

He already owned the forest-green Bentley T2 that had starred in *Killing Floor*.

> It is the most beautiful saloon car ever built. I wrote about it in my first book, because if you can't afford something, at least you can write about it.

And if you could write about it, then perhaps one day you could afford it, not just once but several times over. It was as if his words had conjured his dreams into being.

When I met John Leighton, one of the Grants' neighbours in Kirkby Lonsdale, he told me how he used to work as Retail Director for Clarks Shoes in the United Kingdom and Europe. He did a lot of driving and, like Victor Wilcox and later Lee Child himself, could have whatever car he wanted. In those days he was driving a Land Rover Discovery. It was new out, a massive car with a V8 petrol engine, not the usual diesel, which meant it was quieter but used more fuel. He recalled how Jim liked the sound of the engine. But Jim was also curious. 'Why did you go for this?' he asked. 'Because I could.' John was a quiet man, like the engine of his car.

'Jim thought that was a great answer,' John said, with a quiet smile on his face.

It reminded me of the time I asked Lee why he bought the second, fourth-generation red Mazda in 2015. 'Was it a special occasion?' I wondered.

'No special occasion,' he replied. 'I just wanted it.'

I thought John would think that was a great answer.

Because he could.

20

Easy Rider

'Anywhere I end up, that's where I want to go.'
Echo Burning, 2001

'I don't know where to begin,' Carmen says at the start of *Echo Burning*, as they are riding in her front-wheel-drive white Cadillac. 'At the beginning,' Reacher answers. 'Always works best that way.'

As he sat down to write his fifth novel Lee must have wanted options to play with while he figured out which road to take, which ride to accept, which driver he fancied. There are the three anonymous watchers with their dusty pickup truck. There is Reacher climbing out of his motel-room window with a back story about poor table manners in a bar the night before. There are the three anonymous killers in their 'mud-coloured nothing car', a Crown Vic. And there is Carmen, defined by her luxury car and a bunch of painfully controlling men.

Like Reacher, Lee never plans in advance. He goes where the story leads, hitching a ride on a strong first sentence and following where it takes him. So absolute is the integration of story and discourse that beyond that first sentence he leaves it all up to Reacher: if there's a problem on page 387 because of something that 'happened' on page 38, then it's Reacher's problem, not his, and 'Reacher has to deal with it'. Writing was like getting in a car at night and only being able to see as far ahead as the road picked out by the headlights. You couldn't quite see where you were going but you knew you would get there in the end. It helped if you were an experienced driver.

Reacher asks a direct question: 'You want to tell me where this is heading?'

'This road?' she said, nervously.

'No, this conversation.'

It's a conversation the author is having with himself: *You want to tell me where this book is heading, Reacher?*

In *Echo Burning* the three watchers aren't going anywhere and are soon dispatched by the three killers. Reacher dispatches the four cops. Which leaves Carmen, to whom the writer adds a daughter, Ellie. After that it's up to Reacher. What Reacher does is drive back and forth between Echo and Pecos and Fort Stockton and the mesa until – with the help of an old LeBaron and a 'yellow four-cylinder VW import' that has to be sacrificed and a Jeep Cherokee and a 'tricked-up Crown Victoria' that he commandeers from a bad guy – he figures out the connection between these two separate strands and does what he must to provide a satisfactory resolution, namely defeat Bobby's pickup and save the Cadillac.

He solves the puzzle with a little knowledge of Spanish and French, his recollected readings of Balzac and Marcuse, some reflections on a historic photograph, and his forensic analysis of an entry wound and some bruises. But mostly on the basis of his expert reading of a Mercedes-Benz recently abandoned south of Abilene and an ancient Chevrolet long-since abandoned in the Greers' hellish Red House barn, with the story of its evil past written into the million miles on its clock. 'Probably hadn't been started in a decade. The springs sagged and the tyres were flat and the rubber was perished by the relentless heat.' No more bucking and wallowing and thrusting and bouncing. Inert, silent, guilty: a truck that had made a full confession and told Reacher all he needed to know.

'This is my thing,' Reacher tells his lesbian lawyer sidekick. 'This is what I'm built for. The thrill of the chase. I'm an investigator, Alice, always was, always will be. I'm a *hunter*.'

It was a follow-up to an earlier conversation:

> Then she asked him when he'd been in the Middle East and the Pacific islands, and he responded with the expanded ten-minute version of his autobiography because he found he was enjoying her company. The first thirty-six years were easy enough, as always. They made a nicely linear tale of childhood and adulthood, accomplishment and progress, punctuated and underlined in the military fashion with promotions and medals. The last few years were harder, as usual. The aimlessness, the drifting. He saw them as a triumph of disengagement, but he knew other people didn't. So as always he just told the story and answered the awkward questions and let her think whatever she wanted.

Lee liked the idea of 'a nicely linear tale'. Writing unfolded sequentially along a horizontal, metonymic axis, just as in English books are read from left to right. There had to be a sense of purpose, the promise of a final destination to keep you turning the pages. But if his stories traced a line it wasn't a straight one. It was more like a fractal coastline, 'a saw-tooth itinerary' as Reacher describes it in *Nothing to Lose*, with twists and turns and detours and diversions and digressions, and even the occasional doubling back. It depended on which car stopped to pick Reacher up, or if no car did and he had to walk. Neither Reacher nor Lee wanted to arrive too soon. In the interests of a thrilling climax and a full word count there had to be some holding back or peripeteia first. Like in *The Odyssey*. Like a musician pursuing a far-flung improvisation before resolving back to his theme.

Led Zeppelin, like Aston Villa, was never far from Lee's mind. 'I love both the focus and the discursiveness of Jimmy Page's solos,' he wrote for the *New York Times*. 'I know I'll never play guitar like that, but late at night I think maybe at least I could write like that.'

It was because stories were linear that he couldn't go back to straighten them out. A story had to follow its own path, in the same way that to get from A to X Reacher puts one foot in front of the other and for the writer, one word literally follows the next. The road not taken could always form the basis of the next outing in the series.

'Everyone's life needed an organising principle,' the author writes in *Nothing to Lose*, 'and relentless forward motion was Reacher's.' And a few pages further on. 'Reacher hated turning back. Forward motion was his organising principle.' It was Lee's too, in writing and in life. 'I can't do "xxx" and go back later, because one thing follows on from, and must follow on from another.'

Lee's objective was to capture the reader at the start and keep them going until the end. He would begin with a question, 'then find a rhythm that trips forward, where the beat is always falling just ahead, that subliminally pulls people along by a chain, so it's like riding a bike downhill'.

He liked to quote Henry James: 'Easy reading is hard writing.'

This is why his minor characters are often not referred to by name, something critics sometimes took as a sign of him 'dialling it in'. The opposite was true. He really cared about the reader.

'It's not laziness.' Lee resented the tedium of books where thirty pages in you've forgotten who's who. If he says 'the old guy at the Post Office' (at Mule Crossing in *The Midnight Line*) then the reader is reminded of that character's function in the story. 'Of course Reacher knows his name,' he said. 'He needs to know his name, because he's looking for Porterfield and he needs to find out if this is Porterfield before he can talk to him.' Not only was he looking out for his reader, it was integral to the characterisation of Reacher himself, his easy, familiar, vernacular style.

'I work at this,' Lee said. 'I construct it with aims and purposes.'

But writing a page-turner didn't mean hurtling along at breakneck speed. 'All the Reacher books include episodes of quiet and calm, otherwise the book just batters you to death.' If you had only one pace it was the same as having no pace at all. He explained it to me using two quite different points of comparison. It was like Chuck Berry's song 'Johnny B. Goode', 'which tells the whole story in super-compact form but still has time for redundancy and incidental detail, creating a feeling of expansiveness inside a fast-forward narrative' ('A log cabin made of *earth and wood*'). Or a Manhattan apartment where every square foot is worth $2000, so you make sure to build in the luxury of some unused open space.

Were it not for his dislike of pretension, he might have invoked what nineteenth-century essayist William Hazlitt called the 'super-erogatory' in Shakespeare, the luxurious excess of his style, the first-glance unnecessariness of details that on closer examination rarely were. Lee's prose is seen as 'lean' and 'spare', and mostly (though not always) it is – at sentence level. But he can write whole paragraphs about the electric bell push and wiring and hand-lettered signs and peeling tape ('many layers, applied in strips of generous length, some of which were curled at the corners, and dirty') on the waist-high enquiry counter ('like a miniature version of any government office') of the county records department in Laconia, registered not merely for their own sake but for the snippets of insight they provide into the inner life of non-existent characters ('as if picked at by bored and anxious fingers'). The digital world may be a foreign country to

Reacher, but he has a quasi-robotic capacity for storing and processing information.

You want your prose to keep 'tripping forward', but not at the cost of sacrificing interior monologue, descriptive detail, sociological observation, philosophical reflection and poetic resonance. Hence Lee's love of repetition and lists:

> Jack Reacher caught the last of the summer sun in a small town on the coast of Maine, and then, like the birds in the sky above him, he began his long migration south. But not, he thought, straight down the coast. Not like the orioles and the buntings and the phoebes and the warblers and the ruby-throated hummingbirds. Instead, he decided on a diagonal route, south and west, from the top right-hand corner of the country to the bottom left, maybe through Syracuse, and Cincinnati, and St. Louis, and Oklahoma City, and Albuquerque, and onward all the way to San Diego. Which for an army guy like Reacher was a little too full of Navy people, but which was otherwise a fine spot to start the winter.

This is the opening of *Past Tense*. It doesn't go a mile a minute. It lulls you dreamily into rolling along for the ride, like being wrapped in honeyed tones or rocked in a warm embrace. And since Reacher doesn't go on to do any of these things, it is full of 'Johnny B. Goode' redundancy.

One reason Reacher goes slow is because Lee is a slow writer.

> I'm dragging every word and action out of my head at the time of writing. It's a kind of distributed planning that is very tiring. With a plan writing is boring. Without a plan writing is arduous.

But the stress of constant invention 'totally engages' him. 'It's going slow,' he wrote to me in February 2019. 'I really like going slow.'

'Everything I do I base on my experience as a reader,' Lee told Christopher Wigginton at Sheffield's Off the Shelf festival in 2017:

> What I love as a reader is that factor that makes you keep going. It's a mysterious process: one more chapter, one more chapter, that sensation of immersion on page one that you can't get out of until you finish.

He thought of structure as a retrospective delusion in the mind of the reader, an illusion of intentionality. 'I start with the first line, then I think OK what's the next line, then I keep going and one hundred thousand words later usually the story has worked itself out.' The second half of the book was like a mirror held at right angles to the ink blot of the first, to create an appearance of seductive symmetry.

This aesthetic reaches its peak in *The Midnight Line*. The storyline has an archetypal simplicity, driven by a single specific object from the beginning right through to the end. Despite a string of random encounters, there is nothing Reacher does that is not motivated by his desire to find the owner of the ring. He wants to know the who, what, where, when and why, 'for sure'.

Why? the pawn-shop guy asks him.

> 'I can't tell you exactly.'

A simple answer to a simple question, true to character and intrinsic to the plot. But also effortlessly, unpretentiously self-reflexive.

> 'I guess I want to know the story.'

It's Reacher's voice. But it's also Lee Child, telling us exactly how he writes.

In conversation with Megan Abbott at the Union Square Barnes & Noble on publication day, the two writers considered why Reacher finds it difficult to explain his motives. 'Can he express himself?' Abbott asked. 'Probably not,' Lee conceded: 'I try to make him a twentieth-century guy, if not twenty-first, but he finds it hard to admit why he's affected. Perhaps it's because he's a bit old-fashioned, sympathetic to the woman in a way he might not have been to a man, and to someone dramatically smaller than him.'

True to character, but also solving a fundamental technical problem for the writer. 'He does it mainly because he's got nothing to do.' For which read: *What the hell am I going to write about this time? How do I get him involved?* 'I have to find an aim within the aimlessness of his life.'

Not surprisingly, Reacher encounters scepticism: *A buck gets ten there's no story at all.* The MacGuffin of the ring provides a brilliant beginning, but will the author make it through to the end? Or will this be the novel he most fears, where it all comes crashing down around him? *What if this time I can't pull it off?*

'I'll follow the ring until I find someone who's heard of her.'

There was something Lee said that was often quoted by his disciples: 'The way to write a thriller is to ask a question at the beginning, and answer it at the end.' *The Midnight Line* is the ultimate case study of this theory in practice.

By the time he tracks down Rose Sanderson, Reacher no longer needs to ask for answers to his questions. He no longer needs to know 'the end of the story' because he's already figured it out. This must have been the precise moment when Lee knew for sure – for the twenty-second time in the series – that he was galloping triumphantly down the home straight.

There is another way *The Midnight Line* sweetly marries form to content, through repetition: a series of musical motifs to which the writer returns again and again, tracing not so much a single line as an endlessly intertwining double helix. It's a way of spiralling back and stitching things together and helping readers remember the themes and images that matter. But also playing the reader like some kind of musical instrument. It starts early and easy – unobtrusive, incidental, low-key. Then it becomes soothing, familiar, deliberate, comforting, insistent, demanding. Until finally it builds in metaphoric intensity to the reading equivalent of a mind-blowing opioid high.

He wrote the opening chapter in the Orkneys (using pencil and paper), but *The Midnight Line* is Lee's Wyoming novel. Prompted by the fact that he'd bought a ranch there a few months before (though his lyrical description of a Wyoming sunrise had already impressed reviewers of *Without Fail* fifteen years earlier). 'You have to remember,' he told Abbott, 'to me it's amazing the size of this country. The East and the West are pretty much European in density, but the middle is freaky.'

> [Reacher] liked Wyoming. For its heroic geography, and its heroic climate. And its emptiness. It was the size of the United Kingdom, but it had fewer people in it than Louisville, Kentucky. The Census Bureau called most of it uninhabited. What people there were tended to be straightforward and pleasant. They were happy to leave a person alone.
>
> The first part of the state was high plains. Fall had already started. He gazed across the immense tawny distances, to the spectre of the mountains beyond. The highway was a dark blacktop ribbon, mostly empty.

Abbott liked 'the care and leisure' Lee took in getting Reacher from one place to the next. 'It's both a pleasure and a problem,' he replied. 'I like the long, meandering journeys, his observations along the way, but you don't want it to read like a travel timetable.' Did Homer worry about that too?

For Lee, the best stories were about character. 'Plot is a rental car. You use it for a week. If it's a Jaguar and not a Ford Fiesta all to the good. If I went to the Caribbean with Scarlett Johansson, none of my friends would say "what car did you rent?"'

But cars are a big deal, therefore the analogy intimates that plot is too. And it took him six months to finish a book, so the rental car had to last a lot longer than a week.

Every novel was a road trip and Lee's job was to give the reader one hell of a ride. Easy, but also highly pleasurable. Chopper bikes were cool. But better still a Jaguar.

21

Paperback Writer

Like a condom crammed with walnuts,
is what some girl had said.
Tripwire, 1999

The teenage Jim Grant signed on with a temping agency in search of paid work. Rock bottom was the wrecking crew: the damp, mouldy plaster dust spoiled his lungs for the superior substances he actually chose to inhale. Better was the annual bonanza of wakes week (a religious festival that turned secular during the Industrial Revolution), when local factories shut down for essential maintenance. While the working classes trooped off to Blackpool or Morecambe or Southport to take a salutary dip in the sea, eager, cash-starved school kids would move in to strip, clean and renovate the factories. These were union places: they wouldn't get a look-in any other time.

The classiest job he got was on the basis of his first-class education at Cherry Orchard, where they made sure he could keep his numbers straight. It was in the summer of 1972, in an office on Gas Street, where he was responsible for booking strippers for working men's clubs. His main takeaway was a laconic one-liner – 'I've been around the agented professions all of my life' – guaranteed to entertain future audiences of his own.

Jim liked earning a pound an hour for manual labour, a decent rate before rampant inflation set in at the end of the seventies, especially cash-in-hand in little brown envelopes, but not enough to build up any serious muscle mass. Unlike Reacher, who at the start of *Tripwire* is 'in the best shape of his life' from digging swimming pools under the hot sun in Key West and shifting 'about four tons of earth and rock and sand every day' with a shovel.

Jim didn't want to work up that kind of sweat. Rob Reeves recalled him boasting he would never take physical exercise again, at most he would 'walk from his car'. This was when Rob was going to the YMCA every day to train for the London marathon. 'He'd come up to you, and he'd put his arm around you, slowly. Everything was slow.'

He'd been a strong competitive swimmer. He'd learned aged seven or eight in the Grove Lane Baths in Handsworth, a gracious old building with a gabled roof and first- and second-class baths and a raised wrought-iron viewing gallery. He was in the school swim team until he opted out in Sixth Form and had voluntarily joined Northfields Swimming Club, where he'd been scouted for the Olympic squad. In his 1969 pomp he could beat the time in which Johnny Weissmuller had won gold at the 1924 Olympics but, he said, so could a lot of other people. He had a natural swimmer's physique, but these days was more svelte supermodel than condom crammed with walnuts.

So instead of digging pools he worked for the Birmingham Repertory Theatre at its new home on Broad Street. The original on Station Street had been Britain's first purpose-built rep and was the acknowledged prototype for post-war companies such as the Royal Shakespeare Company and the National.

The production Jim was most proud of was a series of one-act plays for which he rigged up three separate sets of light. The plays were spare, and he wanted the lighting to be spare too, with no excess flesh on the bones. He used only seven lanterns. It was 'very simple, very pure'. But the 'Birmingham bourgeoisie' responded crassly. The council had forked out 'a shedload of money' to get state-of-the-art lighting kit and it wasn't being used. Jim liked simple lighting rigs. He still thinks a lot of stage lighting is over-egged and over-elaborate.

Once upon a time he had dreamed of a place on the stage. He was five years old, sitting in a darkened auditorium at Cherry Orchard Primary watching a group of children a little older than himself perform in one of Miss Lyster's high-octane productions. The children were beaming happily. They were being beamed at by their ecstatic parents. It was hard to know who had started the beaming and who was happiest, but it was like breathing in love instead of oxygen. James wanted some of that surfeit of love for himself. He wanted to be one of those beatific children, basking blissfully in admiration and approval. But it never happened (something to do with being handed a lyric sheet and discovering he couldn't sing). Instead, he was sent backstage to make things. It was a harsh encounter with the reality principle. 'I was disabused of any illusions I may have had about my acting ability by around the age of six.'

Lee didn't need someone else to psychologise him. 'I was drawn to the theatre in my desire for that kind of approval,' he told me. 'I was looking for love.'

It was while working as an unpaid intern at the Royal Shakespeare Company in the summer of 1970, on the cusp of Sixth Form, that Jim first saw *A Midsummer Night's Dream*. Like the first time he heard 'She Loves You' on the radio, it blew his mind and changed his life forever. It was Shakespeare's play, but in the radical version featuring Frances de la Tour and Ben Kingsley that became known as *Peter Brook's Dream*. Jim was lucky to be there. According to the *Sunday Times* it was 'the sort of thing one only sees once in a lifetime, and then only from a man of genius'.

Brook was on a mission to liberate the play from 'encrusted bad tradition'. He wanted to put the emphasis back on the text, to create an atmosphere in which only the poetry mattered, so that audiences would hear 'the sheer incandescent beauty' of Shakespeare's verse (as Lee would describe it) as if for the first time, relying on the power of words to generate a sense of location.

This extract is by John Barber in the *Daily Telegraph*:

> In a production that will surely make theatre history, Peter Brook last night tore through all conventional ideas about how the play should be staged. He found new ways of giving form to its poetry and power.
>
> For setting, he offers a dazzling white box. The only furniture is four white cushions. Trapezes hang from the flies. Iron ladders extend to a platform where musicians are stationed. The naked harshness of this environment is used by Mr Brook as a means to expose the actors' words and emotions.

Titania's bower was a giant red feather.

The costumes were eclectic, but neither Athenian nor Elizabethan. Oberon wore a purple satin gown and Puck a yellow jumpsuit. The mechanicals were dressed as factory workers. The young lovers were in tie-dye shirts and maxi dresses and the fairies were played by adult men. Brook doubled up roles to suggest that the Fairy King and Queen were the alter egos of the mortal rulers, and the conflicts and erotic adventures of the nocturnal wood the uncontrollable eruption of sub-conscious fears and desires. He emphasised sexuality as never before, in tune with the 1960s spirit of permissiveness.

It was around the same time that Jim saw Robert Altman's satirical black comedy *MASH*, and watched his first adult movies at the cinema, though the only one he recalled was soft-core comedy *Au Pair Girls*. 'The sixties didn't really arrive until the seventies,' Lee said. It wasn't a monolithic thing, in lock-step for all people.

At the close of Brook's *Dream*, as Oberon spoke his final lines about the sunrise, the house lights slowly rose, so that members of the audience became visible to each other. Upon Puck's words 'Give me your hands, if we be friends', the entire cast overflowed into the auditorium to embrace the public in what one critic described as a 'lovefest'.

The experience of that midsummer night had a profound impact on the sixteen-year-old Jim. But sometimes you can be inspired *not* to do something. It wasn't until three years later that he got around to reading Peter Brook's *The Empty Space* (based on four lectures endowed by Granada Television and published in 1968), which finally made up his mind, but what he had sensed, even before he was able to articulate it, was that for theatre, 'all you needed was a script, a bunch of actors, and an empty space'. Everything else was an optional extra. He, Jim Grant, technician *par excellence*, was an optional extra. Redundant. Dispensable. *De trop*. He would have to look elsewhere for love.

In *The Hard Way* Lauren Pauling is curious about why Reacher left the army.

> 'As soon as they said that leaving was an option it kind of broke the spell. Made me realise I wasn't personally essential to their plans. I guess they'd have been happy enough if I stayed, but clearly it wasn't going to break their hearts if I went.'

Jim Grant wanted to be essential to what was going on. So it would break their hearts if he went. As Lee Child he had signally achieved that goal.

Jim left King Edward's in 1973 and went travelling in Europe with school friend Mick Cleary (who would become rugby correspondent to the *Daily Telegraph*). Or so he believed. He remembered being in Corsica. He remembered being in Switzerland. There was a train at one point – he remembered sleeping in the corridor. 'It was a bacchanal that lasted all summer long.'

I wrote to Mick Cleary. He remembered being in Corsica with Jim. He remembered hitchhiking and getting lost and pitching a tent halfway up a mountain and going in search of food in the dark. He remembered seeing lights in the distance and climbing some steps to a hotel or bar and opening the door and a hundred shaven heads swivelling round to greet them. A gathering of the Foreign Legion, perhaps. He remembered more than Jim. But this was 1971. Or maybe 1972. They'd landed in Bastia. The Scout Master had told them to bugger off for a few days and reconvene in Ajaccio.

What about 1973? 'Don't remember hooking up with Jim on that trip, but to cite the Marianne Faithfull defence, if you can remember the seventies, you weren't there.'

I went back to Lee. What about 1971 and the Venture Scouts? 'Don't remember that. But you know what they say about the seventies . . .'

'It was 1972,' said Nigel Clay, and showed me a postcard to his girlfriend (now wife) Pat to prove it. According to this report Jim was cross because a wild boar had pissed on his kit.

Jim returned from his grand tour of 1973 in late September. He'd almost forgotten about his A levels. The retakes were passable. He thought: *Ha! I could go to university with these!* But he hadn't applied to any universities and the clearing process that mopped up any remaining candidates was already over and he hadn't a clue. So he did what he always did when he needed answers, and went to the library. The prospectuses were worn and thumbed. One had a picture of a high-rise block against a clear blue sky that it boasted was the tallest university building in the country. It reminded him of that skyscraper he'd fallen for at Elmwood. There was a fantastic theatre that looked like a newly converted chapel. This place was speaking to him, but the front cover of the prospectus was gone. It was saying 'we do this, we do that', but *Who the hell are you?* Jim wanted to know.

He found the name 'Sheffield University' in microscopic print on the back. He rang up and said, 'I got these results at A level.' The woman on the other end of the line was kind and helpful like Susan Turner in *61 Hours*. 'What do you want to study?' she asked. 'What have you got?' There was a momentary pause and then the helpful voice came back on: 'We've got a space in Law.' And that was it. Law covered it, so far as Jim could see – English, History, Maths, Language, Geography, the works. 'It was a total accident.' Canon R. G. Lunt would feel vindicated. Jim's parents would be happy. Maybe he would even get to meet the owner of the voice.

Rex was envious. When he and Audrey moved to Harpenden he did a law degree himself, at night school in London. It was the only time he would follow in his second son's footsteps.

'To be honest,' Lee said, riding roughshod over all sensibilities, 'if you were white and middle-class you were going to get a job. It was inevitable. So I didn't care about my grades. I felt safe. I could pick and choose.'

Really he was still half expecting to do something in the theatre. 'But Peter Brook put an end to that.' Which was when he made 'a conscious intellectual decision' to move into television. There was 'less magic' in film. It was less creative, poetic, romantic. But he would have a proper job to do, instead of just being 'fluff'.

In the meantime it was like Reacher breaking up with Jodie at the end of *The Visitor*. They had a month, or in Jim's case four years, which was more than most people got. Parting was such sweet sorrow. Going to university was one long afternoon off, a fond farewell to his first love. The drama studio was on Shearwood Road, next door to the Law faculty. He got a rave write-up in the Sheffield *Evening Telegraph* for his set for Ibsen's *A Doll's House*. 'It was very minimalist,' Lee said. He was working with a thrust stage with a small amount of seating on each side and the technical problem was how to recreate a

Victorian living room in such a way as to ensure visibility for all. 'My solution was to do it only up to skirting-board height, about six inches, to suggest it by framing.'

The concept makes a comeback in *Past Tense*, when Reacher finally makes it to the spot where his father's house once stood:

> Nothing remained of the lobby's right-hand wall except for stubs of broken brick, low down at floor level. They looked like teeth smashed down to the gum. In the centre was a stone saddle, no taller, but intact. The right-hand ground-floor apartment's front door. Reacher stepped inside. The hallway floor had three trees growing through it. Their trunks were no thicker than his wrist, but they had raced twenty feet high, looking for the light. Beyond them and either side were low lines of smashed brick, showing where the rooms had been, like an architect's floor plan come to life, slightly three dimensional.

It had been a very good set for *A Doll's House*. Maybe his best ever. Worth reviving. He wished he had kept some photographs. But never mind. The power of his words would suffice to generate a sense of location in this empty fictional space.

Lee often went to the theatre with his daughter Ruth. Their approach was eccentric. 'We usually see each show three times, from three different vantage points. Front-row seats, dress circle, mezzanine – because the kinetic presentation can't be fully experienced from just one viewpoint, you can't see it all.'

But three was nothing. Lee made a point of seeking out every new production of Beckett's *Waiting for Godot*. By the time I met him he had seen it more than thirty times. It was a great play. He was still waiting for it to be really well done.

He had an early memory of a show on Broadway. The tickets were a gift from Jane's parents and they had front-row seats. It was a musical that featured a black guy smoking weed, who at a certain point held out the joint towards the audience, 'no doubt expecting to provoke shock, or a horrified recoil'. What he wasn't expecting was Lee, 'acting on pure muscle memory', who held out his hand to take it, like he was hanging out with a bunch of his mates. He'd done that exact same thing so many times before, but this time his hand was slapped away.

Lee Child was made ThrillerMaster (by the International Thriller Writers association) at the ThrillerFest banquet in 2017, hosted by executive director Kimberley (K. J.) Howe. Guests were given mini packs of yellow-and-white M&Ms in which individual sweets were printed with the words 'Lee Child' or 'Jack Reacher' or with a line drawing of the author's face. Heather Graham (2016 ThrillerMaster) said Lee was 'a truly amazing man, the kindest you'll ever meet, so giving, so smart'. Then she turned to him and declared 'We pretty much worship the road you walk on', before breaking into a version of Carly Simon's 'Nobody Does it Better'.

Next, the thriller-writing guitar-playing duo of Parks and Palmer stepped up to sing 'Tiny Jack Reacher', 'Eight Blurbs a Week' and 'Reacher Eating Pie in Diners' to the tune of three chart-topping Beatles hits. Lee was a Brit, so had a divine right to direct association with the Fab Four. But the theme tune he was hearing at that point was more likely a different one: 'I'm fairly shy, so before appearances, in my head I play "Golden Boy" by Natalie Merchant, or "The Lemon Song" by Led Zeppelin – why we were born with ears' (*New Statesman*).

'How can I follow that?' Lee said as he took to the microphone. He hadn't written a speech because he wanted to say 'how it feels to be standing here' and he couldn't do that till 'right now'. He played to the stereotypes, saying he faced two structural handicaps when it came to talking about how he feels: 'I'm English, and I'm a man.' His wife and daughter often urged him to talk more about his feelings, and his response was always: 'If I ever have one, I'll let you know.'

Then he said that 'right here right now' he had a 'warm feeling'. That he was among friends. That writers were the nicest people ever, except for readers ('If you are a reader you are a person of tremendous charm and quality,' he said a week later in Harrogate). That it was astonishing 'to finally find my tribe after so long'.

Lee Child, the artist formerly known as Jim Grant, was standing alone and centre stage. Lean and hungry and very very tall, like he had raced up six feet four inches looking for the light. He was beaming, or as close as he was likely to come. He didn't want to expend too much energy. There were throngs of people beaming back at him. The applause was thunderous and prolonged. There were cheers and whistles and the occasional scream. Maybe someone fainted. It was like breathing love instead of oxygen.

It felt a bit like being a Beatle or a Rolling Stone.

There was only one word to describe the atmosphere in that stifling Manhattan ballroom on Saturday 15 July, 2017.

Lovefest.

22

The Crucible

'You're young, to be married.'
Nothing to Lose, 2008

When Jim met Jane she was just another girl on his 'to be shagged' list. One of two girls he had in his sights the day after Valentine's Day in 1974. He was into his second term at Sheffield. Of the two, 'it turned out to be her'. After the party he went back to her place. She said are you staying and he said may as well. It was a great night. So great that Jim gave the relationship a solid couple of weeks. But the next week it was still great, and the week after that. She was 'unbelievably beautiful, unbelievably exotic. It was no hardship at all.'

He kept two black-and-white photographs in the entrance hall of his Manhattan apartment. The twenty-year-old Jim is bearded with long hair and sideburns and looks like the young James Taylor. Jane has big dark eyes with strong straight brows and sleek dark hair, like a smouldering Cleopatra. They both have the same outsize features. He is lighting a cigarette. Neither of them is looking at the camera.

The photographs had been taken by Adrian Mudd, a drama-studio friend, 'in the first flush of romance', and were mounted in mottled mirror frames illuminated by Gothic silver candlesticks. Others were in an album Ruth had made. Lee pointed to one and said, 'that's my

226

emaciated drug addict look'. He's standing by a cairn in the Lake District with a cigarette in his left hand, wearing a dark plaid shirt, tucked in to flares but unbuttoned to the waist, sleeves rolled up to his biceps. His wavy hair is curling up at the ends. On another page, a triptych of black-and-white images shows Jane seated at her desk, posters tacked to the floral wallpaper behind her. In the first she is pensive, looking down at a book; in the second she has turned slightly to face the camera; in the third she is smiling, her head resting on her left hand, her severely parted hair draped like a heavy silk curtain against the sleeve of her silky dark shirt. Her strong face is partially illuminated; her eyes are in shadow.

Jane reminded me of Andy Saunders's older sister, who had the same haircut and dressed the same, and who just a year before had been rolling spliffs for Jim because he couldn't roll them himself.

In August 1975 Jim and Jane were married.

Jane had just graduated. They went to Bravingtons in Piccadilly to choose their matching gold wedding bands and have them engraved with their initials: 'All the good stuff was in London.' Jane's grandma Claire came over from America. Jim's grandad and grandma Scrafton came from Otley, but not his granpop and granny from Belfast: John Grant hated to be seen in a wheelchair. The two fathers had dinner together in a 'wincingly retro way', but neither set of parents thought much of their offspring's choice of life partner. Jane was 'invisible' to her future in-laws, and Jim was a 'wastrel' with no obvious prospects.

They tied the knot in the morning and had a lunchtime reception at the Dam House restaurant in Crookes Valley Park. Jim wore a broad-collared white shirt, dark blue tie and white carnation with a light blue windowpane-check three-piece two-button suit by Jonathan Silver. The trousers flared out over his brown shoes, the six-button waistcoat was fitted, the jacket was never even intended to be buttoned and had deep pointed lapels as wide as his shoulders. Jane wore a full-length empire-line pale-pink-and-green floral dress she had made herself, with a sweetheart neckline and softly puffed sleeves and a smocked front that her grandmother had shown her how to do. Her accessories were a single pink rose, a pendant necklace and white block-heel sandals. Her hair was centre-parted and tied back in a low ponytail. Jim has a short chin beard. His hair is thick and slightly waved. Jane's head barely reaches his shoulder. His right hand rests on her right hip, and looks twice the size of hers, hanging loose by her side.

The deed was done in the Sheffield Register Office, known as 'the Wedding Cake' because it was circular and white with a flat top. From above it looked as though it had been scored with a knife, ready for slicing. There were red padded seats for guests and white satin-covered chairs placed side by side in front of a polished wooden table for the bride and groom. There was a sign that read: 'Marriage according to the law of this country is the union of one man with one woman, voluntarily entered into for life, to the exclusion of all others.' For their honeymoon they went to Greece and Yugoslavia.

The 'Wedding Cake' was built in 1973, the year Jim moved to Sheffield, and demolished again by a 'muncher digger' in 2004 (according to local newspaper, the *Star*). I doubted Lee would be overly sentimental about its demise. Four decades later his marriage was still going strong, and in interviews he was wont to specify the number of years like he was marvelling at the ever-mounting total: forty-one, forty-two, forty-three, forty-four . . . It seemed unlikely he would forget their anniversary, but the wedding day itself was not a big deal. 'I was happy with Jane, is all. Satisfied. There wasn't a switch that was flicked.' They got married so she wouldn't have to go back to the States.

And so she could take him with her when she did.

The first time Jim and Jane went to America they got a student fare with Air France to Montreal, then flew down to La Guardia on Eastern Airlines. They circled Manhattan for half an hour before landing and Jim thought he had 'died and gone to heaven'. The only thing missing was the soundtrack from all the movies he'd seen.

Lee's abiding memory of that seminal visit was the shock of seeing his soon-to-be father-in-law reading a hardback book he had actually bought new from a shop.

Jane Hope Shiren was born on 24 January 1953 in Mount Vernon in New York State, an upwardly mobile blue-collar city just north of the Bronx. Their neighbours were the Dolans, later of Cablevision and Madison Square Garden Company. When Jane was three years old the family moved north to Schenectady, on the confluence of the Mohawk and Hudson rivers. The town had been founded by Dutch colonists in the seventeenth century on land belonging to the Mahican tribe and had evolved into an industrial city. It was the base of the American Locomotive Company and General Electric, formerly the Edison Machine Works, billed as 'the city that lights and hauls the world'.

Jane's father was a research physicist with General Electric until he joined IBM five years later and relocated back to Westchester County, to Mount Kisco. He did not suffer fools gladly. 'He was blunt to the point of rudeness,' said a friend from Granada; and another, 'Her father was very forceful.' Lee could hold his own and they got on well enough, and anyway, he was used to difficult parents. He was becoming used to losing them too. It seemed only right, in 2018, to dedicate *Past Tense* to *John Reginald Grant, Norman Steven Shiren, and Audrey Grant, deceased*.

An obituary was published in the *New York Times* on 15 August 2017.

SHIREN—

Norman S., born 7th February 1925, beloved husband of Edith, father of Leslie (Joel Litoff) and Jane (Jim Grant), loving grandfather of Ruth, died peacefully in his sleep on 30th July 2017 in Sleepy Hollow, NY, aged 92 years. Norman was an esteemed research physicist, late of Bronx Science, Tufts, the US Navy, Columbia, and Stanford, where he earned his PhD, and where, with his colleague Richard Post, he did crucial early work on the first electron linear accelerator. He went on to a career at Hudson Labs, GE, and IBM, where he worked on semi-conductors and crystal theory. He was an ardent supporter of liberal causes and cared deeply for the arts and his dogs.

The Shirens made a political point of sending their daughters to the more diverse Fox Lane High School in Bedford rather than Horace Greeley at Chappaqua, which was reputed to be better academically but whose students were all white.

Professor Shiren spent the year 1969–70 on leave in Oxford. Jane graduated from high school a year early so she could accompany her parents to England, and she and her older sister were enrolled at Oxford High School for Girls for a taste of English educational life. They left within weeks. But Jane was 'a classic kid seduced by the Academy' and captivated by England, and when it was time to take up her place at the University of Miami she did so reluctantly. She badgered her parents until, at the end of her first semester, they allowed her to return to Oxford. Norman and Edith were 'trepidatious' as she was still so young, but they couldn't fault her lofty aspirations.

Jane signed on at independent sixth-form crammer St Clare's to get the A levels she needed to study archaeology and prehistory at an English university. She resumed her friendship with Angus Alton, younger brother of Roger Alton (of the *Guardian*, *Observer*, *Independent* and *Times*) and son of Reggie, an English don, and Jeannine, a modern linguist. Angus was Oxford born and bred. He advised Jane against Cambridge, one of only three places to offer the course she wanted, and to choose between Southampton and Sheffield instead. Jane chose north rather than south, which meant leaving Angus behind. When Jim met her she was going out with a guy called Nigel.

In the story of the little boy looking out from his Manhattan tower block at the Empire State Building there had never been mention of a little girl looking back at him. Yet it seemed inevitable that Jim should plight his troth to an American girl. Especially one from New York. Even if she didn't live in a skyscraper. Perhaps it was the unacknowledged feeling that it was somehow meant to be that made it conceivable to marry so young.

'They were always "Jim and Jane",' said Rob Reeves. 'I found it weird that he was married.' Rob was a few years older but still flamboyantly single in the Granada days.

This is Reacher talking to Lucy Anderson in *Nothing to Lose* (dedicated 'to my wife, Jane, with a lot of thanks'):

'You're young, to be married.'
'We're in love.'

Jim had started out roughing it in Hillsborough before getting accommodation in Thornsett Road, where Jane's boyfriend was living. When he and Jane began dating he moved in with her at 34 Wadbrough Road, and when they got married they had a ground-floor flat at 329 Crookesmoor, a six-bedroom Victorian terrace with bay windows and shared bathrooms and kitchen and a lounge that opened out onto a wilderness back garden that looked like an abandoned building site. No. 329 is still listed in the *Student Housing Guide* as having 'a great position'. It was close to the centre and a short walk to Shearwood Road via Crookes Valley Park, and from the footpath there were views over the Pennines. Sheffield was hilly enough to keep even a refusenik like Jim pretty fit. According to the *Tab* in 2016, Crookesmoor was 'what the uni experience is all about'.

> In a land far away, at the top of a magical hill in Sheffield, lies Crookesmoor, where the streets are paved with ~~gold~~ empty pizza boxes and smashed bottles of Lambrini. A short walk from Upperthorpe Tesco, and the glittering lights of Walkley, it's been said by some that it's similar to St Tropez, just without the beach, or the sea . . . or the hordes of glamorous people.

The fast-food outlets may have changed since the seventies, but not the hedonistic spirit. Jim was still a committed all-rounder.

> I used to say I was a bad student. Now I just say I was a seventies student. Not only did you not have to pay, you were actually paid to go. University was different back then. You didn't do any work. You just had fun.

'I was nineteen years old,' he told me. 'How can you not have a good time?'

Only about 12 to 15 per cent of school leavers went to university in the 1970s. It distinguished you from the crowd. Once you were in there was nothing left to worry about. You accrued no debt. There was full employment. You could go anywhere on any bus for four pence 'so everybody did, including the white-collar workers', because they were 'cheap, clean and comfortable'.

'Everything is the opposite now,' commented Lee.

He was still desperately in want of cash. In 1974 he spent four weeks in Birmingham as an ice-cream vendor to raise money for that first transatlantic trip. He didn't need a commercial licence, just rocked up at the depot to pick up van and supplies, cranked up the music box (fitted out with a guitar pick-up for amplification) and set off on his rounds, dropping it all back at the end of the day and pocketing the profits. The next year he did the same in Sheffield, parking up outside the Botanical Gardens on Ecclesall Road. Perhaps it was there he got used to people lining up to speak to him. But as he handed over a cone or choc-ice in exchange for a few coins and some chat about the weather or football, what he noticed was how many of his customers were maimed in some way. Between the heavy industry and the legacy of war, missing fingers were routine.

He did a few short stints in factories. Bread and jam were OK. Worst was Batchelors, where they were drying peas. It was seasonal work because of the harvest and already hot outside the shed, but as the peas rolled down a conveyor belt of fine steel mesh over the fearsome flames below the temperature would hit 140 °C. Free orange juice was laid on so workers could rehydrate. It was a brutal job, but at a pound an hour with unlimited shifts was a great earner.

The cardboard-box factory was a breeze. Jim had read an article about how to improve conditions for workers by playing five minutes of rock and roll over the Tannoy at the top of the hour – long enough to reward but not so long as to deflect or distract. The cardboard-box guys were doing it and it was paying off. It felt like by working harder you were making time pass more quickly, and as the countdown began your mood lifted and productivity increased. There were a few dozen middle-aged women on the production line whose job was to cut and fold and glue all the boxes, but carting around the big blanks of cardboard was a job for a man, but only one man, so between five-minute bursts of music Jim would spend fifty-five minutes listening to 'the filthiest crew' he would ever encounter. Before long he had heard 'every sexual fantasy it was possible to have', almost none of it suitable for a novel to which he would willingly put his name. Still, it made light work of the lifting.

'Batchelors was a good job to get,' said Martin Brown, who had drifted back into Jim's life after a year at teacher training college in Winchester. He'd given up on his boyhood dream of working in the Birmingham car industry and was studying to become a mechanical engineer. 'Better than Bassetts and Liquorice Allsorts.' At Lyons you got covered in sugar. Lyons had relocated from London to Barnsley for the cheap site and labour. It was staffed by miners' wives who were members of the Bakers' Union, but in holiday periods the student population took over, maximising their earnings by working double shifts seven days a week. 'We were clearing £100, which was good money back then.' When management tried to put a stop to it they all banded together and said, *We'll bring everybody out.* 'You didn't need a union to do that,' Martin said. 'You just needed student solidarity.'

After Sheffield, Martin got grants to do his MA and PhD then took a job with the Health and Safety Executive as an inspector of Her Majesty's factories.

When Lee returned to Sheffield in 2017 to appear at the Off the Shelf festival he said it was a dream come true to appear at City Hall, where forty years before he had heard David Bowie and Rory Gallagher. He recalled how he would take the night bus out to the moors to watch the sun come up, how both his younger brothers had followed him there as students, and how as a kid the drive north from Birmingham to see his grandparents in Otley would take them right through the centre of Sheffield. It was at a picnic stop on one of those trips that at the age of five he first tasted coffee. 'Hated it with milk – tried it black, and loved it.'

Now he was also a benefactor. The university had got its teeth into him at the same time as King Edward's, around the time he was first making it big in the charts. He'd given Sheffield fifty-two 'Jack Reacher Scholarships' worth £2000 each and they had given him an honorary doctorate and a visiting professorship and brewed a local ale in his name. His father wrote a letter addressed to Prof James D. Grant (instead of James Grant, Esq, LLB) and congratulated him on being 'a great success right from the word Go!'

'If I'd known you could buy a degree I wouldn't have bothered going to university at all,' Lee said laconically, but it wasn't true, because it wasn't the degree he'd gone for.

It wasn't just the dizzying heights of the Arts Tower, which English Heritage called 'the most elegant university tower block in Britain of its period' and was said to be inspired by the Seagram Building in New York. It wasn't just the redemption of the old Glossop Road Baptist Church by its conversion to a theatre. The Birmingham scuffler was attracted to the Steel City for its down-and-dirty affinity with his roots.

'He would like to be thought of as strong and reliable,' neighbour John Leighton said. 'Like a piece of steel.'

'It was part of his dirty protest,' commented ex-Chief Master John Claughton. Birmingham plus. Doubling down on his origins out of a stubborn sense of pride.

Sheffield was more Toledo than Saint-Tropez. Its knives were getting five-star reviews from Chaucer in *The Canterbury Tales*. By the seventeenth century it was the biggest centre of cutlery manufacture outside London, overseen by the Company of Cutlers of Hallamshire from their pillared and porticoed building opposite the cathedral on Church Street. When it was incorporated by an Act of Parliament in 1624 the guild was given jurisdiction over 'all persons using to make Knives, Blades, Scissers, Sheeres, Sickles, Cutlery wares and all other wares and manufacture made or wrought of yron and steele, dwelling or inhabiting within the said Lordship and Liberty of Hallamshire, or within six miles compasse of the same'. Its motto was: *Pour Y Parvenir à Bonne Foi – To Succeed through Honest Endeavour.*

No need to look further to know it was Lee's kind of town.

It was the home of crucible and stainless steel and Sheffield Plate. Thanks to the consequent pollution (and rapid decline of its back-to-back factory housing into slums) it was also, according to George Orwell in 1937, three years before the Sheffield Blitz, 'the ugliest town in the Old World'.

Perhaps those cruel words were still ringing in Sheffield ears. When the coal and steel industries collapsed in the 1980s the city set about planting trees. Soon it was as famed for its green spaces as for silver. But it couldn't win. Now another big-name writer was running it down. Lee missed that raucous prosperity and mourned the loss of the heavy stuff. He regretted that Sheffield now relied almost entirely on retail and dealt mostly in picture postcards, 'like most British towns'. The honest endeavour of making things well had been reduced to an emasculated exercise in period nostalgia.

I thought of Lee's words when I picked up a black-and-white postcard from a city-centre store. Thirteen slender chimneys soaring above as many squat cooling towers and silhouetted against the twilight, the sky festooned with puffballs of sooty smoke drifting smudgily from east to west. The image was captioned 'Beautiful Sheffield'. And it was beautiful, in its dark, Satanic, romanticised way.

It could be that Lee's harsh judgement was in part an ad hoc rationale for his ruthless rejection of his home country. Not everyone would agree with him. Because out of the crucible of destruction arose the new creatives, just as Lee Child himself had arisen from a broken Granada.

In 2013 Chris Watson (of post-punk group Cabaret Voltaire) was commissioned to produce a sound map of the city for the new Millennium Gallery. He told the *Guardian* how the remaining steelworks had been changed by automation: 'The steel mills are still active, to some extent, but they are now much quieter.' Writing for the same paper in 2018, Dave Simpson recalls how in the seventies the 'big hammer', which could be heard for 30 miles, directly inspired Cabaret Voltaire and the Human League's early electronic music: 'it was literally the sound of Sheffield'. The Arctic Monkeys made their first recordings in a disused cutlery finishing room, and when in 2006 their debut album became the fastest-selling record in British pop history they had the same galvanising impact as the Beatles in Liverpool forty years before.

In 2016 BBC journalist Peter Day went to visit the Magna Science Adventure Centre, created out of the old works at Templeborough known locally as Steelos:

> It's far larger than a cathedral or an airship hangar, and once housed six monstrous electric arc furnaces making steel from scrap. It was the biggest concentration of them in the world.
>
> The centrepiece of the vast space is a recreation of the steel production process called the Big Melt. Every hour [. . .] there's a show of simulated sound and gushes of fire from the extraordinary electric arc process that turns scrap metal back into steel.

Lee might see this as a glorified postcard, but it wasn't far removed from his own fabrication of a metal recycling plant in *Nothing to Lose*:

> The line of lights on the far wall ran close to a mile into the distance and dimmed and shrank and blended into a tiny vanishing point in the southwest corner. The far wall itself was at least a half mile away. The total enclosed area must have been three hundred acres. Three hundred football fields.
>
> [. . .] The ground was soaked with oil and rainbow puddles of diesel and littered with curled metal swarf and where it was dry it glittered with shiny dust. Steam and smoke and fumes and sharp chemical smells were drifting everywhere. There was roaring and

hammering rolling outward in waves and beating against the metal perimeter and bouncing straight back in again. Bright flames danced behind open furnace doors.

Like a vision of hell.

Or Lee's homage to Sheffield.

In his first term at university Jim was listening to Van Morrison (*Saint Dominic's Preview*, released July 1972), Pink Floyd (*Dark Side of the Moon*, March 1973) and Mike Oldfield. Perhaps there was no heating in his digs, because 'even now I feel cold when I hear *Tubular Bells*' (May 1973).

Sometimes he would help out at the new Crucible Theatre. It was there that he first used a pseudonym. By the time he arrived at 'Lee Child' he had tested out at least three: Troy Granite, Tony Jackson and Richard Strange. New job, new name – it seemed normal to him. Stage managers belonged to the same union as actors, and Equity had a rule that if you had the same name as an existing member (like James Grant) you would have to change it. Then when he was under contract at Granada, moonlighting on other jobs, he was compelled to go undercover.

'Troy Granite' was a spoof name. But not unconnected. To Homer and Odysseus, like Reacher a man of outstanding wisdom, shrewdness, eloquence, resourcefulness, courage and endurance. The town of Troy wasn't far from Schenectady. Author Kurt Vonnegut lived there and after the Second World War had worked at General Electric. In 1973 he told *Playboy* magazine that his first novel, *Player Piano*, inspired by the introduction of a computer-operated milling machine, was about 'the implications of having everything run by little boxes'.

> To have a little clicking box make all the decisions wasn't a vicious thing to do. But it was too bad for the human beings who got their dignity from their jobs.

Troy was also the site of the first Bessemer converter in the States, an innovative blast furnace that its inventor originally brought from London to Sheffield in the 1850s. It was the Bessemer that had ushered in the industry's age of mass production.

'Tony Jackson' was a musician. Or rather two. One was bass player and lead singer for 1960s Merseybeat group the Searchers. The other was an early twentieth-century jazz pianist from New Orleans who in 2011 was inducted into the Chicago Gay and Lesbian Hall of Fame. A third Tony Jackson was a valiant ex-member of the First Parachute Regiment in *The Hard Way*, 'not quite SAS, but close', and a fourth was a Cold War secret agent in the story 'Grit in My Eye', who though civilised and urbane 'could reach back and still be a caveman'. 'Richard Strange' could have been Richard 'Kid' Strange, frontman of mid-seventies art-rock band Doctors of Madness, but turned out to have been inspired by Ariel's song from *The Tempest*, Lee's favourite, or second favourite, Shakespeare play:

> Full fathom five thy father lies;
> Of his bones are coral made;
> Those are pearls that were his eyes;
> Nothing of him that doth fade,
> But doth suffer a sea-change
> Into something rich and strange.
> Sea-nymphs hourly ring his knell:
> Ding-dong.
> Hark! now I hear them – Ding-dong, bell.

Lee thought everyone should choose their own name when they turned eighteen. The names our parents gave us were a joke. They didn't know us when they named us, and we didn't know them either.

You could use whatever name you liked from a legal point of view, so long as there was 'no intention to mislead'.

Jim was such an outstanding all-rounder that he failed his second year at Sheffield. It didn't matter. He just got one more year in the theatre. Jane was now two years ahead of him, and after a year of teacher training at Sheffield City College took a job in a village primary school in Beighton. They bought the red Beetle and, in 1977, 'a brand-new flat for £7,500 on an awful greenfield housing estate in a town called Halfway'. It was a place of their own with wheels of their own, and like the optimists of *Nothing to Lose* they were setting out on life full of vitality and vigour:

> The wagons had rolled out of Despair with only the optimists aboard, and the town of Halfway reflected their founding spirit. [. . .] There was no real reason why one nearby town rather than another should be chosen for investment and development, except for inherited traits of vibrancy and vigor. Despair had suffered and Halfway had prospered, and the optimists had won, like they sometimes deserved to.

It seemed inevitable that there should be a twist in the tale. 'I had been labouring under a terrible misconception,' Lee said. 'I was in love with America but she was in love with England.' Jim, like Reacher, needed a big empty frontier landscape. Jane felt perfectly at home in a country that would fit snugly inside the state of Wyoming.

They loved each other. But not *to the exclusion of all others*, not if you counted countries. 'She was a rabid Anglophile,' he said, 'and it took me twenty years to get her out of there.' Not that he ever entirely did.

23

Thornsett Road

The kitchen and living room were
spotlessly clean and immaculately tidy.
The Hard Way, 2006

They all agreed that Jim had stolen Jane from Nigel. The two friends were sharing a house at the time, along with Mike.

Nigel was obsessed with Jane. He was 6 foot 2 with a 28-inch waist, and she was dark and delicate and sloe-eyed and foxy and all of 4 foot 11. He'd sat next to her in lectures during her first year as an Archaeology student, which was his second, or maybe his third, and the night before she flew back to the States for the holidays they found themselves in bed together. Later that summer they met up again at a dig in Orkney, which was when he fell for her head over heels.

Nigel Hallam was a couple of years older than Jane Shiren. He might possibly have been taken for Jim's less feline older brother, and like Jim had 'done too much of everything'. As a consequence he too had flunked a year of his degree, in his case the first. He spent his second on social security, which was when he moved into 20 Thornsett Road. Twelve months later he was joined by Mike Gibbons, and the year after that Jim, who was seeing a girl called Lucy – small and wealthy and generous and always laughing.

'I pursued Jane relentlessly,' Nigel said. They argued constantly, but she was the only woman to whom he ever proposed marriage. His eventual wife proposed to him.

No. 20 Thornsett Road was a three-storey Victorian house. On the ground floor lived Miss Grünberg, a Russian Jew in her nineties who claimed a connection to the Romanovs and could remember seeing Lenin on a soapbox. Her family had been evacuated from St Petersburg but wound up in Berlin. Only she and her sister survived the war. Miss Grünberg learned English and took a job as a shorthand typist. She was short and plump and had jet-black hair, which when it wasn't tied back in a bun reached nearly to the floor. She loved having young people about, less so at three in the morning or when neighbours called the police because they were dancing naked on the garage roof, and was a willing confidante. When she invited them down for tea she would give the boys a pack of cigarettes, though she herself didn't smoke. 'A man should smoke,' she said, 'and I like having a man about the place.'

Nigel kept a cat, Sam, who had taken to Miss Grünberg. One weekend the friends had no money for food and all that remained was a mouldy loaf, which they planned to toast. There was a knock at the door: it was Miss Grünberg holding a plate of freshly cooked chicken. She herself was a strict vegetarian. 'I've cooked this for Sam, can you give it to him later?' It took Nigel milliseconds to wrestle with this tricky moral dilemma. Chicken on toast! *Why thank you kindly, Miss G.*

Jim's staple diet consisted of two set menus. At the university cafeteria it was a tub of cottage cheese and a helping of baked beans. At the chippy it was rice and mushrooms. The cheapest options on the board but a step up from Birmingham, where he had been known to suck tomato ketchup off a paper napkin at the Kardomah with a cup of tea on the side.

It was coming out of the chippy one day that he last used the headbutt. He had his dinner in one hand and his change in the other, saw he was about to get mugged, didn't want to lose either, so 'just took a step forward and laid the guy out'. He didn't even have to break stride.

Thornsett Road reeked of Player's No. 6 or Embassy. They all had the same full ashtray. The beds were legless, just frames on the floor. But at least you could sit on the bedroom carpets without catching some virulent disease. The lounge carpet was a serious health hazard. Maybe it had once contained fibre, but now it was nothing but a noxious mix of grime, fag ash, dirt, spilt coffee and beer. To match it they painted the walls purple and brown with orange trim and split the light fittings so the rooms were festooned with pendant lamps and live wires.

Miss Grünberg's rooms were pristine and she kept the front garden full of flowers. But the upstairs digs were squalid. Rubbish and half-built theatre props blocked the landings, attracting the occasional hibernating hedgehog. Washing-up was done before a meal, not after. There was an argument about whose turn it was to wash a pan, which sat under the sink for two terms before someone hurled it out of the window into the garden below. Sometimes the rubbish smelt so bad it would be removed to the first-floor fire escape. 'We never cleaned,' Mike Gibbons said. The wall behind the cooker was covered with mould.

There was a single bathroom with a tub but no shower, and the bath was used for printing posters so the drains were clogged and it was garishly stained, foreshadowing the nightmarish modus operandi of the serial killer in *The Visitor*. But at least the sink was still viable. Once a week Mike would sneak back to his first-year hall of residence to take a shower, on Sunday mornings when it was quiet. Gyms didn't exist. As Lee liked to remind fans squeamish about Reacher's personal hygiene, it wasn't an era when people bathed every day. He himself was proof of humanity's ability to procreate in conditions of imperfect cleanliness, and could clearly remember the days when putting on a fresh set of clothes was still seen as a big deal.

Mike and Nigel met at the Student Union on Western Bank, the base for clubs and societies. Nigel, an ex-cathedral chorister, was chairman of the theatre group, and Mike, a bassoonist and counter-tenor, was chairman of music and debates. Historically the two committees had been deadly rivals, but the two friends chose to bury the hatchet by living under the same roof. All their housemates were recruited the same way. Which was how Jim wound up there, despite being a couple of years younger. It was the golden age of Thornsett Road, said Mike, 'overflowing with creativity'. Nigel went on to form a children's theatre company, and soon after Jim joined Granada both Nigel and Mike were working for the BBC. 'We didn't just print posters. We used to sit around writing music and plays.'

Like the Cannon Hill Arts Centre in Birmingham, the drama studio was a symbol of expansionist sixties dreams. It had a full lighting grid so you could walk across at roof level and when a production was in full swing you could stay on through the night. The manager was Bill Royston, previously of the Welsh National Opera, who took his young company on tour to other cities. Mike got to conduct Gershwin's *Rhapsody in Blue* with dancers: 'You had the chance to explore what was possible.'

Jim worked backstage with Martin Brown. Martin hadn't known his old friend was at Sheffield, but Jim was the first person he saw when he walked into the Union restaurant on his first day and after that they were together the whole time. 'He was definitely my best mate at university,' Martin said. Martin was a rare non-smoker but happy to roll spliffs for Jim like Andy Saunders's sister used to do. 'It was a technical skill,' he said. 'I was always good at making things.' 'He would never smoke,' Lee said, 'but he was a great roller.'

'Jim and Martin were the go-to guys for mad solutions to weird problems,' said Jenny Neesham, a former English student from the drama-studio crowd. 'Like when the park rangers wouldn't lend us a bench and they put on boiler suits and carried one off from under their noses.'

Ticket prices averaged thirty pence. The university archive reveals that make-up for *A Scent of Flowers* and *Loot* was done by Jane Shiren, who partnered with Nigel on publicity and provided 'gymnastic advice' for *Cinderella*. But it was Jane Grant who did make-up for *The Crucible*. Jim was on the technical crew for *Loot*, did lighting for *Peer Gynt* and both set and lighting for *Tiny Alice*. For *Cinderella* he trained the elephants. Lee had blotted the elephants from his memory but there was evidence of the two productions he was most proud of, which judging by their programmes were a cut above the average. The notes for *A Doll's House* were handwritten over four pages of heavy cream parchment paper sealed with wax, in flowing italic script. Nigel made the posters, Martin was technical director and Jane Shiren was manager. Publicity was by 'Richard Strange' and the designer was Jim Grant. 'I thought it looked more professional than having one guy doing two things,' Lee explained. 'It was a signally beautiful production,' recalled Jenny, who later made a career in theatre. Jim was principal designer for *Oh, What a Lovely War!* too, billed on the stylish red and black programme as a 'Robin Petherbridge – Jim Grant' production.

Jim wasn't a typical lawyer. He had the mind, but not the demeanour. He wasn't studious, but no one was (being in the theatre group made you a libertine by definition). It didn't matter whether you got a first (which almost no one did) or a 2:1 (which few did) or a third. 'We had three years to grow up at the taxpayer's expense,' said Mike. 'We may not have been very hygienic but it was a golden time.'

But the law hadn't done Lee any harm. It gave you 'a healthy relationship with the world': you knew what was likely to be true or not and developed a certain self-confidence. Lawyers often made good writers. There was a precision to their use of language and they could see the big picture too. A litigator was telling a story to a jury of ordinary people and was 'fifty per cent of the way there'.

He'd never intended to go into practice but was sorry to let down his parents. It was ironic, and sad, that his success as Lee Child so transcended the aspirations of Rex and Audrey, so astronomically exceeded their expectations that they couldn't grasp it, almost as though it had nothing to do with their son at all. Lee Child was an alien. Jim Grant, barrister manqué, was a disappointment.

It wasn't just Jim who was in thrall to America. 'If you grew up in the fifties and sixties America was all over the place,' Mike said, 'that big clean John Wayne-Lone Ranger-Wells Fargo thing, big cars and big ranch-style houses.' 'Buicks,' Lee added, 'with large fins and loose suspensions.' Not forgetting actual archaeological traces left behind by GIs – a stick of gum or a pack of Lucky Strikes, or the back half of a *Superman* or *Batman* comic, with ads that evoked an unimaginably different, reckless world. And it wasn't just Jim who was in thrall to Jane. 'I had the same view of her as he did,' said Mike. He still remembered the day when, like a magician pulling a rabbit out of a hat, Nigel suddenly introduced his exotic partner into their lives. 'She sparkled,' he said. 'We were all incredibly envious when he rocked up with her.' But she could be sharp too, he added. 'I would have loved to get to know her, but she was with Nigel.'

Which hadn't bothered Jim. He had two inches on Nigel and the self-belief to go with it.

> All his life, to be taller had been to be better. More dominant, more powerful, more noticed, more advantaged. You got credibility, you got treated with respect, you got promoted faster, you earned more, you got elected to things. Statistics bore it out.

> You won fights, you got less hassle, you ruled the yard.
> To be born tall was to win life's lottery. (*61 Hours*)

'There was never any animosity,' Nigel said. Jim had done him a favour, steering him towards his wife Bridget Lokes (who did wardrobe for *A Doll's House*) via a brief reunion with former flame Christine, dumped for Jane on the night of that end-of-term party. Lee was relaxed about it. 'Relationships were so short they were changing all the time.'

'We were the first pill generation,' Jenny said.

> AIDs was still well over the horizon, and antibiotics were effective, so we didn't think much about sexually transmitted diseases. I suspect we presented as sexually and socially confident, dominant, if not actually aggressive. We had a lot of sexual control and the whole contraception thing was still new. Men hadn't got used to it and hadn't begun to think of sex as a right, and any lad who might have hinted to that effect would have got slapped down pretty sharply.

It was another golden moment, when it seemed women had finally achieved some kind of hard-won liberation which they thought would be enduring and could never again be lost. Lee remembered Jenny and Bridget wandering around the flat, 'revelling in their own nakedness'.

Jenny came late to Reacher, on the back of talking about her old friend's life. Immediately he reminded her of Beowulf, an abnormally strong man who comes from outside into a beleaguered community and saves it by ripping monsters apart with his bare hands. She told me that the words 'Thaet waes mothig secg' translated as *That was a brave man*, but that Seamus Heaney had rendered them as *That was a considerate man*. 'Reacher is kind and considerate. I think that may be a bit of Jim. I remember Jim as being gentle in his dealings with other people.'

247

'He was a gentle bloke,' said Martin Brown; 'a gentle, arty bloke', said Chris Springall, who had shared the stage with him at King Edward's. 'He could be hard with it too,' countered Rob Reeves.

Kind, considerate, gentle and protective: these qualities didn't prevent Reacher from indulging in a little Beowulf-style bragging. 'A brag should be faintly preposterous,' said Jenny. 'I'm going to kill Grendel with my bare hands. And his mother. I'm going to stuff Arthur Scorpio into his own tumble dryer. However preposterous, the true hero fulfils it to the letter.' Just like Jim and the flick knife in French class.

Jenny thought the sex in Jim's novels was very seventies, 'no trendy descriptions of sexual athleticism but plenty of post-coital intimacy and tenderness'. Reacher loved and left women who loved and left him; they parted on equal terms. She couldn't help noticing the preponderance of small, delicately built women who were as competent and tough as the men. What did she remember about Jane? *Small, competent and tough* covered it pretty well. Jane was both reserved and forthright. Not a 'gasbag'. She didn't wear her heart on her sleeve.

'The girls Jim went out with were all petite,' said Alison Yeomans.

At Thornsett Road Jim had the first-floor bedroom next to the lounge, where stairs from the balcony led down to the back garden. The other bedrooms were on the top floor under the sloping roof. Until he moved in with her, Jane moved in with him. One night they were having a party. Nigel and Bridget had turned in early after a long run of screenprinting, and at some point Nigel staggered out of bed to ask them to keep it down. Turned out they were playing knots, standing in a circle holding hands and trying to get into as big a tangle as possible without breaking grip. They were all naked. Nigel crept back upstairs to Bridget but they couldn't sleep. Not only was it still noisy, but they were missing out. So they stripped off and went downstairs, threw open the door and leapt into the frivolities, whooping merrily. By which time the others were all fully clothed. 'It was probably the most naked I've ever felt,' Nigel recalled.

They took sex casually and relationships seriously. But relationships took over quickly. There was a lot of short-term serial monogamy.

Which made the early marriage less surprising. 'We were a centre-left house,' said Mike.

> Centre by upbringing, left by youthful ideals. Centre in our descent into middle-class life – married house-owners with kids quite soon, with the eventual paradox of a socialist millionaire living on the Upper West Side.

It was all about Jane getting a visa, said Lee. 'It was so she could stay once she'd finished her degree.'

Mike was from Bath. Like Jim he had gone to a direct-grant grammar school, part of the same foundation as King Edward's in Birmingham. He had never seen anything like the steel towns of the north-east. There were leafy oases around Ecclesall Road and Fulwood and out on the moors, in the poetically named Hathersage, Ladybower and Snake Pass. But venture downhill into industrial Attercliffe, south of the River Don, and 'the steel works were going full pelt. It was like Tolkien could have envisaged the set for Mordor.' Attercliffe was on Jim's bus route from Hillsborough, and Mike went there to sell the student rag magazine. 'We used to walk off the street into the bell factories where the steel was being forged, right on the roadside.' The 1960s image of *Coronation Street* back-to-backs was real. 'Poverty levels were horrendous.'

But there was a sense of vitality too. Sixties tower blocks alongside Victorian terraces, the Arts Tower and paternoster lift (a chain of open chambers moving continuously in a loop), reputed to be the largest in the world, and the Hole in the Road. Built in 1967 under what used to be the market square (obliterated by German bombs in December 1940), the Hole in the Road was a network of underpasses and shops with a central area open to the sky that featured a fish tank with carp and goldfish and bream and rudd and roach. Demolished ten years before the Wedding Cake, the two follies were remembered with the same ambivalent affection.

In Sheffield Mike heard Dvořák and Brahms for the first time.

> I fell in love to the third movement of Brahms' Third Symphony. I saw the biggest bands in the world. I found out how to look after myself. I saw Pelé play for Santos at Sheffield Wednesday. We learned how to deal with people, because we were living close-up to them – their mood swings, their ups and downs. It was a vibrant, slightly risqué, off-the-wall community, and probably the most important part of personal development.

No one remembered Jim talking about books or writing (in *The Hero* he recalls reading *Stone Age Economics* by Marshall Sahlins and *The Descent of Woman* by Elaine Morgan and *Shakespeare Our Contemporary* by Jan Kott). He was always on about Aston Villa. He wasn't involved in politics. He was seen as detached, with that persistent reputation for being a cynical observer that he would never quite throw off. It all struck him as faintly absurd, like the People's Front of Judea in Monty Python's *Life of Brian*. It wasn't the real thing like at Granada, where the unions affected people's livelihoods. 'People always say I'm cynical, but I just think I'm realistic.'

The first time Mike heard about Lee Child was at his wedding anniversary in 2003. Nigel and Bridget were sitting in Mike's conservatory when Nigel said: 'You know Jim is a millionaire author, don't you?' *What?* 'Yeah, he's won all these awards.'

Since then Mike had read all the Reacher books. He liked their obsessive detail and vivid imagery. He had become claustrophobic from living through Reacher's narrow escapes in *Die Trying* and *61 Hours*, which, exceptionally, explored the downside of being tall. Reacher was bigger and harder than Jim, but Mike could hear Jim in his voice. He thought there was a point between *One Shot* and *The Hard Way* where the publishers stopped promoting Lee Child as author and by moving his photograph from the inner flap to the back cover began hinting that he was his hero instead.

Mike thought writing had got Jim exactly where he wanted to be: far away from the Ridgeway Avenue house with the outside toilet, far from Handsworth, Birmingham and Sheffield and across the ocean to another social dimension. When the Grants emigrated to the States in 1998 they sailed on the *Queen Elizabeth II* because Jim wanted to experience that mythic moment when you see the Statue of Liberty silhouetted against the Manhattan skyline, a symbolic marker of the fact that he was consciously setting out on a new phase of his life, putting Thornsett Road behind him forever. His apartment on Central Park West was the kind of place that looked exactly the same from one visit to the next. Though compared to the condo on East 22nd Street (where he lived from 2004 to 2014), which had the wiring embedded in the walls, it was positively cluttered.

In the *Wall Street Journal* ('Reacher's Minimalist Roost', 2010) Lee admits to fantasising about a lifestyle modelled on that of his ascetic, 'possession-free maverick'.

> So if a button falls off his shirt, Mr Child casts the shirt in the garbage, as he doesn't want to store a sewing kit. He doesn't cook, so he sees no need for pots, pans or ingredients. [. . .] 'In principle if I could not have a home I wouldn't. But not having a home would be too difficult procedurally, going from hotel to hotel, the gap of three hours where you're hungry and tired.'

Which didn't explain why he then needed four apartments in the same building (one for living in on the twenty-fifth floor, one for working in on the seventh, one for Jane on the thirtieth, and one for guests on the sixteenth, south-facing, without the views), nor why he later needed four different homes (one in Manhattan, one in France, one in Sussex and one in Wyoming).

> The entire left-hand wall [. . .] is a plane of glossy white laminate cabinetry. Inside the cabinets are some 3,000 books, as Mr Child believes books make a room visually chaotic and that displaying them is pretentious. The books are shelved randomly; Mr Child says his photographic memory allows him to know exactly where each one sits.

By the time I met him the books were back on show, neatly aligned in beautifully crafted white bookcases. Not to display them would have seemed pretentious. But it was true he knew where each one sat, and you messed with them at your peril.

> The source for colour: A large Tom Christopher painting of a New York street scene looking down on Fifth Avenue. The red traffic light in the painting is echoed by a red ashtray on the small balcony outside, where the view up Fifth includes Madison Square Park, the Empire State Building, the Chrysler Building and the Metropolitan Life clock tower.

Lee could detail these iconic landmarks as only the convert could. As a measure of how far he'd travelled, they meant more to him than to a born-and-bred native of his adopted city. According to the *New Yorker*, Christopher 'is to Times Square what Monet was to water lilies', which seemed right for someone en route to investing in the French Impressionists.

Perhaps he bought the paintings in the burst of displaced creativity that came upon him each September, as with the gold bands he wore, which like his dwellings had also multiplied. Now Lee wore three on each ring finger. Two of yellow gold and one of rose, six in total, so he could choose freely between the Fabergé and the Patek Philippe without fear of a fashion faux pas. The five new rings, purchased together to ensure a perfect match, were also engraved, three for his nearest and dearest – Jane 1974, Stanley 1978, Ruth 1980 – and two for milestone events: J.R. 1111 2008 2011 (the two times he'd scored four no. 1s simultaneously, on both sides of the Atlantic) and 8 July 1998 (the date he became a United States resident). 'I like gold,' he said. 'It's a nice chunk of wealth.'

The rose gold bands for Jane and Ruth lay either side of the wedding band, and on his right hand the order of metals was reversed, with Stanley the springer spaniel in the middle.

Extreme minimalism is easier for a fictional vagabond, the *Journal* remarks.

> Mr Child bought the 990-square-foot apartment in this doorman building for $1.5 million in 2005. It then took two and a half years, $800,000 and interviews with twelve architects to satisfy his need for precision.

Consciously or not, this passage from *The Hard Way* could have been written for Nigel and Mike.

> The kitchen and living room were spotlessly clean and immaculately tidy. The décor was mid-century modern, restrained, tasteful, masculine. Dark wood floors, pale walls, thick wool rugs. There was a maple desk. An Eames lounge chair and an ottoman opposite a Florence Knoll sofa. A Le Corbusier chaise and a Noguchi coffee table. [. . .]

'Very elegant,' Pauling said.

'An Englishman in New York,' Reacher said.

The items of furniture were all things Lee had owned, though not in the same place at the same time. It was like a coded message: *Top of the world, Ma!*

Not that Lee was doing any more cleaning than Jim had. He had staff to do that now, and first-world problems like how to recruit them. He didn't know where to find his broom or his ironing board. But he was fussy. No one really ironed things right ('you should press it on both sides'), and one argument for minimalism was to mitigate against the generally poor standard of housekeeping.

At Sheffield they had been relaxed in their habits, but that post-war legacy was driving them to achieve. They would be judged on whether they'd been able to climb the ladder and move on, especially the men. His friends speculated that notwithstanding his outward composure Jim felt this burden more than most, because of his parents. From the day he turned up at Thornsett Road he appeared to have a 'more active' relationship with his family than the others. 'Not close, but busy.'

The Mike of the early 1970s, in a crumpled snap from the Union photo booth, looks like a guy without baggage. His hair and beard are abundant, framing his face in a glorious afro-inflected halo. His smile lights up his face and reaches his eyes. Just to see it makes you cheerful. He's holding a thin-stemmed Falcon pipe.

Had Jim ever looked that carefree, I wondered? 'Never!' said Mike. 'He always looked carefully if happily cautious. Maybe a little youthfully uncertain.' Mostly he was reserved and understated and emanated self-control, but sometimes he would talk 'over a cigarette or something less legal and endless coffees long into the night'. They all drank coffee endlessly and Mike, like Reacher *père et fils*, still did. 'Jim was a good friend and companion and as a younger arrival did well to settle in with the flat.'

I wasn't sure you could call it settling. More like an albatross alighting briefly, just long enough to snatch up the prize.

Few remembered Jim fighting, none beyond his school days. But he was capable of dishing out a verbal beating and many sensed a subdued angry streak in him that would find its voice at Granada. Jim told the same stories of boyhood bundles Lee was telling four decades later. There was a perception he could spool back quite easily. 'Contra mundum, babe,' read an anniversary card from his wife.

When Nigel spooled back it was to the good times, back to when Bridget was still alive and they *just had fun*. He recalled the wedding in Crookes Valley Park and how the best man had put his foot in it by letting slip that Jim and Jane had lived together out of wedlock. 'It's true,' Martin said. 'It was about the first thing I said.' He didn't remember much from the big day except that as usual Jane's older sister Leslie was 'a bit prickly'. 'There's a lot to think about when you're best man.'

There was no music or dancing at the reception. But some time late into the afternoon the friends may have drunkenly re-enacted the Battle of Salamis on the adjacent boating lake. Nigel had done ancient history as a subsidiary subject, and Jim had read about it in a book.

'The Jim I knew was very cool,' Nigel wrote. 'The most laid-back guy I've ever met.'

Except for those cruelly parted by death, all three couples were still married.

But only Jim and Jane were still wedded to nicotine.

24

A Charmed Career

They talked about the past. Escapades,
capers, scandals, outrages.
Bad Luck and Trouble, 2007

It was Wednesday 29 June, 1977. At some point between 2 and 3.55 p.m. Jane was out at work. Jim was out of work, apart from occasional shifts as stage manager at the Crucible. He was lounging at home on the sofa in the soulless new flat in Halfway, mentally constructing the blueprint of a better house and watching the Wimbledon Championships (in those days the women's final was played on Friday and the men's on Saturday). They were so poor they had rented a black-and-white television, but by then the green grass was stamped on his retina.

It was a historic occasion. Thirty-one-year-old local favourite Virginia Wade, three times a losing semi-finalist, was facing her nemesis, US golden girl and defending champion Chris Evert, a decade younger, who had beaten her in twenty-two of their previous twenty-seven meetings. Evert had already dispatched fourteen-year-old Tracy Austin and Billie-Jean King, who was even older than Wade. Ginnie's American coach Jerry Teeguarden was puffing on his pipe in the players' box and Chrissie's on-off love interest Jimmy Connors was poised to face eighteen-year-old John McEnroe.

It's no coincidence that it was to New York-based Chrissie that Reacher so ecstatically surrendered in *High Heat* at the age of sixteen. Chris Evert was Jim's favourite tennis player. Even forty years later he recalled how pleasant it was to watch her 'glow' and how both pleasure and glow increased as the match built to its climax. Miss Evert was retro. She didn't sweat, she 'got damp'. But in some repressed recess of his Americanophile psyche he was happy that the long-suffering Miss Wade went on to beat Betty Stöve in the final, thrashing her 6–1 in the third set and perspiring profusely.

Somehow the tennis focused Jim's mind. That and the holes in the wafer-thin wall, which he'd had to patch, having accidentally drilled through into the neighbour's flat while putting up bookshelves. Jane would be pleased when she got home from work. But it wasn't enough. *I'd better get my act together*, he thought, *and apply for that job.*

At first he hadn't taken any notice. But in the end he couldn't help himself. He was programmed. That was his job. To get a job and support the family, even if for now they were only a family of two. It was in his DNA. And in case he had any notion of breaking the evolutionary mould it had been drummed into him at King Edward's too. It was right there in the school song, like an earworm admonishing him from within. *Die of service, not of rust.*

So when the match was over and Chrissie had gone and while the thought still remained he hauled himself up off the sofa and went in search of the newspaper. Specifically, the *Guardian* of Friday 24 June. There in the media section, he saw an advertisement headed: Granada Television, Trainee, Transmission Control.

That would do very nicely.

He didn't so much apply as notify Granada of his intention to arrive. Which he did, on 12 September, a date he remembered as vividly as he did Chris Evert.

Robert Reeves had got there ahead of him. He had seen the exact same ad a few months before and had started work on 21 June. Granada were after two trainees but had found only one. So the notice Jim saw was a re-advertisement: *Previous applicants need not re-apply.* It was like it was directed at him. *We're waiting just for you, Jim Grant!* 'I knew I'd get it,' he told Rob. 'I knew exactly what to say.'

'I knew I'd get it,' he told me forty years later. 'I knew exactly what to say.'

When asked what he'd written in his letter of application he said: 'I know I'm the person for this job, you won't need to hire anyone else, I know it's me.' Which I interpreted as a concise paraphrase of a considered argument until Nigel Hallam told me it read: 'Look no further, I'm your man.' As Rob put it, there were times when Jim was 'teetering on the edge of arrogance and maybe going over the other side'.

But there was no denying he was right. 'Sure enough, he got it,' Rob said. 'He was cut out for that job. It's a job for cool, almost machine-like people in their thinking, and he was ideally suited to it.' Legend has it Granada were so tantalised by his one-liner that by the time Jim and Jane got home from holiday there was a pile of letters on the doormat all saying something like, 'Why aren't you answering our letters? We're holding the job till we can interview you.'

'He slotted right in,' recalled Stephen Gallagher, who was already established in the same role. Presentation was a hard gig to define. It recruited individuals with a creative bent for a job that allowed little scope for individual creativity. 'We were at the heart of show business, the point crew for the country's leading commercial broadcaster, but when it came down to it we were the traffic managers of other people's art.' Jim's attitude was that he'd fallen backward into this well-remunerated media job where he could sleep in late every day for three out of every four weeks and where the weekend evening shifts were the cue for an elaborate boozy picnic in the control room.

'We called them "soirées".' Gallagher remembered Jim saying how his parents made him swear never to tell his more diligent older brother how much he was earning. It was almost indecent.

In August 1978 Jim and Jane moved to Stalybridge in Greater Manchester and got their first dog, Stanley (for whom Reacher's father was named). Stalybridge was eight miles east of the city and had been one of the first centres of cotton manufacturing but was now semi-rural. Copley Park Mews was the Grants' first house, where Ruth was born, and special for these reasons alone. But, directly opposite Copley Mill in a cobbled courtyard off the Huddersfield Road, it was also of historic interest, judged in a 2013 conservation appraisal to be 'a pocket of character'. No. 13 is in a terrace of 1830s workers' cottages, built back-to-back in local stone with slate roofs but later knocked through into three-bedroom single dwellings with private parking. The robust architectural detail was typical of early nineteenth-century Pennine mill buildings, the watershot cut of the bricks helping rain to run down the exposed masonry. The terrace was built by mill owner James Wilkinson and had outlived his own Brookfield House, whose adjacent grounds, lake and glasshouses had long since been reclaimed by self-seeding woodland.

It was tempting to see the move to Granada as written in the stars. On 5 July 1954 the British Broadcasting Corporation broadcast its first daily news programme, with Richard Baker presenting. In the same year, a few months before James Grant was born, the government passed the Television Act, permitting the creation of the United Kingdom's first commercial network. The weekday franchise for the north of England was granted to Granada Television, which along with Associated-Rediffusion, ATV and ABC quickly became established as one of 'The Big Four' providing the majority of network output. The Conservative government had learned from the American experience that multiple competing stations meant a race to the bottom, so instead awarded a monopoly to the regions. Costs were 100 per cent tax deductible and in the trenchant opinion of plain-speaking newspaper baron Lord Thomson, a stake in commercial television was the equivalent of having 'a licence to print money'.

Granada's rise from zero to hero was spectacular. Just a year after the contract was signed, the inaugural transmission went on air from a state-of-the art studio complex on Quay Street, the first commercial building to be constructed in Manchester after the war, crucial to the city's regeneration and with its illuminated period typeface soon to become a landmark on the skyline. Twenty-odd years after this genesis moment there were many more independent stations but the technology remained largely unchanged, and Jim and Rob were at the sharp end. Jim calculated that there were fifteen thousand pieces of information to process in any one day, all of them timed to the second.

Lee's memories of that time are of how carefree it was. When asked at interview if he had any questions, he replied 'No, I think I've got all I need, thank you.' 'Don't you want to know how much you're going to be paid?' 'Oh yeah, of course, thanks!' Then: 'Wow, really?' Jim couldn't believe how much better it was than selling ice-creams or drying peas or lugging boxes. 'I thought if I earned £100 a week everything would be just fine. Then pretty soon I was earning £500 a week. What more could I possibly want?' He got a 40 per cent pay rise after his first year. It was a period of high inflation, and he soon became accustomed to the rapid escalation in salary.

He contrasted his 'charmed career' with that of his father. 'My father got a job and dutifully went to work every day for the rest of his working life, but never enjoyed what he did.' Whereas Lee had done 'only things he loved doing, in a realm that he loved'. While admitting he sometimes complained, he had never felt unhappy about going to work in the morning. Especially since becoming a writer. 'This job?

It's a dream! Sit around and make shit up and get paid a shedload of money?' *No, I think I've got all I need, thank you.*

Success had contributed retrospectively to this Chrissie-like glow. 'I had a very lovely career in TV,' I heard Lee tell assembled fans more than once. 'I loved every minute of it. By my third day I was being trained by a lovely woman who told me "Come on, we're going to lunch with some actors." And she picked up a Fortnum & Mason wicker hamper and I followed her out of the room and we had lunch with Alec Guinness, John Gielgud, Ralph Richardson and Laurence Olivier.' *What more could I possibly want?* 'Lovely' became a defining word.

'Bollocks!' was Rob's response. 'He wouldn't tell that story if I was in the audience.' It was true that Olivier had made *Cat on a Hot Tin Roof* with Robert Wagner and Natalie Wood, shot at Granada Studios in 1976, and Rob knew someone who could remember Olivier being snubbed by Ena Sharples of *Coronation Street* when he ventured into the canteen. But 'no one in our department knew Alec Guinness *and* John Gielgud *and* Ralph Richardson *and* Laurence Olivier.'

Rob recalled his own first day, which he surmised was typical. He came in wearing a jacket and tie and got introduced to people: Candice Morgan, secretary to David Black, boss of Presentation, and head of Promotions Joe Rigby, brother of actor Terence and known as the fifth Beatle for his haircut, and music hall artist Wilf Parkin, then someone took him down to the canteen for lunch, where he saw no wicker hampers and no Laurence Olivier. 'I would say London to a brick on it's not true,' Rob concluded, emphatically.

We shared a moment of contemplative silence then remembered how Lee would also tell audiences that if you asserted something with sufficient authority people would happily believe you. 'By telling you that story he's just had you,' Rob said. 'You've believed something that isn't true.' The compliant reader was always willing to suspend disbelief.

I confronted Lee with Rob's scepticism. He stood by his recollection but conceded he was hazy on timing. Perhaps it was the third week, or the third month, but in his mind it had definitely happened. I found no evidence of all four actors convening at the Manchester studios on a single day. Harold Pinter's *No Man's Land* aired in early 1978, starring Gielgud and Richardson and overlapping with the prestigious *Laurence Olivier Presents* series – maybe if you discounted Alec Guinness it was all true. Either way it felt like mythic realism in action.

Mainly Lee told the story to set up his punchline. 'I had a very lovely career in TV. I loved every minute of it. Then one day my boss said something to me that made it impossible for me to continue: *You're fired.*' Guinness, Gielgud, Richardson and Olivier would have applauded his determination to deliver a crowd-pleasing performance.

Lee had commended Rob to me for the excellence of his memory. But later Rob wrote to say he was no longer certain, like he too was falling prey to that persuasive authorial voice. 'The weird thing is that when I was driving home a dim remembrance did come back that maybe he'd told me something along those lines one time. But not all four giants of the English stage, in one go on his third day!' When a huge star was filming there (Bowie, Hoffman) 'you generally knew and would talk about it'.

'Not sure why everyone would assume they were all working at GTV,' wrote Lee. 'There was the BBC in Manchester, also theatre, plus nearby cities. Larry was out of seclusion, and if he invited friends to lunch they might have travelled a distance.' It was characteristic that he should want the last word, but there was no disputing his logic.

Training began in the third-floor open-plan office that housed Planning, Presentation and Promotions, where you got a sense of the interlocking whole. Schedules were produced on typewriters and listed programmes, promotions and commercial breaks, with the length of each precisely defined. 'Everything had to be exact,' Rob said. 'It was timed to an absolute second.' There was an area set aside for changes to be made by hand and until you mastered those critical skills there was no way you'd be let loose on the ground floor.

> There was a real sense as we went down to CCR [central control room] that we were the intrepid ones. There was a kudos to working there. It was a totally different world, the nerve centre, something bordering on the sacrosanct about it. Any outsiders who walked in seemed to emit a kind of nervous respect.

Jim and Rob trained together and were made assistant transmission controllers in January 1978, which meant Jim had got there faster. He was promoted faster too. From trainee to assistant to controller by 1981, then presentation director, the youngest by a decade, and finally senior presentation director, lord of all he surveyed. By the time he became Lee Child he was accustomed to being top dog.

Central control room looked like something out of the Starship *Enterprise*, a two-person flight desk facing a six-by-four bank of grey, slightly convex screens. For a lay audience Lee would liken his former job to that of air traffic controller. Rob thought it was more complicated, because the air traffic guy was dealing only with a single source, 'with plane after plane after plane after plane'.

Transmission teams worked in pairs, with the senior partner on the right issuing instructions, and the junior on the left, executing them and operating the desk. The assistant was like the controller's arms and legs. The controller was there to troubleshoot, would answer the red telephone if a problem was called in from across the network or take over the controls if the assistant had to be dispatched to the pub for a bottle of wine, and had always come up through the ranks. There was no such thing as fast-track officer-level entry: you had to have been a foot soldier first.

When I met him in 2018 in Kirkby Lonsdale, Rob brought with him two treasured archaeological artefacts: a pair of old-style faders, one for vision and one for sound, the same as had been used by every assistant transmission controller since the launch of independent television in 1955. When new technology was introduced in 1981 and the old control room was abandoned, Jim and Rob had broken in one night and rummaged around in the ruins until they found them in a box. 'Here,' said Jim. 'You keep those two and I'll have separate sound.'

Rob wanted me to hold the fader in my hand and test it out. He wanted me to feel how heavy it was and how it had a spring that made it resistant to pressure. I pushed down on the lever. Rob explained how when I released it, in that precise instant it would 'take' the next source I had chosen for it – movie, commercial, soap opera, news – and there was no going back. 'See how it's responsive to your touch? That's why I brought it. It's important. This was the job we did. Everything went through here: these two, and separate sound.' The faders were built into the control desk side by side, plugging into the network wires, with separate sound just slightly apart in case you wanted to crossfade.

'Technologically it was the most complicated time for the job we did,' Rob said, because there were so many different sources, including a mix of still and moving images. 'You had film, you had three-inch and two-inch videotape, which ran off fifteen-second rolls, and you had slide commercials on cassettes.' Sometimes you had five cassettes to play in a single break, but the stack only held three, which meant you'd be holding down the sound and vision faders in the ready position with one hand while changing cassettes with the other.

Commercial breaks were insane. They only lasted five minutes but the assistant might have to take up to fifty separate actions, which meant fifty chances of getting it wrong. There might be three and a half minutes of commercial with a one-minute promotion at the head, which could involve cuing a live announcer, and a thirty-second promotion at the end, and since this was before the advent of self-contained television, when promotions would be delivered off-the-peg, you had to juggle all the elements simultaneously and repeatedly – image, jingle, caption, voiceover – like being conductor and orchestra all at once.

Meticulous planning went into the tour de force of those five-minute breaks. The watchword was to do the next thing you had to do as soon as you possibly could. 'When it came up to one minute to the break you would open talkback and say, if the first source was telecine: "One minute stand-by 35 A", which stipulated 35mm film on camera A in the telecine room, and then, at the end of that minute, "35 A roll film". "One minute stand-by VTR A" would mean fifteen-inch tape on machine A.' These were protocols he and Jim had executed thousands of times, so Rob was surprised when in 2015 Jim had asked to be reminded of the exact form of words.

Rob left Granada in 1984. He did seven years to Jim's eighteen. But forty years later both still had the same dream, only it's a nightmare: you're doing everything wrong, and those five-minute breaks are five minutes of unmitigated disaster. A 2015 entry from Rob's diary reads:

> I had returned, and was on with Jim. Frozen by my complete unfamiliarity with the mixer, I floundered around looking for the right buttons and faders. Jim said nothing, except to say that all the faders were different, then he left me there, on my own, to watch another programme run out into interminable black.

'If Jim hadn't become Lee Child I wonder if he would have left me to get on with it?' Rob mused. And if not for Reacher, would he have *said nothing*?

If you got it wrong you'd go in the log. Which explained the subject line of one of Jim's emails to Rob: 'I'm gonna have to log you, mate.' This was a line favoured by previous-generation controller Norman Matthews. The log would read: '15:45 break, finger trouble ATC, missed first two seconds of commercial.' The subtext: *I've got it over you.*

Caroline Gosling worked in Promotions for two years from 1979, around the time continuity announcers first went in-vision, while Jim was still an assistant. She too was from Birmingham and felt drawn to Jim's 'dry sense of humour' and 'slight Brummie drawl'. Promotions worked a day ahead, scheduling trailers and commercials (mostly slides with voiceover) as they were booked in from the Golden Square head-quarters in London or from Local Sales down the corridor. Sometimes they had to mock up promos themselves, as well as supplying captions (white Letraset on black card) for the newly introduced local news bulletin that followed the *News at One* and was always pre-packaged, even though they spoke of putting it out 'live' to 'air'.

One of Caroline's jobs was to prepare a daily 'spot sheet' for Presentation to work from, alerting Jim or Rob to potential gaps. Programmes were cut to a commercial hour, and Promotions would request thirty-, forty-five- or sixty-second slots to fill the remaining time, with any slack taken up by continuity announcements. If it turned out there were twenty seconds unaccounted for going in to *Coronation Street* and thirteen coming out, those two periods could be combined for an additional thirty-second trailer, moving the episode up or down by ten seconds on the spot sheet and incorporating a three-second freeze where it was least intrusive. Often the announcer could self-edit on the hoof or improvise over a programme rundown slide, but sometimes transmission controllers would have to scramble to rewrite a script or cut some film together, troubleshooting on a wing and a prayer to cover their backs, because wasting seconds was the ultimate transgression.

The high stakes gave the job its adrenaline rush and conferred upon those who executed it a heroic glamour, like they were engaging in some death-defying extreme sport. Not only would mistakes be broadcast across the land but they would cost the company serious money. Commercials were a massive source of revenue and the loss of even a second would have to be accounted for. In the 1980s, Lee recalled, they were bringing in a million pounds a day and 'if we screwed up it mattered'. Which meant they wielded tremendous power. As transmission controller you were in 'absolute control' and 'not even the managing director could override you'. 'On the day you were the word of God.'

Jim and Rob had about five years of unforgettable thrills and spills. Then things started becoming automated, which was one of the reasons Rob went. Everything was on tape. You no longer had to use a caption generator or live-mix a promo. The fifty actions were reduced to fifteen and you could start sleeping easy at night. But it was a loss as much as a gain, the end of a swashbuckling era of derring-do. When Channel 4 began in 1982 it was 'basically computerised. They just loaded these cassettes. Every programme they had, every commercial, they just sat there and watched it go out.'

It was like they were watching the creativity go out of it as well.

'Later the job became too slick,' Lee said. 'It was more fun when there was more of a random element to it.' For him the difference was defined in the shift from the Falklands War in 1982 to the Gulf War in 1991. 'In the first case we were having to think on our feet, with information coming at us left, right and centre. There were fifteen telephones and one day they rang incessantly, all day long. That night I heard telephones in my sleep. It was the closest I ever got to too much stress in my life.' Whereas in the second case 'it all came to us pre-packaged by ITN', the Independent Television News channel that the networks owned collectively.

Jim liked being boss. He liked having to take decisions and act on them and defend them. 'There were lots of vectors. We had to protect company revenue, comply with government regulations, consider public taste, respect moral imperatives and accept responsibility.' Whereas the job of assistant was purely operational, that of controller was editorial too. Controllers had to be on-the-spot responsive. 'If we had news film about famine in Ethiopia, it didn't feel right to be pushing Fray Bentos meat pies.' You were 'thinking on behalf of the audience'. Like being a writer of popular novels.

Lee recalled an incident in Ireland. The southern networks weren't interested, but since there was a strong Irish presence in Liverpool and Manchester he and his team took it upon themselves to assemble a news bulletin, and were hauled up next day for treading on the toes of the news team. 'So I said, if you don't want us to step on your toes then you'd better stick around until 1 a.m. every day to do it yourselves.'

'Jim was always calm at work,' said former colleague Janet Brown. 'I never knew him to lose his temper. He would always take control when the system went down.'

Janet was a loggist from the mid-seventies until 1981. She was based at a typewriter with a silencer, and her job was to log every transmission. She would start by typing up the schedule, then systematically check off each item as it went out. If there was a deviation or loss of transmission, however fleeting, she would note it down precisely, including the exact duration. It was painstaking work, accommodating few pauses and no lapses in concentration, with only the assistant to cover for her when she needed a break, which then required the controller to step in at the desk.

It seemed to me that the members of CCR were engaged in a ceaseless ritual dance, or were like the interlocked, interdependent elements of a single complex organism. Like the artillery crews in

Night School, whose coordination Reacher describes as 'almost gymnastic', 'as complicated as a ballet, timed to the tenth of a second'.

Lee and Rob both remembered Jim Grant's finest hour at Granada. But they were two different hours.

'It was the Iranian Embassy siege night,' Rob said. Even though Jim was still an assistant he'd been left on his own. It was bank holiday Monday, 5 May 1980, and Jim's hero, Canadian Cliff Thorburn, had just won the World Snooker Championship at the Crucible. Maybe the controller had gone out to buy drinks or play a game of pool, 'when suddenly the SAS stormed the Iranian Embassy and the news channel took over'. Jim had to completely rewrite the schedule. 'These bombs were going off and it was still all the complicated stuff and he was relatively new, but he held it together. He was ideally suited to do that.' Like Reacher, Jim Grant had grace under pressure.

Lee thought his biggest gig came during the royal wedding of 29 July 1981, when Granada lost their live feed just as Prince Charles was saying 'I do' to Princess Diana. By this time Jim had been promoted to controller (and had moved house again as a result). Quick to recognise a state of emergency, he broke every rule in the book by patching into the BBC for several minutes just to keep the show on the road. He was no royalist, but he had professional standards, and to this day he was proud of that moment.

Later he would pass on to Reacher the benefit of his experience. This is from *Killing Floor* (chapter six), when the character is in the early stages of definition:

> Evaluate. Long experience had taught me to evaluate and assess. When the unexpected gets dumped on you, don't waste time. Don't figure out how or why it happened. Don't recriminate. Don't figure out whose fault it is. Don't work out how to avoid the same mistake next time. All of that you do later. If you survive.

Ian Gerrard was an assistant under Jim in subsequent, less nail-biting years.

> I remember him sat in the Control Room appearing to pay no attention to what was going on, reading books (he was an avid book reader) and papers all the time whilst the ATCs did all the work, but then when an emergency arose he was instantly on it, sorting any problems out. He was definitely the most calm and level-headed TC you could wish to have working with you. His photographic memory and knowledge were his greatest assets, which is borne out with the detail and descriptions in his books.

When he wrote in 2018 Ian was still working part-time in transmission control, but like Lee and Rob was quick to point out how much less interesting it was. 'Computers have taken over and the job is basically list watching. In the past you used to go into work and think about how you could improve transmission – now you go in just to make sure the list keeps running and feed the machine.' We were entering Vonnegut's 'little boxes' future.

On 23 June 2005, at the Fox 6 TV station in Milwaukee for an author interview, Lee Child saw his first studio with robot cameras. 'Made my old trade unionist's blood run cold,' he blogged, 'all those camera operators out of work.'

Jim was the calm at the eye of the storm. Conservation of energy may have been his natural modus operandi but it made a lasting impression on colleagues. Iain Hale was an engineer who worked in the four operational studios: Telecine, VTR, Network Control and ACR. 'ACR25s were video cassette recorders,' he explained, 'which had air-operated transport systems that would sometimes fail, with spectacular consequences for transmission as another source would need to be cued up while the ACR25 was recovered.'

Working in the adjacent control area meant that because of the long shifts (up to fourteen hours) [. . .] we had time to get to know something about each other's personality. Jim was always laid back and never flustered. Always in control. I remember he could be sitting at the control desk reading the paper and he would reach over to open the talkback key: 'That's a minute and ten VTR A.' Having given the standby cue Jim would resume reading until about fifteen seconds before the roll, when he would put down the paper, open talkback and say: 'VTR A roll tape', and bring up the output on the mixer to Air. This was happening on multiple occasions at every programme junction throughout the hours we were broadcasting.

The less time there was, the more he had. It was the equivalent of creating the illusion of space in a tight New York apartment, or writing 'the fast stuff slow and the slow stuff fast'.

By the time he was fired Jim held the title of senior presentation director. It was the same job he'd always done, if a little easier, but he'd risen to the top of the tree. 'Maybe we had a new button to push. But they had to give us new job titles to justify the pay rises.'

Through the law of unintended consequences the word 'director' played right into Lee Child's storytelling hands like a final-salary pension. 'At Granada I was a director, not a writer,' he would say in early interviews, when he was building his new persona and needed to make his mark. He never explicitly claimed to have directed *Brideshead Revisited* or *Jewel in the Crown* or *Prime Suspect* or *Cracker*. But he didn't disabuse those who made that claim on his behalf. Their research was their responsibility. Not his problem. He rarely corrected the misinformation that circulated about him on the internet. It all added to the mystique.

Rob agreed that this was merely to sin by omission. He reviewed in his mind certain times he'd seen his old friend on television, maybe with Richard and Judy or on some other chat show, when he'd been asked about his Granada days. 'He wouldn't really talk about the job he did, not the job I've told you about. He'd just let these things go.' The director of *Brideshead Revisited* was Charles Sturridge. 'We were just rolling tape.'

But rolling tape was a big deal, back in the glory days of British television. Where would the artistic director be without the transmission team? What if the controller at the desk simply chose not to release that all-important fader? What then?

The job title was irrelevant. A rose by any other name would smell as sweet. Jim Grant was still the main man.

25

You're Fired

Eggs get broken, the omelette gets made,
and if it turns out tasty, then all is forgiven.
Night School, 2016

Jim Grant had the distinction of being fired twice from Granada.
The first time was in 1979, before the Iranian Embassy siege and
the royal wedding. He almost didn't make it to controller.

It happened on the day he refused to release that fader. When he
chose, perhaps prematurely, to exercise his controlling power. It was
like he was flexing his muscles.

It wasn't *Brideshead*. It was worse than that.

The date was Wednesday 5 September. The time was 12.59. The
one-minute countdown to the one o'clock news. Jim was on shift
with Norman Matthews. He was twenty-four years old and doing a
job that he loved, poised to take the next action as soon as he possibly
could. But there was a problem.

The National Union of Journalists was involved in a dispute at
ITN, which produced the news bulletins for the independent television
network. A non-union-produced programme had been sent down the
line. Jim's thumb was on the slider. He was programmed to press go.
Standing behind him on one side was the union shop steward, Malcolm
Foster, urging him not to transmit. Standing behind him on the other

273

side was Andrew Quinn, General Manager, ordering him to do the opposite. *Don't transmit! Transmit! Do it! Don't!*

'I didn't transmit,' Lee told me. 'At one o'clock on the dot, the screen went blank. Quinn said: "You're dismissed! Leave the building!" And we were locked out for eleven weeks.'

Ultimately his dismissal got lost in the general lockout. When everyone else returned to work so too did he. But it was an inevitable statement of solidarity. Jim was a member of the ACTT – the Association of Cinematograph, Television and Allied Technicians – it was a closed shop: 'we all automatically were' – one of thousands stood down as screens went blank around the country. They were to stay blank for three months, at best displaying an apologetic notice: 'Normal service will be resumed as soon as possible.'

It was all part of the rough and tumble. 'I struggled to begin with,' said Rob, 'but if one person was cut out for it, it was Jim. He was out-standingly good at his job.'

Presentation consisted of five assistants paired with five controllers, two full-time loggists, a handful of part-timers and four continuity announcers. It was the only department working seven days a week and the unsocial hours and regular switching of teams made for a strong sense of camaraderie: CCR against the world. When Steve Gallagher joined in 1975 an integral part of training was to go to the nearby Post Office Club at lunchtime with the duty controller and supervising assistant and get in a round of large white wines. Another favoured local was the Film Exchange, where in silent-movie days distributors had met to trade 35mm prints. Then Granada reopened the former Stables Club in the old railyard buildings down a side street (where the first full-scale outdoor set for *Coronation Street* would later be built), which did little to reduce alcohol consumption but made for a shorter commute.

For a while Rob was seeing Ann Todd, who worked in Scheduling alongside Caroline in Promotions. Rob really liked Ann but what stood out in his memory was a night with Jim and Jane and another couple at the Sandpipers bar in Fallowfield, where they ordered six rounds of cocktails, thirty-six different cocktails in total, except Ann only had five before she stood up to excuse herself and then crashed into a neighbouring table and passed out. 'She was only eighteen,' Rob said. 'Remember Ann Todd?' Jim asked when they met up again twenty years later. Then added: 'She's a hausfrau now.'

Rob wasn't proud of this story (or the coda). Nor was Jim. But they couldn't go back and change it, even if they wanted to. I was reminded of Jim's schoolgirl sweetheart Dot. Lee had done the best he could, probably, to make things up to the women in his past by writing what he saw as empowering outcomes for the strong, talented individuals he dreamed up in his novels.

It was a drinking culture but Jim still preferred weed. Rob was into amphetamines. Jim had developed a taste for 'white widows' (weed laced with cocaine). His colleagues thought him fearless for heading over to Moss Side – a deprived area of Manchester – in search of the best he could get. When I asked if he felt fearless Lee snorted. 'I was a paying customer. They welcomed me with open arms.' But it was on his return from one of those shopping trips that for the only time in his life he saw a gun fired in anger. It was a clash between some black guys and some white guys who'd come across from the other side of Heaton Park, and Jim was idling peacefully at an intersection with the sunroof open when he heard – glimpsed, sensed – a bullet shoot straight over his head. 'I took off,' he said. 'Didn't think twice about it. Just jumped the red light.'

Jim, Rob and Gallagher were contemporary with Joan Humphries and David Halliday, known as Shirley Temple for his golden curls, and their controllers were Norman Matthews, David Hill, Ken Ashcroft, Paddy Irwin and John Brown.

John Brown was Jim's de facto mentor. He had a 'ruthless sense of humour' and 'no shame', in Gallagher's words. Janet Brown, his then wife, said 'the language would flow'. But John had expertise, which Jim respected, and was battling the legacy of polio, which he respected even more. And he and Janet had been hospitable to the newcomer, inviting Jim and Jane home for dinner and putting them up overnight on the sofa so they wouldn't have to drive all the way back to Sheffield. Sometimes the two men would go to the Stables together. Later, Jim would buy John's immaculately maintained metallic brown Ford Capri.

There is a photograph of John sitting alongside Halliday at the console. He is bearded with a walrus moustache, looking straight at the camera with his chin tilted upwards like he is spoiling for an argument. The thick brown waves of his centre-parted hair are touching the lapels of his tan suit jacket, worn over a wide-collared open-necked black shirt, two or even three buttons undone. 'John Brown was good,' Rob acknowledged, 'but always trying to prove himself.'

'I got on better with Ken,' Rob said. Ken Ashcroft started out as a DJ at the Cavern Club, then got a job working for Brian Epstein. He had acted as stage manager for the Beatles during their 1963–4 Christmas shows at the Finsbury Astoria. According to Epstein, Ashcroft had once accompanied him to the States but was so out of his mind on pills and booze that he couldn't remember. Ken was quick-witted with a sarky sense of humour and a stunning wife called Petal, but he wasn't part of the married set and was constantly at war with Brown over top-dog status.

Rob didn't like John. And Jim didn't like Paddy. Pat Irwin carried a ruler like Miss Dawson and would rap her assistants over the knuckles with it when they got things wrong. She'd been in the Signals Regiment providing communications for Eisenhower's team on D-Day and there were rumours she'd been a driver at the Nuremberg trials. Paddy couldn't be bothered with faders. She favoured the straight cut from source to source: less skilled but foolproof and stress-free. She thought Jim was arrogant because he refused to compromise and he thought she was bad at her job because she lacked finesse and went round whacking people with rulers. For Rob it was enough that Paddy knew all the actors and was fun to hang out with at the bar. A guy would be pouring her a cocktail and when it came to the tonic she'd say, 'I wanted a drink not a bath.' Jim had the last laugh when in 1981 he got her job. 'He got what he'd always wanted,' said Rob, 'to be a transmission controller.'

'That's why she never liked me,' said Lee. 'She was old and I was young. She knew from day one she was training me for her own job. That she was a dinosaur on her way out.' Which chipped away at the reliability of his narrative voice, since this was also 'the lovely woman' with the wicker hamper famed not merely for knowing but picnicking with the most famous actors of all.

Jim wasn't cool, like Rob. Rob was into the Sex Pistols. Jim was into Pink Floyd, 'like John'. He wore a sports jacket and tie, 'like John'. A photograph taken at a party shows him in glasses, clean-shaven and fair-skinned and unlined, wearing a narrow-lapelled suit with a slight sheen to it and a narrow tightly knotted tie over a striped shirt, holding some kind of drink in a can. It's hard to tell if it's tonal dressing in shades of blue or shades of grey. Jane is in vivacious red and white.

The glasses dated from 1981. Not because they added gravitas to his new status. He'd been to an away match at Stoke City's old Victoria Ground and when Villa scored the winning goal at the far end he turned to the guy next to him and said: 'Who was that?' And the guy said 'Gary Shaw', and Jim thought, how come he can see and I can't? He'd worn them until 2011 when a fortuitous bump on the head during a visit to Rudyard Kipling's house corrected his vision. 'It was the nineteenth-century Lancaster linoleum,' Lee explained: 'an oil-based product over hessian or burlap.' It had been dimpled by stiletto heels in the fifties but then women stopped wearing stilettos to visit National Trust properties and the polish of five decades had caused the dimpling to resemble 'archaeological traces'. At which point Jim walked straight into the lintel and like Reacher at the end of *Make Me*, felt sick and dizzy for a day or two afterwards. Later, the optometrist was amazed to find his eyesight almost perfect. Head injuries could go either way, Lee said, and he was lucky.

'He was never totally stylish,' said Rob. 'Now he looks tanned and rugged,' said Caroline Gosling when I met her at the Union Club in London's Soho, 'but back then he was as pale as this white china cup. Some friends who came to the office described him as "a long drink of milk".' Rob moonlighted as a model for a pulp-fiction illustrator and had a tailor make his clothes. He had shirts with bolts through the collar and a replica of the jacket Dylan once wore to a famous press conference in San Francisco. 'Jim would just laugh. He wore the same thing every day.'

'What stood out was his height, and an almost feminine languor. My enduring image is of him contracting his six-foot-four-inch frame into a bucket chair in the CCR, bunching up his legs and rocking back and reading the papers.'

Rob was at home in bed when he heard about the strike. He wasn't sick. It was his day off and he was with his girlfriend. The office staff were jealous. Mainly of the days off. They thought the transmission teams had it easy.

'But we worked Christmas Day and Boxing Day and weekends and covered for each other.' Rob could reel off the five-week cycle in a rhythmic chant that spoke of rigorous routines rolling back through the years: 'Early Tuesday, early Wednesday, early Friday, early Saturday; early Monday, early Friday, late Saturday; late Monday, early Friday, late Saturday, late Sunday; late Tuesday, late Wednesday, late Thursday (Jim wouldn't remember any of this . . .). Then there was an office week where you did schedules and the lunchtime news, came in for one and finished at five.' The other technicians were jealous too, because the transmission guys were better paid. 'The buck stopped with us.'

There had been rumblings, but still the strike happened suddenly. Pay was at the heart of it, on the back of hyperinflation. Between 1975 and 1979 inflation had gone up more than 70 per cent, but the value of commercial television went up even faster. In that same four-year period Granada's share price increased by 1418 per cent and in 1979 it made a profit of £8 million. The ACTT's newspaper compared reluctance to meet pay demands to 'the Rockefellers pleading poverty'.

This retrospective from the *Observer* of 5 September 1999 cites TV executive Barry Cox:

> 'We knew we were [. . .] negotiating from a position of strength as there would be a growing market for our skills. It was totally different for people who were not just fighting for jobs, but for the survival of an industry. But clearly, since the Thatcherite laws on industrial action came in and technical changes have taken place in the UK TV industry, this kind of strike could never happen now.'

Employees voted to return for pay rises of up to 45 per cent. According to the *Observer* the Manchester branch of the ACTT 'smugly suggested that the ITCA [the Independent Television Companies Association] had been deluded in standing up against the broadcasting unions'.

Jeff Turner had just got a job at Granada when the lockout occurred. He was a skilled mechanical engineer, and when he reported for duty four months after his interview it was for a 25 per cent increase in the salary he had first accepted.

It was a triumph. But it was also the beginning of the end.

Rob recalled an editor working Sundays to get *Brideshead* finished. He was on double time, then quadruple in line with union rules, commanding staggering sums of money. If you worked into an additional overtime hour you had to be paid for the whole hour, and it was a combination of these rules that once resulted in Lee getting his best ever rate of pay: £1000 for twelve seconds (half went on tax, the rest on a piano). 'As a rule of thumb,' Lee told *Playboy*, 'we felt good if our salary surpassed that of the prime minister. It always did.' 'We had them over a barrel,' commented Rob. 'It was the last major strike that's ever been won by the unions. Margaret Thatcher had come to power the previous May, and she took note of that.'

But Jim had also taken note of Thatcher and wasn't about to back down. If you saw the monster rising up out of the slime you ran towards it, not away from it. He became increasingly politicised.

'I could feel the stupid breathless urge to win,' says Reacher in chapter two of the first draft of *Killing Floor*. And although these uncharacteristically self-psychologising words didn't survive the final cut the feeling never dies.

Here is Susan Turner grilling Reacher in *Never Go Back*:

'It's always win or lose with you, isn't it?'

'Is there a third option?'

'Does it burn you up to lose?'

'Of course.'

'It's a kind of paralysing arrogance. Normal people don't get all burned up if they lose.'

'Maybe they should,' Reacher said.

Similarly Chang in *Make Me*:

'We can't fight thirty people.' [. . .]

To which Reacher's natural response was: Why the hell not? It was in his DNA. Like breathing. He was an instinctive brawler. His greatest strength, and his greatest weakness.

Blessed or cursed, Jim Grant would, if necessary, take on the whole institution.

In 1985 Granada was voted best commercial station at Canada's Banff Film Festival and described as 'the creamiest, dreamiest television station in the world'. In the words of Raymond Fitzwalter, formerly of *World in Action*, latterly Professor of Media at the University of Salford and author of *The Dream that Died: The Rise and Fall of ITV*, it remained 'the company Sidney Bernstein built; the creation of one man, based on the idea that television could influence people for the better'.

But it was on borrowed time.

In 1986 the Peacock report recommended that television companies be obliged to sell off the hitherto unused night-time hours to the highest bidder. Money for old rope. Audiences would be small but they could buy in external programmes at rock-bottom prices. It was the beginning of the new era of twenty-four-hour broadcasting and a concomitant lowering of standards.

Voices were raised in protest. Denis Forman had been with Granada since the beginning. In the 1987 Richard Dimbleby Lecture he declared that the government no longer valued quality:

> They long to apply the principles of market forces to television [. . .]. Which conflict absolutely with the doctrine enshrined in the Television Act and the BBC Charter, namely that the prime purpose of television is to educate, inform and entertain.

It was around this time that Steve Morrison came to prominence en route to becoming chief executive in 2001. Morrison will be forever despised by Reacher fans as one of the original bad guys, the corrupt chief of police in *Killing Floor*. According to Lee, his real-life boss was 'one of those guys who rises without trace'. He was made 'director' rather than 'controller' of programmes as though the semantic distinction might protect the company from being ravaged. His brief was to sell programmes and maintain Granada's position in the network chain of supply, but it was a tacit acknowledgement that business imperatives would henceforth prevail. Morrison was notorious for playing people off against each other and delivering edicts from within the shower or the lavatory.

By 1990, writes Fitzwalter, permanent staff reduction had reached 529 in five years, or 33 per cent, and the company had moved from overmanning to exploitation. All this before the arrival in 1991 of Robinson and Allen, denounced by Monty Python's John Cleese as 'jumped-up caterers'.

Gerry Robinson, the new chief executive officer of Granada Group, and Charles Allen, his new CEO of Television, brought 'a gust of cold wind'. Did programmes have to be individually made? They demanded replicable templates. At his first meeting Robinson announced that there was no place in his brave new world for anyone who did not put profit first, second and third. Work would be contracted out. Pay would be frozen. In case anyone had missed his meaning, Allen argued that 'an act of senseless brutality' could occasionally be justified because it made others compliant.

Unless they were cut from Reacher cloth.

It turned out that 'Allen Lamaison', which had sprung fully formed to Lee's mind as the name of the bad guy in *Bad Luck and Trouble*, was a composite: a dual tribute to Charles Allen and Julia Lamaison, one of his equally unlikeable sidekicks, who in Lee's memory attracted such epithets as 'scurrilous' and 'nemesis'. He'd already killed her off once in the thinly veiled thinning-haired crooked-toothed form of Julia Lamarr in *The Visitor*, but once wasn't enough.

The voices of protest became more outspoken, and rang on into the future.

In 1998 Martin Bell, ex-BBC war correspondent, formerly of Granada:

> For 35 years *World in Action* exposed wrongdoers, shook politicians, made the unholy tremble – and on occasions even changed the law of the land. It told truths governments did not want told. It withstood corrupt politicians. [. . .] With its passing, [. . .] investigative journalism on television will scarcely happen.

In 2001 David Liddiment, also of Granada but by then ITV Director of Channels:

> Really good television has to do more [. . .] than just bring in the numbers. There has to be a margin for the unexpected, from programmes that the public has no idea it wants until it sees them [. . .]. We must lead audiences as well as be led by them.

In 2007 Jude Kelly, of the Independent Television Commission:

> The great days of Granada were pivotal in exploding the myth that the southern voice must hold sway [and in] bringing to prominence working-class voices, lifestyle and aspirations. [. . .] In less than a decade, that confidence and energy has been savagely depleted without any artistic or strategic benefit.

It was a classic tale of rise and fall. There could be no return to paradise. Freelancers were brought in and people became 'conflicted through fear'.

The culling of staff was 'brutal and violent', there were 'believers' and 'dissenters' with individuals required to commit 'acts of faith'. 'Informing, betrayal and score settling took hold,' Fitzwalter writes, 'as the new management sought to change the culture to something more submissive.' His own department corridor was 'cleansed' overnight.

Administrator Tony Brill chaired meetings between management and unions:

> I made management give reasons for redundancies. Often they did not have one and invented something because they had just been given a number to reach.

This chimes with Lee's accounts of the endgame, when he felt double-crossed by former friends (including Ashcroft and Brown) and deployed an army of spies to keep one step ahead. He had his own way of charting Granada's waning star. Once, as a lowly assistant, he had run into Mike Scott (then director of programming) in the corridor and asked how *Brideshead* was going, and Scott had replied: 'Every frame a Rembrandt.' Now the public was footing the bill for lowest-common-denominator material such as *You've Been Framed*. The artisanal skills Jim held so dear were under threat of extinction.

'There was plenty of political skulduggery behind the scenes.' Specifically Lee meant Thatcher and Murdoch colluding to do away with the 'White Book' of union rules and regulations, which opened the door to night-time programming. Jim joined the union committee in 1988, was elected deputy shop steward, and set about calculating the fifteen thousand pieces of information processed every day by the transmission team so as to negotiate 'a punitive deal' for the anti-social hours. It was 'a sensational deal', his greatest victory in the role, perhaps the greatest ever. If your attention drifted you might have thought he was talking about a contract for the next three Reachers.

The committee consisted of departmental representatives but only the steward and deputy could negotiate with management. The chairman (voted in by the entire workforce) acted as liaison, overseeing meetings and disseminating information. By the time Jim became steward in 1993 the ACTT had become BECTU (the Broadcasting, Entertainment, Cinematograph and Theatre Union). The chairman was Jeff Turner, and lighting director John Scarrott was Jim's second-in-command. Scarrott recalled Jim denouncing the night-time programmes as 'rubbish American series' and saying 'even I could write better than that'. Once when Jim entered the meeting room a member of management commented, 'the negotiator from hell'. 'He could run rings round the lot of them,' said Ian Gerrard.

Shop steward was top dog, but it was also an unpaid job on top of your paid one. For idealists and brawlers, people who weren't afraid to break a few eggs. Like Reacher, Jim would fight dirty if he had to.

'The new management wanted to destroy the union,' Lee said. They fired a shop steward on specious grounds, then fired his replacement a week later. Jim said he would be shop steward and they should try and fire him. A management guy warned he'd be out of work in a week. He lasted 'one hundred and fifteen weeks', fighting 'a desperate, rearguard battle'.

It was a long bad day at the office.

He was fighting for the legacy of the business, which they were trashing from top to bottom. But he was also fighting for the people, who were being trashed as well. He worked furiously on getting outplacements and improved severance deals, like Reacher extracting the maximum for the Shevicks in *Blue Moon*.

I'll show you what the gutter is about, he thought. He would wait till the last member of management had left the parking lot at 5 p.m. then send out his SWAT team of cleaning staff to search every bin and bring him anything that looked like a torn-up first draft of a memo. Others steamed open mail and hacked into computers. When locks were installed on the keyboards his engineering buddies whipped out the hard drives and copied them at home. The law degree gave him the confidence to act. He knew what precedent he would cite in case of a legal showdown.

He was an old-fashioned hero. You were either with him or against him. No grey area.

If ever you asked how he was, Lee was liable to say: *Can't complain*. Which is what Reacher says when the pawn-shop guy asks *how's it going* at the start of *The Midnight Line*. But you don't have to read much further to find out what happens when he's having his own bad day at the office. 'Who the hell are you?' the pawn-shop guy asks.

> 'Just a guy already having a pretty bad day. Not your fault, of course, but if asked to offer advice I would have to say it might prove a dumb idea to make my day worse. You might be the straw that breaks the camel's back.'
>
> 'You threatening me now?'
>
> 'More like a weather report. A public service. Like a tornado warning. Prepare to take cover.'

And that's before he runs up against Jimmy Rat and his bikers and the bad day becomes a very bad day – for them.

One of the more controversial executions in Reacher's career comes at the end of *The Enemy*. For the US Army, read Granada Television. For Willard, read (Pete) Williams ('I didn't want a name ending in "s"'), a technical supervisor who was 'sucked up into management' when they were purging the expensive old guard and promoting compliant collaborators:

'You ruined it for me,' I said. 'You and your damn friends.'

'Ruined what?'

'Everything.'

I stood up. Stepped back. Clicked the Beretta's safety to fire.

He stared at me.

'Goodbye, Colonel Willard,' I said.

I put the gun to my temple. He stared at me.

'Just kidding,' I said.

Then I shot him through the center of the forehead.

This is Scarrott's version of Jim Grant's final play at Granada:

Times were changing thanks to the 'jumped-up caterers', intent on stripping assets and bumping up the share price. [. . .] In early 1995 automation of Transmission Control and the transfer to Leeds was fast approaching. Jim asked if I would accompany him to his redundancy hearing. I asked if I should argue for retraining or saving his job. 'Categorically no,' he said, 'under no circumstances, I'm ready to leave anyway. I've been writing a novel and it's going well. [. . .] Anything extra I can get out of these b★★★★★★s is a bonus.'

So Scarrott pretended that Jim would fight tooth and nail to hold on to his job and only consider redundancy if the package was very good indeed. Looking back Lee would describe this attritional war of resistance as his single worst investment: *Hey, I coulda been two books in already.*

The second time Jim was fired was less dramatic than the first. He knew it was coming. It was almost as though he had willed it on himself. *I hope you're having a lovely holiday in Spain*, said the answerphone message from head of personnel Richard Wilson. *Oh, and your keycard has been cancelled. Don't bother to come in again when you get back.*

Lee described 'three dynamics of emotion':

First: I was feeling fine. I'm a creative and combative person. I knew I could win by force of personality and intelligence.

Second: I was upset for a lot of other people, especially some of the guys in the engineering section who were hopelessly institutionalised. It was going to ruin their lives.

Third: I was disgusted by the hypocrisy, by the betrayal from people within our group, by the scabbing and black-legging, often from the most vociferous union supporters.

Rob's recollection is more downbeat. When they met up at the football in January 1994 they both knew Granada was hitting the buffers. Rob thought Jim looked 'downtrodden, beaten and sad, as though he had the weight of the world on his shoulders'. He was concerned for his friend. 'There was no side to Jim, he was totally genuine. He cared about everyone in the office.' Now he was 'being beaten up on both sides'.

John Scarrott had been a Lee Child fan from the start and read all his books. He was still waiting to appear in one of them like Mike Nendick, another Granada colleague, who had a star turn as 'a small thin nervous guy in Sunday clothes' running video surveillance in *Without Fail*. Scarrott was a good name. It could only be a matter of time. Although if truth be told (and as Nendick could attest) it was a mixed blessing.

Back in the good old days of 1979 when the strike was over and the transmission team returned to work they got a 15 per cent pay rise backdated to July, then 9 per cent the following January and another 15 soon after that. Rob was uneasy about it, even in 2018. 'The miners' strike was about protecting the mines. TV was always going to carry on. The money the companies were making was huge, and we were making good money too. We were very militant, and kind of greedy.'

His words were echoed by the *Observer*:

The action was a landmark as the last hurrah of union power in the television industry. It was significant that in the opening year of Thatcherism, not only was the entire ITV network on strike, so were the printers at the *Times* and *Sunday Times* – the final act that prompted Rupert Murdoch to break the unions and take his papers to Wapping. The striking TV executives and *Sunday Times* journalists used to play football against each other at weekends.

One ITV executive recalls: 'We used to beat them hollow. They were on full pay and spent the weekend sitting around at home or in restaurants. We were earning nothing and had to find extra money during the week, driving taxis or painting houses.'

It was the lean-and-hungry approach Lee Child still advocated (and in a literal sense practised), despite his spectacular profits. If you want to be a writer, he was fond of saying, somehow managing not to sound facetious, 'I recommend you lose your job first.'

> [Reacher] believed hunger kept him sharp. He believed it stimulated creativity in the brain. Another old evolutionary legacy. If you're hungry, you work out a smarter way to get the next woolly mammoth, today, not tomorrow. (*Never Go Back*)

When asked how he spent those three months during the 1979 lockout Lee said: 'I did painting and decorating with John Brown and Shirley Temple.'

But even so he'd had a lot of time on his hands. And like Rob, he spent a lot of it in bed.

Nine months later, on 30 June 1980, Ruth Sadie Grant was born at St Mary's Hospital in Manchester.

26

The Judge

His best friend, possibly, in a guarded way,
if friendship was permission to leave things unsaid.
Night School, 2016

It wasn't just Shirley Temple. Everyone had nicknames. David Hill, who was Australian, was Skippy. Jim was known as the Judge, or sometimes Judge Dread, after the popular ska musician (or Dredd, after the comic). Partly because he had studied law and partly because of his height, which put Rob in mind of a Supreme Court judge – 'almost like Lincoln'. 'We were very interested in the Kennedy assassination and there was a judge down in Florida, Jim Garrison, who was very tall, who appears in the film *JFK*.' But partly too because of his uncompromising moral stance and the strength of his opinions. Jim cared about right and wrong.

Sometimes Rob referred to Jim as J. D. Granite, especially after Jim told him his all-time favourite single was Jimmy Ruffin's 'What Becomes of the Broken-Hearted'.

Rob didn't have a nickname. He had a reputation. Decades later he ran into a girl who had run into Ken Ashcroft at a party. 'He said you were the biggest lothario at Granada,' she said. At heart he was a romantic. He read Camus and Alain-Fournier and idolised James Dean. He had seen the 1967 film of *Le Grand Meaulnes* almost as often as Lee had seen *Mamma Mia!* He had driven down through France to Fournier's old school in Épineuil-le-Fleuriel and the supposed site of the lost domain. 'His tragic early death before the end of the first month of the Great War piles on the poignancy,' he wrote. 'Deaths, certain famous deaths, totally obsess me.' He had visited the place where James Dean crashed, twice. 'Cholame is a Reacheresque location.'

Rob's parents met in Cairo. Ralph was a rear gunner on Wellington bombers, and Betty was in the Women's Auxiliary Air Force. After the war they lived mostly in Guildford, where Rob was born, via a stint as landlords of the Onslow Arms in Cranleigh, which meant Rob was often left on his own. 'My parents were cash poor but rich in style and looks.' Rob sent me a photo taken in 1959. 'Betty has great pins.' She and her husband are seated on the same bench, his right arm holding her close, his left clutching a silver tankard and a cigarette. Her long shapely legs are crossed, elegantly sheathed in what Reacher persists in calling 'nylons'. His hair is dark and glossy, slicked back off his broad forehead, and even in black-and-white hers glows like spun gold.

The young Jim hadn't thought of his parents as good-looking or handsome or charismatic in any way. His mother looked 'like all English women did in the late 1950s', Lee said. 'You know, like Ingrid Bergman.'

There was a second photo where Ralph and Betty were standing proudly behind their six-year-old son, seated on a wooden chair. 'I never felt spoiled,' Rob writes, 'but look at me in that Tyrolean hat and wellies!'

'You should be writing Rob's biography,' Lee said.

'You have a tough job,' said Rob in turn, 'because Jim's life back then wasn't so much about exploits and adventures, more about the person he was, and has remained. He married so young.'

He was working hard too. When he went back after the strike and Jane was pregnant he worked sixty days in a row, got one day off, then worked thirty more straight. He believed in what he was doing. He was building something that would take him right through to retirement with a solid pension to back him up.

At first, because of the John Brown thing and the marriage thing, Rob and Jim weren't that close. Then Jim started calling Rob 'Bobby'. 'No one else calls me Bobby.' Rob was two years older but Jim was 'preternaturally mature', like the Grand Meaulnes, and was used to having brothers. 'He took an interest in what I was doing,' said Rob, like it was a mix of vicarious enjoyment and concern. 'He was always very gentle.'

They were born in the same decade and though it seemed like Rob was still in his teens while Jim was already in his thirties they had a lot in common. They both loved football and had seen the Beatles as their first live band and were academically lazy. Rob had Boxers Café in Guildford to Jim's Kardomah. The girls down south were classy, he said.

> My first girl was Electra. Her phone number was 1812. Her mother was a wacky artist. Her lover left his boots by her bed. They kept a donkey that wandered into her kitchen. She had a sister called Else. Unlike Jim, I only lay with one of them. Electra and I went upstairs while the others stayed downstairs listening to the Beatles' *Magical Mystery Tour*. Many years later I bumped into Else in a mountain-top restaurant in Courchevel. She told me Electra was living in an Irish commune with her kid.

It was easy to see why Jim might be attracted to Rob. Like his father Ralph, who not only looked but 'sounded like Richard Burton', he was a natural raconteur.

All his girlfriends had great names. After Electra there was French *assistante*, Denise Divia, 'very sensual, incredibly nuanced and attuned', whom he later followed to Nice ('I worked for a removal firm and delivered to Chagall and Max Ernst'), but she wanted to marry, 'and unlike Jim I was still too young'. Then after Swansea, where nominally he studied History but 'wasted three years doing drugs', there was the spectacular Hilary Aloof, 'blonde, bright and sexy'.

> We were both into Dylan and pinball. That ended and I was made redundant [from a job in publishing]. It was 1977, the summer of punk and the Jubilee. And that's when a friend told me about the job vacancy at Granada . . .

Jill, Michelle, Sara . . . 'I met Sara at the Conti [New Continental] Club in Manchester on a Tuesday, which was nurses' night. Your soles stuck to the booze-impregnated flooring while you shimmied there. We were on-off lovers for a couple of years and engaged for about a week.' But Rob thought 'Suze Rotolo' (who wasn't his girlfriend) was hard to beat as a name ('she shares the *Freewheelin'* cover with Dylan on a frozen West 4th Street in early '63'), not to mention Dylan's first love, Echo Star Helstrom (the inspiration for 'Girl from the North Country'). Like Andy Saunders, Rob was an idealist and a dreamer. His heroes were lovers, not fighters.

Rob saw Jim as a loving kind of guy. 'The best way of summing Jim up is his quiet solicitude. Even today he will talk about people we worked with. He kept an interest in all their stories.' Especially the tragic ones. It was Jim who told him about Skippy's daughter being run over when she'd gone out to a late shift at a job she'd taken when her father was laid off with stress, and how the pain of it had driven her parents apart. Then Rob got in touch to say Phil Sayer had died. Phil was a station announcer at Granada and then also on London's

Underground, the voice you heard saying 'Mind the gap' when the platform was curved. His widow had posted a message on Facebook: *Unfortunately, the train has come to a halt.* Jim recalled how Phil's mother-in-law had spilt a pan of boiling water over Phil's first child and the child was disfigured and the mother-in-law had committed suicide, and how Phil had remarried and had two more children.

Another time a schoolfriend of Rob's was dying of cancer. He was a big Lee Child fan. 'I wrote to Jim and said I've seen you're in the country on tour, could you sign a book and get it to him, and he said absolutely.' When Rob went to visit, Jeff showed him the book and it said, *For Jeff, something or other, love Lee.* 'Jeff asked, "Why has he written *love*?" And I said, "That's Jim."' Next time Rob saw the book it was on display at the funeral.

I knew what Rob meant. When I asked Lee about his primary-school teachers he told me how Mr Weaver, his old football coach, had failed to return to Cherry Orchard in September 1964 because he'd drowned while on holiday in Spain.

'I remember the good stuff too,' Lee said. 'But it's harder to sum up.' He told me how at quiet times Rob and station announcer Graham James would break out into 'Blue Moon' (the title of the book he was then working on), singing together in exquisite harmony. 'They both had beautiful voices.' Graham was older and had sung in West End musicals, so he took the main melody, with Rob doubling as a kind of vocal instrumental backing, filling in between lyrics.

I caught up with Graham near his home just south of London, where he was nursing his convalescent husband. He shuddered at the name of Paddy Irwin. 'She was horrible, an absolute tyrant.' On his very first shift she had marched in, taken one look at him and said: *Oh for Christ's sake, what've we got here?* But 'Jim was gorgeous. I adored him.' He and Rob had got Graham through the darkest period of his life, when he was splitting from his wife and family. Rob would tease him gently (John Brown brutally), but never Jim, who was empathetic: 'Jim had the gay gene.' Jim and Jane were 'earnest and learned, on a different level to the rest of us intellectually'. Their house was crammed floor to ceiling with books. He'd once asked how many books Jim read, and the answer came: 'Oh, at least one a day.' 'He was never without a book in his hand.' He wasn't 'showbizzy' like Rob. He wasn't the 'warmest, fuzziest' man you could meet. He could be lugubrious. He took some getting to know. But his brain was like blotting paper.

It was only around the time Rob and Jim joined Granada that the company first started recruiting graduates. Books weren't exactly common currency. Jim would come back from lunch carrying a magazine and John Brown would say, disparagingly, 'Got another book then, have you?' Lee remembered how much it annoyed him.

Jim the controller didn't mind stepping up as the word of God. But he also liked being part of a well-oiled machine. Indispensable. Responsible. A star team player. As a writer he could go four or five days without leaving his apartment and seven or eight without saying a word to another human being, and he missed working in an intensely social, close-knit group – which was why he had Reacher 'put the old unit back together' in *Bad Luck and Trouble*, conceived ten years to the day after he was sacked. They'd had a lot of fun in presentation, a lot of it at the expense of others, much as it was back at school. 'We were gossipy and bitchy, classic TV folk,' said Rob cheerily.

Jim was friendly with everyone. But his affection for Rob was unique and enduring, like the perfect emotional equivalence described in Montaigne's essay 'Of Friendship': 'a knot so hard, so fast and durable', 'no commerce or business depending on the same, but itself'.

I showed Lee a photograph of the two of them together, taken by Marilyn Gallagher. He said: 'Look at the difference in our eyes.' I agreed that Rob's expression was open and untroubled, Jim's more watchful and guarded. But Lee saw himself as 'manipulative', like he was forever calculating what he could get out of a situation. Rob was 'smart' and 'attractive', with 'tremendous charisma', a product of the home counties who 'breezed through life with absolute confidence'; his own 101 per cent confidence was mere bravado by comparison, which perhaps explained his need to assert it so fiercely. The Midlands was so recent a concept, 'so amorphous', and so invisible to the rest of the country, that it bestowed no secure sense of identity or belonging.

Later I showed Rob the same photograph. 'You can see the closeness between us,' he said, warmly.

The pattern of shifts meant their paths might cross only at handover but in 1981 Jim was promoted and Rob wasn't, so there was a golden period when Rob was working as Jim's glamorous assistant. Those were the halcyon days and the two friends would always look out for each other. In 1983 Rob ran the marathon to raise money for a children's hospital. Jim sponsored him £2 a mile (more than anyone else) and on his triumphant return presented him with a cheque for £52. The same year they had a bet on which team would finish higher in the Football League: Spurs or Villa. When Villa drew 1–1 away to Liverpool on 7 May Jim knew he was doomed. He wrote out a cheque for £200. Rob was costing him a lot of money.

Except he wasn't. Thirty-five years later in the Royal Hotel in Kirkby Lonsdale, Rob whipped the crumpled cheque out of his pocket: candy-floss pink, the turquoise-blue ink smudged almost beyond legibility, drawn on the Deansgate branch of the National Westminster Bank and signed James D. Grant on behalf of J D & Mrs J H Grant. When he and Lee Child met up again, his old friend said how much he appreciated Rob never cashing that cheque. It was serious money for a man with a wife, a child and a mortgage, however generous the pay deal.

Tottenham Hotspur finished fourth in the table and Aston Villa sixth. For the two friends it had gone down to the wire. Rob got so worked up he thought he was going to lose it, in more ways than one. Jim was cooler. It was an era of unsurpassed sporting interest in the UK because of the success of English teams in Europe. Liverpool won the European Cup in 1977, 1978, 1981 and 1984. In 1979 and 1980 it was the turn of Nottingham Forest, then in 1982, gloriously, as immortalised in *Die Trying*, Aston Villa. The only blot in the record book was 1983, which went to the Germans – Hamburg, which city has a suitably shady role in *Night School*.

'It was the pinnacle,' Rob said. In 1981 Villa won the League using only fourteen players all season, including Jim's all-time hero Gordon Cowans. The manager was 'granite-faced' Ron Saunders. Jim loved Saunders, 'one of his quiet, monolithic heroes like Clint Eastwood, who never said anything'. As a sidebar there was Botham, and the legendary rivalry between middle-distance runners Coe and Ovett. Coe was Rob's idol (he followed him to the Moscow Olympics), but Jim was drawn to the rebel figure and dismissed Coe as 'a goody two-shoes'.

Those were the pool years at the Stables, inspired by Thorburn and his maximum break at the Crucible, the first ever 147 at a World Championship. But Jim didn't have very good hand–eye coordination. Or in Rob's words – 'I was OK and he was crap.'

It was hardly surprising that when I went to Manchester the city should seem so steeped in romance, not least down by the River Irwell, with its railway line and bridges and warehouses and cranes silhouetted against the sunset and blurry in the misty morning light. It was easy to picture Rob and Jim working there and to imagine the creative buzz.

Rob had sent photos of the old Granada Studios so even for me it felt like going back. There was poignancy in the ghost signs, barely visible above the main entrance and at the top of the high section of the building, particularly since Lee had once told me that even after Granada closed in 2013 they could not be removed. GTV had hosted the first television appearance by the Beatles, and David Bowie had starred on the last *Marc* show, around the time Jim joined and – Rob informed me – 'a couple of weeks before Marc Bolan was killed in a car crash near Barnes Common in London'. Bowie had stayed over in Sidney Bernstein's penthouse flat.

In July 2018 the main building was still standing, though ragged chunks were being torn out of the art deco annexe across the street, due to be replaced by a luxury hotel. There were guards proactively preventing any drift towards the *Coronation Street* set: *You can't come in here, miss, it's private property.* There was a café in the foyer of the Atherton Street entrance and from my table I could see the lift doors painted with their iconic black block-print arrows, pointing up and down, and the wide wooden staircase with its chrome handrail swooping down towards the canteen, where Little Elsie would be perched behind the till: '*That's you and me straight, luv*, she would say, once you'd settled up for your meal.' But I wasn't allowed in until I met Kerry Clark, onsite project manager for developers Allied London. Kerry was a Granada fan with a strong sense of history and had secured permission for the new mixed-use building to include a professional film studio for hire. The canteen was now an open workspace, and the revamped studios were state-of-the-art, but the old control rooms and smaller vacated suites resembled an apocalyptic scene from a dystopian movie: smashed consoles, muted screens, exposed circuit boards, loose-hanging plugs and thick multi-coloured bunches of ripped-out wires. It was hot, airless, and deathly silent.

Jim and Rob both moved house in 1981. Jim and Jane were living at 47 The Circuit in Alderley Edge, on the outer fringe of the area now known as the playground of footballers and millionaires. The house was situated at one end of a road shaped like an oval race track so had a big garden to play in and was an easy commute to Wilmslow Prep, where Ruth would be enrolled. A photograph taken by Rob that summer shows a heavily bearded impossibly long-legged Jim leaning back against a tree trunk ('like he's having a day off from fronting the Eagles'), both arms around Jane, drawing her close. The still-new parents are tanned and smiling in the dappled sunlight. Jane is wearing shorts and a white T-shirt; she is slim-waisted, her shorter hair swept behind her ears. Sometimes Jim would take the train to work rather than drive so he could eavesdrop on what people were saying about the previous night's television.

Rob had a small place in Didsbury: 'lots of musicians, students and singles' (like Tony Wilson, aka Mr Manchester, a one-time Granada employee who became boss of Factory Records). Previously he had lived in Rusholme near the university, where his landlord was Jim Roberts, a film editor at GTV. Once they hosted a party that the Grants attended: a multi-media louche affair, with a music room and video room 'plus my bedroom with its two pinball tables'. Rob was living it up. 'You were the guy,' Jim said when they met up again, 'who bought a house [for £25,000] and a car [a Scirocco Storm for £4000] in the same year.'

About two years after Jim, Rob became a controller by default. But that only strengthened his resolve to move on. Jim was happy in a way Rob wasn't, and even after he made it as Lee Child insisted – though Rob didn't believe him – he would swap it all to be back curled up in his chair at Granada. If Granada still existed and hadn't been trashed. But Jim was also more cautious. They both applied for jobs at new cable TV company Screensport and both got them, but only Rob was dissatisfied enough to take a 50 per cent pay cut. He, like Gallagher, felt Presentation was heading nowhere except for a dead end.

Gallagher had left in 1980. People said they couldn't understand how he could walk out on a well-paid job-for-life. Which it turned out it wasn't, not even for Jim Grant, who lasted another fifteen years. But during the strike Gallagher had sold a play to the BBC and picked up some novelisations, which persuaded him he could make a go of it.

He'd bought a 16mm Beaulieu camera with his earnings and set about shooting his first film. Jim offered to handle the lights. The Piccadilly Hotel let them shoot in the bar and after Jim had lit the scene he and Jane and Rob sat in as extras. Joan Humphries lent her place for night interiors and then the whole department decamped for a week to an old timber shooting lodge in the Lake District that had been built for the Earl of Lonsdale for the visit of Kaiser Wilhelm. People would drive up between shifts to muck in, bringing ribs of beef and malt whisky and wine.

Gallagher found it hard to picture Jim in the controller's chair. But he knew he himself wouldn't have been any good at it. He wasn't even a good assistant, he said. One time he put out a thirty-second cat-food commercial instead of an ad for a chocolate bar – *Kit Kat, Kitekat* – and cost the company £5000. His aim had always been to navigate his way into drama, but he soon realised all the serving controllers had washed up in Presentation from other jobs. The tipping point was when he applied to become a director and was told he'd have to start as a trainee floor manager in the studio. Even once he'd worked his way up again he'd be lumbered with grunt work, as the showcase dramas were now being used as carrots to lure in big-name freelancers.

Jim was too comfortable to care. He had landed in the department without any bigger plan, and it would take a tectonic shift to jolt him onto a new trajectory. But he agreed about the impossibility of sideways movement. If they'd had it in them, Granada might have spotted the larger-than-life creative streak in him.

At his leaving party Rob was presented with a framed poster of the 1984 Olympics. Everyone signed it. But Jim's message stood out. Partly because it had clearly been written with a ruler, perhaps the very ruler Paddy Irwin had used to rap him over the knuckles. Rob hadn't noticed, to him it was so routine as to be invisible, but he knew immediately why it was. 'Jim must have signed it when he was amending the next day's schedule. The use of the ruler was originated by Ken Ashcroft. There was something reassuring about the process and it became an idiosyncratic detail peculiar to that job.' The CCR had its arcane discipline and rituals, just like the army.

But set aside the ruler and the fastidious style. What really stood out was what Jim had written. Which was astoundingly simple.

What can I say?
I love you.

I was tempted to ask why Jim had used the word 'love'. But I already knew. And I already knew what Rob would say. *That's Jim.*

The strength of feeling reminded me of Stingo, from Lee's all-time favourite novel, *Sophie's Choice* (1979):

I adored Jack Brown. There are friends one makes at a youthful age in whom one simply rejoices, for whom one possesses a love and loyalty mysteriously lacking in the friendships made in after-years, no matter how genuine.

In 2018 Rob wrote to me that you could 'pretty much sum up his feelings about Jim' in these lines from the Bob Dylan song 'I'll Remember You':

There's some people that
You can't forget
Even though you only met 'em
One time or two
In the end
My dear sweet friend
I'll remember you.

They hadn't lived in each other's pockets. They had met only a handful of times since going their separate ways.

Later he sent a postscript apologising for 'mangling the lyrics'. Which he had a bit, but I liked them just fine as they were.

I didn't need to ask why he would use those words. I knew. *That's Rob.*

27

Like Winning the Nobel

Being a father seemed both straightforward
and infinitely complex.
Never Go Back, 2013

The day Ruth was born was the day everything changed. From the moment he held her in his arms, he knew two things more clearly than he had ever known anything in the twenty-five years of his life. From that moment onwards all he would ever want was for her to be OK. And from that moment until his dying day he would feel responsible.

Maybe it would be difficult, but it wasn't complicated. Nor was it new. Like the desire for revenge, what he was feeling was something humans had felt since the beginning of time. But it was a first for him. And even though he was feeling something universal, it was also uniquely personal, in the same way his daughter herself was unique. Uniquely his and Jane's, but also uniquely herself.

'Sadie' came from the Jewish tradition of naming a baby after the last family member to have died, which happened to be Jane's grandmother. 'Ruth' was the only first name they could agree on.

Jim was present at the birth. All twelve hours of it. 'Stanley [the springer spaniel] was at home on his own and didn't even pee on the carpet. He did really well.' The year 1980 was 'on that glorious cusp

303

between old and new', and Jim chain-smoked in the delivery room. He recalls three visceral responses on first seeing his new daughter: relief, joy, and 'the almost auditory sensation of the prison door slamming shut'.

'It'll be fine,' he told his anxious wife throughout the pregnancy. He was being supportive, but statistically he also believed it to be true, despite the medical profession categorising his twenty-seven-year-old wife as an 'elderly primigravida'. But as the baby's head crowned he experienced an instant of heart-stopping panic. The statistics had let him down: 'There was purple goo everywhere and the top of her head looked exactly like an exposed brain.' It wasn't going to be fine at all. He cradled the newborn in his arms and wondered how he was going to break the news to Jane. Then the midwife cleaned Ruth up, revealing a full head of long black hair, 'like a style, like she'd just come out of the salon'. She was perfect.

Only trouble was, he felt like he'd been sent down for the next eighteen years. Till later, when he realised it was a life sentence.

He hadn't looked forward to becoming a father. He hadn't not looked forward to it either. It just wasn't something he had planned for. Nor had Jane. For him, the switch had been flicked on that fateful day in St Mary's Hospital. For Jane it had happened a year earlier, when she had gone to visit a friend who had recently become a mother. She left the house as one person and came back another. But once that wire had been tripped there was no going back, for either of them.

Luckily he felt equipped 'with the minutiae of being a parent' thanks to the arrival of his youngest brother Andrew in 1968, when he was fourteen years old (and Stanley, ten years later). The birth of Rex and Audrey's third son, three years his junior, had mostly passed him by. The only thing he remembered was that his parents had asked Richard and James what to call the new addition to the household, and when they said 'Goliath', had promptly named him David instead.

Audrey was in her early forties when her fourth child was born. She legitimately qualified as an elderly primigravida and in those days her situation was deemed 'grotesque'. But Andrew was 'a cute kid' and 'a happy experience'. Even at the precognitive stage his personality seemed set. He was stubborn and obstinate and chafed against his parents just like Jim did, as though it was innate, rather than merely wilful. Which was a relief to both of them, but especially Jim, who had felt so estranged from the family that he sometimes wondered if he could be a changeling. Andrew was proof, physically and psychologically, that they really did share the same DNA. Rex and Audrey came to fear the return visits of their renegade second son, because Andrew so stubbornly and obstinately copied all his habits.

When Andrew grew up he studied English at Sheffield and hung out at the drama studio and got married and ran a touring theatre company before getting divorced and moving to Chicago to marry an American historical novelist and become a full-time thriller writer. The two brothers remained close and from 2016 shared adjacent properties in Wyoming, like a couple of out-of-state guys come to find themselves: 'We get those, from time to time. Maybe they're writing a novel' (*The Midnight Line*). 'It's tough to evaluate,' Lee said, 'because I am very self-reliant, but that question of who you would turn to if the chips were down – if you needed a thousand dollars and an unregistered handgun and a trip to the border – that would be him.' Conversely, he felt responsible for Andrew, like he did for Ruth, who was two years closer to her uncle in age.

'I remember when Jim got a new baby,' said Alison, his barn-dance date from Handsworth Wood. She wasn't talking about Ruth. It was like she'd been thrown back fifty years and was even then acknowledging his fatherly disposition. It was true that Jim had tried to compensate for the lack of warmth in his own boyhood by lavishing plenty on his baby brother. He remembered taking a ten-year-old Andrew to see

Star Wars in 1978, in London's Leicester Square, never imagining that one day he would return to attend not just one, but two red-carpet premieres of movies based on books he had written.

A photograph taken outside Underwood Road shows a fifteen-year-old Jim wearing a maroon polo shirt and sea-green fisherman's jumper and an infant Andrew in a cable-knit cardigan, both beaming. But it's Richard, wearing a tweed jacket and also smiling (but not beaming), who's holding the baby. A second, taken four years later under a hazy blue sky against a background of wooded mountains in Switzerland, shows a taller, lankier Jim, wearing a slim-fit blue T-shirt with some kind of Hawaiian-vibe all-over pattern and aviator-style sunglasses, still smiling, his hair turning up on his shoulders, his right hand resting on Andrew's gleaming golden head. The five-year-old, who would grow to the same height, stands level with the top of his big brother's low-slung jeans. It was a Grant family holiday, Lee said, except Richard wasn't there.

Andrew calls Lee, Jim. Richard and David still call him James, like their parents did.

When Jim became a father for real he brought a box of American Baby Ruth candy bars into work. The Snickers-style bar had been named after President Cleveland's daughter and launched when baseball hall-of-famer Babe Ruth was at the top of his game. Jim, like Reacher, was well versed in trivia about the American presidents, though he had never used one of their names as an alias.

The Gallaghers gave 'Lee Baby' an inscribed book of fairy tales, and when their own daughter was born the Grants reciprocated with an illustrated copy of *Alice in Wonderland*. Steve recalled the new father telling the story of how on a trip to America to show off their precious new acquisition to relatives the flight attendant had run through the safety routine about what to do if the plane ditched in the ocean and then blithely announced, 'and for your entertainment, our in-flight movie is *Jaws*'.

Reacher had 'never fathered any children' (*Tripwire*). 'He knew very little about children' (*A Wanted Man*). Until *Never Go Back*.

> Fatherhood was up there as one of the most commonplace male experiences in all of human history. But to Reacher it had always seemed unlikely. Just purely theoretical. Like winning the Nobel Prize, or playing in the World Series, or being able to sing. Possible in principle, but always likely to pass him by. A destination for other people, but not for him. He had known fathers, starting with his own, and his grandfathers, and his childhood friends' fathers, and then some of his own friends, as they got married and started to raise families. Being a father seemed both straightforward and infinitely complex. Easy enough on the surface. Underneath, simply too immense to worry about. So generally it seemed to come out as a day-to-day thing. Hope for the best, one foot in front of the other. His own father had always seemed in charge. But looking back, it was clear he was just making it up as he went along.

Much like writing a book. Lee was once asked at a Q&A whether being a father would have changed Reacher. 'Yes,' he answered, 'he would have felt responsible.'

It was clear that Reacher didn't know about children the way he didn't know about cars. He wasn't a car owner or a father, but *he knew someone who was*.

In a 2018 interview for *The Big Thrill* Lee cited biographer G. K. Chesterton's argument as to why Charles Dickens 'wasn't just a hack': '"Dickens did not write what the audience wanted. Dickens wanted what the audience wanted."' Lee felt an affinity with his nineteenth-century forebear: 'I'm a completely normal person in every possible way – except that I can also write. Whatever interests other completely normal people – of which there are billions – interests me too, and I write about it.'

The claim to normality is always suspect. But presumably here it encompasses all those people who are born without having asked to be born, who mostly die in ways over which they have little or no control, who to a greater or lesser extent are motivated by lust, lucre or loathing, and who at some stage are likely, perhaps without having planned it, to become parents.

The fact is that a Reacher novel has never been written by someone who wasn't a father. Such a thing simply doesn't exist. So the unmistakable quality of fatherliness that permeates the novels is not only not surprising, but inescapable.

Most of the books place children at risk, and most of those children are daughters – as in 2019's *Blue Moon*.

It starts at the beginning, with *Killing Floor*.

> 'It was a nightmare,' Hubble said. [. . .] 'He said it wouldn't be just me who got cut up. It would be Charlie too. [. . .] Then after we were dead, which of the children would he start with? Lucy or Ben?'

Hard reading for Lee's old Granada colleague, Ian Gerrard.

Ian had sent me a photograph of the title page of a UK first edition of *Killing Floor*, with a dedication by the author. The book was inscribed: 'For Ben and Lucy, the origin of the names, Lee Child' (an accompanying note read: 'Feel free to buy hundreds of copies, love Jim'). One day at work Jim had asked what Ian's son and daughter were called, 'because he always had a problem with names'.

'They were a nice pair of kids,' Reacher said, when he met Lucy and Ben in Margrave. 'Polite and quiet.' You know it's only a matter of time before he has to save them. Twenty-three more chapters of reading time, to be precise, when he finds them fast asleep on the floor of the bad guys' warehouse, 'wide open and innocent like only sleeping children can be'.

> The children had been worrying the hell out of me. [. . .] I'd thought it through a thousand times. [. . .] I'd always come up with some kind of bad outcome. What the staff colleges call unsatisfactory results. I'd always come up with the children splattered all over the place by the big shotguns. Children and shotguns don't mix.

In Reacher's world children and shotguns mixed far too often.

It all ends well. No ghoulish splattering, just happy verbs exploding on the page like celebratory confetti. Ben and Lucy are 'scooped up', like little children always are, except when they're 'swung up' instead, and there's a collective outbreak of hugging and kissing and laughing and dancing and back-slapping. The closest Reacher gets to ice creams in the park.

When children are involved, it's all right to express emotion.

> He kept his eyes wide open so he wouldn't have to see it, but he saw it anyway. Not Marines this time, not hard men camped out in the heat to do a job, but soft people, women and children, small and smaller, camped out in a city park to watch fireworks, vaporising and bursting into a hazy pink dew like his friends had done thirteen years before. [. . .]
>
> They were all staring at him. He realised tears were rolling down his cheeks and splashing onto his shirt.
>
> 'I'm sorry,' he said.

The closest Reacher gets to PTSD. This is *Die Trying*. The plot is driven by the imperative to recover a kidnapped daughter.

Tripwire is dedicated to 'my daughter, Ruth. Once the world's greatest kid, now a woman I'm proud to call my friend.'

David Highfill was Lee's editor at G. P. Putnam's Sons for the first six Reacher novels, his first editor ever. For him, the scenes with the ageing parents in *Tripwire*, desperate for news of their long-lost soldier son, are among the most poignant Lee has written. It breaks Reacher's heart that they may have to 'live out the short balance of their lives with whatever dignity they could find in being just two out of the tens of millions of parents who gave up their children to the night and the fog swirling through a ghastly century'. Spooling back two decades these two characters were still achingly present in David's mind. 'I know these people,' he said. 'I've been there, I've seen them, I care deeply about them.' It was only a handful of short passages in a manuscript of 148,629 words, but when David told Lee how he felt, Lee said: 'Yes, that's exactly what the book's about.'

Reacher is 'huge, gorgeous, clever', Highfill said. 'You think Sherlock Holmes is smart? But there's always a point at which his emotions are engaged, and that's what grabs the reader, when Reacher's emotions come into play.'

His emotions are fully engaged in *Echo Burning*, especially by Ellie, Carmen's six-year-old daughter, with her little short steps and her hair lit from behind, glowing 'gold and red like an angel'. The first time Reacher sees her she is being picked up from school, and her mother 'skips' round the car to greet her.

> [Carmen] scooped her up in a wild hug. Spun her around and around. Her little feet windmilled outward and her blue lunch box swung and hit her mother on the back. Reacher could see the child laughing and tears in Carmen's eyes.

Ellie immediately adopts Reacher. She insists on him carrying her up to bed. 'She held up her arms, more or less vertical. He paused a beat and then swung her into the air and settled her in the crook of his elbow. Kissed her cheek, gently.'

Asleep, she is vulnerable, 'innocently barrelling on toward the day' when her 'little life' would change forever.

> [The nightlight] showed the child sprawled on her back with her arms thrown up around her head. She had kicked off her sheet and the rabbit T-shirt had ridden up and was showing a band of plump pink skin at her waist. Her hair was tumbled over the pillow. Long dark eyelashes rested on her cheeks like fans. Her mouth was open a fraction.

The book writer may be six-foot-four and a man, but must be able to see through the eyes of a little girl who, when trying to escape her kidnapper, has to stand on the points of her carefully buckled shoes and strain and stretch to 'reach' the door handle. Or deduce from the absence of toy bears with their stuffing out and chipped dolls with their arms off that the eight-year-old Jade from *The Hard Way* had not been abducted at all.

Here is Reacher reading clues in the kidnap vehicle of *A Wanted Man*:

> There was a sparkly pink hair band on the floor. Not the kind of thing an adult woman would wear, in Reacher's opinion. There was a small fur animal in a tray on the console. Most of its stuffing was compressed to flatness, and its fur was matted, as if it was regularly chewed. One daughter, Reacher figured. Somewhere between eight and twelve years old. He couldn't be more precise than that. He knew very little about children.

What he knows is they belong in the category of small creatures that need protecting.

Ellie Greer is 'a smart kid', and like Reacher, good at hide and seek.

Ruth was a smart kid too. When she was twelve she made her first solo trip by rail, from Oxenholme in the Lake District to Wilmslow, south of Manchester, to visit a friend. Two hours after he put her on the train Jim got a call from the friend's mother to say she hadn't arrived. The train had decided to skip a load of stations and go straight on to Poole or Bournemouth, way off on the south coast. In that split second Jim thought: *I would give anything for another day with her.* He rang the rail company saying *What the hell?* The staff said not to worry, they'd made an announcement telling passengers to change at Preston and then at Manchester Victoria. When it turned out she was fine, his euphoria was commensurate with his fear. Not just because he would get another day with her, but because he knew 'she was smart, a survivor'.

Eleven years and twelve books after *Tripwire*, *Worth Dying For* is again dedicated to 'Ruth, my daughter'. In context, this is the most explicit of Lee's titles.

Here Dorothy Coe recalls the day her child went missing:

> There's a kind of crazy period at first, when everyone is mad and worried but can't bring themselves to believe the worst. You know, a couple of hours, maybe three or four, you think she's playing somewhere, maybe out picking flowers, she's lost track of time, she'll be home soon, right as rain. No one had cell phones back then, of course. Some people didn't even have regular phones. Then you think the girl has gotten lost, and everyone starts driving around, looking for her. Then it goes dark, and then you call the cops.

Reacher 'figured there was nothing worse than the Coe family story. Nothing at all.'

In *Never Go Back* Reacher endures his own what-if parental nightmare:

Reacher dreamed about the girl, at a much younger age, maybe three, chubby not bony, dressed in the same outfit but miniaturised, with tiny laceless tennis shoes. They were walking on a street somewhere, her small hand soft and warm in his giant paw, her little legs going like crazy, trying to keep up, and he was glancing over his shoulder all the time, anxious about something, worried about how she was going to run if she had to, in her laceless shoes, and then realising he could just scoop her up in his arms, and run for her, maybe for ever, her fragrant weightless body no burden at all, and relief flooded through him, and the dream faded away, as if its job was done.

It helps to be father-sized.

The author draws parallels between the teenage Sam and Reacher to tease his hero (and reader) with the semblance of a genetic relationship. But she's more like Lee himself. Thin and bony with a 'quizzical half-smile, as if her life was full of petty annoyances best tolerated with patience and goodwill', and a mother defined by 'her whole stressed-out martyr shtick'.

Reacher watched her as he walked. All legs and arms, knees and elbows, the jean jacket, the pants, the new blue T-shirt, matching shoes, no socks, no laces, the hair like summer straw, halfway down her back, the eyes, and the smile. Fatherhood. Always unlikely. Like winning the Nobel Prize, or playing in the World Series. Not for him.

But there is something that binds Sam to Reacher more intimately than any accident of birth. Like him, she doesn't fear 'the howling wolf'. The hobo demon is calling her, just like it called Jim Grant to write *Killing Floor* and Jack Reacher to head to Georgia in search of Blind Blake. The kinship of the clan.

Millions of years ago, Reacher hypothesises (as Lee Child might), 'a gene evolved where every generation [. . .] had at least one person who had to wander', so as to mix up the gene pool (Major Turner is unimpressed).

> 'I think ninety-nine of us grow up to love the campfire, and one grows up to hate it. Ninety-nine of us grow up to fear the howling wolf, and one grows up to envy it. And I'm that guy.'

Fathering, possibly. Fatherhood? Like being able to sing. *Not for him.* *Gone Tomorrow* isn't dedicated to Ruth. But she makes an anonymous appearance, twice, as the girl with the rat terrier walking south on Broadway towards 22nd Street. She enters the high-rise apartment building where the Grant family used to live just as the police turn up in the black Crown Vic the Grant family used to drive. But this time it's the girl who saves the father figure rather than the other way round: it's when Reacher turns around to reassure the barking dog that he spots the car in the corner of his eye, and he knows when he sits on the low brick wall in front of the building that the police won't shoot for fear of collateral damage. Ruth really did have a rat terrier, called Mr B., so oblivious to rats that they ran right underneath its belly without it turning a hair. Sometimes Mr B. would send Ruth's dad Father's Day cards, thanking him for the treats and tummy rubs.

People are weighed in the balance by reference to children. In *Without Fail* there is nothing more important to cleaners Julio and Anita, which puts them in the clear; Nendick and his wife don't have any, which flags up a warning. Carmen's wicked mother-in-law gave Ellie to her kidnappers. 'My grandmother would have died before she let her grandchildren get taken away,' Reacher said. But Lee's great aunt Hettie got taken away as a girl. She was the oldest of eight and the parents were struggling to make ends meet. So when childless relatives came calling, the Scotts gave them Hettie and one of her siblings – 'it was common practice at the time'. Hettie ended up living with her cousin Millicent Vandeleur, known as Millie; neither of them married, because after the war there weren't enough men to go round. They'd been given up to the night and the fog.

Motherhood done right conferred a special quality on a woman, gave her 'a weight [. . .], a gravity, a heft, not physical, but somewhere deep inside her' (*The Hard Way*). Made her someone you might spend more than a day with, maybe even a week. Which was all Jim had envisaged spending with Jane, back when the two of them first met.

The domestic fantasy is evanescent but seductive, linked to sowing seeds and growing things.

> He liked California. He figured he could live there, if he lived anywhere. It was warm, and no one knew him. He could have a dog. They could have a dog. He pictured Turner, maybe in a back yard somewhere, pruning a rose or planting a tree. (*Never Go Back*)

> And there was Kate Lane's dream to think about, the new extended family farming together, growing hay, leaching the old chemicals out of the Norfolk soil, planting wholesome vegetables five years in the future. (*The Hard Way*)

The conjunction of Lee and a vegetable patch seemed as likely as that of Reacher and a sparkly pink hair band, though he had once taken a chainsaw to a tree that was blocking his view of Colorado's Diamond Peak from his mezzanine office in Wyoming. But Jane loved gardening. Perhaps Lee had *Jane Grant's dream* to think about when in 2012 he bought a 1920s arts-and-crafts-style house with a farm and a bluebell wood in Sussex, and employed a land manager to do 'the agricultural work': 'Organic wildflower hay mostly. Also hedges, paths, ponds.' His anniversary card that year was simple (and looked distinctly like he'd written it with a ruler):

> 37 years!!
> 32 acres!!

The acreage had since been increased to 45, so as to incorporate a whole postcode.

Lee's dream was to retire to a beach and grow a beard (he hated having to shave, but felt he owed it to his readers to look smart).

Jim and Jane decided against having a second child. They liked being parents, though it was hard work. But they hadn't much liked being siblings. Why inflict one of those on their beloved daughter? And Ruth was perfect. Why tempt fate?

But Lee liked kids. 'I used to have one of these,' he said, posing for a photograph in Harrogate with a mystified little girl in his arms and managing not to sound like a politician. His face lit up when he heard news of his friends' children and he never forgot their names. Names mattered. There were plenty of dogs and babies called Reacher, but it worked both ways. Lee had named a barely literate motel owner in *Never Go Back* after the erudite John Claughton, and I couldn't help wondering if he might also have named Reacher's putative daughter after Claughton's autistic youngest son. He hadn't. But the metaphoric resonance was there all the same, so then I thought it must be writerly empathy at a subconscious level or some kind of sixth sense. John had sent me a contemporary photograph and the hair like summer straw and the new blue T-shirt and the quizzical half-smile were firmly in evidence. 'Sam worships Lee,' John said. Lee had got on his wavelength from the moment they met and had sent him a card describing him as his 'favourite Englishman'. 'I really like Sam,' Lee said. 'He's the only person I know who says exactly what he thinks.'

'One's first response,' Claughton said thoughtfully, 'is that Lee is quite austere and remote and difficult, but that couldn't be further from the truth.'

When Ruth Sadie Grant was born Jim bought his first camera. There's a picture of Grandma Scrafton from Otley cradling the newborn, peaceful in a pink babygro, her eyes firmly closed, a serious, half-frown on her face, and one of Rex in a festive red shirt and patterned tie, where Ruth is lying in his arms and waving her open hands about, as though on the point of waking to her grandfather's dazzling smile.

Janet Brown had visited Jane at St Mary's when Ruth was one day old. She sent me a faded photograph of the young family grouped around the table of her former cottage in Worsley. Little Ruthie, as Janet called her, is nestled on her father's lap, in the crook of his elbow, his arms locked loosely around her, her chubby left hand on his big left paw, her right raised as though in greeting. Not even Jim was bony then. Their faces look similar in shape, and their hair is similarly styled. He is looking down at his smiling daughter as though about to kiss her on the cheek and his beard is brushing against her head. Ruth is wearing a red-and-white checked summer frock with little puffed sleeves edged with ribbon or braid, with a built-in open collar and knotted red tie. She has *trust and merriment in her eyes*. She was *worth dying for*.

Jane is seated opposite, in a checked shirt with straight elbow-length sleeves over a white T-shirt, with a weight and a gravity and a heft about her, looking across at her husband and child, smiling. His hair and beard dated the photo, Lee said. It was late in the fall of 1980. They were preparing to shoot the army scenes of *Brideshead Revisited* and the make-up team needed to practise 1940s military-style haircuts. 'I was so busy I decided to volunteer, and ended up almost bald.'

'I'm very sentimental about my daughter,' Lee told *SAGA* magazine in 2016.

> I love her. I think she's the best ever, like any father. She's always entranced me, partly because obviously she's DNA-related to me, but what I always loved, even from the earliest months, was the sensation that she had a private existence that I didn't know about, which, of course, escalates exponentially once they start school and stuff. She is me, in a way, but is also so radically different and knows things that I don't.

'Like Spanish,' he told me.

Privately I suspected he would have passed on his own fair share of knowledge too, like Reacher, who in *Never Go Back* figured that 'if the kid had been his, he would have had a discussion. No point in being a pedant, unless you got it exactly right.' This when inwardly critiquing Sam's description of Shrago's ears as hexagons when 'they were irregular polygons, more accurately'.

Little Ruthie, aka 'Toot' to her father, is sentimental too. 'Doof' is her 'best buddy', 'the world's greatest father'; he teaches her 'boy stuff' and she restocks his larder (Rice Krispies, tinned peaches, pineapple chunks, Coke) – 'Welcome back! Come see me whenever you want. Love you!'

On day one, Jim knew his daughter '100 per cent'. He knew 'everything about her', everything there was to know. But with each day that passed she blossomed into an independent being and gradually 'it tailed off', and then more quickly, and he knew her less and less and she became more and more of an entrancing mystery. It was the inverse of all other relationships. He wasn't sad about it.

Sometimes it felt like sitting out in the sun. Sometimes like looking out through the bars. But he'd sown the seed. And now he would watch it grow.

28

Ruskin's View

I looked out of the window. Georgia.
Killing Floor, 1997

In 1991 the Grant family moved away from Alderley Edge to Kirkby Lonsdale in Carnforth, in the South Lakeland district of Cumbria.

Maybe Jane felt more at home there. Her parents had lived at Stoop House on Back Lane when Professor Shiren spent his sabbatical year of 1983–4 at the University of Lancaster and they liked the place so much they rented it again in 1998, for Christmas and New Year. They saw it as a typical English village, like something off a chocolate box or postcard. They loved the brass band. Lee liked the brass band too, but thought Kirkby Lonsdale belonged in EPCOT (Experimental Prototype Community of Tomorrow) at Disney World in Florida.

The Shirens were not alone in being seduced by Kirkby Lonsdale, documented in the Domesday Book as a 'cherchibi' – a village with a church. The view over the Lune Valley from Church Brow, a short walk from 10 Abbotsgate where Jim and Jane lived, was described by art critic John Ruskin in 1875 as 'one of the loveliest in England, therefore in the world'. The tourist information plaque lauds 'a gentle panorama of river, meadow, woods and hills in almost perfect balance', as though the natural landscape were already a work of art.

Ruskin first encountered the scene in a watercolour painting of 1822 by Turner, which became known as *Ruskin's View*. He deemed it 'priceless', but in 2012 it sold at auction for £217,250. 'I do not know in all my own country, still less in France or Italy, a place more naturally divine.'

It was looking out over this idyllic landscape that Lee Child wrote his debut novel, set in fictional Margrave in real Georgia, roughly four thousand miles away and a place he'd never been. It was a feat of imagination that still amazed his New York editor David Highfill.

> I looked out of the window. Georgia. I saw rich land. Heavy, damp red earth. Very long and straight rows of low bushes in the fields. Peanuts, maybe. Belly crops, but valuable to the grower. Or to the owner. Did people own their land here? Or did giant corporations? I didn't know. [. . .]
>
> After maybe a half mile I saw two neat buildings, both new, both with tidy landscaping. The police station and the fire house. They stood alone together, behind a wide lawn with a statue, north edge of town. Attractive county architecture on a generous budget. Roads were smooth tarmac, sidewalks were red blocks. Three hundred yards south, I could see a blinding white church steeple behind a small huddle of buildings. I could see flagpoles, awnings, crisp paint, green lawns. Everything refreshed by the heavy rain. Now steaming and somehow intense in the heat. A prosperous community. Built, I guessed, on prosperous farm incomes and high taxes on the commuters who worked up in Atlanta.

The use of the first person stakes a claim to authenticity. More audacious is the admission of ignorance – *I didn't know* – and invention: *I guessed*. It was one reason Reacher was born to a displaced military family. He was and he wasn't American, he did and he didn't know.

Passing through San Francisco ten years later, Lee would have lunch with Martin Cruz Smith. 'He was a huge inspiration for me,' he wrote in his *One Shot* tour blog. 'When I was in England starting to write about America and wondering if I could get away with it I would think back to *Gorky Park* and say, hey, for sure I've been to the States more times than he's been to Russia, and it worked for him.'

Lee calculated that between his first trip in 1974 and the day he got his US residency in 1998 he had visited America precisely one hundred times.

From Church Brow I walked down the Radical Steps through the wooded valley to the fourteenth-century Devil's Bridge. Most likely the work of monks from St Mary's Abbey in York, according to legend the devil had appeared to an old woman and promised to build a bridge in exchange for the first soul to cross over it. When the bridge was finished the woman threw bread over it and her dog set off in pursuit, thereby outwitting the devil while still gaining a crossing.

I saw more dogs in Kirkby Lonsdale than I'd seen in my life, often outnumbering their walkers three to one, and I doubted their owners would be so willing to sacrifice them. There were bowls of water and biscuits outside every other shop and home. From the canine point of view there was surely no place more divine.

It wasn't hard to find ideas, Lee said. Stories were all around us, written on the wind.

Like Rex and Audrey, like Stan and Josie, Jim and Jane cared about education. One of the big attractions of Kirkby Lonsdale was Queen Elizabeth School, a former grammar turned secondary comprehensive. Not that there weren't equally good schools in Manchester, but Queen Elizabeth was free. Since negotiating the punitive deal in 1988 Jim had known his days were numbered. He preferred to anticipate his straitened circumstances rather than see history repeat itself and Ruth yanked out of school as a traumatic consequence of redundancy as her grandmother had been before her.

Abbotsgate was a new development minutes from the centre of town, a right turn off picturesque Mitchelgate, where the flower boxes were made from recycled French wine crates. The houses had been sympathetically built of local stone, paler in colour than their historic counterparts. No. 10 was on a corner, the first house on the right-hand side. No blue plaque, yet. You could see over the side fence into the downward-sloping back garden and out to the sweeping views towards Casterton beyond. I knew Jim had carved two miniature headstones and installed them at the far end, one for Ruth's guinea pig, Giz, and one for Stanley. But the garden had been recently land-scaped and I doubted they were still there.

It was while I was knocking vainly on the door that Dave appeared on his driveway at no. 8 and told me the occupants were away. He volunteered that the low stone wall protecting the patch of lawn outside the dining room where *Killing Floor* had been written was new, and that in days gone by people would randomly park there, and Jim Grant would open the window and say, *Do I know you?* When the answer was 'no', he would add: *Well then fuck off out of my garden.* The next day I had happy-hour drinks with Dave and his wife Mary at Plato's on Mill Brow, near where the road plunges dramatically down into the Lune Valley.

The Sapsfords had moved in about four weeks before Jim and Jane. When the Grants stopped by to introduce themselves they discovered they had daughters of the same age. Ruth and Nicky started school together, along with Anna Leighton, and practised juggling in the Sapsfords' back garden, and when the girls finished their GCSE examinations the Grants took Nicky with them on holiday to Florida.

There were only about fifteen hundred people in the town back then and when he went to pick up fish and chips for supper the day they arrived it seemed to Jim that most of them already knew who he was. According to Mary and Dave, the Grants had always wanted to live in Kirkby Lonsdale. They wanted to stay there 'forever'.

By the time I left the locals knew who I was too: *Are you the lady I gave directions to yesterday, to Abbotsgate?* asked a helpful gentleman wheeling his bicycle past the open window of the Royal Hotel where I was sitting with my notebook. This was after I had walked back from Lower Biggins and stumbled across Queen Elizabeth School. There were pupils milling about in the street and I stopped to ask an affable young teacher whether the girls' uniform had changed since the nineties. It hadn't: green pullover and tie over a white shirt with a knee-length pleated plaid skirt. The teacher turned out to be the son of the local doctor and a former pupil, from the same year group as Ruth.

Dave was a Professor of Economics at Liverpool University, and then Lancaster, where Jim attended his inaugural lecture on 'Econometricks'. Sometimes they would go to gigs together at Kendal Brewery, or in Manchester, where they saw American blues guitarist Buddy Guy, and for a while Jane and Mary went to bridge classes. On 1 May 1997, six weeks after the publication of *Killing Floor*, the Grants went next door to celebrate the election of Labour Prime Minister Tony Blair. Dave played in a covers band and owned forty guitars.

Their local watering hole was the Snooty Fox, just off the market square next to the Tourist Information Centre, but once a week the two couples formed a team of four at weekly quiz nights at the Pheasant, in the adjoining village of Casterton. There were half a dozen regular teams but their only real rivals were the teachers from Casterton School, dourly described in its school song as 'the grey child of an ageless fell'. Its claim to fame rested on having educated the first four Brontë sisters, but this was an ambiguous distinction since the two eldest had died of tuberculosis aged ten and eleven as a direct result of the cold and hunger suffered there.

Publicans Mel and May Mackie ran quiz nights on winter Thursdays in aid of Guide Dogs for the Blind. One time Jim's team got to name a dog, which they called Otis. Dave did music and culture, Mary geography, Jane history and architecture, and Jim sport and television, though books must surely have got in there somewhere. The arch rivals were segregated by the bar, bad guys on the right, good guys on the left, with the other teams occupying the neutral zone in between. 'We won about eighty per cent of the time,' said Dave, a wiry guy who shared Jim's compulsion to emerge victorious from a fight.

There was a happy hour at 8 p.m. before the quiz at nine. Which was why Jim and Dave had stuck in May's mind. They double-ordered, buying twice as much as they could drink of the house red at bargain prices. 'The two lads would stand at the bar together and walk away with two bottles and four glasses,' she said, still sounding a little annoyed, then go and sit in the corner next to the fire. They got free food too, because it was traditional to 'wheel out the chips and sandwiches'. Dave and Mary were chatty, Jim and Jane quieter. 'He kept himself to himself, he didn't spill himself all over the place.' The way May remembered it Jim wore a green sweater and did all the scribing.

There was debate around the bar but no one fell out. Mel recalled canvassing during the general election and 'running into the two lads with their left-wing lapels'. *Why don't you join us?* they cheeked him, but there was no animosity. 'Mind you,' said Mel, who was into his eighties when I met him, 'if I hadn't been landlord of the Pheasant I probably would have said *F-off*.' We were drinking tea from dainty china cups. On a side table by his winged armchair was a well-thumbed copy of *Make Me*.

Mel liked the Reacher books and thought 'those scenes' were 'quite tasteful'. Sometimes you wanted Reacher to get more serious about a girl, but 'you didn't want too much detail'.

As I took my leave May Mackie said: 'Now friends are always amazed when we say *we used to have that Lee Child in our pub.*'

In Kirkby Lonsdale every prospect pleases. I felt I could have spent the rest of my life sitting in the rear garden of the Pheasant gazing out over the sun-kissed meadows and watching the sheep safely graze under the spreading oak. Even Reacher might have enjoyed it, for a day.

According to John Leighton, Jim was 'never the noisiest person in the room' but could be 'bolshy at times'. His default position was to be anti-management on principle, irrespective of circumstances. Politically, John was at the opposite end of the spectrum. He and his Birmingham wife Jacquie had lived in London in the 1970s and 'suffered from the strikes in a way Jim never did'. 'It was hell on earth,' John said, especially on the Underground, and in his view tube drivers were pretty well paid. But Jim saw them as 'defending their rights' and participating in 'the workers' struggle'.

John remembered Jim's 'scientific approach' to his first book, how he had chosen the market and was writing for 'the airport business', using short, sharp sentences for readers with 'a short concentration span'. One night over dinner at his house with the Grants and the Sapsfords there had been discussion about what the title should be. Jim had come up with 'Killing Floor', but 'most of us thought it was too brutal'.

John was a Lee Child fan and had bought every book he'd written. He liked to alternate Reacher with books about history and politics and the Second World War. He was gratified to be cast as a likeable prison governor in *The Visitor*. Jim had explained how he liked to use real names for authenticity, and that he had chosen 'John Leighton' because he wanted something 'solid and dependable, representing authority'.

> The captain [. . .] was a head shorter than Reacher had ever been, but he was broad and he looked fit. Dark hair neatly combed, plain steel

eyeglasses. His uniform jacket was buttoned, but his face looked open enough. [. . .]

'Come in out of the rain,' the captain called.

His accent was East Coast urban. Bright and alert. He had an amiable smile. Looked like a decent guy. [. . .]

'Pleased to meet you,' the captain said. 'I'm John Leighton.'

Next time, he asked Jim, 'could you make me chairman of the joint chiefs of staff?' He thought he could make the cut in matters of strategy.

He could see his old friend in Jack Reacher: 'they're all his values'.

Bruce Woods Jack had lived in Kirkby Lonsdale since 1971 and for many years ran the Art Store on the High Street, which doubled as a Christian Science bookshop. He once sold Jim a Merriam-Webster's *Collegiate Dictionary*, which he stocked because it 'included and acknowledged the seven synonyms for God'. He had been about to instruct his customer on this point when Jim got in ahead and recited without hesitation: 'love, spirit, substance, truth, life, soul, principle'. His father had been a Christian Scientist, so he already knew them. Which meant Reacher would know them too. ('Is Jack Reacher a communicant?' Rex asks his son, in a letter written shortly after book one.)

Bruce took a proprietorial interest in *Killing Floor*. One day Jim had walked into the shop with a bunch of pages typed up and ready to go. This was when he and Highfill were faxing page edits back and forth between Kirkby and New York, but the technology was slow and the process lengthy so there had been plenty of opportunity to shoot the breeze about religious and other matters in the back office. Then there was that chance meeting in New Zealand, when Bruce and his wife were visiting family. They were walking past a bookshop in Wellington when Gina called out, 'Come and see who's here!' So Bruce backtracked and 'there was Lee Child signing books in the store'. They joined the queue and then Jim looked up and did a double-take and said: 'What are you doing here?' And announced to his assembled fans: 'Here's Bruce – without him and his Webster's dictionary, without Bruce and his fax machine, I wouldn't be where I am today.'

'I fell in love with Jack Reacher,' Bruce said. 'Here I am with five children and seven grandchildren, a business to run, church and care work – it was a form of escapism.'

Gina – who made a traditional afternoon tea with cucumber sandwiches laid out on a hand-embroidered runner – had a soft spot for Jim because her father, like his, had been present at the liberation of Belsen. She and Bruce bought a chaise longue from the Grants (when he'd lost his job, they thought, and was strapped for cash), and were invited to dinner at Stoop House by Professor and Mrs Shiren. Jane's father was forceful, they said, uneasy at the memory, and not very tolerant of their rejection of the Beaujolais nouveau on the grounds of being teetotal. '*You know where the kitchen is, get yourselves a glass of water,* he said. So we did.'

David Firth used to run the Lunesdale Pet Stores next to the Spar supermarket, across the market square from the Art Store, where he also had a job dropping off textbooks to local schools. Ruth would pop in on Saturday mornings to get food for her guinea pig. Sometimes her father would come with her. Jim put him in mind of an accountant or solicitor. 'He wasn't at all swashbuckling.'

David was from Lytham St Annes. He had a degree in Geography from Liverpool, where he had been president of the Geography Society, and had taught at schools in Dunstable and Portsmouth before being diagnosed with bipolar disorder. He took photographs and wrote poetry and one day Jim Grant had paused from looking at the pictures and poems pasted on the pet-shop wall and remarked: 'I can see you're an educated bloke.' He was 'caring and quiet, a nice, modest man', and they would have long conversations about upstate New York and minimalist music, or John Updike and Steinbeck and Alistair Cooke's *Letter from America*. Jim had a Gibson and David had a Fender Gold Stratocaster.

'It was like meeting a bloke at the university again,' said David, wistfully. 'You see the best side of people if you have a pet shop.'

David had a glossy black-and-white border collie called Stella that he took on long walks, wearing a flat cap and carrying a stout cane. He gave me a smart photograph of Stella to pass on to Lee. 'Dogs are therapy for me,' he said. He was happy to learn from an article he'd read, and cut out and kept, that Ruth had 'continued her love of animals' and that rather than going into the secret service, as had been an early wish, was working with dogs as an animal behaviourist.

One day Jim had come into the shop and said: 'Granada has folded up. I've got to write a bestseller, an airport-style bestseller.' David was struck by his friend's clarity of purpose. 'It was this new genre that was taking off,' he told me. Jim had explained how he was writing for people who can't concentrate: 'if you do subordinate clauses you're a bit old hat, aren't you,' said David, again a little wistful.

On one of his visits Jim might well have seen this extract from Robert Browning's 'Shop' that David sent me:

> Because a man has shop to mind
> In time and place, since flesh must live,
> Needs spirit lack all life behind,
> All stray thoughts, fancies fugitive,
> All loves except what trade can give?
>
> I want to know a butcher paints,
> A baker rhymes for his pursuit,
> Candlestick-maker much acquaints
> His soul with song, or, haply mute,
> Blows out his brains upon the flute!

Like David, like Browning, Jim knew instinctively that being one thing didn't stop you from being – or becoming – another.

David loved landscape and 'understanding the world' and wasn't much of a reader, 'certainly not of thrillers'. His own poetry was tender and subtle and spiritual, about coastal lowlands and sandstone and the mind of God. But Jim had got the book done and David had read it and thought, 'There's a lot of Kirkby in this, the small town life with dark secrets and machinations.' He appreciated Jim's sense of location: 'He likes detail, and I like that.' David's favourite book was *Zen and the Art of Motorcycle Maintenance*. He had lived a stone's throw from Abbotsgate since 1979, but now it seemed to him that everyone was selling the same thing and it had become 'tinselly'. Too Disney. Too many nostalgic postcards, just like Sheffield.

David was present at Lee's first book signing and had taken a picture of the debut author in John Lennon glasses and a blue jacket and blue-checked shirt signing his treasured first edition of *Killing Floor* with Ruth – also wearing blue, and with her father's jawline and features – standing proudly by his side. The shop at 9 Market Street was aptly named the Bookstore, and behind the signing table is a poster headed:

LOCAL AUTHOR
LEE CHILD

It was 'a real rags to riches tale', David told me, happy for this kind and courteous man's stellar success. Later he sent me a photocopy of the autographed title page, which read: *Your friend Jim Grant aka Lee Child, June 1997*.

While I was in Kirkby Lonsdale I took a side trip by bus to the Asda Superstore in Kendal, famously the place where Jim had once accompanied his wife shopping and they came up with the name of his hero. Or rather she did: 'It was a gift from her to me.' Whenever he went to a supermarket (*and that must be at least, what . . . a dozen times by now?*) a little old lady would approach him and say: *You're a nice tall gentleman. Would you reach me that can from the shelf?* On this occasion Jane had quipped: *Well if this writing gig doesn't work out, you can always be a reacher in a supermarket.*

Jane Grant gave her husband a year to pursue his quixotic dream (Ruth had the insouciant faith of a daughter in her father). Twenty-three had passed since that historic encounter with an innocent old lady in the Kendal Asda that helped unleash Jack Reacher on an unsuspecting world. The shelves were still stacked unfeasibly high with cans and cartons and rolls of kitchen towel, and almost the first thing I saw was a reacher, then another, two reachers, standing on custom-built aluminium steps and even so, stretching and straining like little Ellie Greer. I couldn't resist snapping them on my iPhone, which brought security running. I explained myself to the store manager. 'Shall we see if there are any Lee Childs on the shelf?' I asked brightly, as though it were possible there might not be. And there they were: handsome blue-and-gold paperbacks of *Gone Tomorrow* on a £4 promotion, between James Patterson's *Haunted* and Wilbur Smith's *The Tiger's Prey*. Lee's name was also dotted liberally over the Patterson–Clinton collaboration *The President is Missing*, on bright red stickers reading, *'The political thriller of the decade.' Lee Child.* Soon the store manager would be telling his friends, *that Lee Child used to shop in our Asda.*

Jim wasn't especially motivated by money, said John Leighton. He 'just wanted to provide for his family'. But 'he did once say he'd always wanted to turn left on the plane'.

So I told John about the first time Lee had hired a private jet, in 2005, for a flight from New York to the south of France. He wanted to shield his nervous lurcher-Labrador Jenny, a rescue dog, from unnecessary separation anxiety.

It was during a quiz night at the Pheasant that the call came through. Thursday 7 December, 1995. Lee's agent, Darley Anderson, who'd phoned home first and been informed by Ruth that her parents were out at the pub.

'There's a call for a Lee Child,' May said, or maybe it was Mel. Everyone looked around blankly. They didn't know any Lee Child.

Then Jim Grant stood up and walked to the phone.

After a while he came back. It had finally happened. Darley had received an offer from G. P. Putnam's in New York for *Killing Floor* and a follow-up book. Jim told his wife and friends about the deal. Then asked: 'Should I take it?'

On 18 December he opened his first business account with the Midland Bank: 'Mr J Grant trading as Lee Child.'

29

The Apprenticeship

Long years of training, absorbed right down at the cellular level,
permanently written in his DNA.
The Hard Way, 2006

Lee calculates that during the totality of his time at Granada he was responsible for over forty thousand hours of programme transmission. His skills were highly specialised and not directly transferable. He wanted to retire – *I'm a Brit, and the point of life is to retire* – but he was thirty-nine years old and had only seven house payments left in the bank and couldn't make the numbers work.

It was 'the usual 1990s downsizing thing'. He was an expensive veteran and as union organiser had been making his presence felt, just like in Mr Rigby's classroom. He wasn't going to be on any employers' wish lists. He became a writer 'because he couldn't think of anything else to do'. As luck would have it he'd come up with this idea for a character who had suffered a downsizing experience but was taking it completely in his stride. All he had to do was bring the same total commitment to his audience that defined the television industry and maybe he could get something going.

Mostly he argued there was little crossover between his consecutive careers. But those forty thousand hours had 'taught him a thing or two about telling a story' and 'the rhythms and grammar of storytelling had been imprinted on his DNA'. He'd written thousands of links, trailers, commercials and news stories on deadlines that ranged from fifteen minutes to fourteen seconds. The thought of a novel a year didn't faze the controller.

He'd seen how to engage human curiosity and control suspense.

> When I was working in television there was something no one had in 1980 that everyone had in 1990 and it changed everything. Notice I haven't told you what it is? And you're all wondering . . . *What is it?* That's how you create suspense. The remote control. It used to be that having to haul yourself off the sofa was a major disincentive to changing the channel. Capture your audience at peak time and you'd keep them for the rest of the night. Suddenly you could change at whim and you'd run into very vulnerable times. Like heading into a commercial break. So we started asking a trivia question – like, who was the first choice to play Dirty Harry? – and at the end of the break we would answer it.
>
> The psychology was that people would stick around for one of three reasons. If they know the answer, they enjoy the gratification of being right. If they don't, they're curious. And even if they don't care they still stick around, because we're hardwired like that. (ThrillerFest)

With television you had a big audience and fast feedback. There was ample opportunity to learn what audiences wanted, and how to please them. 'The entire purpose of story is to manipulate,' he would later write in *The Hero*.

Lee measured success by numbers. How many copies does the book sell? Not because he was greedy for money, but because the only true measure was: are real people actually reading this book? Or are they changing the channel? If you're not selling, you're just not doing it. Writers were there to entertain the audience, like the Anglo-Saxon gleeman. If you lost sight of that, you were sunk.

If readers were coming back for more, so too would publishers. If readers were talking to their friends, publishers would talk louder. Increase of appetite grew by what it fed on. It made sense to invest in a winner.

Most of what Jim learned at Granada he learned from the people around him, and what he learned most about was people. Their joys and their sorrows, their hopes and their fears, their crazy ambitions and their failed dreams and their secrets and their scandals.

Like Rob said, he remembered all the stories, even years afterwards. How Elspeth died of cancer and Candy had Huntington's chorea like her mother and Rita had been beaten up by her husband. The man whose wife had been killed in an accident when an exhausted stage manager crashed his minibus after a twelve-hour shift and the one who insisted on a surprise party for his spouse even though she hated surprises, only for her to faint from shock and hit her head on the kitchen table and die in hospital the very same night.

There was the attractive married woman who worked in the office who'd been to Florida on holiday and met another man and started an affair and agreed to go out there and live with him. She had everything packed and ready and one day when her husband went off to work she flew to Florida and never came back. Jim admired her courage. Not many would follow through like she did, leaving behind her happy-but-dull life and everything she had, including her children.

There was the woman from management who'd driven Jim to the point where he told her he was going to say he'd had an affair with her and he was going to spill the beans and even though none of it was true he was going to do it anyway and she wouldn't be able to disprove it, so she would have to back down and he would win, which he must at any cost, because he was right and she was wrong. You don't think twice about crushing a cockroach, says Reacher in *Echo Burning*, and human beings often made cockroaches look good.

334

Sitting in the lobby of the Grand Hyatt, Lee told me the one thing he felt seriously guilty about.

> The hardest thing I've ever done was something I didn't do. It was my turn to interview for an in-vision announcer. People sent in old VHS demo tapes, mostly amateur things. My favourite was a woman with a perfect face and voice, warm, with great presence. The tape started with a close-up on her face, a very tight zoom. Gradually, as the demo progressed, the camera pulled back and I saw she was sitting in a car. Then the camera kept pulling back and I saw she was a thalidomide victim, with little hands poking out of her shoulders. I was afraid it would make viewers feel uncomfortable, so I gave the job to a black woman instead, trying to compensate. She had beautiful liquid eyes and she was good, but not as good, not so fluent, and she stumbled over some words and pronunciations. She lasted a couple of years before going back to Trinidad, where she was greeted as a celebrity like Trevor McDonald and her family home was robbed and all of them were shot dead.

And then there were the Janet and John stories.

Janet's partner Conrad picked me up from Eccles station in Manchester. Janet told me about her job as loggist and how Jim was so cool under pressure.

Then she told me about her life. I'd heard some of it already, when Lee was explaining how different the world had been when he was growing up. Janet was not so lucky as Jim. She hadn't been able to dodge the bullets the way he had, and her story deeply moved him.

Janet Brown (née Speers) was born to working-class parents in Hope Hospital in Salford. She was the oldest of three daughters. Her father worked shifts for the Manchester Ship Canal Company, on the Locks and then as Bridgemaster on Barton Swing Bridge. Money was scarce, but they were well fed and cared for. Janet had piano lessons. Her mother had a part-time job in a mail-order warehouse. Her grandfather would take her for walks in the pushchair.

The summer of 1947 was a hot one (just as winter had been exceptionally cold). Janet had recently started school. She spent the afternoon at the park and when she got home she fell suddenly ill with flu-like symptoms. She was put to bed and when she got up again her legs gave way and she fell to the floor. It was the time of the polio epidemic and the doctor sent her straight to the local fever hospital. This hospital was called Ladywell.

Janet was placed on the 'free-list', which meant she wasn't expected to make it. Once, she dreamed she was falling down and down into blackness, and afterwards wondered if this was the moment the fever broke, and she was really 'coming up instead of going down'. She wasn't ready to shuffle off her mortal coil. She didn't want to be set free.

Her mother and father could look at her through the glass of her isolation cubicle. Janet still remembers that cubicle. She still remembers the pain when they tried to straighten her legs by forcing them into splints, bandaging them to keep them immobilised, which only helped the virus do its damage. There was a button at the side of her bed and sometimes she pressed it. She was only five years old. Then a nurse threatened her with another enema if she ever did it again, so she didn't. A 'nice nurse' told her she would soon be able to dance on the lawn outside her hospital window.

Janet was in isolation for eight weeks. Back home in Salford neighbours would cross the street when her mother went shopping.

When she was no longer infectious she was sent to Biddulph Grange in Staffordshire. The ward was separated by age group into a 'big end' and a 'little end' and contained about thirty beds. Sister Burgess had an all-glass office at the centre, where she could see everything that went on and ruled with a rod of iron. If a child misbehaved – hopped out of bed when she shouldn't or didn't do as she was told – she was put under a restrainer, a canvas sheet that was stretched across the mid-section of the body and fastened tightly under the bed so that she couldn't sit up.

They were woken at six with breakfast at seven. They had to eat everything that was put in front of them. The day staff arrived and remade the beds. The bedridden were lifted onto a trolley, the rest sat around a table waiting for lessons to start. The ward was scrubbed and the wooden floor polished. Bed pans were provided after each meal and to ask for one at another time was a form of not behaving. There was no toilet paper, only tow (a coarse fibre used in upholstery stuffing). After tea an enamel bowl was brought round, with warm water for the girls to wash their hands and faces.

When Matron did her round, or the consultant, the beds were lined up perfectly, with the corners tucked in just so. 'We had to keep very still. It was like a military operation and these people were treated like gods.'

Visiting was one weekend a month for adults only, so Janet never saw her sisters. Her parents didn't have a car but so many children were afflicted that a coach was laid on. The doors opened at 2 p.m. Janet still remembers the thrill of anticipation, and her mother's loving hugs. She remembers how she hated it when they had to leave. But crying was a form of misbehaviour too. Any sweets the visitors brought were taken away and doled out one by one. She had no toys of her own.

Janet made friends with Marjorie in the bed next to hers. They came from the same part of town and maybe when they were better they could go to the park or dance together on the lawn. One night she heard a strange noise and called the night nurse. Marjorie, unable to sit up or raise her head, had choked on her own vomit. The next morning the bed was empty, and Janet was told she had gone home. It was only later she realised that her friend had died.

At Biddulph Grange Janet learned to walk again, with the aid of two callipers, two walking sticks, and two stiff legs. In those days callipers didn't have knee joints to enable them to bend. John Grant senior would have empathised. On summer nights the beds were pushed outside, but it wasn't exciting or fun. The gardens had been divided into themed areas inspired by China and Egypt, and many years later Janet would visit them again with her best friend Jane Grant, but for a sickly child they were full of shadows and ghosts and Buddhas that seemed to glow red in the dark.

Janet wasn't bitter. She didn't feel abandoned or unwanted. When she was home again her mother took her on a coach trip to see a faith healer called Percy, who put his hand on her back and spoke some words over her and made no perceptible difference but at least they had tried. Marjorie's family came to visit. Janet continued to go to hospital three times a week, travelling on her own by ambulance, and her grandfather paid for someone from the local football club to come to the house for physiotherapy. Janet liked that, because it meant she didn't have to go to bed so early and afterwards her father would carry her upstairs, because without the callipers she couldn't walk. She was still full of hope.

Janet spent eighteen months at Biddulph Grange. Then a further nine months in hospital when she was fourteen and three when she was seventeen, for operations on her feet and legs. When I met her she was in a wheelchair. Bright, bubbly, glowing, and with Conrad, flirtatious. Jane Grant had taken her horse-riding, she told me, and made her feel that 'anything was possible'.

'John Brown wore a calliper too,' Rob said. 'I can still hear the click, as he adjusted it.'

Janet and John had met when they were seventeen years old at St Loye's College in Exeter – 'for the training and rehabilitation of the disabled' – where they were doing a course in Pitman shorthand, typing, English and general office procedures. John's parents owned their own home and car and his mother had paid help twice a week. His father was a clerk in the Assistant Magistrates' office and wrote a column for the *Bournemouth Echo*.

John's father was cold and hard. John had to go to church three times on Sundays. He was made to catch a bus and take the long walk up the hill for singing lessons he didn't want, even after he too contracted polio at the age of ten and spent ten months in hospital, one for every year of his life. John struggled to accept his disability, 'though it was slight compared to many'.

They were both determined that polio should not define them. The strength of that determination came from the polio itself.

Jim often thought about what it must have been like for a boy to be deprived overnight of his freedom and mobility on the cusp of adolescence. He rejected Rob's notion that he had been in thrall to John Brown. But it was true that he had been fascinated by him. Looking back, he thought it was his writer's brain beginning to crank up.

He'd always done 'the Walter Mitty thing'. As a kid he daydreamed, drifting through vaguely heroic stories that were shifting and fluid. As he grew older the stories became obsessively detailed, plausible, and correct. Commuting to and from Granada he would think of what he should have said at the meeting he'd just come out of, and say that thing in his head or even aloud, and pretend it had happened that way, and rewrite history from that point on. He'd mentally write complex narratives about how to break some manager's leg. How to contact the tough guys and where, and what sort of place it was, what to say to them and how to pay them off without revealing his identity. He edited reality in a way he wouldn't dream of editing his fiction.

It was like he'd always been a writer, but hadn't yet made the connection between his brain and the page.

Once Jim said he'd been breathalysed on the way back to Stalybridge after dinner with the Browns. 'I was well over the limit and somehow

I summoned myself to breathe in a certain way and I passed it.' You can't do that, Rob thought, but it was 'classic Jim'.

Jim had a great turn of phrase. Rob remembered him saying the snow on top of a brick wall looked like the crust on a loaf of bread, and how a moustachioed footballer resembled a First World War officer and four hens emerging from a shed reminded him of a bunch of old ladies going out for a walk. But he hadn't expected Jim to become a writer. Rob was a Hemingway fan and not uncritical of Lee Child, but thought he was better than Grisham. He especially liked the first few pages of *61 Hours* and 'the skid-panning of the coach as it slews out of control'.

This is how Jim responded when, out of the blue, Rob emailed him in September 2014:

> So great to hear from you. I'm not very nostalgic or sentimental but, like you, those times we shared have a huge place in my memories. A lot of random fun. I remember being bored one day and writing endless versions of 'It's our title, says Big Ron' on the Aston caption generator. Might be the first fiction I ever wrote.

He wasn't owning up to *10-inch Cyril*. Rob too remembered writing spoof headlines about Manchester United and their manager Ron Atkinson but on the cruder Riley, which preceded the Aston (which became the industry standard). The new character generators allowed you to type words in and superimpose them over anything, where previously the graphics department would mock something up with white letters on black board. This was around 1981, when a brand new cutting-edge Quantel Paintbox was parked outside the CCR and like the big kids they were Jim and Rob would go out and play with it.

It was easy to make things up or tell other people's stories. The greater mysteries were closer to home. How well had he known his own father? Lee wondered, when he set about writing his twenty-third book, *Past Tense*. How well did he know his brothers? In a 2019 interview with the *Sunday Times* in South Africa, Lee revealed that with the surprising character of Mark Reacher he wanted to provide 'a bit of moral colour for Jack'. 'If you start looking at your family, you might not like what you find.' Not all stories could be told, not all could be known. Had he ever really seen beyond the tip of the iceberg? 'There was a list of things never to be talked about,' Lee told me, looking back on life with his parents, 'and number one on the list was the list itself.'

David Grant was the fittest of the four brothers. 'He was a better Scout than Jim,' recalled Mr Rigby, Scoutmaster as well as Biology teacher. But he got no obvious aesthetic joy out of the countryside or sensual pleasure from fresh air. It was all about challenge and endurance and self-punishment. He belonged to the Brecon Mountain Rescue Team, but if he spent days trekking Reacher-like through the snow or trawling the waters of the Severn it wasn't, so far as Lee could tell, because he derived any deep human satisfaction from saving lives or restoring the missing to their grieving families. He was in it 'for the geeky stuff, the vehicles and equipment'. David taught Chemistry at a local secondary school. He owned a Porsche and like Lee had a weakness for cars. But he and Richard, who after Cambridge had rejected a job at Pratt & Whitney (the US manufacturer of jet engine turbines) and gone to work for the Central Electricity Generating Board instead, 'had no concept of human emotions'. Yet correspondence suggests that Richard, like Rex, read each of the Reacher books as they came out, and he never forgot a birthday card: 'Many happy returns of your birthday', read his annual message to brother James, only exceptionally hinting at toy cars once played with, or long-lost episodes of *Doctor Who*.

In 2012 Lee (who had recently become the first British author to sell a million ebooks for Kindle) donated £10,000 towards a £65,000 replacement vehicle for the Brecon Mountain team when their existing one was written off in a collision. '[They] wouldn't dream of singing their own praises,' he told *BBC News Mid Wales*, 'but the truth is they're real experts – intrepid on the mountains and innovative in river searches. Their control vehicle was world class [. . .] and copied by the police and the military.' Mr Child's brother would help design the new interior.

It was as close as Lee would come to acknowledging that the almost invisible third son, often omitted by acquaintances when listing the Grant brothers, and of whom at time of writing I had seen no photographs, could be said to be doing in the real world just a little of what he, the second son, was only writing about.

The first time Jim mentioned his intention to write a book to anyone outside his immediate family was at a New Year's Eve party in 1989. He'd recently discovered John D. MacDonald in an airport bookstore (starting with *The Long Silver Rain*) and was talking to Anne Wilkie Millar, then shop steward to his deputy. It was soon after they'd negotiated the twenty-four-hour deal, 'like printing our own money'. Not only had they screwed the company on pay but Jim hadn't let up. Shift workers would miss TV programmes and phone calls so would need answerphones and video recorders, one each for every employee, all on the company dime. He didn't just know the writing was on the wall, he'd put it there. 'What are you going to do afterwards?' Anne asked him under the mistletoe. 'I'm going to write a book.' MacDonald was like a how-to manual, for plot but also for character, and Jim thought, *I'd like to do this too.* He'd always been that way. *This music is incredible – I want to play the guitar. This show is great – I want to be on stage.*

It would take another five years for Jim to act on those words and pass on to Reacher that 'strange, weary blend of nobility and cynicism' that had so attracted him to Travis McGee (as he later wrote in his

1981, the Granada Years: Jim and his glamorous assistant and partner in crime, Rob 'Bobby' Reeves, at the Piccadilly Hotel, Manchester. *(Marilyn Gallagher)*

Jim Grant, Transmission Controller – aka 'The Judge'. *(BACW, UEA)*

The all-important faders, salvaged by Jim and Rob when technology changed in the early eighties. 'On the day, you were the word of God.' *(HM)*

Central Control Room, Granada Television, early eighties. Station announcer Graham James is in vision. *(Robert Reeves)*

CHAPTER ONE 1st draft

~~I slept on the bus~~ right ~~sleeping through~~ the long
~~haul from —. It had rained all night It was~~
~~cold The bus droned and hissed and vibrated~~
~~The passengers dozed and snored and stank I knew~~
~~none of them. I hated them all~~
CH

I was arrested in Eno's diner. At twelve o'clock.
~~I had~~ ordered lunch ~~but not eaten it yet.~~ I was
eating ~~toast~~ eggs, drinking coffee. A late breakfast, not ~~a~~
lunch. // This was a small ~~place~~ diner, but bright and clean.
Looked brand new. ~~Neat, I think.~~ Built to resemble a converted railroad car. //
I was at a window. I saw the police cruisers pull
into the gravel lot. They were moving fast and
crunched to a stop. Light bars flashing and popping. ~~didn't park~~ Doors burst open,
policemen came out. Two from each car, weapons out. Two
revolvers, two shotguns. This was heavy stuff. One
revolver, one shotgun ran to the back. One of each
rushed the door. I knew who was in the diner
A cook in back. Two waitresses and two old men. And
me. This major operation had to be for me. I had
been in town about four hours. The others had
probably been here all their lives. Any problem with
any of them and a sergeant would have shuffled
in apologetically. He would ~~give~~ be embarrassed and
~~murmur~~ to them. Ask them to come to the station, house
The heavy, weapons and the rush weren't for
them. They were for me. So I crammed egg into my mouth and
trapped a five under my saucer. I kept my hands
above the table and drained my cup. Well, You never
know where your next meal is coming from.

The revolver stayed at the door. He was in a
crouch and pointed the weapon two handed. At my
head. The shotgun approached close. These were

First page of the first handwritten draft of *Killing Floor*, September 1994. *(BACW, UEA)*

They came for me

I was arrested in Eno's diner. At twelve noon. I was
eating eggs, drinking coffee and reading somebody else's newspaper
about the campaign for a president I hadn't voted for last time
and wasn't going to vote for this time. Twelve noon, but it was ~~late~~
breakfast, not lunch. I was late and wet and tired after a
long walk in heavy rain. All the way down into town from the
highway.

I was sitting there reading an abandoned newspaper about
the campaign for a president I hadn't voted for last time
and wasn't going to vote for this time. Outside,

Redrafting the opening of *Killing Floor*. (BACW, UEA)

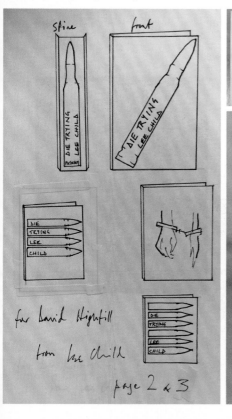

Spine

front

DIE TRYING
LEE CHILD
PUSHAM

DIE TRYING
LEE CHILD

DIE
TRYING
LEE
CHILD

DIE
TRYING
LEE
CHILD

for David Highfill

from Lee Child

page 2 & 3

They want a Reacher sequel!

(above) Book #2, 'They,
The People', starring
John Pemberton Trent,
becomes *Die Trying*.
(BACW, UEA)

(far left) 1997: Lee has a
go at designing his own
book cover for *Die Trying*
– the one that almost
got away. Note the early
signature. *(BACW, UEA)*

(left) What's left of the
pencil that started it all.
(HM)

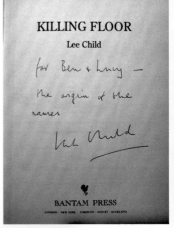

(above left) June 1997: First public signing, with Ruth at The Bookstore, Kirkby Lonsdale. Picture taken by David Firth of Lunesdale Pet Stores: 'Jim wasn't at all swashbuckling.' *(Courtesy of David Firth)*

(above right) A note to Ian Gerrard, Jim's assistant transmission controller at Granada. *(Courtesy of Ian Gerrard)*

(right) 'They were a nice pair of kids,' Reacher said, when he met Lucy and Ben in Margrave. 'Polite and quiet.' *(Courtesy of Ian Gerrard)*

3 July 1998: Jim and Jane Grant set sail on the Queen Elizabeth 2 from Southampton, bound for the United States of America. It was a forty-four-year-old dream come true. *(BACW, UEA)*

(above) Scott and Jen Smith of Naked Blue with Lee, working on their 2018 album, 'Just the Clothes On My Back'. *(Courtesy of Lee Child)*

(left) 2017: Being filmed writing 'My Rules' (for 92Y with Xerox) in his office on Central Park West. 'Somewhere inside Lee's head there's violent brutality.' *(HM)*

July 2019: The writer at work, Central Park West. 'I don't want to be remembered.' *(HM)*

1. 20 Ridgeway Avenue, Stivichall, Coventry. The house where James Grant was born. *(HM)*

2. 29 Queen's Terrace, Otley, where Lee's maternal grandparents lived. 'James felt safe with grandma and grandad Scrafton.' *(HM)*

3. 125 Hyndford Street, East Belfast. Where Lee's father (and later Van Morrison) grew up. *(HM)*

4. 13 Kingsway Avenue, Cherryvalley, East Belfast. Where John and Winnie Grant lived after Van Morrison's parents bought their old house. *(HM)*

5. 6 Underwood Road, Handsworth Wood, Birmingham. Where Jim Grant grew up. *(HM)*

6. 20 Thornsett Road, Sheffield. 'The upstairs digs were squalid.'

7. 329 Crookesmoor Road, Sheffield. Jim and Jane Grant moved here as newlyweds, while still at university. *(HM)*

8. 13 Copley Park Mews, Stalybridge. On the right, the house where Ruth was born. The first house Jim and Jane owned. *(HM)*

9. 47 The Circuit, Alderley Edge. The house the Grants moved to when Jim was promoted to Controller. *(HM)*

10. 10 Abbotsgate, Kirkby Lonsdale, showing the corner where the dining room was. *Killing Floor* to *The Visitor. (HM)*

11. The view from the back garden of 10 Abbotsgate. 'I looked out of the window. Georgia.' *(HM)*

12. The dining table where *Killing Floor* was written, in pencil. *(LC)*

13. The new office, funded by the advance for *Killing Floor*. *(LC)*

14. 110 Upper Shad Road, Pound Ridge, New York. From *The Visitor* to *The Enemy*.

15. South of France. Fleeing family and George W. Bush. *(LC)*

16. 5 East 22nd Street, Manhattan (with Flatiron Building), where Jim and Jane had four apartments.
From *One Shot* to *Personal*. *(HM)*

17. Minimalist room with a view. *(LC)*

18. The view (cropped) from East 22nd Street. 'My Home in America.' *(LC)*

19. Sussex. The house with its own postcode.

20. Sussex. Jane Grant's bluebell wood. *(LC)*

21. Central Park West, Manhattan. From *Make Me* to *Blue Moon*. *(HM)*

22. The office that is no more, dismantled after *Blue Moon* was written. *(HM)*

23. Lee Child has left the building. 'Let someone else have a go.' *(HM)*

24. Wyoming. Where Lee Child is now. *(LC)*

July 2019: At home, Central Park West. 'My desire has always been to be shown with something between me and the viewer … through a window, for instance.' *(HM)*

introduction to the reissue of *The Deep Blue Good-by*). But in his final months as an underemployed underappreciated senior presentation director he started taking the draft manuscript into work and typing it up on Ruth's laptop, a monochrome Lexmark 486/25 given to her by Jane's father, lazily extending a paw now and then to flick the occasional switch at the control desk. Colleagues would ask questions, maybe tease him a little; one fell in love with his hero Jack before he became famous and named her first-born son after him without the published author ever even knowing. Others said no way would he make it and were duly logged and slated for a nasty run-in with Reacher's skull or the sharp end of his elbow.

Jim Grant's last day at Granada was 21 June 1995 ('Jack Reacher's birthday, in a very real way,' he blogged ten years later). He left with a severance package of £30,000 (half of which went on settling debts) that with frugal living would give him just about long enough to negotiate a life-saving deal for his first two books. The family thought about relocating to the Loire Valley. But instead Ruth got a Sunday job as a waitress and Jane joined the Tourist Information Office, and when they began to run out of money Jim took on some highly paid work as a freelance transmission controller at NBC in London. He did twenty-one shifts, staying in the cheapest hotel he could find near the Central line so as to get to Tower Hill or Bank and connect with the Docklands Light Railway to the Isle of Dogs. By coincidence, Rob was drafted in to produce some tennis one Sunday and they said: 'We had this other guy from Granada in here recently, Jim Grant. He's writing a book and we all think it's going to really take off.'

The year 1994 was one of new beginnings.

But this rebirth took place in the shadow of the valley of death, and 1994 was also the year that broke Jim's heart. First, Stanley the springer spaniel died of old age. Jim and Jane had two rules for Stan: wait two days, and was he still eating? After two days he still wasn't eating and they called out the country vet. Then Giz the guinea pig contracted cancer and the vet couldn't locate a vein and had to inject straight into the cavity. Lee still remembered how the tiny animal took twenty excruciating minutes to die, all the while looking helplessly into his eyes.

Most of what Jim learned at Granada he'd learned by staying alive. It was what Lee told creative writing students who asked for advice. The essential thing was to read. Other than that, all they could really do was go away and live a bit longer, wait until the gas tank was full.

'Nineteen ninety-four was a terrible year,' Lee said, gloomily. 'My Otley grandma died too [in November], at the same time I was getting it in the neck from Granada.'

No wonder he wanted to escape to Georgia.

30

How Hard Could It Be?

*Where he matched his talents with unrelenting hard work and
made himself a star, in a shadowy, black-ops kind of a way.*
Personal, 2014

'I know, I'll write a book. I'd read a few. How hard could it be?'
It was lunchtime. Thursday 1 September, 1994. Jim Grant left
the building. The sun was shining. He wasn't hungry. He was heading
for WHSmith at the Arndale Centre. He didn't want a magazine. He
wasn't planning to come back with yet another book. Instead, he
bought three pads of lined paper, one pencil, one pencil sharpener
and an eraser for a total of £3.99. He was thinking of William Styron.
Twenty years later he would nominate *Sophie's Choice* for the *Wall
Street Journal* Book Club. Five years after that he would tell me that
the red house in *Echo Burning* was an echo of the pink rooming house
where Stingo embarks on his writing career. Stingo is a recent émigré
to New York with a threescore-a-day Camel habit who records in
his diary:

> My first morning – a Saturday – I rose late and strolled over to a
> stationery store on Flatbush Avenue and bought two dozen Number
> 2 Venus Velvet pencils, ten lined yellow legal pads and a 'Boston'
> pencil sharpener . . .

Contrary to popular mythology, Lee Child did not begin writing *Killing Floor* on 1 September. He didn't even begin working on it. He'd already done a day's work. Same on Friday. Saturday and Sunday were out too. He was on the weekend shift.

'September 1st just made for a better story,' Lee said. Like Reacher being born on Friday instead of Tuesday or Wednesday.

It wasn't until Monday 5 September that Jim Grant sat down at the round chrome-and-glass dining-room table and wrote the first sentence of his first novel.

Anything was possible. He wrote:

CHAPTER ONE 1st draft

I had slept on the bus right through the long haul from _____ . It had rained all night. It was cold. The bus droned and hissed and vibrated. The passengers dozed and snored and stank. I knew none of them. I hated them all.

He stood and paced and smoked. Something didn't feel quite right. His *I'm heading down a blind alley* detector was already twitching. Later he could rely on picking up on it within seven words. He sat down again, crossed out each sentence with a horizontal line and then a single diagonal cutting across the middle.

Then he wrote:

CH 1

I was arrested in Eno's diner.

That felt better. Looked better too. He read it aloud. It sounded good. He wrote:

At twelve o'clock.

The third sentence – 'I had ordered lunch but not eaten it yet.' – had been crossed out and replaced with:

> I was eating eggs ['lunch' is crossed out], drinking coffee. A late breakfast, not lunch. // This was a small diner, but bright and clean. Looked brand new. Built to resemble a converted railway car. // I was at a window.

The fragmentary, choppy style was deliberate. It seemed right for a hero who would use words sparingly, but with precision: naming the diner, stating the time, caring which meal it was. It was also deliberately exaggerated. He needed to attract attention, stand out from the crowd. He figured he had the length of a television commercial to make himself unforgettable, unputdownable. To grab his audience and hold on to it. According to Philip Pullman, it worked: *Killing Floor* was his first Reacher too, sometime around 2009, and a year or so later he'd caught up with them all. What he especially liked was the way 'nothing comes between the reader and the story'.

But it took a while to get that first paragraph right. Here is 'new para 1', undated (and still not final), written up in red ink on a separate page:

> I was arrested in Eno's diner. They came for me at twelve noon. I was eating eggs, drinking coffee, and reading somebody else's newspaper about the campaign for a president I hadn't voted for last time and wasn't going to vote for this time. Twelve noon, but it was breakfast, not lunch. I was late and wet and tired after a long walk in heavy rain. All the way down into town from the highway.

Then he began to compress his sentences. It was subtle. 'Looked brand new' (replacing 'New, I think.') became simply 'Brand new';

'This major operation had to be for me' became 'This operation was for me'. At the same time, he introduced more on Reacher's point of view, more descriptive and sensory detail – about the lunch counter bumped out back and the booths and the rain pebbling the windows with red and blue light and the car hissing over smooth soaked tarmac. Reacher gradually becomes less explicit about his feelings, cooler and less hot-headed. He stops saying he hates people, and muttering 'smug bastard' under his breath. He stops analysing his shortcomings and agonising over his failures.

Lee had thought hard about his hero. Character was top of his list of priorities. It literally came before plot on the first page of his planning notes (British Archive of Contemporary Writing KF1011A). He'd written a whole paragraph about it, notable for its use of urgent, imperative verbs:

> Character of H –
>
> This is vitally important. It will be make-or-break. Must be such that it arouses envy in male readers. They must admire him & want to <u>be</u> him. Women readers must be fascinated by him. They must want to be <u>with</u> him. Must be some moral base albeit probably bleak & cynical to a degree. Needs to be alienated, outsider, loner, tough, resourceful. There must be a very subtle portrayal of superman powers. Must be unfeasibly tough & strong & invulnerable, to provide escapist identification. Gets away with things, possibly unrealistic but serious & convincing. Always knows better. Things turn out OK.

That would do. Quite enough to get him started and propel him through to the end. At the foot of the same page he has written:

> H had tried it their way. Now he is trying it his way. To hell with them.

I had tried it their way. To hell with them. Now I am trying it my way.

And on the flip side, an emphatic note-to-self: 'H can't just be an investigator, too clichéd. H must establish alienation, oppression etc.'

He settled on first-person narrative. It was the natural way of telling a story. It was intimate and beguiling and seductive. But there was another compelling reason: at this point he still had no idea what 'H' – the hero – was called. Jane hadn't yet dragged him off to Asda to help with the weekly shop. He hadn't yet answered the cry for help from that little old lady. He'd been toying with 'Franklin', but he wasn't convinced. Somehow Franklin didn't feel quite right.

It wasn't until 2272 words into chapter two that he wrote:

'My name is Jack Reacher,' I said. 'No middle name. No address.'

It was purely accidental. But the subliminal echo of 'Richard' was resonant. With a touch of Richard III thrown in – by no means a good man, but undoubtedly charismatic. The only one of Shakespeare's major characters to open his own play and capture the crowd through soliloquy.

Lee was his own sternest taskmaster. After he'd completed the first draft, and written it all out a second time, again by hand, and typed it up a first time, single-spaced, he decided to run a check. He sat down at the laptop and typed:

Reacher was arrested in Eno's diner. At twelve o'clock. He was eating eggs and drinking black coffee. A late breakfast, not lunch. He was wet and tired after a long walk in heavy rain. All the way down into town from the highway.

He retyped the whole of the first chapter in the third person, read it aloud and dismissed it. Tossed it into a box he was using for filing stuff. Which is how I came to read it twenty-five years later.

Apart from the wholesale deletion of the opening paragraph it was a remarkably clean first-draft first page of a first-time novel. At this primal stage only six more words were cut, and a couple of dozen inserted. It was like the three-year-old sitting on that beast of a tricycle or the seventeen-year-old getting behind the wheel of a car: he was off and running, and nothing and no one was going to stand in his way. About four days in he experienced 'a frisson of disappointment and irritation' when his wife reminded him they had to go out and do something. It was then he knew he was doing the right thing with his life. It was the same feeling he had when he was obliged to tear himself away from reading a good book.

That was the last time he would scratch an opening paragraph. 'I'd rather hang myself than waste the start of a novel,' he said. First sentences set the tone and raised questions: 'They found out about him in July and stayed angry all through August' (*Without Fail*). *Who? Why?* More, they would come to dictate where the novel was going. Like in *Past Tense*, where felicitous mentions of 'Maine' and 'birds' told Lee his twenty-third book would couple a spooky Stephen King-style strand with the back story of Reacher's birdwatching father. Or *Blue Moon*, where the simplicity of 'The city looked small on a map of America' determined the architectural feel of the whole.

From the outset, Lee knows what he 'must' do. Here are his first-time plot notes (KF1011A):

Features of plot –

Must be action, adventure, <u>ingenuity</u>, unbeatable self-defence. Must be a surrogate, vicarious, escapist mood but deadly serious. Integral action & adventure necessary, ingenuity & self-confidence in all predicaments vital to provide escapist feeling. Need to appeal to power-less, unconfident readers who would secretly like to enact fantasies e.g. survive outside a job, beat up their boss, be unafraid etc. etc.

At the top of KF1013 is this short paragraph:

Barest possible outline: H is an alienated loner, redundant from job, becomes involved in some kind of [activity] which provides a deter-mined loner the opportunity of appropriating large amount of cash, which he does, after dangers and contests, subsequently leaving the area, revenged against oppression, and enriched.

On the flip side, in a darker pencil, are some sketchy thoughts around chapter two. Williams hasn't yet become Morrison and Jones hasn't yet become Baker, but X (Hubble) and H have now been named:

Jones did it.

Tapes are important. Removed with files Fri pm by Williams. Finlay and Roscoe can't find them Sat. Eventually they are found in Williams's house – doctored re confession from Reacher, Hubble re hit. Also report written by Williams re death of Hubble & Reacher in prison i.e. Reacher strangled Hubble, Reacher killed by intervention of other prisoners.

Mon am Williams is found killed. Hubble disappears. Finlay is not promoted. Mayor makes Jones Chief.

Lunch at Eno's – two waitresses, one wears glasses.

Hubble's tape cannot be found therefore no pursuit of Hubble.

KF1014 begins with a selection of possible titles. The second makes 'Killing Floor' seem positively upbeat, and the third suggests that Reacher, at this point, is more *cursed* than *blessed*:

> Bad Luck and Trouble
> No Luck at all
> Born under a Bad Sign
> Down to the Crossroads
> Got no Place to Go

The reverse is pure structuralist theory. Like Canon R. G. Lunt had once said, Jim Grant was showing signs of being a real intellectual. The untitled list has its origins in Vladimir Propp's thirty-one narrative functions in *Morphology of the Folktale* (1928), mediated via Joseph Campbell's *The Hero with a Thousand Faces* (1949), which articulates the seventeen stages of the 'hero's journey', and Christopher Vogler's Hollywood manual, *The Writer's Journey: Mythic Structure for Writers* (2007), which reduces the seventeen to a more manageable twelve.

> Ordinary World / Status Quo
> Call to Adventure / description of problem
> Refusal of the Call / reluctance
> Meeting the Mentor / i.e. what is the motivator
> Crossing the first threshold / i.e. precipitator
> Tests, Allies, Enemies / initial alignment of characters
> Approach to the Innermost Cave
> Supreme Ordeal – climactic danger
> Reward
> The Road Back – not without difficulties
> Resurrection – reaching the uplands
> Return with elixir – happy & enriched ending

Lee was laying the foundations for his signature brand of mythic realism.

There are pages and pages of painstaking calculations. It was almost like he was missing school. Only a few have to do with plot:

> A dollar bill weighs 0.94 gram (♎1)
> 1064 dollars = 2.2 pounds
> 1,083,345 dollars = 1 ton
> 1 pound of single dollar bills = $480
> 1 ton of single dollar bills = approx $1 million
> 30 dollars = 1 oz
> $480 = 1 lb
> airconditioner box = ? 200 lbs = $96,000

Most, densely covered, are obsessively concerned with the internal economy of the text. A 'schedule' lists page counts for each chapter across different drafts. There is a comparison of his own pen draft with books by James Patterson and Patricia Cornwell: overall number of pages, number of lines per page and number of characters per line. A note reads '257 words per page (on my draft)'.

On the facing page Lee has written:

> What the writer needs is a sixty-two character line
> What this page needs is a line of sixty-two characters
> What this page needs are lines of sixty-two characters each
> *What these lines need are lengths of sixty-two characters each

Patterson's lines were typically 63 characters long. Lee notes that Grisham's *The Firm* has 62 characters x 40 lines, whereas his 'Bad Luck and Trouble' ('Bad' for short) has 79 characters x 28 lines. He is happy with the ratios. He tots up the total number of letters in 189 words (ranging between 1 and 13 characters in length) and calculates an average word length of 4.15 characters – 'call it 4'. He concludes: 'Aim for 472 pages or more of my m/s.'

Finally, in March 1995, he is satisfied. Jane reads it. Ruth reads it. Andrew reads it. They are all satisfied. Lee types up chapters one, six and nine and sends them off to two literary agents. Darley Anderson bites immediately. Blake Friedmann, like Cambridge's Sidney Sussex College, misses out.

Then comes the to and fro of consultation with agents and editors. Summaries of objections from readers. Responses to those objections: an 'x' in the margin where he thinks they've got it wrong, the single word 'think' when he thinks it's worth thinking about. There are maps of Margrave and 'to do' lists and itemised accounts of proposed changes, both planned and executed. There are synopses batted back and forth. Jim practises writing the word 'Lee', initially opting to form the vowels in the style of the lower-case epsilon.

Most revealing is the correspondence from Putnam's David Highfill: critical, demanding, insistent, encouraging, cajoling, nurturing. His seven-page letter of 22 February 1996 in response to the first major redraft concludes thus:

> I know some of these issues are complex, but I'm confident you can write thrillers with the best of them. I mean that. You have enormous talent. I know I'm spending more time here with what I don't like, but you know what I love in this.

With the tiniest reservation, the debut author takes it on the chin (4 March). 'Excellent points, no problems at all with most of them. I'm about halfway through the edit, your suggestions are in place, and I'm on course to lose around 125 pages.' And: 'You're the boss, and as you know, I'll do whatever it takes.'

This is the same Lee Child who twenty years later would say: 'I tell my editor she can make three comments and I'll act on one of them.' For Reacher no. 7, *Persuader*, Transworld's Marianne Velmans was still valiantly covering slips of A6 paper in detailed handwritten notes. On one she has written thirteen carefully reasoned lines on continuity issues, to do with time phrases and plates of food and 'the best way to create clarity'. At the foot of the page Lee has added three words in block capitals: 'KEEP AS IS.'

Highfill's main concern is with pacing. He wants to sell the book as a thriller, not a mystery. Chapters need to be shorter, more like Thomas Harris. Reacher needs to be more active. He needs to stop telling us his plan in advance of executing it. 'This is a habit of yours. Watch it in other places too.' There is too much dialogue. 'If the total now is 625 pages and we're cutting 150 pages, then most scenes should come down about 25%.'

Here is his note on p. 547:

> R sits down to eat at Eno's with Picard guarding him. R figures out how he can beat the clock and Kliner. This is brilliant deduction on Reacher's part [. . .] but it's a step back from the action. Can he think about this in half the number of pages? While he's driving with Picard? Can he just think about one challenge at a time instead of ticking them all off in his mind over 10 pages? He doesn't leave Eno's for 10 pages. This has all been thinking. It's slowing it down.

Judiciously, he throws in the odd carrot of praise: 'p. 526: Kliner is the "Henry Ford of counterfeiting". Love it.' Or 'p. 544: Wonderful scene [. . .]. Kliner's dilemma is delicious. [. . .] Very, very smart plotting on your part.' And 'p. 584: R. breaks Finlay out with the Bentley! Terrific.'

Lee cuts eight pages of dialogue between Reacher and Charley Hubble in chapter eleven down to one. His conversations with Finlay are similarly abbreviated.

On 19 April Highfill writes that the streamlined version is 'so much stronger'. Lee has done 'a terrific job'. But . . . it could be stronger still. This letter is a mere two pages, but accompanied by brutal line-edits. 'I've cut down some of your section and chapter endings.' Highfill wants the action to 'speak for itself'. He doesn't want Lee 'leading the reader too much' ('let me know if you disagree'). He is most ruthless towards the end, where 'the plot really needs to get cooking'.

They've clearly spoken on the phone. In his response dated 27 May Lee's final paragraph reads:

> I totally agree with you about the attraction of a more resonant, more up-scale, bookstore-rather-than-supermarket-rack type of title. Having said that, I think *Killing Floor* has a number of virtues . . . it's terse, hard-edged, slightly quirky, menacing. Main problem is, right now I can't think of a real alternative except possibly *The World All Changed* . . . which relates well in terms of the upheaval in Reacher's life, his brother dying, the nature of the counterfeiting method, the international source, the changes in the other characters' lives, etc. etc., but it's a bit *soft* perhaps . . .

Third go round (16 July), just prior to the production of galley proofs, Highfill shortens some of the sex scenes, which are a touch 'melodramatic' and 'make the book look more "downmarket", as we say'. He wants *Killing Floor* to be read as 'an important hardcover debut', not 'a down and dirty paperback original'.

Lee responds promptly, on 18 July, after another phone call, his first letter on headed paper, including an early adoption of American spelling. 'Meanwhile, back to the T-word [. . .] Anything here you like?'

TITLES WHICH TRY TO SUM UP THE BOOK:

Over the Line

The Threshold

Exact Retribution

Hard Currency

Method of Payment

Provocation

The Toll

The First Rule (. . . this is Jane's favorite – I like it too . . . poses the basic read-on question, what is the first rule?)

Loaded

Circulation

Dead Line

The Velocity of Money

TITLES WHICH TRY TO SUM UP JACK REACHER:

Unconditional

The Unconditional

Unconditional Loyalty

The Troublemaker

The Uncompromiser

Uncompromised

No Compromise

The Adjudicator

Really, how hard could it be? There is no response archived, but elsewhere I came across other signs of Jane's unobtrusive input, like the handwritten list of birds she supplied when Lee began writing *Past Tense*.

Four days later anxiety levels are running high. Lee writes a two-page letter that can only be described as impassioned. He is bitterly annoyed at a dilatory courier, who embodies all the shameful failings of 'merrie olde England': 'We're stuck in the post-industrial, pre-service-industry quiet zone. I guess they understand the concept of service, like they know there are such things as poisonous spiders or decent burgers, but it's all theoretical, it's something which exists in other parts of the world, nothing to do with them.'

But this rant is all displacement. 'I'm still moderately agitated about the title.'

His UK publishers feared the title might be off-putting to women readers, who might 'never pick it up'. Lee had done some 'seriously flawed anecdotal research' among his female friends, who tended to agree they might pass.

> I've tried hard to think of alternatives. It seems to me there are two routes to go down. The first is to try to sum up the feeling of the whole book – which I think 'Killing Floor' does pretty well. It captures the violence, the thrills, the hard edge, the tight location, as well as being an intriguing pair of words, somewhat musical, even slightly poetic. The only alternative would be something like 'Reasonable Force' or 'Justice Zone'.
>
> The second route is to try to sum up the character of Reacher, to capture the tough-guy-with-attitude, latent-danger type of thing. My favorite would be 'Forbidden Door'. From p. 106, '. . . tough shit. He started it, right? Attacking me was like pushing open a forbidden door. What waited on the other side was his problem. His risk. If he didn't like it, he shouldn't have pushed open the damn door . . .'. I like this approach. I think it's equally valid to try to sum Reacher up as it is to sum the whole story up. Maybe more valid, if Reacher is to be a serial character.

All those he asked favoured 'Forbidden Door' over 'Killing Floor'.

The final paragraph is raw and emotional: 'Anyway, to save my brain from exploding, I'm going to stop worrying over it.' Whatever the final decision, he would support 'the boss' 100 per cent. Transworld would just have to 'suck it up'.

> It's very, very important to me that there is no misunderstanding between the two of us – my position is that your view is binding, and I need you to understand that I am totally happy with that situation, and I definitely wouldn't want it any other way. OK?

This (possibly unique) expression of need was reassuring. As was the reticent request for reassurance in turn at the end. He was human after all.

Somehow, over the course of his illustrious career, Lee Child had done what the best musicians and ballet dancers do: make a truly staggering amount of hard graft look easy. It was excellence, but not without effort.

He had written the whole of *Killing Floor* in seven months, on his days off, while holding down a full-time job in the pitiless face of imminent redundancy. He'd written it out twice by hand, in pencil and blue ink and red ink, Tippexing and revising and annotating. He'd produced at least two typewritten drafts.

'The work you put in was epic,' I wrote to Lee after my first week in the archive. 'I know,' he answered. 'Unimaginable now. Got very lazy.'

I was reminded of his old form master: 'Only his own efforts can ensure success.' But Jim Grant didn't really care what the masters thought. They were the educational equivalent of newspaper critics. The motivational words he harked back to came from one of his sixth-form contemporaries, S. D. 'Sid' Jones. Sid wore a cravat. He liked to flaunt his manhood on the diving board of the outdoor swimming pool, and would don a fresh pair of ironed, neatly folded, sparkling white Y-fronts after every shower. He smoked John Player Special cigarettes. His mother had a green Triumph TR4A and Sid himself drove an orange MG 1100. All in all he was the kind of guy who left a lasting impression. He was only a middling rugby player, but had once given a terrific team talk that had stuck with Jim for ever.

'My motto,' Lee wrote to me, quoting Sid: 'I can't grow any more talent, but I can out-work you.'

'It's something they teach you in the army,' said Reacher in *Blue Moon*.

> The only thing under your direct control is how hard you work. In other words, if you really, really buckle down today, and you get the intelligence, the planning, and the execution each a hundred percent exactly correct, then you are bound to prevail.

31

The Plan

'I don't plan to fail.'
Without Fail, 2002

As his fanbase grew and he told more and more stories about how he got started and how he worked, or told the same stories over and over again, at first finessing and refining, then later embellishing and retouching and heightening, Lee Child became famed as the mysterious *man with no plot*.

'I never plot,' he would say blithely, stretching out his long legs and lying back on the sofa and lighting another cigarette and yawning. Plotting was a bore.

He'd forgotten about those hours of industry at the dining-room table.

'Everyone has a plan, until they get punched in the mouth,' says Reacher in *The Affair*. Lee had something of the magpie in him, and didn't think twice about pinching a pretty line from Mike Tyson, or Clive James (the walnut-stuffed condom) or his old friend E. L. Doctorow (writing is like driving a car at night). Jim Grant's plan had been to stay in the job he loved, doing the thing he was good at, making more money than he'd ever imagined. Until, that is, his boss said something that made it impossible for him to continue. Which was when he fell back on Plan B.

Plan B was to write a bestseller.

Trouble was, he didn't feel like planning any more. Life in television had been about nothing else, planning every second of every shift, and now he was all planned out. He was done with planning. From now on he would be footloose and fancy-free, Reacher-style. *No plans, no drafts.*

Or at least he would be, after a little planning. He'd been good at that job. More than good, outstanding. Maybe even the best. He'd excelled in his class. They'd been crazy to get rid of him. He'd learned a lot of things at Granada, but the one thing he'd mastered was planning.

Why not play to his strengths? It was his scientific approach. He would plan now so as to be free of it later. He would come up with the masterplan to end all masterplans, and more importantly, all planning.

Right at the top was *no more early morning shifts*. 'The idea of getting up at five in the morning to start writing? I'd rather hang myself.'

Lee told me that strictly speaking, the single biggest influence on him at Granada was Steve Gallagher, who had shown him 'it could be done, that it was possible'. Gallagher remembered an early conversation about writing, but with Jane as well, who was toying with the idea of a historical novel on William the Conqueror's mother, Queen Emma of Normandy. Jim thought it was a great subject. Jane tested out a few pages on her husband, who rewrote them with added violence, whereupon she returned to academia. Gallagher said:

> Much later there was the 'I hate those bastards at Granada' conversation where Jim described a plan to study bestsellers and analyse their moving parts with a view to writing one of his own. Using a pseudonym would free him to change name and take a second crack at the market if the first try didn't work out.

His agent was impressed by the pseudonym. Not just because it would slot neatly on the shelf alongside stablemate Martina Cole. Not just because it was short typographically and 'could get bigger as he got bigger'. It was the fact he'd chosen it at all. 'Usually I have to be the one who suggests a better writing name,' said Darley Anderson when I met him in London. But Lee was 'a lot of moves ahead of the game'. So far ahead that they were well into their working relationship before Darley discovered Lee was not who he said he was. The first he knew of James Grant was when they were booking hotels for a tour and everyone assumed it was a mistake or that Lee was a fugitive from the law. For years the author would pass off 'Lee Child' with foreign publishers as 'my middle names'.

Back in September 1994 Jim had tested out a few pages on Jane and she hadn't felt the need to rewrite them. She told him to keep going and since then he hadn't looked back. But he *had* redrafted, diligently. 'Who sends in a manuscript saying THIRD DRAFT?' Darley was still bowled over by it. 'Nobody. Especially not a debut author. The guy is so clever. He was telling me this had been worked on and polished.'

Lee was accustomed to talking about how he'd come up with his series character.

Sometimes he made it sound like a blind process. You couldn't overthink it, or tailor it for male or female readers. The irruption of Reacher into Jim Grant's life, and the success that followed in his wake, was a happy accident over which the author had minimal control. He just wrote Reacher. Reacher was *what came out*.

> I'd been in show business long enough to know if you set out to do something deliberately you end up with a laundry list. I did the first book unconsciously. (To Christopher Wigginton)

You talk as if I designed Reacher with more care than I did. I learned long ago that with an audience you can't predict anything. If you over-design you end up with a laundry list, and it comes out artificial. So I just closed my eyes, metaphorically, and typed – or wrote with a pencil, in fact. Reacher came fully formed out of my instinctive approach. (To Janet Maslin)

At other times he was frank about how he had forensically examined certain strategic choices. He'd read Michael Connelly (*The Black Echo* was published in 1992) and recognised that he was looking at the next big publishing phenomenon. To go head-to-head with Connelly would be inviting hubris. So instead he planned to do the opposite. 'Hieronymous' was a complicated name, so Lee would choose the simplest name imaginable. Bosch had a job and home in Los Angeles, so Jack would be homeless and unemployed. There would be no ex-wives and no drunkenness and no deep psychological trauma. Reacher would not be a dysfunctional character, because that trend was 'out of control'. Did we really want to read books about increasingly miserable people? Lee hated a bandwagon, and the alcoholic-with-regrets trope had become a parody of itself. The only problem he foresaw was that the good Goliath – decent, untroubled, indomitable, fearless – was potentially boring. So Reacher had his flaws, but was oblivious to them, which was one way the reader could gain an edge. Reacher had only two moods, as Maslin observed, 'angry and not angry'.

It was a kind of reverse homage, a reactive move in the long-term game. 'I wanted to go back to a much simpler, plainer kind of guy,' said Lee, putting it simply and plainly. It was 'unreal', but why become a writer 'merely to reproduce the conditions of reality'?

'Why set your books in America?' Lee was asked at ThrillerFest 2017. To which he answered: 'Because like the bank robbers say when asked why they robbed the bank – *that's where the money is.*'

Then, showing traces of the righteous anger that fuelled him:

> I'd already lived in Britain for thirty-nine years, which is enough for anyone I'd say. I was pissed off at Britain and wanted to escape. British people are stubbornly illiterate. I read somewhere that six out of ten have never read a book. You all think that we're born having read Jane Austen, but it's not true. Plus there was a great independent bookshop trade in the US, selling by word of mouth. British attitudes to money are weird, no one will ever spend their money on someone else's recommendation.

But 'the real reason'?

> My wanderer needed a big empty frontier landscape. That landscape used to exist in Europe, around five hundred years ago, for example in the Black Forest, where there were bears and wolves. But that feeling has been forced out of Europe and migrated to the States. My character couldn't work anywhere except America.

Australia had the landscape. But the population was paltry. The market just didn't compare. In Canada 'you might not find enough trouble'. Canadians were never bad guys in his books, but Reacher tended to view them as 'hapless'.

Both reasons were real. There was no conflict between business and art. The aesthetic imperative was not incompatible with a 'shameless, meretricious ambition to penetrate that enormous, glamorous market'.

On 21 March 1995, one Lee Child (c/o 10 Abbotsgate, Kirkby Lonsdale) wrote his first ever letter, and signed his name (officially) for the very first time. It would not be the last. He was a mysterious, shadowy figure. But his words were plain and his message clear:

Dear Darley Anderson

I'm writing to you because I've got a novel to sell. It's a thriller, lots of action and suspense, an attractive main character, a hard enough edge to make it competitive, and a 'big' epic focus to the plot. [. . .]

I'm not new to the entertainment media – I worked in commercial television for nearly eighteen years – but this is my first novel. I'm planning to spend the next three years doing whatever it takes to become a successful writer of commercial fiction. I want to offer strong plots, tough characters, realistic action, fresh perspectives – all written in a way which is accessible to anybody, but with enough inherent style to satisfy readers who look for more.

The manuscript is completed and ready now. It has not been offered to anybody before.

Yours

Lee Child

In response he received an even more direct handwritten postcard dated 23 March:

Dear Mr Child

Your ms looks interesting. Please send me the first consecutive five chps. At present you sent chp 1 and chp 6, but I need consecutive chps to get a proper feel of the flow of the novel please.

Sincerely, D. Anderson

Darley prided himself on reading a manuscript the day it came in and reacting swiftly. That way there was less risk of missing out on the big coup. That way he was sure to get in ahead of Blake Friedmann, to whom Lee Child had written on the very same day (and whose lukewarm response on 7 April read: 'I'm sorry to say we don't feel that strongly about your work, but please do persevere').

366

Lee had found Darley in the 1995 *Writers and Artists Yearbook*. It was the next step in his military campaign but there was a whiff of destiny about it too, like they'd been looking for each other and it was meant to be. You must have come across me quickly, Darley said. No, Lee replied: he'd started at the end and read backwards, so he wasn't influenced by alphabetical bias. It was a habit of his (but fortunately not of the average bookshop browser).

By the time he got to Anderson, he told me in Bristol at the 2018 CrimeFest, he had trawled through 'loads of poncey, posh, precious London agent blurbs about poetry and what-not, all self-penned in the third-person'. It was making him sick just thinking about it. Three things stood out about Darley. He used the words 'commercial' and 'hard-boiled' and cited figures for deals secured for previous debut authors. First impressions were not merely positive but a blessed relief.

'I was the only agent to mention a sum of money,' Darley recalled. It was the £150,000 advance he'd got for Martina Cole in 1991, the only other time in his thirty-year career as an agent that he'd known with absolute certainty he'd struck gold.

'We all know the English are uptight about money,' Darley said.

> But if Caradoc King at AP Watt Literary Agency had mentioned the sums of money he got for 'The Horse Whisperer' by Nicholas Evans in 1995 – two million dollars for US film rights, £360,000 for his book in the UK, these were records at the time – then maybe he would have got Lee instead.

Lee made it clear he wanted 'to sell a lot of copies and make a lot of money'. Which was exactly what Darley wanted too.

> We both had chips on our shoulders. His was being fired from Granada. Never forgive, never forget. It became a spur to him.

He wanted to make sure that his second career wouldn't be a fuck-up too. He felt he should have anticipated and evaded the first fuck-up, and was trying to do everything in his power to stay ahead of the game. And twenty years in commercial television had made him a commercial animal, just like Patterson, who came into the writing business as an ad man.

Darley described his own previous career in publishing as niche. Nobody identified his talent and he tired of working for nobodies. When he decided to strike out on his own he started with no money and an overdraft, just like Lee. 'I had to succeed,' he said. 'I had no choice. I had to make it work.' It was a marriage made in heaven.

In a 2009 interview for *Parade* Lee explained the 'fuck-up' in his own terms.

> I felt betrayed. Not by the people I had worked for – they went in the very first wave. I felt betrayed by my own naiveté. The modern world had snuck up on me, and I hadn't seen it coming. The rules had changed, and I hadn't noticed.

Being sucker-punched would henceforth be a thing of the past.

From the beginning Darley had focused on commercial fiction. 'I have nil interest in literary fiction,' he said. 'I'm the only agent in London who doesn't care about winning prizes.'

Lee remembered their first meeting, in March 1995 at Darley's office, which occupied the basement of his house in south-west London. Later Darley would buy another house, two houses in fact, proportionate to Lee's four, and his offices would expand to fill the whole of the original building. They had a 'vigorous discussion of business'. Darley, with his 'roll up your sleeves and get on with it mentality', was 'obviously the guy'. But as if testing each other's mettle they also had an argument. Darley had cited Ken Follett's *Eye of the Needle* as a paradigm of the perfect balance between pacing and plausibility and an example of seamless action. 'I disagreed, because there's one big implausibility in that book.' Darley was 'a Cambridge guy' and ten years older, but deferred increasingly to Lee. 'We still talk tropes and trends, and what other writers should be doing. Now he thinks I know better than him, and obviously I do.'

Recognising that 'Bad Luck and Trouble' (as it then was) was 'very visual, very filmic' and bearing in mind *The Horse Whisperer*, Darley went straight to Hollywood. He wanted to sell the film rights first, then the US book rights, and only then the UK rights. 'But it backfired spectacularly.'

Steve Fisher (then of the H. N. Swanson Literary Agency) had been in the business about five years when he got a call out of the blue from Darley, who said he was looking for film representation for his agency and by the way he was representing this new thriller writer named Lee Child. He hadn't sent him out for publishing yet but thought he was really terrific. Steve's eyes 'rolled back a bit', because: no name, no track record, 'it's very much a challenge'. But for some reason he agreed. It was one of the best thrillers he'd ever read. 'I said to Darley, and I wasn't kidding, that it quite literally gave me nightmares. The men in the overshoes, I'll never forget that, that really did me in.'

So he sent it out. But there were no takers. What's more, he reported back, 'for now the book is dead in the water'.

Why didn't Hollywood want it? No name, no track record, Steve thought, looking back on it, but then hypothesised that Lee's books were cinematic in 'a more modest way'. The studios were into 'four-quadrant big tentpole' movies, and 'that means you're blowing up the world' space odyssey-style. The Reacher books would make terrific movies but wouldn't be 'quote unquote big' in the way *Transformers* or *Batman* were.

Lee and Darley had played for high stakes, but were forced to regroup.

Darley wasn't a man to give up. He realised he had to agent the book as though he were a New York agent living in New York. He had to position himself mentally where Lee Child wanted to be. 'He was in Cumbria and I was in London, but I had to think *I'm an American agent and he's an American writer.*' The agent was buying into the author's story.

'His ambition was to be on the *New York Times* bestseller list, not the *Times* or *Sunday Times*.' It was crucial that his primary editor should be based in America. 'We always considered the United Kingdom a subsidiary market.'

It was then that Darley decided to target Irwyn Applebaum, boss of Bantam, on an exclusive. He was poised to say the words *a million dollars for two*. Applebaum was in London and agreed to read the manuscript over the weekend. On Monday morning he was on the phone saying: 'Darley, I read it, but it's not for me. We get offered everything. This isn't even worth taking on editorially.'

Applebaum and Child would have a good laugh over it later.

'I was in shock,' Darley said. But he dusted himself down and got back on the horse. Plenty of publishers had turned down Grisham's first novel, and even Frederick Forsyth's. 'Who would turn down *The Day of the Jackal*?' Ludicrous, but somehow to be expected in the commercial sector. A commercial book had to be well written, he hastened to clarify, but that meant writing that worked as a vehicle for story and character.

Soon after, Fisher was having lunch in Los Angeles with David Highfill, 'the first to pick up on the quality and commercial appeal of *Killing Floor*'. David said *I love thrillers and have you got anything for me?* and Steve said *That's funny, because a week ago I read this terrific thriller and I don't think there's a publishing deal yet*. Then Steve called Darley and said, 'I've met this terrific-sounding editor.' 'I pitched the novel like a movie and he really liked the idea.'

'Everyone else who had read it passed,' Highfill said, meaning other US publishers, when I spoke to him in New York in 2018. But he was seduced right away. It was fresh, but all the right touches were there: voice, language, tempo. It was new, but with echoes of all the old familiar heroes: Joseph Campbell, Clint Eastwood, James Bond.

'You know it, it's there on the page.' He was then just thirty years old and had only recently moved into publishing, but he knew it all the same. 'I was the new kid on the block and I was saying to the sales force: *You don't know me, but this guy is going to be a superstar.*'

Lee's faux-naif style had given his writing a distinctive fingerprint, just as he'd planned. Literary voice was a metaphor he took literally, and he considered this his single biggest breakthrough at the beginning. 'It had to be like someone was speaking a story to me.' The *New York Times* no. 1 of fifty thousand years ago was the guy you most enjoyed listening to, and Lee wanted to tap straight into that ancient collective memory. He'd read too many books to cite a dominant influence, but there were two voiceovers he couldn't get out of his head: the stilted, staccato expression of Kevin Costner in *Dances with Wolves* (1990) and the unpolished, melancholy narration, both innocent and knowing, of seventeen-year-old Linda Manz in Terrence Malick's *Days of Heaven* (1978). Lee wanted that same authenticity for Reacher (and also loved Malick's painterly style and his Hopper house set in a never-ending sea of wheat).

Highfill felt he had 'barely touched' the manuscript. Archival evidence indicates otherwise, but in his view the changes were superficial. You could edit for plot, momentum, pace, maybe even character, but not for voice.

Imagine there comes to you a man in a suit: handsome, well put together – cut, colour, fabric, image, design, all there. My intervention came down to cuffs or no cuffs, or a slightly narrower lapel. Maybe I might move a button.

It wasn't entirely clear if Highfill was talking about the man or his book, but 'part of publishing is falling in love'. 'When it comes to debut novels, no one's ever come up to that level for me.'

He would say to you that he did it like in a fever dream, very fast, that it came to him fully formed. But his instincts and choices and decisions were all right.

Highfill claimed titles were 95 per cent of marketing. 'Bad Luck and Trouble' wasn't well received. For Darley it was too negative and for Highfill too jaunty, 'with an Elmore Leonard style humour that wasn't Lee'. When you were established fans would buy your book regardless, but for a debut *Killing Floor* 'was more masculine and fitted the target audience better'. Putnam, he admitted, had been slow to realise 'how viscerally Lee connected to women'.

Die Trying started life as 'They, The People'. For no. 3 Lee, Darley and Transworld wanted 'The Hook' ('too pared back for an American audience, almost cartoonish') but settled on *Tripwire* in the interests of transatlantic harmony (Darley still preferred the nod to one of Lee's greatest characters). No one could agree over no. 4 ('Doom Changes', 'Smokescreen', 'None So Blind'), which was published as both *The Visitor* (UK) and *Running Blind* (US). Highfill was in awe of 'the green paint one' (whose villain was a consummate planner), which 'seemed like something from outer space but was a total locked-room mystery, all logic, all right there to be figured out'.

But his favourite would always be *Killing Floor*, 'my first love, like your first child'. He sent a card with the first physical copy: 'Lee! The baby! It's been delivered!! Isn't it the most beautiful?'

Darley was happy with Putnam as Lee's first home in America. They had four or five authors shifting five hundred thousand hardbacks a year and the same number shifting four hundred thousand: in Highfill's words, 'we were mammoth'. Lee had provided a figure for how much he needed to earn and Darley had said he couldn't promise ('if you promise a sum that sum takes on a reality and with thrillers it's feast or famine') and then gone out and got 50 per cent more ('$150,000 – a ridiculously small amount of money even then'), and with that as ammunition, the same figure again but in sterling.

Highfill recalled Darley telling him about a taxi ride to Transworld. Marianne Velmans had expressed qualified interest early on, but now agent and author were buoyed by a strong revised manuscript and the finalised American deal and had secured a face-to-face meeting. It was 22 May 1996, Lee's father's seventy-second birthday. 'Are you nervous?' Darley asked. Lee said: 'This is a ride. It might take a few years, but we're all gonna be awash with money.' Which was a ballsy thing to say, yet apt, since that was precisely the ending of *Killing Floor*, 'where they are literally wading through mountains of cash'. Highfill was worried it made Lee sound mercenary, whereas he was 'just a lovely guy coming off the dole'.

Free of such qualms, Darley had also recounted this story. He knew Lee was sceptical about British business, so had asked himself: *Which is the UK company that Lee Child will approve of in terms of their effectiveness?* Easy. Transworld stood head and shoulders above the rest. They had been going fifty years but despite a succession of managing directors had retained the same ethos, and though their list was small they had more no. 1s than any other publisher. 'I needed Lee to think this was an impressive outfit.' If anyone was nervous it was Darley. He was like a jittery matchmaker counting on the two parties doing the Highfill thing and falling in love.

When they arrived at Transworld there were six or seven of them lined up on the other side of the table like they were interviewing for the post of vice chancellor at a university. Darley said *Killing Floor* wasn't on offer to anyone else, then handed the floor to Lee. The effect was instantaneous. 'They were stunned, starstruck, spellbound: it turned into a seminar on the art of the thriller and the history of thriller writing and they were totally captivated.' A week to the day after this meeting the publisher made an offer for two books and Darley said no. They made a second offer and Darley said no again. They came back with a note of exasperation and said this was the end of it, and Darley said no. Then seized the initiative. 'I took the fight to them and said, another twenty thousand on top. They were not happy, but they did it. It was never an auction. It was them against me, and we closed on that deal.'

Lee remembered trying to shut Darley up by saying it was in the bag and how they would soon be awash with money. But that was on the way back. On the way there, he was supremely confident. 'I was going to eat it up with a spoon, they were going to be my absolute slaves, in ten minutes I would have them eating out of my hand.'

It was me sitting on one side of a long table, with about ten of them on the other side, including [then marketing director] Larry [Finlay] and [publicity director] Patsy [Irwin] and [editor] Marianne [Velmans, all of whom would be with him till the end]. Darley was there as a silent observer. But you have to remember, I was practised. I'd been doing it for years at Granada. Big meetings, just me against management, against the bosses, getting the deal that I needed to get, much bigger, more critical deals that affected lots of people, not just me, much higher stakes. This was child's play by comparison. I knew what I was doing. I knew I would win. I always knew.

It was almost the first thing Highfill had said: 'He has a mammoth ego.' But it was equally fair to say that he gave himself no airs and graces.

'It's like I've got these killer beams,' Lee added. 'I can make people do what I want them to, I can bend them to my will. It's a despicable skill.'

> It's not difficult. No, not difficult at all [thinks the Moriarty-like villain in *The Visitor*]. It's meticulous, is what it is. It's like everything else. If you plan it properly, if you think it through, if you prepare correctly, if you rehearse, then it's easy. It's a technical process, just like you knew it would be. Like a science. It can't be anything else.

Lee and Darley talked percentages. The usual deal for agents was 15 per cent for the home market and 20 for foreign. 'Even though we were both English the US was our primary market. Our foreign market was the UK, but Darley was expecting me to treat it as domestic.' Banking on a long-term investment Lee instructed him to treat both countries as foreign. Which put Darley doubly in his corner.

It was a mutual admiration society. No one thought more highly of Darley than Lee, unless it was Fisher. Darley had 'an unerring sense of taste' and had been Lee's *consigliere*. 'He's a phenomenal individual. In the same way that Darley is lucky to have found Lee, Lee is lucky to have found Darley. It was a career-defining moment for both of them.'

'If you measure it in chart weeks [as dominated by his big four – Lee Child, Martina Cole, John Connolly, Tana French],' Lee said, as someone in the habit of measuring things, 'he has to be the most successful agent in the whole world through sheer force of character and his ability to spot talent.' He was deadly, but civilised too. 'It was wonderful to see him doing his English gentleman thing with US publishers. We were a formidable team.' Darley had a gift for making the author believe he was great and making the publisher believe it too.

With other agents, it's like they hold out a toad in the palm of their hand and say, if you treat this toad right you'll have a beautiful princess. But Darley holds out his palm and says look, here, this is already a beautiful princess, and I'm offering it to you.

There was no written agreement. 'Never has been, never will be.' It was all done on a handshake. 'He sends me running updates, so he's self-auditing all the time, but it's remarkable, when you think that there's a nine-figure cash flow. Well over one hundred million dollars have flowed through that office on my behalf.' The liquid metaphor harked back to the long-gone days of grubby minicabs, before the advent of the Jaguars and Bentleys.

On 31 May 1996 Larry Finlay of Transworld addressed his first letter to Lee Child. There is both pain and admiration to be read in his opening exclamations.

Dear Lee

Great news! I'm really pleased that we got you in the end – Darley drives a hard sell!

As we said when we met, at Transworld we really believe that the relationship between author and publisher works best as a collaborative partnership – and I very much look forward to working with you in the years to come to help you achieve your (and now our) ambition to get you to the top of the bestsellers lists.

Attached to the letter in the archive is a page of partially typed, partially handwritten calculations and projections for 'Killing Floor and Untitled Lee Child 2nd novel' – a copy of the 'pink form' used at Transworld's internal acquisitions meeting.

Under 'Comments' Finlay has written: 'Would definitely like to buy Lee Child. Think we could really have a success on our hands.'

He asks his team to run more figures (15,000 hardbacks at £9.99 as opposed to 7000 at £15.99, and to consider a trade paperback for airports) and signs off: 'But whatever, let's get him!!'

Marketing propose an initial budget of £15,000 for the hardback and £10,000 for the paperback, going up to £40,000 and £30,000 for Book 2, where the projected print runs and sales figures increase by roughly 50 per cent. Unsigned comment: 'We need to spend high on Book 1, possibly more than £15,000 if it all comes together.'

Dated 4 June, Lee's reply reads:

> Dear Larry
>
> Thanks very much for your letter – I'm thrilled and delighted that you took me on. The money is great – can't deny it – but what really does it for me is to see the words 'the marketing of your first novel' under the Transworld letterhead and over your signature – like a dream come true.
>
> As you know, my intention was to find the best team in town and then collaborate every step of the way. So – if there's anything at all, big or small, now or later, that I can do to improve my books or to help in their marketing, don't hesitate to let me know. I'm going to give this whole thing at least two hundred per cent – and I'm going to enjoy it.
>
> It was great meeting all of you. I've been in the media for a long time, but I can't ever remember meeting a team which was so on-the-ball yet so charming. I'm looking forward to a long and prosperous relationship.

The letter was circulated with the note: 'We have one enthusiastic author!'

Get yourself a good agent, Lee urged his acolytes at ThrillerFest. 'There is no greater distance in the world than between a good agent and a bad agent.' When someone asked how, he said: 'Go where the love is. Be guided by who respects you and what it's going to feel like. That's my yardstick for making all business decisions now.'

It was striking how freely the business invoked the concept of love. Highfill said:

> Publishing is hard. You do it for love, you don't always make a lot of money. Having a warm relationship makes all the difference. With Lee, there was an immediate connection, right from the start. I remember thinking: I just got so fucking lucky.

Lee:

> Perhaps David had more of that woman's sensibility. He fell in love with Reacher. You have to remember back then I was young and beautiful. I had intellect, and Englishness too.

There was heartache for David in the break-up. But he was a generous man. So often success comes to people for no good reason, he said, but 'this feels right'. Gallagher shared his sentiments. I asked if he'd been surprised by his old friend's success.

> In the sense that the odds in this business are so stacked against anyone taking their shot, then yes. But not if your definition of success is also bound up with the recognition and respect of your peers. That's earned.

If anyone could understand it, Rob would. But he was still marvelling over Jim's planning powers. The sheer audacity of it blew his mind.

I think he planned everything meticulously. I think he thought, 'OK, this is happening to me, so what am I gonna do about it? I know, I'll go get these foolscap pads and write a novel, and I'll aim it at America, because that's where the biggest market is, and I'll make this transcendent quantum leap . . . I'm not gonna go halfway house and write something for the Brits, I'm gonna set this in America and everyone's gonna react to this guy. I'm gonna create a superhero, a superstar, a Robin Hood.' I mean – who else would think of doing that?

Conscious intention was like the frame, as thoughtfully designed and fit for purpose as Jim's minimalist set for *A Doll's House*. But intention was not the same as execution. For that he would trust to his subconscious.

'When contemplating an offensive,' said Lila Hoth in *Gone Tomorrow*, citing a British book on empire, 'the very first thing you must plan is your inevitable retreat.'

But Lee wasn't Lila and he wasn't planning to fail. 'He had staked everything on it, [Reacher, *Echo Burning*]. He had no plan B.'

Hope for the best, plan for the worst. 'Reacher got that from me,' Lee said, as though that wasn't true of everything else.

32

Four Thousand Tons

A gigantic dune of money filled the whole shed.
Killing Floor, 1997

Highfill was Lee's first editor. But the first person to give him detailed editorial feedback was the official reader from the Darley Anderson Literary Agency: Elizabeth Wright.

On 11 May 1995 Mr Child received a three-page letter from Wright saying there was money to be made from 'a big thriller'. She said Darley thought Lee had it in him to write one and cited Jeffrey Archer as a redrafting role model ('We can all agree that the most annoying author in the world is Jeffrey Archer,' said Lee at the Theakston Old Peculier Crime Festival twenty-two years later). Then she got him started on doing *whatever it takes*.

Wright set out three main requirements: character, plot (which should be a chase) and pace (citing Forsyth, Follett and Lionel Davidson as exemplars). She had 'no worries' about the pace of 'Bad Luck and Trouble' and thought Reacher could 'potentially' meet the criteria for 'an exceptional central character'. It was step two that concerned her.

> Your chase [. . .] is for Reacher to get to Hubble first to prevent his penis being cut off and his family being brutally mutilated in front of his, Hubble's, eyes. But this is not strong enough. It is not earth

shattering enough. The plot is not good enough, neither is it written in a sufficiently nail-biting way.

I thought Ben and Lucy's dad Ian Gerrard, from Granada, was unlikely to agree that the stakes were too low, but Wright wanted a Hollywood-style climax.

Her letter ends:

> Roll on when the film rights are sold and we can all have dinner at the Ritz, better than scrambled eggs at Eno's!

Killing Floor was an immediate hit. The Transworld marketing team sold Lee Child as the British answer to John Grisham (the hardback sported a bellyband proclaiming 'As good as Grisham or your money back'), and in 2018 the two writers would share a stage at the Royal Hall in Harrogate. The year before, *Killing Floor* scooped a Specsavers Platinum Award for selling more than one million units in the United Kingdom alone.

Lee explained how, when he first started, he wanted to record Reacher's movements exhaustively, to leave no gaps. He shouldn't be on a bus one minute and in a diner the next with no idea how he got there, or how long it took. No more Jim Grant/Mick Cleary-style blackouts. He aspired to a punctilious verisimilitude. It was a hangover from his years in transmission control and the imperative to account for every second of every day.

He soon came to realise the futility of this heroic approach. When he could see his first draft spiralling out of control in the direction of a one-thousand-page doorstopper he began to cut back and pare down and skip and omit and elide and withhold. But both Wright and Highfill still found it too long. It was hard, but once he'd cut the first word it was like he was hacking his way through with a machete.

The 600-plus pages were reduced to 425, the 217,459 words to 142,185.

He resolved never to get himself into that kind of tangle again. 'I might cut seven words,' he told David Remnick of the *New Yorker* in 2018. 'And even that hurts.'

After *Killing Floor* it typically took him eighty to ninety working days to write a book, spread over six months. 'I don't see any virtue in spending too long on a book. It just becomes an excuse for procrastination.'

Wright objects to the two Hispanic men being lured into a copse in chapter eighteen and the hero never being seriously endangered. 'It is just about as eventful as consuming a plate of eggs in Eno's. It does not work.' In later drafts the suits are exchanged for loud shirts but Reacher is still 101 per cent in control. Dispatching a couple of small-time thugs was no more taxing than eating eggs at Eno's, and quite possibly less noteworthy. Character is king. Lee Child was laying it out from the start. But at least he was ready for Highfill:

> I want the frisson in this scene not to come from any danger Reacher is in – or any tension he feels – but to come from the reader's reaction to what a ruthless and cold-blooded guy Reacher is – and how competent he is. I feel it's important that the reader is slightly lulled, so the casual shooting stands out.

Next, Wright objects to Reacher riding around in a Bentley. But the Bentley was there for Lee's personal gratification, so by way of compromise he delegates that problem to Reacher.

> The Bentley was a lovely automobile, but it was not what I needed if the surveillance went mobile. It was about as distinctive as the most distinctive thing you could ever think of.

The prosaic refusal of simile would become a defining grace note of his style.

There was no denying the Bentley was an eyeful. But if Lee couldn't own it in fiction then what was the point? Why become a writer *to reproduce the conditions of reality*? He'd already had to sacrifice the fantasy ending where Reacher had driven away in a Bentley – 'my Bentley' – as part payment (along with a bounty of £5 million – 'my five million dollars') for tracking down Hubble and some kind of consolatory compensation for giving up Roscoe. He wasn't about to send it to the literary scrapyard just because some mean-spirited agency reader told him to. There had to be a solution. Reacher would arrive at it through *a thought process*.

> Picard had made me use the Bentley. Not his own car. Had to be a reason for that. Not just because he wanted the extra legroom. Because it was a very distinctive car.

Reacher temporarily exchanges it for 'an eight-year-old Cadillac the color of an old avocado pear', but twenty-three years later the Bentley would make a return in the short story 'Smile', written in December 2018 for Maxim Jakubowski's anthology *Invisible Blood* and set mostly in the first-class lounge at Heathrow Airport. Reacher was 'not a first-class kind of guy'. But Lee Child was.

Novelist Jakubowski was the creative entrepreneur behind London's legendary Murder One bookshop on the Charing Cross Road, and (with Mike Ripley) published Lee's first ever short story, 'James Penney's New Identity' (recycled from 'They, The People') in *Fresh Blood 3*, in 1999.

Wright objects that:

> Reacher tracks Hubble down in Augusta and no-one follows him. [. . .] Not stomach churning stuff at all.

Lee raises the stakes by having Picard usher Reacher into the car with a stubby gun barrel.

> I was closer to panic than I'd ever been in my whole life. My heart was thumping and I was taking little short breaths. I was putting one foot in front of the other and using every ounce of everything I had just to stay in control. (Chapter 28)

They go to Eno's.

> I was screaming at myself to listen to what I'd learned through thirteen hard years. The shorter the time, the cooler you've got to be. If you've only got one shot, you've got to make it count. You can't afford to miss because you screwed up the planning. [. . .] I had to find him inside my head. It had to be a thought process.

Wright complains that Reacher seems indifferent to Roscoe's fate once she is removed to the safe house. 'Even a so-called hard man would have to be totally abnormal not to be concerned.'

In response, the (relatively) compliant debutant teeters towards the opposite extreme. He has Reacher find a phone booth and check in with Finlay:

> 'Roscoe's safely installed. [. . . Picard] said she sends her love.'
>
> 'Send mine back if you get the chance,' I said. 'Take care, Harvard guy.'

Such explicit sentimentality would not be permitted in later novels, where feelings are stronger but mostly left unexpressed, allowed to resonate in the interstices of dialogue as in the silences between notes in a line of melody.

Wright denounces Reacher for not looking in the boxes at Oates' house. So the author replaces Oates by Stoller and presents the boxes already open and empty, but Reacher detects a 'faintly sour smell' that sets him off on the trail like an unstoppable springer spaniel. She denounces the citizens of Margrave for failing to report back to their paymaster Alan Charles (aka Granada's Charles Allen), so the author deletes Charles altogether, a satisfactory form of revenge.

Lee and Highfill collaborated closely on the edit before the book was finally accepted, faxing annotated pages across the Atlantic, in Lee's case from the back office of the Art Store. One of the first things Lee learned was that every book had to have a three-word description, and the first two words were always *It's about*.

'Bad Luck and Trouble' was about drugs.

Lee was fascinated by the scale of the narcotics trade, said to be worth twice the amount of legal money in circulation. He gave the fifteen-year-old Ruth some American banknotes he had lying around and asked her to weigh them in her school chemistry lab. On that basis he came up with a figure of 4000 tons. The logistical implications of shifting that volume of money were difficult to compute, the physical reality difficult to visualise. Roberto Escobar, brother of kingpin Pablo, had acted as accountant to the Medellín Cartel – which at its apogee was responsible for up to 80 per cent of cocaine smuggled into the US – and claimed they spent $2500 a month on rubber bands alone.

But as a sales pitch, *It's about drugs* was tired. It wouldn't cut any ice, wouldn't generate a buzz, wouldn't press the right buttons. They needed a better third word.

Lee had bought Jeffrey Robinson's *The Laundrymen* (1994) mainly because it had a real dollar bill laminated into the jacket. The book was an in-depth exposé of the trade in illegal money and claimed more was spent worldwide on illicit drugs than food and that deprived of this income, many countries would collapse. In October 1995, when the new series $100 bills were introduced, he read an article in the *New Yorker* ('fanatically well researched') about how this first major redesign since 1929 was intended to deter counterfeiting. In addition to the interwoven fibres and micro-printing and a plastic security thread, it incorporated a watermark and optically variable ink that changed from green to black when viewed from different angles. The dollar was the world's reserve currency and any loss of confidence – the mere suggestion that you might exchange a hundred dollars of gold for a worthless piece of paper – could prove catastrophic.

Drug running and illegal money were two sides of the same grubby coin. It was the shortest of short steps from one to the other.

Just six weeks before Darley made the call that interrupted quiz night at the Pheasant in Casterton, Lee faxed Highfill and said, try this: *It's about counterfeiting.*

Highfill was enthusiastic. 'This is great. This is new, fresh, I haven't seen it before.' Which may not have been strictly accurate, but it felt right. There was something in the air. Robert Crais's *Indigo Slam* came out three months later.

Lee didn't mind about changing the plot (though he hated waste, so drugs would make a return in *61 Hours* and *The Midnight Line*). 'For me it was the image of the warehouse full of cash. That was where I was heading. I didn't care how I got there.'

When Reacher gets there and the author delivers an ending that is both surprising and inevitable, he enters the Kliner warehouse at upper-floor level. Looking down, he sees a sight that he would 'never ever forget'.

> A gigantic dune of money filled the whole shed. It was piled maybe fifty feet high into the back far corner. It sloped down to the floor like a mountainside. It was a mountain of cash. It reared up like a gigantic green iceberg.

The people were dwarfed like ants. The cars were like toys on the beach.

> It was a fantastic scene from a fairy tale. Like a huge underground cavern in an emerald mine from some glittering fable. [. . .] Hubble had said a million dollars in singles was a hell of a sight. I was looking at forty million.

But there is 'an appalling stink'.

> A heavy, sour, greasy smell. The smell of money. Millions and millions of crumpled and greasy dollar bills were seeping out the stink of sweaty hands and sour pockets.

Teale and Kliner were in possession of their hearts' desire, but 'the enormous drift of cash was [. . .] going to engulf them and choke them to death'.

Actually it blew up and burned them (with a little help from Reacher), which would later prompt Stephen King to recommend an award for Best Exploding Warehouse.

Warehouses became a regular feature of both books and life. In 2011 Lee drove to Westminster, Virginia, to sign stock for bookstores across the county. The staff formed a conga line to process hardcover copies of *The Affair*: one person to unpack the boxes, a second to check the books were in perfect condition, a third to fold the flaps in to mark the title page, and a fourth to line up each volume under Lee's poised right hand. The signed book was then passed to a fifth person to check that the jacket was neatly aligned before being repacked by the sixth in line. They signed 2,500 books in three hours. Lee liked the smell of new books. They didn't stink like old money.

By 2018 technology had changed. The books stayed in the warehouse and 27,500 individual tip sheets (for insertion in *Past Tense* before sale) were delivered to the peace and quiet of his apartment. He was a one-man factory all by himself. It depended on whether the stack of papers was moving well, but on a good day he could get through around a thousand an hour, signing blind while listening to music or watching YouTube.

His hand never got tired. He got tired of people saying it must. Maybe his little finger felt sore, where the weight of his hand rested on it. Once when he'd been walking to the 21 Club in the rain, holding an umbrella, he'd slipped on the midtown paving, and instinctively broken his fall by 'punching the sidewalk'. He wrote: 'Bone was sticking out. Ancient men's room attendant patched it up. The cut healed but the bone never knit.' Then added: 'You'll be glad to hear I stayed for lunch.'

After much deliberation the editorial team of Highfill, Anderson and Child agreed on the title *Killing Floor*, which first appeared as number nineteen on a handwritten list of twenty-two possibilities. Heading the list was 'My Only Friend', followed by 'The Weimar Drop' ('Weimar' as code word was later replaced by 'Pluribus'), 'Country Road', 'The Forbidden Door', 'Unfinished Business', 'The Warehouse', 'Jack Reacher's Story', 'Cloverleaf', 'Margrave Story', 'The Kliner Scam', 'Blue Creek' and 'The Menorah Shape'. Already crossed out, with a single line in blue ink, were 'Blue Skies', 'Like a Rolling Stone', 'The Weimar Operation', 'The Open Road', 'The Scam', 'Further On Up the Road', 'No Place to Go' and 'To Hell with Them'.

Second last on the list was 'Four Thousand Tons'.

It was like Lee was conjuring his future wealth into being.

33

My Home in America

Then he felt the roof soar away above him.
Die Trying, 1998

It took more than an American wife for Jim Grant to escape. It took him longer than the Beatles. But on Friday 3 July, 1998, Jim, Jane, Ruth and Jenny the lurcher-Labrador set sail on the *Queen Elizabeth II* from Southampton, bound for the New World. Five days later, having supplied the obligatory X-rays to prove he was free of tuberculosis, Jim was granted residency and became a legal immigrant. It was a forty-four-year-old dream come true. He was no longer trapped in the wrong body, even if he would have to wait another six years for a bird's-eye view of Manhattan. Jane had been missing her family and Ruth was looking forward to starting at Wesleyan University in Middletown, Connecticut, where she had secured early acceptance for a four-year degree in linguistics (to be funded by Reacher film options) and would soon meet Lin-Manuel Miranda.

The picture-postcard perfection of Kirkby Lonsdale had worn thin. 'The weather was crushingly bad.' They'd sold the house and its contents for £165,000 to a couple who, like them, were starting over, and Lee had begun work on his fourth book, *The Visitor*. He wasn't sitting at the dining table any more. They had used some of the *Killing Floor* money to provide Ruth with a bigger bedroom and Jim had taken over her playroom for his office. The room with the view. The final line he wrote before shutting down his computer for the last time on Abbotsgate was Jodie Garber scolding Reacher for engineering the demise of a local gangster: '"I told you not to do that," she said.'

This is Lee's account from the introduction to the Mysterious edition of *The Visitor*:

> We went by ocean liner for two reasons: we had a dog, and we didn't want to put her in an airplane hold, and because insurance on container consignments was compulsory, expensive, and pro-rata with the value of the contents. The ocean liner allowed unlimited baggage [. . .] so we bought trunks and hand-carried the most expensive stuff, thereby lowering the container insurance to the point where the saving more or less paid for the liner tickets. And it was a perfect emigration–immigration experience – very reminiscent of history, very relaxing, and a very well-defined transition between old and new. We watched England disappear behind the stern, and then five days later we saw the Statue of Liberty approaching through the morning mist.

It is characteristic of his autobiographical writing that he should focus more on the minutiae of travel than the poetry of the journey. When they docked on the west side of Manhattan, Jane and Ruth waited on deck with Jenny while Jim dashed off to hire a truck.

A day after disembarking, Lee set off on his first ever promotional tour, for *Die Trying*.

> Crowds were small, and events were intimate. But I loved every minute. I saw places I hadn't been before, and I realised the lovely truth of book touring: no one shows up who doesn't already like you. It's a warm bath.

The 'warm bath' would become a go-to metaphor for the pleasures of the writer's life, even though in real life it lost out to a hot shower: 'the full 22-minute routine, including brushing my hair', he blogs for *The Hard Way*, channelling the Reacher of *Tripwire*. As with habits of dress it wasn't clear if this was life imitating art or the other way round.

There had been no tour for *Killing Floor*. Lee signed stock at Partners & Crime bookstore on Greenwich Avenue in the West Village (one of the partners, Maggie Griffin, would soon become his personal assistant and website manager) and at the Deansgate branch of Waterstones in Manchester, but the only sit-and-sign public event had been at Kirkby Lonsdale's Bookstore, attended almost literally by one man (David Firth) and his dog (back then a sheltie collie cross called Lucky). But these were all firsts, with a charm all their own, and the thrill of seeing his book on the shelves.

After that 'it was quite rapid-fire'. It felt 'new and fresh and exciting', getting a new house and new cars, 'frothy and extremely lovely'. Home was now 110 Upper Shad Road, Pound Ridge, in Westchester, about one hour north of Manhattan (not far from West Point), which Jane had found in February that year and they'd bought for $475,000. ('Shad', Lee instructed me, was Old English for 'boundary'.) It was a four-bedroom detached house, to which they added a heated pool, built in 1980 and set in 2.4 acres of wooded countryside, not far from Jane's parents and their private beach on Stillwater Lake in Ossining. A photograph taken by Janet Brown at the Shiren family home shows Jim stretched out on a pillowed lilo smoking a cigarette, a blue-painted rowing boat tied to a wooden jetty in the background, surrounded by weeping willows.

Pound Ridge gets eight mentions in *Tripwire* (finished the previous December). Its function is to signify affluence:

> A rich woman living in Pound Ridge like Marilyn has many contacts in the real estate business.

'We were happy to move to that house,' Lee said. 'We'd come from the UK with a very conventional idea of living in a house with a garden. It would never have occurred to us to live in the city.'

Lee went back to *The Visitor*, stopping each evening for the first pitch in the baseball game. It was an amazing season. The Yankees had been his team ever since Norman and Jane had first taken him to the original Yankee Stadium in 1976. In 1998 they won the World Series – and in 1999 and 2000 too, like a lucky charm, until 9/11 came and the world was upended and they went down at the last gasp to the Arizona Diamondbacks. It was easy to work in his office overlooking the pond, even with the family about, and writing 'was kind of idyllic'.

Graham James from Granada came to stay. It was his first trip to New York. He'd always wanted to go. Jim picked him up at JFK and, casting his mind back to his own first time, as they drove across the Whitestone Bridge and Manhattan came into view he pushed a button on the radio and Sinatra's voice poured out of the speakers. The Pound Ridge house was 'fabulous' and Graham was thrilled 'to see such a successful writer's office'. Jim took him to a diner – 'he knew I loved diners!' – and Graham wanted to pay, but Jim stopped him, laying a hand on his arm and saying: *Graham, I'm a millionaire now.* 'He wasn't boasting. He sounded like a little boy, enjoying the moment.'

It had taken a while to adjust to their newfound wealth, Lee admitted, and for a long time Jane refused to fly first class with him. Two years after Graham's visit he told the 'Money' section of the *Sunday Times* that six books in he now had twenty-one credit cards (though for practical purposes used only two), 'simply as a reaction to the times when I could not get one'. 'I definitely think,' he added, 'that the amount you earn has nothing at all to do with your quality as a person. At various times I have had some, none and a lot of money, but I've always been the same person.' Wasn't there a risk of becoming the 'big man' he so railed against? I asked. No, he would reply: he was 'a poor man with a lot of money'.

In October 1998 Lee attended genre festival Bouchercon XXIX in Philadelphia, scooping the Anthony Award for Best First Novel and the Barry Award from *Deadly Pleasures* magazine. He recalled sitting around with a bunch of other nobodies – Harlan Coben, Dennis Lehane, Laura Lippman, George Pelecanos – thinking obscurity would be a step up, but if they just kept showing up maybe one of them might make it big (in five years' time he would be toastmaster). Back in England he had scored an invitation to the Authors of the Year party at Hatchards, 'the Ritz' of London bookshops next to Fortnum & Mason on Piccadilly.

The plan was working, and he was feeling lucky.

'You have a loving, close-textured feel for America,' Stephen King said when the two friends did a joint event for the Harvard Book Store in September 2015. 'You really understand nowhere.' From the start Lee had been seduced by the unaccustomed emptiness of the country, 'thousands and thousands of square miles of it, mostly in the west' (*Daily Mail*, 2010). The distances travelled were reflected in attitudes too.

> The US is home to some of the world's most eminent scientists, and they have studied radioactive half-lives, and they have proved that the world is almost four billion years old. Other people say no, it's only 6,422 years old – exactly – because they've worked through the Bible and added it all up. And both sides of the debate are utterly, implacably, immovably serious. And neither side is hidden away on the fringes.

Some visual constants were suggestive of homogeneity – dollar bills, road signs, cars – but in fact 'the nation is a mosaic, a crazy patch-work quilt, insanely scaled from end to end, in every dimension, both physical and intellectual'.

When Lee wrote this he'd lived in New York for eleven years, longer than half his neighbours. As well as a beach house on Long

Island he now had the four apartments on East 22nd Street (which he'd persuaded the taxman to treat as a single dwelling) and officially was that rather large little boy sitting on the window sill gazing out at the Empire State Building beyond the almost Parisian Madison Park. He spoke a version of English. He blended in fine. He loved the diversity of the people he saw around him, their vividness, so much more vital than his memories of the inbred, pasty-faced people of Britain. Outside New York he didn't stand out any more than anyone else on the road. To the 'leathery lizard-lady' who had to travel 250 miles to the store for anything she didn't kill or grow herself he came across 'as a funny-looking guy with a strange accent. [. . .] To her, a guy from Oregon or Ohio or even Oklahoma would have seemed just as foreign.'

For a writer it was immensely liberating. 'Every crazy thing happens here. I could just make everything up and inevitably it would all be true in some far corner of America.'

His favourite example came from *A Wanted Man*, where he'd made up an involuntary witness-protection facility that one of his FBI contacts later inadvertently confirmed was real: *How did you know about that?* But in a small way I'd seen it for myself. In 2017 I'd read 'My Rules', his story about a silver-tongued scammer who fleeces a couple of middle-class managerial types on Barrow Street in Greenwich Village, relieving them of their wallets while purporting to mediate a dispute on smoking in the workplace. A year or so later we were standing on West 3rd Street just up from 6th Avenue when a silver-tongued scammer with a strong Irish accent approached us (we weren't arguing) and told Lee how he looked like Peter O'Toole, or maybe Robert Redford, and what a pleasure it was to engage in cultured conversation with such a fine gentleman from the old world, and how no thank you, he didn't smoke and therefore had no real need of a light, but yes he was down on his luck as it happens, and might this fine gentleman be able to spare him enough to buy a Big Mac?

Lee admired a skilled operative in any field, and liked to acknowledge talent when he stumbled across it. 'That'll get you several Big Macs,' he said, handing over a crisp $5 bill.

'I definitely checked I still had my wallet after he'd gone,' Lee said.

In a narrowly biographical sense, he was indifferent to the old world. Emigrating was all about 'shaking the dust of Britain off our feet'. Coventry had no hold over him. Birmingham – traditionally anti-royalist, non-conformist, home to the first free traders and trade unionists, dedicated to the automobile and to commerce – 'was almost American'. The anti-Irish feeling he'd grown up with had only alienated him further.

But aesthetically and intellectually, his heart was with the ancients. Among his greatest treasures was a 250,000-year-old Neanderthal hand axe. At Granada he and Gallagher left notes for each other in Latin, and much later he would have the Latin translation of his most renowned catchphrase, 'Reacher said nothing', carved into a sundial in his Sussex garden. He regretted not being in Classical A at King Edward's, which meant you would study Greek (they'd written him off because of his background), except when he regretted not being in Science A ('for one question in O-level Physics they asked for your workings and I took it right back to Heisenberg's uncertainty principle'). He resented the two cultures divide that frustrated his Renaissance instincts and applauded the visionary Claughton, who helped with the sundial, for having the plain good sense to introduce the International Baccalaureate.

It was possible to discern a trace of romantic nostalgia in his acquisition of a rare copy of the Kelmscott Chaucer (considered one of the world's most beautiful books), illustrated by William Morris and old Edwardian Edward Burne-Jones, who also donated to Birmingham's St Philips its exquisite red-and-blue stained-glass windows. When I visited King Edward's in 2019, acting chief master Keith Phillips told me how he'd based an assembly on the unexpected juxtaposition of Burne-Jones and Lee Child at Reading railway station, one poster advertising an exhibition at Tate Britain and the other *Past Tense*: *Reacher never looks back . . . Until now*. The autumnal shades of the book harmonise with the rich orange-reds of the pre-Raphaelite painting (Venus pining for her lover), positing a secret kinship.

To Americans Lee was the quintessential Englishman, and he played on his accent just as he once had as a schoolboy in France. They were flattered by his adoption of their country and in awe of his ability to *write American*. How did he do it? First, Lee would credit his wife, and her *house committee on un-American activities*, which when he was starting out vetted every word he wrote. Then he would note that it was natural for a writer to be attuned to variations in language, and the job of a fiction writer to write fiction. You were already leaping into an invented world, so to leap into a world you didn't live in made it easier. That way you had to think about everything equally intently, which made for a more organic whole, rather than grafting fictional action onto a factual environment, which would seem 'very uneasy'.

Sometimes it felt uneasily like he was grafting a largely 'factual' character onto a fictional environment. Reacher was heavier and no longer smoked, but they had more in common than not. Lee had never been in the army, not even the cadets, but he had been a high-ranking member of an elite unit who had then been downsized. Neither liked running. They were both classicists and mathematicians manqués who had their heads full of once-heard-never-to-be-forgotten esoterica. They listened to the same music and supported the same teams. They shared the same birthday. They both had nerdy big brothers in need of protection, drank copious amounts of black coffee and liked peach pie. They were both restless loners who would travel in search of the sun.

Like Lee, Reacher was more old than new. Forget recent partial precursor James Bond (Lee had twice turned down the offer to take over the franchise), the melancholy issue of his Mayfair-born Eton-educated creator's sense of post-war irrelevance, who Lee eloquently defined in a 2012 essay for the *Daily Mail* as a boiled-down lone-man single-operative personification of a lost imperial England. Forget the new-fangled johnny-come-lately Western. Reacher went right back to the origins of Western civilisation.

Only Reacher would make a connection between 'xeric' or 'xerophilous' desert plants – 'from the Greek prefix xero-, meaning dry' – and Xeroxing, or 'copying without wet chemicals'. Only Reacher would think of Zeno as he gears up for a fight:

> *Dum spero speri.* Where there's breath, there's hope. Not an aphorism Zeno of Cittium would have understood or approved of. He spoke Greek, not Latin, and preferred passive resignation to reckless optimism.

The allegorical *Nothing to Lose* was a philosophical meditation poised between Hope and Despair. Reacher was not a stoic: 'I take challenges personally.' But he appreciated a woman he could talk stoicism with, like small-town cop Vaughan.

This was not idle self-indulgence. The subtext was the bedrock of Lee's existential and literary aesthetic. As a species we were only recently modern. The lizard brain was only thinly papered over by the veneer of civilisation. We were closer to the Stone Age than the stars.

> He considered himself a modern man, born in the twentieth century, living in the twenty-first, but he also knew he had some kind of a wide-open portal in his head, a wormhole to humanity's primitive past, where for millions of years every living thing could be a predator,

or a rival, and therefore had to be assessed, and judged, instantly, and accurately. Who was the superior animal? Who would submit? (*Blue Moon*)

According to Lee there was only one genre, and only two stories, deriving directly from Plato. The thriller was not *a* genre, but *the* genre, not one in a series of parallel streams, but the river itself. Stories took place either inside or outside of the cave. You were either inside, worrying about what was going on outside (serial killer on the loose), or you were outside sorting it out (avenging hero). The thriller was 'the central way that humans tell stories'. Everything else was decadent accretion.

> My guess is that early fiction was about perils survived. As everything has got more civilised, then all these other genres grew up alongside it, including literary fiction, as a luxury, as a kind of barnacle on our boat.

Inside the cave was Europe – as cramped and claustrophobic as the tunnel in *Die Trying* or the disused military bunker in *61 Hours* – where for want of space and freedom it was all going on inside your head.

Outside the cave was America, which still had room for the old-world heroes – for Odysseus and Beowulf and Don Quixote, for Lancelot and Gawain and Robin Hood.

When Lee explained his innate affinity for America on the back of growing up in 'progressive' Birmingham it didn't quite ring true. No one would place Reacher at the cutting edge of technology. What Lee wanted from America was its primitiveness. When he caught the ship out of Southampton to the new world he was heading back in time to the old, to the world of myth and legend.

It was only out west he could walk into a store and buy pants and shirts that fitted him. But it wasn't just clothes. For all his formative years Jim Grant had been forcing himself into a space that was way too small for him. Like Reacher he needed room to move, space to wander, a chance to spread his wings. His character 'couldn't work anywhere except America'. When he said those words he was referring to Jack Reacher. But Reacher wasn't his only fictional character. He might as well have been talking about Lee Child.

34

Out of One, Many

'Is it Latin?' she asked.
Killing Floor, 1997

'If you think like that, you're a lunatic,' Lee said. It would have been nothing short of insane, when he sat down to write his first novel, to imagine that a quarter of a century later he'd be writing the twenty-fourth book in the series. How crazy would you have to be, to dream of that kind of success?

Twenty-one, on the other hand, was a reasonable number. John D. MacDonald had written twenty-one Travis McGee books (and sold an estimated 70 million), so at best he might aspire to emulate, but never surpass, his role model.

At Reacher's twenty-first birthday party Larry Finlay recalled their first meeting, when he asked Lee, *what next?* and Lee responded: 'This is the first of twenty-one books.' Cue mild amusement from sceptical publishers. But it wasn't long before twenty-one seemed quite a small number. Lee signed for books no. 22 through no. 24. 'When he said *I'm gonna give you another three*, it was the best night of my whole career,' said Finlay. 'Think of it as the dead author contract,' Lee admonished him, as though they had happened across three books in his desk drawer when he died, like stumbling on a gold mine.

Sometimes it felt like they were flogging him to death.

By the end of 2018, at a conservative estimate of one every nine seconds, Lee Child was selling an approximate average of four hundred books an hour. When it came to numbers of readers, he'd long since passed what at ThrillerFest he referred to as 'the magic threshold'.

> You're a writer as soon as someone else has read your book, but two thousand is a significant number because it's outside our tribal consciousness. That's more readers than you can personally know and more than you would have in your address book. The good thing is that most of us [writers] will get there.

He once tried to calculate how long it would take to take each one of those first two thousand readers out to dinner, individually, and concluded it would be about five years, or rather five and half years, or in fact 5.4794. There would be a lot of fighting to establish precedence.

Lee loved the additional frisson that commerce brought to writing. He admired the designers of the Ford Taurus more than the designers of a Rolls-Royce, because they were dealing with the serious business of selling a million cars and pleasing a million people, rather than a meaningless, trivial thousand. By analogy, and much as he respected their work, it was a far greater challenge to be Lee Child than Martin Amis or Ian McEwan: 'They can't write our [crime fiction] books, because they try all the time and usually they don't get it right,' he told the *Evening Standard* in March 2010, when McEwan's *Solar* and *61 Hours* were 'slogging it out' in the bookshops: final score after first week sales, McEwan 14,176–Child 26,247. To be fair, McEwan didn't stand a chance. The dissertation-length planning document for the Transworld publicity and marketing campaign ended with the aggressive rallying cry: PRE-AWARENESS STARTS NOW!

Highfill was right, Lee's instincts had been sound. Rob Reeves surmised that Jim had absorbed the winning concept of a popular, replicable formula at Granada, that 'he cleverly set up this template from the get-go'. It wasn't an implausible theory. But mostly Lee had chosen to write about a character who transcended time and place because that was the kind of character he liked.

The decision turned out to have unplanned benefits. Reacher wasn't tied to anything and nor therefore was Lee. The character could go wherever he wanted and do whatever he pleased, which increased his longevity because it allowed the author to continue 'smoothly pursuing his own way', as the *Standard* put it, and stopped him from getting bored. Though Lee knew better than most the value of soap opera, its repertory cast and unifying milieu made it 'fundamentally restrictive'. For many years (in compliance with his own myth) he had sat down at his desk on 1 September 'with great excitement'. It was a new adventure for him, as it was for the reader. It never got stale. 'I can't even remember the other books.' In the last week of August 2017, when he was about to start *Past Tense* but didn't yet have the title, he wrote and asked: 'When was R's father's funeral and did he go?'

There was an assumption that Reacher was a quintessentially American hero in a more melancholy revisionist Western. This was true, Lee allowed, citing the scenario of a remote cattle station where the men are absent and the women and children have been left alone and trouble comes calling and the lone rider, in exchange for a woman-cooked meal, will save the day before riding away again. But this story was not exclusive to America. Zane Grey hadn't invented it. It went back to tales of pilgrims being ambushed in the Black Forest and saved by a knight who appears out of the trees only to disappear as mysteriously as he came. The Western was a modern iteration of a classical paradigm from medieval Europe, and before that Scandinavia, and before that the Anglo-Saxons and the Greeks. And that trajectory should surprise no one, because what was America other than 'a place full of people that have come from somewhere else?'

America was big, which was why he'd chosen it for Reacher. But not big enough. Lee needed the whole world to roam free in, and the whole of human history. We saw Reacher not only in every Reacher book but in every generation and country too.

Like all writing, his own grew out of other writing. He pulled what he had off his mental shelf and adapted it. His second book drew on his reading about separatist and militia movements, the third on his reading about Vietnam MIAs; the fourth was a blend of the locked-room mystery and a serial killer novel, and the fifth was inspired by Benjamin Franklin's assertion that 'three people can keep a secret if two of them are dead'. What were we, he said tersely, standing outside the Union Square Café at East 19th Street and sounding like a professor about to launch into a lecture on Roland Barthes, other than the sum total of our reading? His head was a place full of words that had come from somewhere else.

At first Lee didn't think about where Reacher came from: 'I just wrote him.' But when he felt secure enough to reflect on his own practice, he realised that his hero had emerged rough-hewn from the collective unconscious. He'd been market-tested for three thousand years. 'People must really want this character,' he thought. Even Reacher's moral ambiguity was part of 'a tradition of taint, of rust in the armour'. There was a reason the guy was wandering lonely as a cloud, a reason the Ronin had been disowned by the emperor and exiled from his court and pushed out towards the frontier. It was a story that tapped into a deep human need. Which was how he had summoned it up in the first place, because it tapped deep into a need of his own.

In *The Hero*, Lee argues that the concept behind the noun must have been shaped by the needs, concerns, desires, prejudices, aspirations and fears of ancient Greek culture. 'All stories have a purpose, and the older and more durable the story, the more elemental the purpose is likely to be.' It was simply a matter of figuring out what it was.

He gave Reacher the minimum of back story. Not because Reacher was an archetype, or to keep his options open. In real life we found out about each other slowly; we didn't have a CV pinned to our chests like a medal. Even in the closest relationships, what we learned was a minute fraction of what there was to know. Reacher would grow organically, just as his creator would. At first, his background as a West Pointer and major in the military police had taken Lee by surprise – Jim came from a generation where any affection for military culture was taboo. But to be a knight errant Reacher had first to have been a knight, and to be expelled from the court there had to have been a court for him to be expelled from. The ambiguity over his departure (which persists beyond *The Affair*) – did he jump or was he pushed? – ensured his hero could never be mistaken for GI Joe.

Some fans assumed Reacher was ex-military because Lee was a nationalist, ready for appropriation by the Republican cause. The opposite was true. He wanted to poke and prod and needle his right-wing readers into contemplating Reacher's more liberal point of view (*Echo Burning* on immigration, *The Enemy* on homophobia, *Nothing to Lose* on desertion, *The Midnight Line* on addiction). Reacher was American, but not all-American; he sees America through a stranger's eyes. Lee wanted to explore the sense of alienation, and who in modern society was more alienated than the military brat who is suddenly returned to civilian life? Reacher has a strong moral code but is habituated to a degree of lawlessness and casual violence. He is cast adrift with an overdeveloped set of skills in a very narrow arena. He was born and raised in an enclosed, ritualised society but has always moved around. He is both insider and outsider, rooted and rootless.

Jim hadn't done much moving around at Granada apart from the daily commute. But for eighteen years he had lived and worked in the tight-knit, clannish community of the central control room and been one of its commanding officers for longer than Reacher had spent in the army. It was weird being at home all the time, sitting at the dining-room table with a pad and pencil and looking out over the dales and thinking about Georgia. Sometimes he even had to go shopping.

As Reacher entered his third decade interviewers began to ask whether he had learned anything. 'He knows it all already,' was Lee's stock answer. He'd never forgotten his father saying he looked for books that were 'the same but different', and he wanted his readers to experience that 'rush of pleasure' you got when you found a series by an author you liked and were set 'for a couple of weeks'. Satisfying that desire was 'immensely gratifying'.

> All my effort goes into keeping Reacher the same, even though I myself am growing older and changing. The image of Reacher should be impregnable. I say bullshit to the character arc – I'm not trying to get an MFA here. I'm trying to do for people what I love for myself.

It wasn't just his father he was pleasing. In September 2014, Haruki Murakami was asked by Steven Poole (for the *Guardian*) which modern crime writers he enjoyed reading.

> 'I like Lee Child,' he announces decisively, and laughs. So do I, I say. 'Oh you like him? That's good! So far I have read 10 of them!' What do you like about them? He moves his hands in the air as though running his fingers over an invisible piano keyboard, and grins. 'Everything's the same!'

It was like Lee was tapping into a deep human need. But the 'different' mattered too. In his 2013 introduction to *Die Trying* he writes:

The book's overall shape and approach were based on an instinctive decision to make it as fundamentally different as possible from *Killing Floor* while at the same time keeping it clearly part of a coherent series. I felt that authors could become as stereotyped as actors, and that if I did two similar books in a row I might get locked into a narrower channel than I wanted. I felt that if I used *Killing Floor* as a kind of 'left field', and the new work as a kind of 'right field', then I would be staking out a wide territory in between, in which I could roam free forever.

In *Tripwire* he switched it up by having someone come looking for Reacher, which indirectly enriched him as a character – what made him worth searching for? – while guarding against any accusation that the author was over-reliant on coincidence. Where *Killing Floor* was a single-track first-person narrative set in a backwater town, *Die Trying* was a third-person exercise in multiple points of view drawing on the glossy apparatus of central government. He started writing it by hand because he 'didn't want to jinx it', but once satisfied he still had the voice he made the transition to the new (still monochrome) Compaq 486/50 he had bought – with cash – on a trip to New York. He remembered how Steve Gallagher had shelled out for an expensive camera before he left Granada, but Jim was a cautious man. It was a point of principle not to spend a penny more than he had to before proving himself as a published author.

Lee wasn't worried about spoilers. There was no such thing as a Reacher spoiler – collectively the novels might as well be called *The Epic Adventures and Ultimate Triumph of the Fearless Hero, Jack Reacher (Parts 1 through 24)*. He didn't even much mind when reviewers revealed the ending. The thing they were giving away – that the hero comes out on top – was not unexpected, and to know you could count on it was reassuring. That's what he sought, like his infant daughter demanding the same story night after night: recognition and familiarity. He wanted picking up a Reacher book to be like pulling on an old sweater. He wanted fans to feel 'welcomed and comfortable when they come into the book'.

These enveloping images of grace and domesticity, verging on the feminine and maternal, are curiously – and disarmingly – at odds with the appearance and perception of his hulking hobo hero. It's Reacher as seen through the eyes of the 'twenty-one white-haired seniors' on the South Dakota bus at the start of *61 Hours*:

> He was quiet and polite. He was a foot taller than any of the other passengers and evidently very strong. Not handsome like a movie star, but not ugly, either. [. . .] Not the best dressed of individuals. [. . .] He had no bag, which was strange. But overall it was vaguely reassuring to have such a man on board, especially after he had proved himself civilised and not in any way threatening. Threatening behaviour from a man that size would have been unseemly. Good manners from a man that size were charming.

It was the same effect the six-foot-four Lee had on members of the public. Emma Bryson blogged about it for 'The Reader' after his 2018 tour to New Zealand. She'd attended 'An Evening with Lee Child' in Christchurch, where a couple of fans had purportedly fainted with excitement, and hadn't yet read any of his books. She'd watched the movies and the bar scene between Reacher and not-a-hooker Sandy had made her 'squirm, recoil, and lose a little faith in humanity'. She was 'primed to not particularly like Reacher'. But that night she was won round. The man had undone the damage done by Hollywood. 'Lee Child has a very likeable way of being around people,' she wrote. 'It was impossible not to get sucked in by his genuine concern for his readers.'

This would resonate with Darley Anderson. Not enough credence was given to Lee's foresight and achievement. He was only the second foreigner after Simenon to be elected President of the Mystery Writers of America (in 2009) and it was no coincidence that the Frenchman should have defined success as finding a formula that pleases the reading public and once you've found it, writing the same book for the next forty years. Too many writers wanted 'to take time off to do something different'. Lee and Martina Cole were 'rare beasts', finding variety within formula. 'It astonishes me that commercial writers, working as they are in the entertainment sector, aren't more disciplined.' Such dilettantes were saying 'we are not first and foremost about our readers'. Child and Cole always put their readers first.

Reacher may owe his longevity to his universality, but – despite the killer beams and despicable skills – Lee owed his to being an easy guy to like. Early on what mattered most was how you behaved, he told Maslin at ThrillerFest, especially with people who might go into a shop and buy your book.

> Never talk about the book. Just make them like you and then they'll buy the book anyway. Like the woman at a signing who told me she'd read several of my books and when I asked what made her buy the first one said: 'I saw you open the door for someone and thought, what a polite gentleman, I'll buy his book.' If this writing gig doesn't work out I'll become a doorman.

When the UK cover for *Killing Floor* came in from Transworld, Darley was 'horrified that they should do such a bad job' (a metallic silver background with debossed bullet holes). It 'cost them a couple of years'. But rather than jeopardise the relationship, he and Lee would ride it out. They said nothing, but I could hear Lee thinking, *I'm gonna have to log you, mate*. It helped that Putnam's cover – whose colour scheme, a red handprint on a white background, picked up on the blood-spattered white bodysuits worn by the Kliner crew – was 'an instant classic'. Lee considered it one of the biggest pieces of luck he had. 'The handprint looked instantly iconic, and the whole thing was direct and unadorned.' When Highfill questioned whether the bad guys wouldn't wear something more inconspicuous, Lee explained: 'They're white because I want a ghostly, nightmare feel – also to pick up on the Quentin Tarantino image – e.g. the *Reservoir Dogs* cinema poster – bright red blood smeared on pure white.'

He was easy to work with, said film agent Steve Fisher. The movie representation business itself wasn't easy. You were dealing with big egos and bigger expectations. Lee had big expectations, not least of himself, but was never less than 'decent and honourable and fair'. 'I've never hung up the phone and cringed, or got an email and gone *oh my god he just punched me in the gut*.'

The bigger your expectations, the more you had to play the long game. Delivering the manuscript was only a first, relatively simple step. An agent was looking for the complete package, which was more elusive. 'I'm very good at it,' Lee said.

> A great manuscript, yes. But equally, someone they can work with. Who's easy to work with. With a sense of humour. Someone who's not going to give them a hard time. Someone who's going to put in the hours. Do the legwork. Pull their weight.

However many doors you opened, Lee knew his was a 'classic last-era career'. The first US hardcover print run for *Killing Floor* was a generous eighteen thousand (which by 2019 was roughly the number of Reacher books shoplifted each year in Manhattan alone), but in 1999 Lee and Darley joined forces to buy back and give away hundreds of remaindered paperbacks at Grand Central and Penn stations, and in the UK, with echoes of 1997's Harry Potter, to travellers en route to Heathrow and Gatwick – *All aboard the Reacher Express!* Support from genre conventions and the Mystery Writers of America helped make the book a cult hit. In those pre-internet days there were lots of independent stores and 'a network of people talking about what's good, what's hot'. But still it was small-scale. There had been five or six years of upfront investment – of money, work and emotion – before things really started to happen. 'For a long time it was like being published by the witness protection programme.'

The horizon was shorter now. High-street rents were determined by cosmetics and handbags. Bookstores were no longer a sustainable model: 'even my books might sit in the shop for a day or two'. The industry had become risk averse. Publishers couldn't afford to wait ten years for an overnight success. The International Thriller Writers association tried to help authors break out by creating a big-mouth community, but Lee still believed that 'the only thing that really works is eyeballing a physical book and saying, *I'll give that a try*'. 'My career could not exist if I was starting today.' Ebooks, he thought, had peaked around 2012. 'The physicality of the book is germane to our culture' and 'deep in our souls'. Going out to get a book appealed to the hunter-gatherer in us, and we hurried home quickly with our prize to devour it in our lair.

Lee lamented being born too late to be a Beatle. But he felt that all his life he'd arrived too late on the scene. His first few years at Granada were golden, but with that darkening, narrowing glow of a sun that is already setting. His sideways move into writing coincided with the demise of the UK's Net Book Agreement (which sought to protect the cultural value of books by preventing them being sold at a discount), since when big-name booksellers and authors had thrived at the expense of newcomers and independents. For a few joyous years the business had been a blast, but ever since the recession of 2008 the mood had been 'terrible'. Lee couldn't deny he was doing well out of it, and was not surprised that the first peak of his possession-free hero's 'megapopularity' should have coincided with the financial crisis, but that only made him more uneasy. Other writers were liable to resent him, and though he embraced his fame (he despised people who courted and then complained about it), he didn't enjoy standing out as an anomalous exception, a throwback, like some kind of 'grotesque dinosaur'.

When Reacher began to age gracefully, it was noticeable that other characters began to assume greater importance in his novels. It was a characteristic of Lee's writing to weave micro-stories throughout the macro plot, a device facilitated by Reacher's peripatetic habits, but the subplots, or twin plots, of the Sanderson sisters in *The Midnight Line* and Patty and Shorty in *Past Tense* hinted at books Lee might have written had he ever been tempted to 'take time off'.

The plot of *Killing Floor* hinges on the phrase '*E pluribus unum*'. The United States motto, as Reacher explains, asserting his American credentials, 'adopted in 1776 by the Second Continental Congress'. 'It means out of many, one. One nation built out of many colonies.' In fact the plot hinges on a reversal of the second and third words, which in Latin makes no difference but is ingeniously interpreted by Reacher and Roscoe as suggesting 'out of one, many'.

The Latin master could not condone such egregious liberties. Claughton threw up his hands in horror and wrote at length, concluding his rigorous report with the indignant sign-off: *Thank you and good afternoon*. Impressed by his vehemence I ran his critique past my younger son, who likewise read Classics at Oxford. He empathised, but was similarly emphatic: 'I side with Lee, in that I feel it works as an *English* reordering of a once-Latin phrase now fully interpolated into the *English* language as an *English* phrase. Compare, for example, "clichéd" – English grammatical rules being applied to a once-foreign, now-native word.'

I saw it as a Freudian slip revealing the heart and soul of Lee's creative enterprise, the cornerstone of his authorial empire. Like Reacher said, 'it must mean something'.

> *E unum pluribus.* Out of one comes many. That was Joe Reacher, in three words. Something important, all bound up in a wry little pun.

From *Killing Floor* to *Blue Moon*.

Out of one book comes twenty-four, or one hundred million and counting, if you included sales.

The same but different, just like his father wanted.

35

Great Expectations

It was like watching a movie unfold in front of him.
Echo Burning, 2001

Lee Child had the patience of an impatient man, said Darley Anderson. 'When I told him it was going to take ten years to become an overnight success he was horrified.'

'I'm there at last,' Lee blogged on 11 July 2006 after an event at Foyles, 'the famous London bookstore. They always said it would take ten years.' *The Hard Way* entered the *Sunday Times* bestsellers list at no. 2. In 2007 *Bad Luck and Trouble* was his first UK no. 1, reprinted four times before it even hit the shops. Getting a true first edition was no longer a given. Then in 2008 he went straight to no. 1 in the *New York Times* with *Nothing to Lose* and blogged about 'the smallest number of all (apart from zero, that is)'.

It was the only difficult thing about working with Lee, the scale of his ambition. 'That has been challenging, both sales-wise and money-wise.' But it was a challenge Darley relished.

> Once when I was staying with him in New York he said to me, looking a bit concerned: 'Darley, do you know how ambitious I am?' 'Yes Lee, I do. I always got that.' But I honestly don't think anyone else does.

The problem they faced in those simmering slow-build days was plain to see on Lee's website. With the exception of trade journals, all the reviews for his fourth book came from independent bookshops, which he respected because they had limited shelf space and rent to pay and faced up to commercial realities, but which by definition were staffed by dedicated, motivated readers. Then at last the fifth, *Echo Burning*, was praised by Marilyn Stasio in the *New York Times Book Review*.

> Child uses the forbidding landscape of West Texas as both a metaphor for Carmen's sense of desolation and an excuse for Reacher's pragmatic brutality. But Child writes with more than his knuckles. His words are spare, but well chosen; the action is violent, but well calculated; and the ingenuity of the plot is especially suited to a cool character like Reacher, who always thinks before he strikes.

Putnam had seemed like the right publisher, but agent and author gradually became aware that 'they were never going to break him out'. At first it was only a sneaking suspicion. Putnam loved his work. They kept saying *Lee Child can become a bestselling author*, but even though they had a strong thriller list 'we didn't believe they were ever going to do it'.

'Putnam didn't really know what they'd got,' Darley said.

> I said to David Highfill, you need to put on the cover that these are stories about Jack Reacher. But he said it would make the novel seem 'too small'. Crazy, no? It's all about character – did they not get that? Jack Reacher is the James Bond of the twenty-first century, I told them, and they reacted with absolute horror. Now what do I read, looking inside the cover of *The Midnight Line*? Ken Follett: 'Jack Reacher is today's James Bond.' Part of the time I've just been waiting for people to catch up.

Fisher felt the same way. Lee 'was not an overnight success' (except in New Zealand, where he'd topped the charts ever since *Die Trying*). 'He built convincingly from book to book, but it was steps, not leaps.'

> Once I was pitching him to a guy who was a friend of mine and I said, you gotta get behind Lee Child, I'm telling you this guy is a star, and this is a movie franchise right here. And to this day I remember his words: 'Gotta disagree with you there, Steve.'

Years later Fisher ran across this same friend on the set of *Never Go Back*. The guy had other business with Tom Cruise. Fisher said hey, and thought about rubbing his face in it, and then thought – he's running a studio now so no, I think I won't. The scenario spoke for itself.

If Lee and Darley had been less loyal they might have switched after the tug-of-love over book four. Transworld had respected Lee's choice of title, *The Visitor*, which Lee considered benign, and by juxtaposition with the genre implications sinister too, but Putnam thought it was too science fiction and insisted on *Running Blind* instead (which Lee referred to as *Running Bland*). In a global market it caused trouble among fans, who felt they were being sold the same book twice. Lee realised he should have mandated uniformity and resolved thenceforth never to have a title dictated to him again.

Transworld had excelled at generating excitement among booksellers, but they too had made mistakes, when they were positioning him too narrowly for the male market.

> Lee Child has given them a character with equal appeal to men and women, and – excuse me – that's bloody difficult to do. It's taken them years to grasp that fifty to sixty per cent of his readership is women. You have to have the same talent and instinct he has to parlay

415

his book accordingly. The good thing is he is still alive. I would have been spitting mad if he had died before they worked it out, before they spotted and appreciated and understood his talent.

Darley had the passion of a lioness defending her cub.

By the time the writing was on the wall for Putnam, Lee was being courted by Peter Olson, an early Reacher Creature who was also chief executive officer of Random House. 'Go get me that author,' he told the publisher at his commercial imprint Bantam, Irwyn *not-even-worth-taking-it-on-editorially* Applebaum. So Applebaum swallowed his pride and bid hard, which was what he was best at. He was a money man at heart.

> The beginning of Lee Child's success has to be attributed to Irwyn Applebaum, a salesman. It was Irwyn Applebaum who broke him out, who got him into Walmart. Recognising new talent wasn't what he was about, but selling books was, and he sold the hell out of Lee Child.

'Olson got what he wanted, but you bet they had to pay through the nose for it,' Darley said. 'I got my own back.'

Persuader, Lee's seventh book, with its spectacular evocations of the ocean ('to noir roughly what *Paradise Lost* was to poetry', said Malcolm Gladwell), was his first to come out with Bantam, in May 2003. He marked the rebirth by returning, for the only time for two books in succession, to the first-person voice. *Without Fail*, the sixth, which is dedicated to his three brothers and posits a threat against the life of the vice president, completed Lee's third two-book contract with Putnam and became 'an orphan', expelled into a hostile environment without any fanfare, with the publisher exacting petty revenge by breaking the unwritten rule never to show Reacher's face on the cover. Especially not wearing shades above a white collar and tie. There was no disputing that branding wasn't yet in place. Tradition demanded the orphan book should get 'no marketing, no promotion, no publicity'. But 'it didn't sell too badly', said Lee, helped on by the wave of patriotism that followed 9/11.

In those days Lee was systematically a year ahead of schedule. When *The Visitor* came out in May 2000, *Echo Burning* was already in the bag with the publisher. Lee wrote the second half of *Without Fail* in a few weeks. He was going where the love was, where not only 'the nuts and bolts' but 'the intangibles' felt right.

As if to seal the deal, *Playboy* got on board for *Persuader*:

> The secret to writing a great scene: Start in the middle of the action, then leave the reader hanging. Child has coupled that formula to a razor-sharp style and crafted seven perfect thrillers. One press clip boasted that he's 'The best thriller writer you're probably not reading – yet.' Time to start.

'Any thriller fan who has yet to read Lee Child should start now,' said *Publishers Weekly*, right on cue.

Nearly wasn't good enough for Lee. Not any more.

'I wouldn't have wanted to talk about this ten years ago,' said Highfill, when we met in downtown Manhattan. 'It felt like our failure.' The first deal Highfill had done with Lee and Darley 'was OK, but they pushed us really hard for the second and third'. But he 'would have got out from behind the desk and in Phyllis Grann's face had she turned him down'.

Phyllis E. Grann was head of Putnam, had been since 1987, the first woman CEO of a major publishing company. She had backed Highfill's judgement from the start and was proud to have published Lee's books. But ever since the day she had run into Olson on the streets of London with a galley proof of *Killing Floor* in his hand (Transworld was part of sister company Random House UK) they had known they had competition.

> It was so ironic that he left us for Bantam, who had rejected him in the first place, and kind of bitter and painful, too. Darley said we didn't make it happen. I said be patient, it took Michael Connelly years to break out. Darley said maybe you're not doing it right, and even though it was Darley Anderson speaking I knew it was Lee Child speaking too. He was always fully involved in the business side and why not, he was good at it.

'We're going to lose this guy,' Highfill said to Grann about a year before it happened. A four-page fax addressed to Darley dated 12 December 2001 details a desperate rearguard action, offering 'a more aggressive *New York Times* bonus' (\$25,000 for a top-15 spot in the first week, and \$25,000 for each subsequent week up to a cap of \$100,000), shipping bonuses for the first year capped at \$150,000, a 'major six-figure marketing campaign' and 'a more defining look' that was guaranteed to 'take up more real estate' in bookstores. They even retrospectively changed the packaging of *Echo Burning* in a vain attempt to turn the tide, but 'we didn't succeed with that jacket design either'. It still hurt even now.

Fisher and Lee, who were realists, were more pragmatic and forgiving. 'There's a downside to being a homegrown artist,' Steve said. 'It wasn't really a failure on David's part, or Phyllis Grann's,' Lee said, somewhat impatiently (Grann moved on to become vice chairman of Random House but left the company around six months later).

> It was inevitable. I was always going to leave. Putnam made a great offer to try and keep me, then Random House doubled it, then

Putnam matched it, then Random House doubled it again. The only thing I hold against Putnam was that they pulled out of the bidding process. They could have made me a much richer man much sooner. Olson was never going to pull out. He was going to pay whatever it took.

But he agreed it was better to be head-hunted. Putnam could remember him when he was a nobody, whereas he walked into Bantam 'a huge success'. It was a power play, a big man arriving with a big reputation. He was a winner, someone who had cost a lot, in whom Bantam would therefore invest a lot, so he could keep on winning, for them. 'They wanted to buy, and they bought big.'

It was big talk. But grounded in fact. Applebaum's six-page fax of 7 January 2002 easily outguns Highfill's. The advance is more than 50 per cent bigger, across four books instead of two, and goes up by $100,000 per book, the marketing budget is a 'minimum total of one million dollars'. But the genius of Applebaum is that he doesn't even mention money until page six. He starts out by praising Putnam Berkley (they're great at selling established bestsellers!) before subtly, then lethally undermining them (they're rubbish at making them!). Yes they can handle 'predictable bestsellerdom', but the 'perfunctory' effort Lee has received – 'unexceptional covers, modest distributions, meager advertising' – also yields 'predictable results: *palookaville*'.

> I know he is understandably fed up with sluggish results. Lee is in desperate need of a concerted, muscular, full-court-press hardcover and paperback publication. And that is exactly what we aim to give him.

Lee Child will be one of their 'major "make" hardcovers', and what's more, notes Applebaum happily, the title *Persuader* plays right into their promotional hand.

I couldn't help recognising some of Lee's turns of phrase in Applebaum's letter. But since I knew they'd had a clandestine meeting somewhere out in Westchester I couldn't be sure who was quoting whom. Either way I was persuaded. So too was Darley, as is clear from his handwritten notes. But his response to Applebaum is measured: characteristically prompt, polite and appreciative, but incidentally musing over the many exciting ways in which Putnam were now upping their game.

Transworld survived the cut. But they had to work at it. In 2006 they launched a major marketing campaign with a twenty-page booklet-style mission statement featuring a softer, 'woman-friendly' font and colour scheme. The statement leaves no room for failure or doubt:

1. We will make Lee Child our No. 1 priority for 2006 and beyond
2. We will give even greater focus to Lee Child's books by separating hardback and paperback publication
3. We will target the best possible promotion with every major retailer
4. We will repackage the backlist with the new *One Shot* cover look
5. We will expand Lee Child's readership by targeting women readers
6. We will build the Lee Child brand name
7. We will increase Lee Child's media profile
8. We will mount an unmissable advertising campaign to attract new readers
9. We will increase Lee Child's sales in Europe and other global markets
10. We will make Lee Child a No. 1 bestseller

The back cover read simply: 'We will do it.' And they did. It seems fitting that it should be with *Bad Luck and Trouble*, the first of the Transworld editions to feature – at Lee's suggestion – the shadow figure of Reacher on the cover, and the book that finally reclaimed his first-choice title.

Darley described it as 'a great, great author–publisher relationship'.

On publication of his thirteenth novel Lee addressed the assembled workforce at a party. I love Transworld, he said. You do the hard work. I do the easy bit. I promise you now that you will be my publishers for the next eight books. (Everyone believed he would stop at twenty-one, like John D. MacDonald.) 'It was a huge public statement of loyalty.' The big guns looked at Darley with raised eyebrows: 'That's fine,' he responded coolly, 'but you'll still have to pay top dollar.'

Meantime Hollywood had come to its senses. On 17 March 1997, US publication day for *Killing Floor*, 'they all fell down like dominos' (Lee's words). Steve Fisher called to say he'd done a deal with Polygram Filmed Entertainment, with Mark Johnson – Oscar-winning producer of *Rain Man* – as producer of record. He'd turned down a bigger offer from someone they liked less. Lee liked Johnson because he favoured the classic storytelling virtues of character and dialogue over special effects. Maybe a guy like Howie Long, ex-NFL defensive end turned actor, could do Reacher (his original model had been England rugby player Lawrence Dallaglio, or alternatively, 'the body of Bruce Willis with the head of William Hurt').

'Hollywood's movie moguls have been frantically bidding to buy the exclusive rights to a blockbuster penned by an unknown writer,' wrote the *Lancashire Evening Post*, Jim Grant's local newspaper, collaborating in cranking up the machine.

Polygram developed *Killing Floor* for eighteen months, then dropped it and went under, part of a bigger story. The second big bite came in 2003, from independent producers Don Granger and Kevin Messick, who made mid-range movies and attracted a bid from New Line. 'We made an exponentially better deal,' said Fisher. 'We had more books to sell and it was clear that Lee was not a one-trick pony.' New Line put a writer on it and developed the script but couldn't get anyone to buy it on casting.

By this time it was 2005. Lee had just published *One Shot*, on which *Jack Reacher* (the first of the two Cruise movies) was based. Fisher recalled:

> Don and Kevin came to me and said: 'We think we may have a sale – would you give us Paramount?' I said sure, that sounds great, and Paramount bid right away. They made a very very lucrative deal for us. I would say much much better. Not just incrementally, much much better. Lee and Darley were very very happy with it. They felt this was a deal that was commensurate with the first rank of authors out there.

Lee took Fisher out for lunch at the Beverly Wilshire and they had 'a really really nice time and it was a really really nice moment'. Like the dollars, the adverbs increased exponentially.

'It wasn't life-changing,' Lee said, looking back. 'But it was worth having. Like publishing two books a year instead of one.' He'd got bigger since then. By now it was all a little old hat.

One Shot got a rave review from Janet Maslin in the *New York Times.*

> Mr. Child's idea of heroism has nihilism around the edges but a fierce, fighting spirit at its core. In marked contrast to the brooding figures who otherwise dominate contemporary detective stories, Reacher is not one for self-doubt. His is a two-fisted decency. But Mr. Child also gives him amazing powers of deduction, a serious conscience and the occasional touch of tenderness. It's a wildly improbable mixture, one that can't be beat.

It was a watershed moment. (Though she outdid herself for *Nothing to Lose* three years later: 'Colossal. Earthshaking. Stupendous. Reacher's

422

minimalist character is perfect. One of the most enduring action heroes on the American landscape.') Maslin had previously been the paper's movie reviewer and was read and respected in Hollywood. Her review sparked 'a minor four-day feeding frenzy', ushering in six years of on–off development before cameras finally rolled in September 2011.

Lee still had his eye on the bread and butter. His blog for 5 April 2005, Day 2 of his *One Shot* tour, sees him up early.

> Brad the driver took me to meet legendary south-of-London sales guy Gary Perry and then we hit Gatwick airport for the annual drive-by stock signings . . . total of nine stops, landside and airside. Unglamorous? Don't forget that one out of five UK Reacher books sells at either Gatwick or Heathrow.

On Day 5 he was recording one-minute video clips for Sainsbury's to use at the interactive terminals in their supermarkets: *Not sure if you're going to like the book? Just hit the button and let the author convince you!*

Lee's blogging days ran from 2005 to 2011, from striking a deal with Cruise to making the first movie. He wrote mostly from internet cafés, mostly about the irritations of travel. The bleached, tanned beach-bum look (he was briefly based in the south of France) – faded ripped jeans with sky-blue or sand-coloured shirts unbuttoned over white or gold T-shirts, tucked in and belted – gradually gave way to the pared down black on black he has cultivated ever since. In 2005 he is fifty years old but the world is fresh and new. 'His gaze was like a child's again' (*One Shot*). In London he professes faux relief at not blundering on 'highbrow' Radio 4: 'Did OK. Didn't swear or embarrass myself.' In New Zealand he marvels at it getting colder the further south you go. In Australia he enthuses about the Sydney Opera House and the disposition of the stars in the sky, buys a pearl necklace in Fremantle and teases his public with talk of Mel Gibson, Russell Crowe and Hugh Jackman. At Heathrow Airport he ran into a guy in the smoking room carrying a copy of *The Visitor*.

> 'You like that book?' I said. 'It's great,' the guy said. 'Have you read it?' 'Yes,' I said. 'I read it a while ago.' 'Check out the others,' the guy said. 'They're all good.' 'OK,' I said. 'I will.'

Up until then the highlight had been the time he saw someone reading Reacher on the beach. It was all going according to plan. His scientific approach was working out fine.

Back in New York, after the inaugural dinner of the newly founded International Thriller Writers on 14 June, he teases and tantalises:

> I had drinks with my Hollywood agent Steve Fisher at the Algonquin Hotel . . . two major new offers on the table. I was on the phone all Sunday morning with producers. The doormen in my building were deluged under packages bearing DVDs of their work.

'More movie news' (a few days later). 'Seems like the *NYT* piece stirred things up a little.' And then: 'I'm lucky in a lot of ways, and one of those ways is my movie agent. The proposed deal he just outlined to me hits every plus point a writer could dream of.' That night he went to bed dreaming of tomorrow, wondering if his cellphone would be ringing when he left for La Guardia next morning. (It was.)

One Shot took a risk in the way it postponed Reacher's first appearance. The convention with character-driven series was to introduce the protagonist on page one. 'The returning reader needs a sense of comfort and familiarity, and the new reader needs to know who the book is about, and both needs are usually met simultaneously and without delay,' Lee wrote in 2015 (for the Mysterious edition).

[Paramount] chose *One Shot* as the first movie partly because it was the book that grabbed their attention in the first place, but mostly because Reacher's long-delayed entrance gave them time to 'explain' the character by third-party references and descriptions before he actually appeared. [. . .] They thought the structure was perfect for the first outing in what they hoped would become a long-running franchise.

While Steve and Lee and Darley were papering the movie deal, Don Granger took a job with Cruise/Wagner. The company had an exclusive deal with Paramount. Don said to Fisher: 'I've talked to Paula Wagner, what do you think about folding this deal into Cruise/Wagner?'

Paula had gone away for a vacation some place tropical [Fisher said] and she was sitting poolside and she said there were three people poolside who were reading Lee Child novels. So she thought OK this is absolutely a sign, this guy is clearly bigger than I realise, and she came back from vacation and said yes, we're in, let's be part of this.

Cruise/Wagner were power producers on the studio lots, so in his amenable, upbeat way Fisher agreed: sure, why not, 'the more producing clout around this project the better'. Like Lee always said, it would sell more books in Brazil. (It did.)

One time on holiday Darley's accountant saw an eighty-year-old woman reading one of Lee's books. 'I wish I'd met that Jack Reacher fifty years ago,' she said. Another time he overheard a woman at the bookstore: 'I want the new Jack Reacher book.' The accountant told the assistant to look up 'Lee Child'. 'Who's that?' was the response, from both parties. The woman said, 'Is he the man who writes Jack's stories?' Like Jack was a real guy and Lee his amanuensis, Doctor

Watson to Reacher's Sherlock. Darley said: 'We knew Lee would be a mega-seller when Jack Reacher took on a life of his own.'

Lee described the shift to fellow Brummie Mark Billingham, in a wide-ranging conversation around the publication of *Bloodline*, Billingham's ninth book but his first with newly launched Little, Brown imprint Mulholland Books (Lee had written an early blurb – 'Morse, Rebus and now Thorne. The next superstar detective is already with us. Don't miss him.' – and in 2020 would write the foreword to the twentieth-anniversary edition of Billingham's debut, *Sleepyhead*):

> On Day 1, nobody in the world knows anything about Reacher apart from me. [. . .] Then the first book gets published and then the second and the third. And gradually the ownership of the character migrates outwards into the public realm. Previously people were deferential. They thought Reacher was an independent entity but they knew somehow he belonged to me. After about the tenth book he became totally publicly owned to the point where I now get abused just like any other fan with a different opinion. I count for nothing any more.

This was 2011, in the context of casting:

> My attitude was that 99 per cent of fans would be outraged because it would be a sheer coincidence if whoever it was matched their own personal image. I think it's proof of how tightly owned a series character becomes by the readers, which is great. This is a tough trade. Launching one book every year is a new mountain to climb every time and if you can get any help at all carried over from previous years you need it. If it is a series the new book is kind of 'pre-approved'. It's a much lower hurdle to get over.

426

Reacher was flourishing and like Jim's daughter Ruth, increasingly detached from his father. He was entering the culture from other directions, popping up in Stephen King's *Under the Dome*, where he is called upon to vouch for the military bona fides of the hero, and even muscling his way into the New Zealand parliament: *hope for the best, but plan for the worst*.

I asked Darley what he thought about Lee's appropriation by the establishment – Malcolm Gladwell and Haruki Murakami, Lady Antonia Fraser and Dame Margaret Drabble, culminating in Cambridge don Andy Martin's *Reacher Said Nothing*, a book-length fly-on-the-wall study of the making of *Make Me*. Darley said he thought nothing about it. 'It amuses me. The genius of Lee Child is that he's created a character for everybody, and that includes the literary types.' They were just harmless barnacles on his boat. The way I saw it the story had come full circle. In 1997 the *Lancaster Guardian* had likened Lee's style to that of Graham Greene, a comparison Lee welcomed (and was glad to be reminded of), since the highly cultured Greene had shared his respect for entertainment and written thrillers too. It was as though in between times the critics had been dazzled and blinded by his sales figures: it was simply inconceivable that any writer could be that popular and also be that good.

The key to understanding Lee Child, Darley said – he almost always used his full name – lay in how clever he was.

> His basic philosophy about commercial fiction can be summed up in his words to me right at the beginning: 'Darley, everybody remembers the Lone Ranger, but nobody remembers the Lone Ranger story.' Eighty per cent of the massive sales is down to the character of Jack Reacher. This is what accounts for his success, from the eighty-year-old woman to the intellectual. It all depends on what you as a reader bring to a Jack Reacher story.

'Lee is as clever as Reacher,' Highfill said. 'But he never makes you feel small.' In his 2014 preface to *Without Fail* (for the Mysterious edition), Lee wrote that his old Putnam comrade-in-arms deserved 'credit (or blame, I suppose) for being the single most significant influence on the Reacher series (after the author) as a whole, even today'.

A year or so after they folded the movie deal in with Cruise/Wagner there was 'the whole thing with Tom and the couch-jumping and Scientology,' said Fisher. 'Terrible timing from our point of view.' In August 2006, Sumner Redstone, head of Viacom (Paramount's parent company), terminated the relationship with Cruise/Wagner and kicked them off the lot, citing Cruise's much-publicised comments about psychiatry and postpartum depression.

> We started out with one of the premier production companies on the lot and then we were out there in limbo. We had producers that had a relationship to the studio that had suddenly gotten very complicated. That's one reason it took so long for the first film to be made. Paramount were financing the scripts and the options so they had a huge say in how this went down, and it took a mending of the relationship between them and Cruise/Wagner, and Tom Cruise and Sumner Redstone, before they could come to an agreement on how they were going to move forward with the franchise.

Then Cruise decided he wanted to play Reacher. When I asked why Lee said simply: 'Because Christopher McQuarrie's screenplay was so good.'

In a Q&A in the *Globe and Mail* (September 2011) Lee was still optimistic. The interviewer had been 'bombarded by disbelieving complaints'. Reacher was an intimidating physical presence; Cruise was not. How was this going to be handled?

Lee answered as he had a thousand times since. There were no actors approaching Reacher's size. All actors were small; the camera liked small actors better. Size was a metaphor. Cruise was one of the few true A-listers, probably the best character actor of his generation. It was a Venn diagram that didn't meet in the middle: they needed a guy who was 6 foot 5 inches and 250 pounds, an actor who had the talent to put on screen a character that was almost entirely internal, and a star who was sufficiently bankable to attract investment. It was like trying to square the circle. 'My guess is the acting ability will carry the day, but possibly I'm guilty of thinking too far ahead of the books' audience.' People would be 'weirded out in the first five minutes, but the test is, will they forget that and get wrapped up in the story'.

People never forgot. It was one of the few times he was wrong, on a grand scale. Or was forced to appear wrong, through contractual obligation. It would be a relief when he was finally able to say so. In his heart he knew. He was people. In his heart he wished they'd been making the movie forty years ago, when there would have been a choice of great actors who'd been in the service and had 'a certain gravity because they've had an intense life outside of acting': Lee Marvin, James Coburn, Gene Hackman (who was a fan). 'That generation is where my emotional centre is.'

Lee would never forget the day in March 2011 when Granger and McQuarrie flew in from Los Angeles and took him to lunch at the Gotham Bar and Grill on East 12th Street and plied him with expensive champagne and broke the news.

He'd always loved the movies. The idea that a little piece of him would be forever part of movie history was irresistible. He didn't need to worry. He didn't even really care. They could cast Katie Holmes as Reacher as far as he was concerned. It wouldn't impact on the book. The book was inviolate, invulnerable. The movie was a peripheral sidebar, someone else's take on his work – an opinion, an interpretation. Like the time a Polish thrash metal band had made an album featuring twelve tracks based on his first twelve novels. Like a cover of a no. 1 hit single.

And wasn't someone just offering to spend $120 million promoting his brand?

He had about a split second to make up his mind whether to say yes or no, whether to roll with Tom or kiss goodbye to Hollywood for a third and perhaps final time.

Right afterwards he was on the phone to his media team to say: *Stand by. You're gonna be buried.* The Reacher Creatures would be on the warpath.

'When you're reading [the book],' he said at a 2018 talk at New York University's Center for Publishing, 'it's just you. It's your private possession. A movie blasts it wide open.'

A few months later, Lee Child had Tom Cruise on speed dial.

Like he blogged on 27 June, *It's life, Jim, but not as we know it.*

36

The Treadmill

He had gone from being a big fish in a
small pond to being nobody.
Tripwire, 1999

Lee Child started writing his third book before the launch of his first. The response had been promising, but so far he had zero sales by which to begin measuring his success.

> Strictly speaking I was writing it on spec – I had no contract for anything beyond *Die Trying*. But whereas publishers were always gloomy (like farmers, no year is ever a good year, and next year will probably be worse) this was still early 1997 and the industry was nothing like it is now, so I saw no real reason to anticipate insecurity. (Mysterious edition)

Two books in he was effectively invisible. Despite his ambition, despite his 'creative and combative' personality, part of him – the part wounded by Granada – welcomed that invisibility (and missed it when it was gone). In adopting a new name he was retreating inwards as much as fleeing outwards. But he didn't want being invisible to become a habit, as it had for Reacher. Not least because he couldn't afford it.

Two years ago, everything had turned upside down. [Reacher] had gone from being a big fish in a small pond to being nobody. From being a senior and valued member of a highly structured community to being just one of two hundred and seventy million anonymous civilians. From being necessary and wanted to being one person too many. From being where someone told him to be every minute of every day to being confronted with three million square miles and maybe forty more years and no map and no schedule. (*Tripwire*)

When asked 'what next' during an interview in 1998, he says: 'Book 4 is Reacher again,' like it could have been something else.

Perhaps he was only just starting to believe it himself. Early drafts of book two, 'They, The People' ('I think that putting a comma after the first word sometimes works well,' Lee wrote, comparing 'Walking on the Country Road' and 'Walking, On the Country Road', hearing the words in his head like music), introduce the character of Trent: John Trent. Colonel John Pemberton Trent ('just some name I made up as a kid') is a Special Forces officer who bumps into Holly Johnson as she is being snatched by a well-organised three-man kidnap squad. Trent 'had some pretty unusual skills'.

A Special Forces officer is required. The Army says John Trent is the man. But Trent is already in Montana. Nobody knows why. Nobody knows whose side he is on.

Alone, isolated, distrusted by both sides, Trent takes his own decision. Penney must be stopped. While Army units mass on the perimeter, Trent does what Washington would want him to do. He goes to work as a 'magic bullet', taking out the militia's command structure, one by one. Secession fails. The militia is defeated.

But as a fictional hero, the-same-but-different Trent was doomed.

On the back of the final page of the extended synopsis, in red ink, the still fledgling author has written five, life-changing words:

They want a Reacher sequel!

It was a rare use of the exclamation mark: a marvellous, awestruck moment of realisation, the second best thing to the birth of his daughter sixteen years before, but also like he could hear the door clanging shut behind him, just as he had then. There would be no escaping Reacher. He was going down for a long stretch – he might as well enjoy it.

These were the 'Neophyte Years' (1997 to 2000), when Lee came closest to escaping through Reacher the way his readers did. A time of respite, of renewed innocence almost, when looking out over the pond and the woods all he had to do was write. He was working closely with Highfill, finding out what he could and couldn't do, what was and was not acceptable. They were learning together. No one knew the name Lee Child. No one was calling him up asking for interviews or endorsements, or wanting to write books about him, or swooning in signing queues. No one was denouncing him for selling out to Hollywood or hogging more than his share of the market.

Being nobody was liberating. But he still had that nagging sense of responsibility. He was still a husband and father: still breadwinner, provider, worker. It had been a wonderful moment at the Bookstore, signing his first books for the book-buying public. The signature and delivery payments for the first deal had started to repair his 'unemployed-broke-guy status' and he was feeling good about himself and the future. But in that very same moment he had the sense he was about to step on a treadmill that once started would never stop, and if ever he paused he was liable to be bawled out like the guys on the shaft lift at Hamstead Colliery.

For a while he was jogging along at a comfortable pace. If those things weren't mutually exclusive. Then the machine began to crank up, at first slowly and steadily, then madly, as though some mischievous puppeteer was itching to see him sweat.

The 'Early Middle Period' (2000–10) started with the move to Bantam-Dell and Applebaum *selling the hell out of him*. Suddenly, and literally, he had a following.

In 2004 he went on a four-day cross-genre cruise out of Galveston, Texas – 'Get Caught Reading at Sea'. Not a holiday. Part of a deal with Merchandiser, a wholesale distributor to non-traditional venues such as truck stops and gas stations, pharmacies and supermarkets. In exchange for participation in a daily round of panels and talks, and eating at a different table every night, he would get the major boost of a nine-month mass-market promotion campaign.

By 2005 the fan forum is in full swing. His first blogs are a shout-out to 'long-time forumites' and 'stalkers from way back': 'Reacher Creatures galore' in Glasgow, 'hardcore down-under Reacher Creatures' Helen and Linda and Ashleigh, and 'lurker Libby' ('these Aussies take some beating'), Tina and Teri and their mom, 'the crazy trio from Michigan', and Marcia, who bakes him a box of cookies. The tours get bigger and so too the venues. By 2010 the Lincoln Triangle Barnes & Noble is breaking fire codes for *61 Hours*, with the overflow watching on monitors outside.

The books creep up the bestsellers list. It's still a big deal. On 24 May 2006 he blogs:

> The second Wednesday after a book's release is a tense one: The *New York Times* day, when the bestseller list for the book's first sale week is released, to be published in the paper 10 days hence. Way back I would make it on to what's called the 'extended' list, i.e. places 16 and worse, where a book has measurable sales but isn't burning the place

down. *Without Fail* made it to #17, then *Persuader* made it to the dreaded #15 equal, which actually hits what's called the printed list, i.e. it appears in the Sunday paper, with the curiously stilted little synopsis that someone comes up with. *The Enemy* crept up to #11 . . . *One Shot* peaked at #10.

So, where was *The Hard Way* going to hit?

On 3 June he finds out: 'Either #2 or #3 nationwide, with the *Denver Post* bringing it in at #1. Did I mention I love Denver?'

The blogs read like a man courting his fans. But none of it was strategic, Lee said. He was just riding the wave, having the best time of his life, making good on his promise to pack more into his sixty years than the rest of us would in a lifetime. Everything was on the up, but he was still fresh-faced, still had the time and energy and freedom to hang out at the bar or turn up for champagne and chocolate surprise parties 'plotted by Rae and Janine, held in Cornelia's room'.

In 2007 it was Rae and Janine (groupies who became friends) who came up with the title *Nothing to Lose* (when it turned out 'Play Dirty' was taken) by trawling through Hendrix lyrics in search of a one-liner ('very Reacher-ish', comments Lee). So they must have experienced a proprietorial thrill when a year later, theirs was the first Reacher to hit the all-important no. 1 spot in the *New York Times*.

When Cruise bought the rights to the Reacher franchise it wasn't only the star's height that caused fans to freak out. It was his stardom. A man mixing with TC wasn't quite so likely to be found propping up the bar with Tina and Teri's mom. They were lovely people, Lee told me, and he had been their special secret.

> But once you became big and everyone knew about you they began
> to drift away. It probably started around 2006, or 2008 when I became
> a bestseller, and Reacher wasn't a niche thing any more. It doesn't

apply to me. If I like Camel cigarettes and then suddenly the whole world likes Camel cigarettes, I still like Camel cigarettes – but for other people, it changes everything. The movie became both a symbol and a driver of that divorce.

It was time to let his fictional alter ego take over. Lee wrote his last blog in 2011, the year before Paramount released *Jack Reacher*. The movie turned both Reacher and Lee into public property. Both got bigger, but the power dynamic changed.

In 2013 Lee was awarded the Diamond Dagger by the UK Crime Writers' Association: the first in what would become a procession of lifetime achievement awards. Indifferent to such industry accolades, a nameless faceless fandom began to assume a twisted authority over the author. They still demanded their book a year, but no longer accepted what Lee wrote as the last word. Online reviews read like an unending stream of school reports. *Another excellent year, well done sir, full marks, top of the class, keep it up.* Or (of the same book): *just not good enough sir, not up to your usual standard, can do better, we've read them all so we should know.* And: *We strongly suspect you are using a ghostwriter! Shame on you, sir.* One person put pen to paper for the sole purpose of correcting Lee's use of 'juddering' to 'shuddering'.

It was the onset of the 'Late Period'. People began talking about Tom Cruise's *Jack Reacher*, like a new celebrity manager had taken over the team. Tom's face appeared on book covers. Old-fashioned book readers were affronted. There were people who didn't know Reacher was a book character at all. New markets opened up, in Latin America and Japan, Indonesia and Korea.

Financially, it was all good. Lee calculated that in 2016, the year of the second movie, he earned 90 cents per second. But personally, he was baffled by the backlash. It was unsettling. He began to wonder if some of his readers weren't really *book people* at all. Didn't they understand that the movie would always be worse? That the book was the thing? Last time he'd taken his copy of *One Shot* down from the shelf and opened it, all the words were still exactly where they always had been. Nothing had changed. Except everything had. The hate mail was worse than for controversial chart-topper *Nothing to Lose*, when he'd given a voice to real American soldiers (quoting emails and letters he'd received from servicemen in Iraq and Afghanistan) and the 'patriots' who purportedly supported them had turned on him as a traitor, tearing out the offending pages and using them as toilet paper before putting them in the post with his name on. He was convinced that if his team wrote on his Facebook page: *Lee Child has fallen down the stairs and broken his leg*, the first response would be: *Ask him why he sold out.*

He'd always loved the movies, but sometimes he hated them too. The movies were a cross the book writer had to bear. If someone asked what you did for a living and you answered 'writer', the next question was always: *Have any of your books been made into movies?* At least now he could answer in the affirmative. But it wasn't the unadulterated unalloyed pleasure he once naively thought it would be.

Was it possible, I asked, that with Tom Cruise – paradoxically, and on the face of it ridiculous – he hadn't, for the first time, been quite so lucky? The very definition of a first-world problem, Lee answered, but he didn't deny it. It had not been a 'joyful experience'. 'I regarded it as a chore.' It had all taken too long, which was partly why he felt compelled to plump for Tom in the first place. But from the start he'd sensed it was not going to be 'fun' or 'delightful', as he'd imagined it might be. 'It was taking us off on a tangent. I knew it was not going to produce what I wanted it to.' It also felt strangely unreal, like he'd been shunted into a parallel universe. But not one of infinite possibility. More a dead end.

It was in 2017 at Sheffield City Hall that I first heard him say: 'I made a mistake.' Not in rubber-stamping the casting – the original reasoning still stood. But in 'underestimating reader reaction, how offended readers would be'. His view, the writer's view, was 'not shared by all readers'. *I know, I know*, he would say to later audiences, getting his retaliation in first – *he belongs to you.*

He lost a small percentage of readers who couldn't get Tom out of their heads. But he gained far more. Everyone was talking about it. You would be reading Reacher in a café and instead of *how may I help you?* the waitress would open with: 'Tom Cruise isn't big enough to be Reacher!' The truant hero had become a cultural reference point. He got into crosswords and quiz shows. He was used as a benchmark for video games – 'solidly constructed, expertly polished, easy to consume, and immensely satisfying' (*Eurogamer*). He was used to sell mattresses in Pakistan and Alexa on Amazon (*Alexa, when did Lee Child's new book come out?*). He was cited in *Vogue* (ahead of Jack Vettriano and Liam Neeson) as an analogy for the phenomenal success of Australian fashion designers Ralph & Russo. He rode to the rescue of a beleaguered education system in the UK's *Times Educational Supplement* – 'in desperate need of a Jack Reacher'. A lecturer ran a course at Massey University in New Zealand: 'Jack Reacher and thinking inside the box', 'Jack Reacher's thoughts about leadership', 'Jack Reacher and leading within your comfort zone', 'Jack Reacher and leading by taking action', 'Jack Reacher and the call to leadership'. A guy on Twitter aspired to be the Lee Child of drumming.

At the same time there was a growing category of admirers more interested in the writer than his character. They were in thrall to the perfection of the bookwright's craft. They were going into the bookstore asking for the new Lee Child. Other writers were wishing they had half his skill. When asked what book she wished she'd written, esteemed novelist and critic Margaret Drabble was rapturous in her response:

> Anything by Lee Child. What page turners, what prose, what landscapes, what motorways and motels, what mythic dimensions! He

does all the things I could never do, and I read, awestruck, waiting impatiently for the next. (*Guardian*, January 2019).

For Steve Cavanagh (winner, 2018 CWA Gold Dagger) Lee was 'one of the best authors in the world, if not THE best'.

Stav Sherez (winner, 2018 Theakston Old Peculier Crime Novel of the Year) extolled the subtle brilliance of his voice (*Spectator*, October 2016):

> Child is a deliberate stylist and his prose is taut, dynamic and highly-sprung. The sentences have a rhythmic sophistication lacking in most other bestsellers and a minimalism that is highly conceptual. The opening of 'Without Fail' is a perfect example of this: 'They found out about him in July and stayed angry all through August. They tried to kill him in September. It was way too soon. They weren't ready. The attempt was a failure. It could have been a disaster, but it was actually a miracle. Because no one noticed.' The way each sentence suggests the next mirrors the inexorable unfolding of fate and plot and plays a large part in making the books so compelling.

Similarly Steven Poole, reviewing *Personal* in the *Guardian*:

> [Child] is so good. He makes 'literary' writing seem orotund. Flabby. His sawn-off sentences pile up. He generates relentless momentum. At the same time, breathing space. Educational interludes. A whole paragraph on how to kick down a door. Sardonic riffs on consumerism. Always rhythmically placed in the ebb and flow of information. Contributing to the suspense. Child's dedication to suspense. It approaches the Hitchcockian.

Andy Martin wrote pages on Child's use of the double-tap

double-negative four-word sentence. The first ever such sentence, in chapter two of *Killing Floor* is: 'No address, no history.' In the original draft this is two sentences, and the first, equally defining example doesn't arise until chapter four, on page thirty-six of the handwritten manuscript: 'No milk, no sugar.' (Which on publication becomes the more American 'No cream, no sugar.')

Lee began to feel like Cuthbert Jackson, the black piano player in his story 'New Blank Document' (written for Jonathan Santlofer's anthology *It Occurs to Me that I Am America*, in support of the American Civil Liberties Union), exiled in Paris after the war. Jackson merely spoke plain common sense and people had started treating him like Socrates. 'One guy wrote a whole book about Jackson's five-word answer to a question about the likely future of mankind.'

'I may have written 10,000 things [at Granada],' Lee told *Maclean's* magazine in 2017, 'but most of them were four words long.' But the roots went further back. In 1960s Birmingham it was common to see four-word signs displayed in the windows of houses with rooms to let: 'no dogs, no blacks'; 'no n******, no Irish'. Such messages would certainly have registered on a boy with James Grant's susceptibility to language, story and injustice.

In 2014 *Forbes* magazine declared Lee Child to be 'the strongest brand in publishing', commanding the greatest loyalty among returning readers. He had mastered the art of crafting books that people wanted to read and were willing to pay for. In this he was literally second to none. But now he was also a writer's writer.

The coup was to do it all without being labelled a 'literary' author. 'I didn't want to be James Joyce,' he told Barbara Peters (of Arizona's Poisoned Pen bookstore) back in 2002.

> I would be horrified if I became literary. If I won the respect of literary magazines and was selling three thousand copies, that's no

good to me. What I want is to be ignored by the literary magazines and to sell three hundred thousand copies. This is a business, a living.

Not much had changed. Except that Lee had caught the attention of the *London Review of Books* and the *Times Literary Supplement* and the *New Yorker* (even the *Paris Review* had come nibbling) while selling three *million*, then thirty million copies and more. What could be more literary than referencing Joyce? He was having his cake and eating it too. But he was diligent and saw positive reviews as his due, like a restaurant serving quality food at affordable prices with good service in decent surroundings.

'It was the study of Latin poetry that taught me all I needed to know about genre writing,' Lee said provocatively at the CUNY Graduate Center in 2018 to a bunch of assembled academics. 'That's how I learned my trade.'

He was eleven, reading on the bus going home from King Edward's, when it struck him that 'Theseus and the Minotaur' and *Dr No* were 'exactly the same story in every beat and every plot point'. Everything had already been done. Which taught him two things: 'First, there are certain enduring themes that people love, so the fact that something's been done before isn't a bad thing, and second, you can't worry about it – just do it again, only better.' The same two lessons he would learn from Led Zeppelin.

In 2010 he wrote an essay on Theseus for *Thrillers: 100 Must Reads* (Morrell and Wagner, with a chapter on *Killing Floor* by Marcus Sakey). His lucid analysis lays bare the prototype:

> I first read this tale, in Latin, as a schoolboy. There was something about the story elements that nagged at me. I tried to reduce the specifics to generalities and arrived at a basic shape: Two superpowers in an uneasy standoff; a young man of rank acting alone and shouldering

personal responsibility for a crucial outcome; a strategic alliance with a young woman from the other side; a major role for a gadget; an underground facility; an all-powerful opponent with a grotesque sidekick; a fight to the death; an escape; the cynical abandonment of the temporary female ally; the return home to a welcome that was partly grateful and partly scandalised.

Which taught me two things: first, Lee was a loss to the teaching profession; and second, he was happy to use the semi-colon when the conventions of the genre permitted it.

All the while the treadmill was turning. By 2008 he had scaled the heights of Mount Olympus and was comparing notes with Homer: *who would win in a fight, Odysseus or Reacher?*

But he had to keep running to stay there. Which saddened him, a little. Tom Cruise might like running, but honestly, he really really didn't. It was great to make no. 1. Publishers took you more seriously. They said *we need this guy for another four books.* Foreign deals were easier to come by. You got better placement in stores. You got into stores in the first place. 'If you're in anything where there's a league table you want to be at the top.' But where do you go from there? How long will you stay there: two weeks, four, six? For a few years in Bulgaria he had occupied the no. 1 spot from one October to the next thanks to a peak-time talk-show host who talked Reacher five nights a week. 'Unless you're no. 1 for fifty-two weeks a year in every country on earth, there's always something else to aim for.'

'One regret is not being able to enjoy it,' Lee told me. 'You were always asking: how do we make this bigger and better?'

The alternative to bigger and better was smaller and worse. Lee didn't like the sound of that. Escalation was the name of the game. Once when he and Darley were negotiating a new deal Lee was asked: 'Why are you doing this to us?' The answer was simple, he told me:

'Because I can. But also because I have to. Because it's set up as an adversarial system.'

It was always win or lose, with him. Was there a third option?

By 2018 the third option was looming larger on Lee's mental horizon. Retirement. Whisper it softly, the fallout wasn't worth thinking about. It would be worse than Cruise playing Reacher. His old sparring partner Irwyn Applebaum had already gone, downsized ten years before in 2008: 'As I straddle the line between Bad Luck and Trouble and Gone Tomorrow,' he wrote in response to a note from Lee, 'I take it as a mark of a job well done here that I am leaving and you and your books stay on. I am grateful for having your trust that allowed the Bantam-Dell team to get you to the top.'

'I always thought,' Lee told me over brunch on Columbus, 'that it was going to be an easy choice between a better thing and a worse thing.' Turned out it was a choice between two good things. He liked what he was doing, and the attention that came with it. But he liked doing nothing as well. Hadn't retirement been his first thought when he was laid off by Granada, and writing just the fallback?

The only real difference was he'd done the writing for twenty-five years, and he'd hardly done nothing at all. He'd always worked, like his father before him. He'd never had the luxury of a stretch of time ahead where there was no obligation to go into work the next day, or the next week. Maybe it was time to hop off the treadmill, before he fell off. Like he told the 'Money' pages of the *Sunday Times* back in 2002: 'There's a lot of fun to be had in life outside work.'

That's why he agreed to a return trip Down Under, where Reacher Creatures had not yet followed the giant moa into extinction. A victory lap. The *Past Tense* tour started with the big names – Bill Clinton and George R. R. Martin in New York and Santa Fe, Ian Rankin at the Queen Elizabeth Hall on London's South Bank – and ended with the big crowds and full rock-star extravaganza, with fans in Australia and New Zealand ('the world capital of Reacher madness') reaching out to touch the hem of his leather biker jacket (a gift from Idris Elba after they'd met at a party) as he glided past. I was following it on social media from New York:

'I just got to meet one of my fave writers. Side note: his fashion sense is bangin'.'

'OMG, I think he's the sexiest author alive.'

'I can't believe we're going to meet Lee Child. It's the stuff that dreams are made of.'

'Lee Child: Jack Reacher is the modern version of the knight errant. Me, already taking my clothes off: Mr Child, you're a fucking genius.'

It had been pretty great, he admitted on his return. The US ambassador to New Zealand had even crashed one of his television interviews. But he was tired of touring. The world had become too hostile to smoking. Especially Australia and New Zealand. 'All part of the collapse of society. No goodwill, no convenience. No joy.' ('My First Drug Trial', *The Marijuana Chronicles*)

'Just because you like one thing,' Lee said, 'it doesn't follow that you might not like another thing equally.'

I recalled his answer the last time I'd asked if it would be hard to stop. *Hard would be to keep going.*

There was another thing. Once again the world had changed around him, and responses to his books were shifting in light of a new, ugly politics. The discourse of toxic masculinity 'makes Reacher look worse' and the rise of right-wing nationalism 'casts a shadow over my type of fiction'. There was no tolerance for argument or nuance, no appreciation of the 'various bipolar tightropes' his hero was so delicately walking. The fundamental reality of his character – that he's a decent man who shows respect and sensitivity towards others and treats women as equals – was 'not accurately reported', with certain lazy

444

readers preferring to draw 'cheap and easy comparisons' between Reacher and America's scourge of trigger-happy lone-wolf shooters armed with automatic weapons. In the past Reacher had been perceived and accepted as a rough, tough aberration, a metaphor, but now more combative interviewers would jump gleefully in and say: *Isn't this all a bit Trumpian?*

So when in 2019 Andrew Grant told *Read It Forward* he had created the main character of *Invisible* (the first in his new series about an elite former military intelligence officer who'll go to any lengths to see justice done) because 'we were collectively in need of a new kind of hero' who 'resonated with the time that we live in', it was hard not to feel he might be twenty years too late.

The change had come in like the tide and left Lee exposed. Emotionally, there were shades of Granada, and Reacher's alienation in *The Enemy*.

> I had always been a loner, but at that point I started to feel lonely. And I had always been a cynic, but at that point I began to feel hopelessly naive. [. . .] I felt like a man who wakes alone on a deserted island to find that the rest of the world has stolen away in boats in the night. I felt like I was standing on a shore, watching small receding shapes on the horizon. I felt like I had been speaking English, and now I realised everyone else had been speaking a different language entirely. The world was changing. And I didn't want it to.

Lee wasn't fazed by hard talk. But it had stolen the innocence and joy from his knight-errant hero, who was defined by his two-fisted justice and his ability to distinguish unequivocally between right and wrong (what writer and critic Paraic O'Donnell would call his 'artisanal fascism'). He was fairly certain crime had been around before books and television were invented. He was scrupulously careful about showing the full physical effects of violence – none of that being knocked down and bouncing back up again like *Tom and Jerry*. But despite all this reviewers now chastised him for setting a bad example. 'Really?' he said to me, incredulous, but actually addressing an otherwise warm review of *Past Tense* in the *Times Literary Supplement*: 'You don't want me to kill the bad guys *before* they do more evil? Not even in fiction?'

Why write fiction merely to reproduce a deplorable reality?

'It's moronic,' Lee said. 'I'm all in favour of an open mind, but don't keep your mind so open your brain falls out.'

'It's like this,' he concluded, wistfully. 'When the sun is shining on Reacher from the left, then people emphasise his moral compass and his heart of gold. When it's shining from the right, then he's a violent vigilante.'

Truth was getting too close to fiction, and the sensitivity around it was 'frankly depressing'.

Reacher wouldn't stand in the way of Lee laying down his pen. He had no trouble letting go. He never looked back over past cases. He wasn't nostalgic or proud. He had the skills; he didn't mind exercising them; increasingly, he was curious to see if he was still up to the mark, but he didn't need to be involved, he didn't depend on it, he's quite happy when it all comes to an end.

Much like James Grant.

Retirement was no big deal. He would have to get used to 'not having infinite money'. But he couldn't complain. And he had no compulsion to be heard. 'They're pulling it out of me.' Let publishers find new authors, let someone else have a go. We needed new voices to refresh the culture.

He wouldn't hang on grimly like a spectre at the feast, either. Once he was done he was done. You wouldn't see him again. No more festivals, no more interviews, no more early mornings on the road. *I'd rather hang myself than get up at five in the morning.*

He was standing at the crossroads. As I listened to him contemplate which way to turn, his words for the *New York Times* echoed again in my mind:

> That's the real rite of passage: knowing that you've written and spoken your lines [. . .] and now it's someone else's play.

Lee could be peaceful with his efforts. Not only had he been at the beating heart of the golden age of British television, he'd done a good job as a storyteller too. It had been an amazing second act. 'I've told twenty-four decent stories in the course of my life,' he said, then added: 'Not written twenty-four novels. The novel as a physical artefact was very far from my mind.'

It was time for the family that had steamed into New York twenty-one years before to fan out across the country like people had a hundred years ago. Ruth was selling up in New York and heading for Colorado. Jim and Jane had their hideaway in Wyoming. They could get cigarettes there for $4 a pack.

And Reacher?

Maybe Reacher would go to the Pyrenees, or rent out a beach shack and get a dog.

37

The Happiness Business

'OK,' Reacher said. 'I'm always happy to help.'
A Wanted Man, 2012

Lee didn't much like lawyers. Especially divorce lawyers. Divorce lawyers made their money out of other people's misery. He supposed there was happiness in it for some people, mainly the lawyers, but there was a whole lot of misery along the way. Misery and penury. While the lawyers were getting richer, their clients were generally getting poorer.

He didn't want to peddle in all those synonyms for misery so mercilessly listed in the *Oxford English Dictionary*:

> Unhappiness, distress, wretchedness, hardship, suffering, affliction, anguish, anxiety, angst, torment, torture, hell, agony, pain, discomfort, deprivation, poverty, grief, heartache, heartbreak, heartbrokenness, despair, despondency, dejection, depression, desolation, gloom, gloominess, moroseness, melancholy, melancholia, woe, sadness, sorrow.

Lee wanted 'to do something that makes people happy'.

A passing UFO, he wrote in the *New Yorker* (2016), would once have written us off as sickly, shabby toolmakers.

Then we developed language, and everything changed. We had grammar and syntax, which turned out to be the best tools of all. Now we could plan, and discuss, and theorize, and speculate. We could coordinate ahead of time, with a plan B and a plan C already in place. A cooperative pack of early humans was suddenly the most powerful animal on Earth.

At first we prospered through truth-telling. But at some point we started talking about things that hadn't happened to people who didn't exist.

Not for entertainment during our leisure time. [. . .] We had no leisure time. Everything was a desperate struggle for survival. We did nothing unless it had a chance of keeping us alive until morning. Fiction evolved for a purpose. Warnings and cautionary tales could be sourced from the grim nonfiction world. A sabre-toothed tiger will kill you. OK, got it. Fiction pushed the pendulum the other way. It inspired, and empowered, and emboldened. It said, No, actually, there was a guy, a friend of a friend, who came face to face with a sabre-toothed tiger, a huge one, and he turned and outran it, all the way back to the cave, safe as can be.

The action-hero story was escapism in the face of a brutal realism. At the St Hilda's Mystery & Crime Conference in Oxford, 2016, Lee was succinct:

We're still using stories to get us through life, because real life is shit. Real life is miserable. Real life is frustrating. Telling stories which provide closure is immensely satisfying.

Stories weren't just for bedtime, or around the campfire. We didn't grow out of them. Maybe we didn't have to fight the Minotaur, but we each had demons of our own and dragons within. We still needed an arm around our shoulder. A book of verse to transform the wilderness and help us transcend the terminal 'grey' of desolation. Either that or we needed football.

Critics questioned Reacher's vigilante violence. But the books were not 'textbooks for how we ought to live', rather 'consolation and compensation for how we have to live'. Lee loved to surmise that we all had ten, twenty, fifty guys we would 'happily walk up to and shoot in the head'. Most interlocutors chose to demur. Not so Bill Clinton: 'That wouldn't get me started,' he commented at the launch of *Past Tense*, where he was interviewing Lee on stage. Clinton had just published *The President is Missing* and had been known to call on Lee for late-night writing advice.

'Reacher's a bad guy,' Lee admitted. But not as bad as the bad guys.

> Credit readers with sophistication. We love that he shoots the bad guy in the head while simultaneously understanding that can't happen in real life. We all respect and value the rule of law, due process, etc. – but it is frustrating. Justice is so often not done, but it's the price of a civilised society.

Lee thought his most important work as a writer was to have told the story of Kirk Bloodsworth – the first person in the US to be exonerated on the basis of DNA evidence – for the anthology *Anatomy of Innocence: Testimonies of the Wrongfully Convicted*.

Even when justice was done it was slow and ponderous and costly. Reacher's ferocious violence was 'a metaphor for the ongoing criminal process', short-circuiting the tedium of the trial and, much to Lee's satisfaction, bypassing the lawyers. He felt no calling to write the legal thriller.

Reacher was an idealised agent of desire. You're walking down the street and there's some guy abusing his girlfriend. Mostly, we do nothing. Doing nothing produces 'a corrosive unsatisfied feeling', because mostly we want to do the right thing. Not just men: 'It's a gender-neutral fantasy, being free, and acting on your best impulses.' Reacher stands for our better (as opposed to most law-abiding) self. The satisfaction readers get from this is 'very organic', because it corresponds to 'a deep-down inchoate feeling that you should be doing something yourself'. It's not an abstract, theoretical appreciation, but primal: 'you love that novel in your gut'.

We didn't like being afraid for real. But we could enjoy the simulation of fear if we knew deep down we were safe. It was a way of discharging anxiety without actually getting hurt. Lee had learned this from his daughter. It went back to when Ruth was little and he used to lift her out of the bath and while she was still all wet and slippery toss her up in the air and catch her again, and she would squeal with delight. 'You want to feel scared when you know it's going to be OK.'

Broadcaster and former BBC Radio 5 Live presenter Phil Williams, who bonded with Lee over Aston Villa, put it very simply: 'I always enjoy Lee's books. Pacey, easy to read and leave you feeling better about life.'

For that to happen and for us to experience that satisfying sense of closure Reacher had to get his hands dirty first. He dealt with all those synonyms for misery so that we wouldn't have to. Not being able to change his clothes as often as the rest of us merely served to emphasise that. As did the showers he took whenever he could, sometimes two in a row, using a whole bar of (motel-sized) soap each time. Lee is not shy of spelling it out:

> First they took long hot showers, obviously and overtly symbolic, but also warming and comforting and necessary and practical. They got

out smelling clean and fresh and fragrant. Innocent. Like flowers. (*Blue Moon*)

Lee was happy to be making his money out of increasing the sum total of happiness in the world. Or at least, given pause for thought, out of not causing harm to others or the planet. What he did for a living wasn't going to hurt anyone, not like dealing in weapons or drugs or divorces. And there was freedom of choice: take it or leave it, he wasn't forcing anyone to read his books.

There was no harm in gentle persuasion though. The Reacher machine was a 'juggernaut'. In 2018 his Transworld publicist tweeted of a 'publicity blitzkrieg' and their reliance on a driver 'henchman'. They had invested such astronomical sums of money they would stop at little to claw some back. 'It takes the publisher three or four years to earn back my advance,' Lee said. 'After that it's all gravy. The backlist is long, and fully amortized. Pure profit.'

But there was another, more serious problem. Which was Lee's fault. They were his books, after all. And he had made them dangerously addictive. You might even say it was borderline coercive. More than once his novels had been described as 'the crack cocaine' of mystery fiction, like this was a good thing. Fans waited anxiously for their annual fix, tore off the wrapper and devoured it in a single sitting, then almost without drawing breath set about sweating on the sequel: *When's the next one coming, Lee?* The comparisons – and pairings – with chocolate were legion.

It was something Lee could relate to. Even back when he could only afford 10p books from the secondhand bookshop he would still buy drugs 'when necessary' ('mostly I tried to blag them'): such was 'the reality of an addict's life – they always come first'. He didn't dare experiment with pure opium. He feared 'the joy plant' and the wave of warm contentment that was liable to wash unstoppably over him until it carried him irresistibly out to sea. And no sooner had he told himself a story than he was bored and looking around for the next one. It was why he never mapped out his books in advance, and one reason he cited for not wanting to write the story of his own life: he knew it all already.

Lee was regularly asked what makes a bestseller. His first response was always to delay his response. 'All I know about creating a bestseller is you write a thriller and it sells a lot.' 'Everyone agrees there are two things you need – unfortunately nobody knows what they are.' He might hat-tip Grisham for his command of the narrative engine before concluding that it's all about engaging human curiosity, because human beings are hardwired to want the answers to questions.

Then he got down to basics (ThrillerFest 2017):

> A lot of people have baked a cake. I never have. But I know in theory. First you need ingredients, and the better the quality, the better the outcome. Then you need to mix them together, and the better you mix it the better the cake. Then you need something I've seen but never used, which is an oven. Then getting the timing and the temperature exactly right. Great cake.
>
> But creating suspense is not like baking a cake. Wrong question. The right question is: 'How do you make your family hungry?' Easy, you don't give them dinner for five hours. Set up a situation and don't resolve it, make it last for as many pages as you can.

The principle applied not just to the overriding arc but likewise to 'smaller bites' – to each phrase, sentence, paragraph, page, chapter. He served up a simple illustrative example. *The train was late and therefore John was angry* was 'a perfectly serviceable sentence'. Far stronger was *John was angry because the train was late*. Which made it 'a curiosity issue' and 'a better way forwards'. Then all you had to do was 'keep that going at every level' or 'bake it in'.

When he spelled it out the message was Machiavellian, verging on Sadeian. 'You have to train the reader to expect and desire and crave constant gratification.' Or in more abstract terms, in *The Hero*: 'The story proceeds based on the teller's aims and the reader's needs.'

Lee had trained his readers all too well, rendering many helpless. The worst afflicted signed up for online pre-orders before the book existed, when it was little more than a notional title, a shadowy, unformed embryo in the author's plan-free mind. It didn't make any difference to how soon they could lay their hands on the physical object, but they felt comforted – happier – all the same.

When they did get their hands on it they cancelled dates and called in sick and stayed up all night. They were powerless against the compulsion. There was nothing they could do to fight it. Like Sanderson in *The Midnight Line*, they were *hooked up*. The fix was 'more important than family and friends and any kind of a regular, trustworthy life'.

Reacher was the equivalent of an over-the-counter painkiller. Once, Lee's argument ran, a degree of pain was accepted. We were stoic. Then pharmaceutical companies isolated morphine from heroin (named for the German 'heroic') and introduced it into everyday medicines. They made money. They educated us into regarding no level of pain as acceptable. They educated the medical profession into accepting that pain can't be measured from the outside. They created a demand, a dependency, an addiction. Then they fed that addiction. They created oxycodone, whose 'only purpose was to make you high'. They made a lot more money.

Fortunately, the outcomes from feeding a Lee Child addiction were (mostly) positive.

Once he was signing books at the Mysterious Bookshop when a man approached him and said: 'You saved my marriage.' Something to do with how reading Reacher books on the plane had pacified his anger. 'I'll add that to my resumé,' Lee replied. 'Marriage therapist.' But the chances were that as many had been driven apart. Couples who stopped listening to each other or forgot anniversaries, or who preferred – men and women – to take Reacher, rather than their partner, to bed.

One woman tweeted in annoyance: 'Well, well, well, if it isn't THE Lee Child, destroyer of dates.' She included a screenshot of two terse texts from her boyfriend: 'Can't make it.' 'Completely addicted to a Lee Child I picked up recently.'

As Reacher took pains to remind us: 'No one should ever under-estimate the appeal of an opiate high.'

Here is the deeply flawed, deeply human first-person narrator of 'My First Drug Trial':

> I felt the tiny thrills, in my chest first, near my lungs. I felt each cell in my body flutter and swell. I felt the light brighten and my head clear. [. . .]
>
> I could feel the roots of my hair growing. The follicles were thrashing with microscopic activity. [...] My spine felt like steel, warm and straight and unbending, with brain commands rushing up and down its mysterious tubular interior, fast, precise, logical, targeted.
>
> I was *functioning*.

The orthodoxy among fans was that Lee's novels were a fast read, a score you could go on social media and boast about. Self-restraint didn't enter into it, rather there was an unofficial competition to see who could finish first. 'You don't write the kind of book that you want to sit by the bed for six months,' Naughtie said in Harrogate, 'with people picking it up and putting it down and reading a paragraph at a time.' He believed a thriller should 'thrill from beginning to completion in a relatively short space of time'.

But not everyone saw it that way. Serious addicts were often abstemious readers, spacing out the highs and rationing themselves and setting targets before the next hit like Sanderson on the road: 'a hundred miles, maybe [. . .], or five red trucks, or a rest area, or a hybrid car'.

Crime writer Holly Seddon allowed herself three sentences of Lee Child every night before bed, maybe a paragraph if she was bingeing.

> [Sanderson] took scissors from her cabinet, and she cut a quarter-inch strip off her [fentanyl] patch, and she stuck it behind her bottom lip. A maintenance dose. It would keep her asleep all night. It would keep her warm, and gentle, and relaxed, and at peace, and cradled, and happy.

Sanderson/Seddon was 'doing OK' because she got high every day. She would probably continue to do OK as long as her supplier kept showing up on time.

Lee had found a way of writing that was fast and slow all at once. Both focused and discursive, like guitarist Jimmy Page. You could opt for the precision-tooled plot-driven page-turner or alternatively, the more reflective character-driven analysis of the Jungian subconscious. It was twin-track writing that appealed to the few as well as the many, like a super audio CD, and quite likely more instructive than any university course in prose style. 'Maybe if there's something unique about my books it's this.'

Smart readers were 'relaxing' to write for, because they 'already liked reading'. The rest, if you weren't canny about it, might stop.

He once itemised the three crucial elements of a successful book (that people would buy regardless of genre), addressed to the would-be writer in question form.

1. Can you deliver the reader to the end of the story?

2. Can you write dialogue?

3. Can you become a reader of your own book?

It was 'all about the reader – 1, 2 and 3'. He dismissed the idea that the character had to want something on every page. The character wasn't *real*. 'There are only two real people in this transaction. The writer and the reader.' It was the *reader* who had to want something on every page, and the writer had first to create and then cater to that need.

That was the fundamental answer to the question: *How has Lee Child sold more than one hundred million books?* (Nearer two hundred, perhaps; they were losing count.) He had established a seamless synchronicity between writer and reader. He spoke with the reader's voice.

It was around the publication of *The Midnight Line* that Lee started talking more and more about an emotional contract with the reader. It was directly connected with the conundrum of retirement. He was 'an old showbiz person' who believed you should always leave people wanting more. But he was also 'the servant of the reader', and who was he to say no? *You want more? OK, I'll give you more. You need more? OK, I'm always happy to help.*

There was no denying pandemic dependency was good for business. In the first week of UK sales *Past Tense* sold 58,710 copies and topped the *Sunday Times* bestsellers list; no. 2 on the list scraped just over 10,000; *Blue Moon* broke further records (after what was claimed to be Transworld's biggest ever outdoor advertising campaign). Like Stackley with the Wyoming cowboys ogling the boxes in the back of his truck, Lee could feel 'the hum of desire' over his shoulder when he was sitting typing at his desk. 'Which was good. He needed his new pals to feel what he had to offer.' But great power brings great responsibility, and Lee found himself having to manage his readers' addiction through an artful balance of supply and demand.

He would always deliver on time. But stood firm in the face of escalation (in 2010 Random House US had tried to nudge him towards two books a year when they shifted the release date from March to September, and brought out *Worth Dying For* just six months after *61 Hours*). Ultimately, only 365 Reachers a year would ever be sufficient. To cushion readers from the worst withdrawal symptoms his publishers would drip-feed short stories or teaser trailers into the ether like Stackley peeling back the blanket to let the client take a glimpse at the heady riches beneath.

Lee famously disliked neediness. But he had created a hydra-headed monster of need that he would spend the rest of his life taming and holding in check. By 2016, like Frankenstein, he was squaring up to the beast and exploring his own growing sense of unease. Fiction had helped us survive. But it had also led us astray. We had wandered too far from the straight and narrow path of truth.

> Every bad thing depends on the same two components as every good thing: people prepared to lie, and other people prepared to believe them. The habit of credulity, bred into us, albeit inspiring and empowering and emboldening, has led to some very bad outcomes throughout what we know of our history. From small things, like a father believing a son, to much larger things, like a billion miserable and terrified dead. All balanced against the good things. Is it fifty–fifty? Or worse than that? And what about babies and bathwater? Could we give up the stunning joy that the good side of storytelling brings in order to erase the appalling horrors of the bad side? Where does the balance lie?
>
> It's ironic, given my profession, but the more I learn the more I would uninvent fiction.

The title of his *New Yorker* essay was 'The Frightening Power of Fiction'.

As time went on, and one Reacher book followed another regular as clockwork and reliable as a doctor's prescription, readers began to worry about Lee killing off his character or worse, dying himself. 'How long before the supply cuts off, do you think?' they would ask nervously, like Sanderson grilling Reacher on his power to provide. Lee stopped telling the hypothetical story about a final episode entitled 'Die Lonely', in which Reacher bleeds out on a bathroom floor somewhere in the back of beyond. It was just too distressing all round. Getting him a dog was a better idea.

There was a fantasy in *The Midnight Line* about unlimited supply. What would Sanderson do if she didn't have to worry about the stream running dry? 'I would party at first. Big time. No more rationing. No more cutting patches. I would bathe in the stuff.' Then she breathed a deep sigh of release and contentment, like she was having the best day of her life just thinking about it, like she'd discovered the new gold standard for affluence.

> High-dose time-release oxycodone, and transdermal fentanyl patches
> [...] The boxes were made of high-gloss card, antiseptic white, pharmaceutical grade. They had brand names. They were the real thing. Made in America, straight from the factory.
>
> Solid gold.

Add some eye-popping colour and foil and an embossed font and it wasn't far off a description of the glossy, highly branded Reacher books themselves.

The great virtue stories had over drugs was they never ran out. They were cut-and-come-again miracles, like Norman Lindsay's *The Magic Pudding*, which had been my own favourite book as a child. You could bathe in them any time you liked. Even if Lee never published another word, there were around three million in print that weren't going anywhere. The books would never dry up. Next time you needed a fix, all you had to do was take one down from the shelf. Even after the author was gone. It was as García Márquez said: *When writers die they become books.*

Lots of people characterised the Reacher books as being about revenge. Lee was one of them. 'But you could just as easily say they're about altruism,' he countered: 'love on a public scale.'

It reminded me of a song by Nat King Cole.

> There was a boy
> A very strange, enchanted boy
> They say he wandered very far
> Very far, over land and sea
> A little shy and sad of eye
> But very wise was he
>
> And then one day
> One magic day he passed my way
> While we spoke of many things
> Fools and kings
> This he said to me:
>
> 'The greatest thing you'll ever learn
> Is just to love and be loved in return.'

Lee Child had never forgotten the public adulation that once made him dream of becoming the fifth Beatle. Nor had he forgotten James Grant, sitting in the audience at Cherry Orchard Primary School when he was five years old. All those happy children. All those beaming parents. It was why the two of them had gone into the entertainment business in the first place.

To love, and be loved in return.

38

The Servant King

'They called him the Gentleman Gunfighter,' she said.
Echo Burning, 2001

He'd written it down because he'd found it so fascinating. 'I read somewhere,' said the BBC's Stephen Sackur in December 2018, 'that you see yourself as the servant of the reader.'

Sackur was shocked by this. He could appreciate a successful business formula: the logic of supply and demand would never grow old. But didn't 'servant' imply 'servitude'? Didn't this mean Lee was trapped, like he'd been locked up by his readers, who loved him too much? 'You can't escape!'

It wasn't that he couldn't escape, Lee said. It was more that he had a function. 'Suppose you've got some fantasy medieval court where the king has his own storyteller – that guy's job is to entertain the king.'

'But that guy doesn't have liberty,' exclaimed Sackur, aghast. Which seemed to run against the spirit of Reacher himself. 'That guy might have some other stories in his head that he really wants to tell but the king says *No! I want another of those ones you told last week.*'

That was exactly right, Lee agreed. It would be 'utterly perverse' to say 'I know you're looking forward to it but you can't have it. You can have this completely different thing instead because of my own personal arrogant choice.'

Sackur suspected that Jim Grant was being repressed in favour of Lee Child. 'If you look deep into Jim Grant maybe he's got some other stuff he wants to say and write.'

That was possible, Lee Child allowed, but Jim Grant could say and write it to himself any time he wanted. 'Suppose you are Harry Kane, an athlete who plays football. Your fans don't want the stress of turning up at the ground wondering if you're suddenly going to play hockey or rugby instead. I think the audience needs to be able to trust the writer to deliver what the audience wants.'

Far from being repressed, this was Jim Grant speaking loud and clear. Lee Child was the supreme stylist and literary theorist, the no. 1 bestseller, the rock star, the king ('the Manchester United of the writing world'; 'I don't have rivals'), but Jim Grant insisted on keeping it real ('I think of myself as your lawnmower man'). All he really wanted was a decent job entertaining the court. He liked doing something he was good at. He respected the need to earn a living. He wasn't above providing a service. It was a Birmingham thing.

Sackur didn't pick up on the word 'audience'. Lee had to spell it out. He was perfectly fulfilled by 'continually churning out Jack Reachers' (quoting Sackur, by way of logging him – the implied judgement revealed the stigma of success and he'd had enough of being categorised as a 'guilty pleasure') because he was an entertainer and in entertainment there had to be 'some kind of reliability'. You had only to look around the entertainment scene to see people 'doing their thing'.

Some people 'don't value what you do', said Sackur. 'They see it as junk food.' Lee wasn't bothered. He liked junk food. He would always stop off at the Chambers Street Schnippers (for a blue cheese burger: no lettuce, no tomato) when he had business at the Mysterious Bookshop. 'Suppose you're a gourmet,' he said patiently. 'Wouldn't you sacrifice just one meal to provide for your children and grandchildren?' Literary writers should be humble enough to take a year off to make a fortune instead of catching yet another ride on his boat: 'Is that not an irresistible proposition?' If they didn't, either they were incredibly selfish or they couldn't.

Reacher too was content with providing a public service. He didn't need fame and fortune, medals, prizes and plaudits. Some things had to stay under the radar. It didn't worry him if others took the credit, like the new police commissioner at the end of *Blue Moon*. He was fulfilled by the satisfaction of a job well done. He never killed a man that did not need killing, and certain it was that many of his stern deeds were for the right as he understood that right to be.

> 'A fine obituary,' Reacher said. [. . .] 'As good as you can get, probably.'
> (*Echo Burning*)

It was something many readers – in and out of the industry – found it hard to get their heads round. Superficially the embodiment of stereotypical masculinity, Reacher was emotionally very (stereo-typically) feminine. He already had more of Josie than Stan in him. He instinctively understood the value of service to others, even if this did run up against the principle of personal freedom.

The service he provided was morally delicate, and this was why the reality Reacher had assumed in the popular imagination had become a problem. People forgot he was a fictional character operating in a fictional world, doing things that shouldn't be done in real life. Guns were a tool of his trade. He didn't think they were fun.

But wasn't Lee using guns to entertain his audience? Lee wouldn't fall into this trap. He credited book readers, who in his view were by definition more intelligent than non-book readers, with being able to tell the difference between reality and fiction. Why deny them (or himself) a little harmless wish fulfilment?

'Do you like the idea of summary justice?' Sackur asked. 'Clear absolute lines between right and wrong, a black-and-white view of the world which doesn't allow for much relativism or much shilly-shallying around?'

'I'm a bit like that,' Lee said. He understood about constructing a balanced argument *in utramque partem*. But he was 'tired of constantly re-debating the same questions': 'If Reacher met somebody dressed up in a Nazi uniform giving a Nazi salute, sure, he'd punch him in the face because there is nothing more to be said.'

Sackur expressed righteous scepticism. But when Lee turned the tables – 'What would you do? Every year open a fresh inquiry into whether being a Nazi is a good idea or not? Or do we think we already know the answer to that?' – he moved on to another question.

'Too many rules,' a detective comments in 'Smile'. 'But those don't apply to everyone.'

Lee didn't need to use his writing to signal his own virtues. He wasn't seeking approbation from like-minded people. His power lay in having created a character that bridged the intellectual and political divide and could address those who might not normally listen. He cited *The Enemy* as an example of subliminal messaging to challenge prejudice against gays in the military. 'I use Reacher to give the message there's nothing wrong with that. Are you surprised that there are gay people in the military?'

> I remember my own father, who was not particularly homophobic but just a very repressed and conventional man. He served in World War Two. I once asked him were there gays in the military. And he said we had fourteen million men in uniform, of course plenty of them were gay. I asked did it bother him and he said, why on earth would it bother me? If somebody brings me a can of ammunition in my foxhole, what do I care what his sexual orientation is?

John Reginald Grant hadn't been much fun to hang out with. He was stiff and straight and dour and cheerless. He was emotionally withholding and had no concept of play. But still he was a fundamentally decent, and pragmatic, human being.

Did that make Lee a liberal? Sackur wanted to know, as though this were almost as scandalous as the risk of fetishising violence.

Yes, Lee said, and supplied an argument his linguistically sensitive father could have got right behind. He was a writer, so words meant something to him. 'Liberal? Yeah – based on liberty. I completely believe in liberty.' Then before the BBC man could reduce his concept of freedom to the freedom to kill, he added: 'I believe in democracy, so I'm a democrat.'

I knew a brilliant young woman named Rachel who worked at Westminster and dreamed of Lee Child running for leader of the Labour Party. He was flattered but not tempted. In an interview for his Otley grandma's old favourite, the *Reader's Digest*, entitled 'If I ruled the world', he said he would 'immediately investigate the abdication option'. Canon R. G. Lunt would have been disappointed.

But if he were to articulate a manifesto it might be to increase the sum total of readers in what would then be a marginally less stupid world. He would make teachers the highest-paid professionals because education is 'all we've got'. He would build libraries and protect bookstores:

> Landlords have been jacking the rent up to the point where only certain kinds of stores can survive and bookstores are not that kind of store. Not because people don't want to buy books – they love them, but they don't buy them quite fast enough and there's not enough margin in each sale to compete. Books are really important and I think that even now, in 2018, there's nothing better than getting lost in one: you've got the whole world in your hands.

He would abolish all existing political parties and start afresh. Most of the population were 'lovely people, full of decency', but nobody was representing them: 'We only represent the lunatic fringes – the people on the right or the left – while the people in the middle are left to make their own way.' The royal family were no doubt 'lovely people' too, he said. 'Princess Kate' had invited him to an event celebrating the Queen's Jubilee, but he'd had to turn her down as he was already committed to the Literary Lions Gala hosted by the King County Library System in Seattle the day before.

> But a hierarchical structure like that, where you're born to something, alters the shape of people's expectations. Even now in Britain, there's a feeling that if you're born in the wrong place and the wrong class, you're going to have a limit to what you can do. The royal family gives the country the wrong shape.

Lee would always prioritise the library, even if the Yankees came calling. 'Nobody gets to go to university unless they have been to the library when they are three or four years old,' and nobody gets to be a writer unless they have already read 'tens of thousands of books by the time they are thirty or forty'.

When Lee Child emigrated to the US in 1998 Bill Clinton was president. Three years later he wasn't president any more but had become a big Jack Reacher fan. One day he'd telephoned Lee to tell him so. It was the start of a beautiful friendship and occasional correspondence. Clinton invited Lee to lunch and sent him a note after every Reacher book.

This one is dated 16 June 2010:

> Dear Lee
>
> I really enjoyed the *Chicago Tribune* article on you, it was reprinted in the local paper. What a story you have – almost as good as

Reacher's! And I loved *61 Hours*. As you know, I've read them all.
Hope you're well.

    Best, Bill Clinton

One time, Lee dropped a signed copy at Clinton's house, driving up in his Crown Vic and parking in line with three other identical cars from the Secret Service ('They were practically saluting when I got out'). The inscription read:

> For Bill Clinton —
> the greatest President of my lifetime
>   Admiringly, appreciatively, and affectionately
>   Lee Child

He'd drafted the dedication on a piece of lined notepaper.

Then in 2018 Clinton published a book of his own.

'Dear Lee,' he wrote on 16 May:

> Thanks so much for the great quote you wrote for *The President is Missing*. Writing the book with Jim [Patterson] was a lot of fun, and as a huge admirer of your work, your kind words about it mean more than you know.

And again on 21 June:

> Thank you very much for leading our conversation about *The President is Missing* earlier this month in Philadelphia – what a privilege to talk writing with you and Jim!

The A5 notepaper is headed WILLIAM JEFFERSON CLINTON under a variation of the gold presidential seal. At the foot of the second is a postscript: *You were great. Thanks. Waiting for Reacher . . .*

No politician was ever going to be perfect. Lee thought Clinton better than most. Not least because – like his own father – Clinton read books: in his own words (*New York Times*, May 2018), 'to learn how to do it better'.

In 2002 the Grants bought a pied-à-terre in the south of France (Lee's notebooks reference 'chez nous' and 'l'aeroport'; a card from his wife reads 'Je t'aime'). Jane was having second thoughts about living so close to her family and George W. Bush was no Bill Clinton. Lee Child wrote a letter to the *New York Times* (3 May 2001, 'Bush in the Mirror'). Partly he was scoring points off his father-in-law, who was always firing off letters but never got them published, and partly he was getting his name out to a book-buying readership, but the message was nonetheless sincere.

To the Editor:

In 'Blocking Judicial Ideologues' (editorial, April 27), you write, 'As a general rule, the president's choices for judgeships deserve significant deference.' But the general rule does not apply here, and the only deference expected now is that which President Bush owes in the face of reality.

He should say to himself each morning: 'I lost the popular vote. A man of honor and integrity does not pretend that he won by a landslide when he barely won at all. Therefore, my appointments should please as many people as possible, especially in matters that will endure long after my time in office.'

But clearly, Mr. Bush does not say these things to himself every morning, and I, for one, find that omission both unattractive and unacceptable.

LEE CHILD

Pound Ridge, N.Y., April 27, 2001

Nine months later he wrote again. (8 January 2002, 'Bush Has Changed. No, He Hasn't.')

> Re 'Bush, on Offense, Says He Will Fight to Keep Tax Cuts' (front page, Jan. 6):
> Actually, the president said, 'Not over my dead body will they raise your taxes.' This might represent his normal muddled syntax, but on the other hand it might be a clever get-out clause for later use, because inasmuch as it means anything, it seems to mean, 'If they raise your taxes, it won't be over my dead body.'
> LEE CHILD
> Pound Ridge, N.Y., Jan. 6, 2002

Dubya was as much an offence to the English language as to honour and integrity. In November Lee writes on cynicism around the timing of the Iraq War, then again in January 2004, on duplicity around terrorism and fake news, before presumably throwing his hands up in despair.

Lee's last letter to the *Times* – 'Who's an Exemplary Evangelical' – appeared on 3 December 2004, almost a month to the day after Bush was re-elected with an absolute majority of the popular vote, mainly due to points scored from 9/11 (from which – it was bittersweet – Reacher also benefited). Four years later he would publish *Nothing to Lose*, whose bad guy Thurman presumably has roots in Stott and Falwell:

> Unlike David Brooks ('Who Is John Stott?', column, Nov. 30), I don't see any real difference between the evangelists John Stott and Jerry Falwell. Both would say to me, 'I believe something you don't, and I'm right, and you're wrong.'
>
> Of course, I would say the same thing back to them. So far, so good, and hooray for diversity.

469

But: Whereas I would then be happy to let them go on their way, they have decided they must stop me, change my mind, modify my behavior and regulate my access to rights, freedoms and services. That's not humility. That's arrogance. And it doesn't need 'understanding'. It needs opposition.

LEE CHILD

Pound Ridge, N.Y., Nov. 30, 2004

He didn't really need to get his name out there any more. Jim and Jane sold Pound Ridge and fled the country, hiring a private jet to fly them to Saint-Tropez. When they finally moved back to New York in 2008 they could never quite recapture the innocence or purity of their first arrival ten years before. It wasn't only the residual sourness of the Bush years. Their own world had changed too, especially after Tom Cruise and that first no. 1. Lee was now a celebrity. Soon he would become an institution. And having unrestricted choice (of houses, countries, transport, what Lee came to describe as *distributed living*), or rather not having to choose at all, only increased the risk of domestic entropy.

The first time Lee met Barack Obama, the new president was apologetic: he'd been a little too busy to read Reacher. It was something he hoped to rectify. Lee was magnanimous. It didn't stop him supporting each of Obama's campaigns with maximum donations. He liked his dog Bo (whose Wikipedia page rivals Lee's in detail), and appreciated the president's honesty. At least he was another reader, like Clinton, which Lee doubted Trump was. Lee didn't have Obama on speed dial, but he was definitely on the president's guest list each December for the Holiday Reception at the White House.

One time he joined a select group of four for afternoon tea at a midtown hotel owned by the Tisch dynasty (also represented), ostensibly because Obama was eager to solicit their views on foreign policy. 'Really it was just a stroking thing for donors.' Lee was sitting next to Obama, but last in line to speak. When it was his turn he said: 'I want to know why your watch is ten minutes fast.' He was genuinely curious about the Jorg Gray JG6500 presented to Obama by the Secret Service. But mainly he wanted to puncture the pomposity, which Obama seemed to welcome, explaining it was a habit he'd developed long before becoming president, and the only way he managed to get anywhere on time.

It still blew Lee away that for the launch of his penultimate novel he'd been interviewed by a man who had once been president of the United States of America ('I would have paid to be here,' said Clinton). Even Jane wanted to come along to that one. Even Rex and Audrey might have sat up and paid attention.

But he wasn't going to let it go to his head.

'I don't think of myself as a writer *per se*. I'm not trying to be Albert Camus. I'm the guy that writes Jack Reacher. It's just that simple.'

Jorge Luis Borges famously posited that all men who recite a line of Shakespeare are William Shakespeare. I thought something similar applied to Lee. He had read so much that he was inhabited by the spirit of literature. He didn't have to try to be Albert Camus, because in so many ways he already was.

They both had a poetic sense of place and wrote a spare prose that was nonetheless lyrical and lingeringly attentive to detail. Both suffered from a defining physical frailty (lungs, heart) but were also smokers. Both loved the sun and the dissolution of self they experienced swimming in the sea, drops of water that in the ocean are confounded. Both were popular with women. Both were acutely conscious of the futility of individual endeavour without losing their profound respect for it. Both rejected the philosophical suicide of religion and embraced a form of creative nihilism. Both loved football and the theatre for their invitation to surrender, their in-the-moment intensity and their power to blast away the noise of everyday life. Both had known relative poverty and had the craftsman's appreciation for what worked. Both had experienced the intimacy of teamwork (the Resistance, the central control room) and the isolation of betrayal (ideology, politics).

Lee couldn't recall reading Camus at school. But he did remember Hervé Bazin's *Vipère au poing*. Not only because it was about a son rebelling against his mother but because it had impressed him that his French teacher John Hatton was a personal friend of the (living) author and had smuggled it into the classroom among the more orthodox set texts. Hatton had started his days at King Edward's as Brother John, with a monk's habit and a crewcut. He would stand with his back against the south-facing windows with the sun pouring in behind him and ask the squinting boys: 'Is my halo blinding you?' Later he threw off his habit. He would make the boys sing the 'Marseillaise' and start each lesson by drawing a flamboyant map of Paris on the chalkboard. Hatton taught with a D. H. Lawrence level of intensity and commitment to notions of sincerity and openness: 'Let's talk about sex, boys! Come on, it's nothing to be embarrassed about.'

When I assured Lee that the balance of evidence suggested he had read *The Outsider* he speculated that he had absorbed the text so fully it had become an indistinguishable part of the intertextual being he was. He remembered how one day he was trying on reading glasses in the local pharmacy and had tested out a pair with round lenses and how the thought had popped unbidden into his head that they made him look like Albert Camus.

Writing a book was easier than digging a ditch, he told interviewers more than once. But it was still a Sisyphean task. He prided himself on treating each new novel as if it were both the first and the last. 'It's fun for the first half-hour and then it's a slog.' It hadn't got any easier either, which was a source of deep disappointment. Hitting 'send' on the finished manuscript was always a relief, because every year was like 'climbing a mountain' and 'rolling a boulder up a hill'.

He hadn't set out to be a writer. But when he told Sackur that he 'didn't buy a black polo neck and black leather jacket' it wasn't strictly true. There were at least three black leather jackets in his wardrobe, and what was a (black) T-shirt if not a chopped down (black) polo neck?

I'd heard him say it many times. 'I'm the guy who writes the Reacher books.'

'I'm the Reacher guy.'

39

Die Lonely

Face it. The pathology meter was twitching.
The Midnight Line, 2017

The word 'alone' appears on average roughly thirty-five times in every Reacher book (peaking at sixty in *The Hard Way*). It's not surprising. Reacher travels alone. Victims are often alone, and sometimes the bad guy is too. The word is functional and descriptive.

'Lonely', carrying more emotional weight, appears on average roughly five times (peaking at thirteen in *A Wanted Man*).

There is no Reacher book in which neither word appears.

Roads were lonely. Drivers were lonely. Cars and kerbs and crossroads were lonely. Headlights and tail-lights and pools of yellow light were lonely. Billboards were lonely. Exits off the long and lonely Interstate were lonely too. Iowa was a lonely state. Each exit was an event in its own right. The vast, empty interior was lonely. Echo in Texas was hot, lonely, valueless country, where the lonely guttural cries of cougars and coyotes filled the dark and lonely night.

Houses and motel rooms were lonely. Empty subway cars were vast and cavernous and lonely. Stray dimes in pockets were lonely, so too items on the shelves of lonely stores. Burner phones and English poets were lonely. Bullets in flight were lonely. Death was lonely.

The bereaved were loneliest of all.

Lonely people kept lonely vigils in the lonely darkness. Individuals were by definition lonely. That's why they sought each other out. Like Patti Joseph and Brewer in *The Hard Way*, or Reacher and Eileen Hutton in *One Shot* – two lonely people in the Middle Eastern desert. 'We had a good thing going. Three great months. She was a nice person. Still is, probably. Terrific in the sack.'

Reacher admits to feeling lonely when Peterson asks in *61 Hours*. The grandmotherly Janet Salter doesn't need to ask.

> 'You're lonely.'
> 'Aren't you?'

'Can I come in?' Karla Dixon asks in *Bad Luck and Trouble*.

> 'I was on my way to the phone.'
> 'Why?'
> 'Lonely.'

He gives the exact same reason for calling Summer at midnight in Paris. New York is the natural habitat for a lonely man.

> [Reacher] liked to sit outside in the summer, in New York City. Especially at night. He liked the electric darkness and the hot dirty air and the blasts of noise and traffic and the manic barking sirens and the crush of people. It helped a lonely man feel connected and isolated both at the same time. (*The Hard Way*)

Mostly, Reacher is comfortable with what I once heard Lee refer to as his (own) *solitudinous* state. 'Don't you get lonely?' Hubble asks in *Killing Floor*. 'I told him no, I enjoyed it.' It's not as bad as it sounds, he tells Carmen in *Echo Burning*. 'I like being alone.'

'Loneliness' is a bigger word. Used only four times, and never more than once in a book. Once each in *Nothing to Lose* and *61 Hours*, with reference to waiting women. Twice with reference to Reacher himself. In *Tripwire* he is defined for the first time as 'a man who liked solitude but was worried by loneliness'. In *The Enemy*, he has just lost his mother.

Reacher loved Jodie Garber. The feeling that buzzed through him when he saw her after a fifteen-year separation was as powerful as an electric shock. He'd rarely felt it before.

> Rarely, but not never. He had felt the same thing on random days since he left the Army. He remembered stepping off buses in towns he had never heard of in states he had never visited. He remembered the feel of sun on his back and dust at his feet, long roads stretching out straight and endless in front of him. He remembered peeling crumpled dollar bills off his roll at lonely motel desks, the feel of old brass keys, the musty smell of cheap rooms, the creak of springs as he dropped down on anonymous beds. Cheerful curious waitresses in old diners. Ten-minute conversations with drivers who stopped to pick him up, tiny random slices of contact between two of the planet's teeming billions. The drifter's life. Its charm was a big part of him, and he missed it when he was stuck in Garrison or holed up in the city with Jodie. He missed it bad. Real bad. About as bad as he was missing her right now. (*The Visitor*)

He hated eating dinner on his own in the fancy Italian restaurant while Jodie worked late at the office. He hated beating back rampant nature in his unwanted garden. The loneliness of the road revitalised him. The loneliness of domesticity depleted him.

In *Never Go Back* Reacher finds a woman more like himself. She's holding down his old job with the 110th MPs. He can call her by her last name. He's hitchhiked all the way from South Dakota to Washington DC to reach Major Turner, his Penelope, setting out four books earlier, at the end of *61 Hours*. It's a long way. He would have got there sooner, except for having to clear up a few messes on the way.

It's peak romance, but it doesn't work out. Reacher doesn't want to stay with Turner, and she doesn't want to go with him. The song 'Canvas and Lace' (on the album *Just the Clothes on My Back*) could have been written for her – or Chang, from *Make Me*, or Abby, from *Blue Moon*:

> I say run with me
> Come and be free
> You say no
> You're not gonna go

Lee refuted the idea that Reacher was the 'love them and leave them' type. Reacher was attracted to strong, intelligent women; smart women, with meaningful careers and full lives. These strong, intelligent women saw him as the ideal man – to spend a few days with. Long-term prospects were nil. Let's face it, the pathology meter was twitching.

Chang left him a note, like they often did.

> She had used a simile, to explain and flatter and apologise all at once. She had written, 'You're like New York City. I love to visit, but I could never live there.'
>
> He did what he always did. He let her go. He understood. No apology required. He couldn't live anywhere. His whole life was a visit. Who could put up with that?

The fault was his. Yet there was something unsettling about this chivalrous assumption of blame and responsibility. On the face of it the woman had agency. The choice was all hers. But it put her in a near impossible position. She couldn't choose to stick around (or get on the bus) and give it her best shot without simultaneously damning herself as something less than strong – and a whole lot less than smart. The object of her affection would be immediately disenchanted. Lose–lose.

And insofar as Reacher 'let her go', was the choice really 101 per cent hers?

No getting away from it. The wandering knight's code kept the woman firmly at arm's length. Feeling abandoned and unloved was essential to Reacher's nature. Both blessed and cursed.

The book writer, on the other hand, was blessed: settling down and raising kids would spell the end of his alter ego once and for all. *Why become a writer merely to reproduce the conditions of real life?*

Lee didn't have a favourite among his female characters. 'Mostly I feel like Reacher does, happy to spend time with them and happy to move on.' If forced to choose it would be reader favourite Frances Neagley. Neagley was strong and smart. She had a meaningful career in the army, and later as a private investigator. What distinguished her from all other Reacher women was her dislike of being touched, and what distinguished Reacher was he never asked why. The erotic charge is all the greater for this restraint.

Since Reacher never asks why, he never knows why. And since we see most characters through his eyes (whether first or third person), we know them only to the extent that he does. This was realistic, in Lee's view. For better or worse, a person – especially Reacher – would not necessarily ask why, in real life. He lacked knowledge because he was not lacking in respect, sensitivity and awareness.

The strict control of narrative point of view insulates the author from having to represent complexity of character in mimetic detail. It was an inbuilt lack of presumption that would also deter Lee from writing a novel from the female perspective. It wasn't that he saw women as fundamentally unknowable – no more so than any other human being, even those related to us by blood. But the female experience was intimately removed from his own and was, he felt, better represented by women.

He experimented briefly with a female point of view in 'Everyone Talks', written in 2012 for *Esquire* magazine, but only as a framing device for a story otherwise narrated by Reacher from a hospital bed – an unlikely place to find him, but allowing the female gaze to rest on his half-naked body, and deduce from his scars that 'he knew a hundred ways to help me, and a hundred ways to kill me' (perhaps the writer's POV on the number of stories he could make up). The detective is defined by her status as a new recruit, so it's less an opportunity to see into her soul than to see the familiar hero anew through her fresh eyes. But we see how the world looks different too. Rules were rules, 'times two for a woman in a man's world'. She got the worst car, 'obviously'. She put in plenty of overtime, because not only was she a rookie, and keen, but 'women have to work twice as hard, to get half the credit'.

The same premise drives *The Midnight Line*, where Reacher knows how hard the mysterious West Point graduate must have worked for the gold filigree class ring with its black stone and its tiny size. Every day they would have tried to break her, he told Nakamura. *Times two for a woman*. Nakamura is a five-foot-nothing detective from Rapid City trying to nail local hoodlum Arthur Scorpio. She writes up her report but feels bad about using an exclamation mark. 'It looked girlish. But it had to. Really she meant for her boss to read her note and order an immediate resumption of surveillance. [. . .] But her boss claimed all executive authority as his own. [. . .] Hence the giggly deflection, to take the sting away. To make the guy think it was his own idea all along.'

Lee had conducted an impromptu survey once, at a bookstore event. One hundred and twenty people had turned up and they were all women. Or so it seemed when he looked out at the sea of excited faces. He drew the conclusion that the survey generated four main reasons for Reacher's popularity with women readers.

1. For structural reasons endemic in society, women still found it hard to express anger, and liked doing so vicariously.
2. They appeared to be more sensitive than men to injustice, and yearned to see it put right.
3. They liked that he respected women.
4. They fantasised about freedom as much as the next man.

'The female characters in the books are not bimbos who need saving,' Lee says in a 2018 interview for Penguin.

> Most of them are tough as hell, as tough as Reacher a lot of the time. Even now in the 21st century, there's still this issue about assertive women. They're seen as shrill and somehow not as acceptable as assertive men. So I think women take vicarious pleasure in Reacher's assertiveness.

There was a fifth reason. Reacher was hot. The idea of a no-strings dalliance with a guy they could count on never to turn up on their doorstep, far less text or email, was, to many, irresistible. Social media bears out this hypothesis. But some women think it's about mothering too. They're the ones who bake Lee cookies and cakes and knit scarves for him, instead of sending him their underwear. 'I'm in love with my pressure cooker and Jack Reacher,' one writes.

'I have more than my fair share of women readers,' Lee said, laconically.

When asked about his practical preference for the third-person point of view Lee would explain how it not only facilitated suspense but there were certain things you couldn't easily say in the first person. He invariably gave the same example. *You can't say* [he said while saying it] *I'm a good-looking guy and women are attracted to me.* But you could under cover of the third person.

Not that you had to be good-looking to be a successful knight errant or writer. But every little helps. 'Do good-looking people automatically get more credibility?' Reacher asks the disconcertingly named (Theresa) Lee in *Gone Tomorrow*. *The Midnight Line* stood out not only for its classical narrative, musical form, subtle self-reflexivity and social challenge, but also for the writer's bold attempt to grapple with the inequality of appearances and the harsh realities of the beauty myth.

Lee was baffled when people expressed surprise over his strong female characters. 'I'm just doing reportage,' he told *The Writer* in 2019. 'Women are just as strong and tough as men. If you're going to have an honest portrayal of women, you have to recognize that.'

He might conversely have volunteered that men were just as weak and vulnerable as women, and that the unremitting obligation to be strong and tough was wearing no matter the gender – a truth he finally surrenders to in the song 'Sanctuary' (his own favourite from his album):

> Will you be my sanctuary
> My harbor in this wild and bitter sea
> You always need me strong
> Will you let me be weak

But book-Reacher knows (or can entertain) no such weakness. It's permissible for him to get the odd headache (a detail Philip Pullman remembered being struck by in *Killing Floor*). But he can't afford a bad back or a cold. He can't say: *No, I just don't fancy beating up the bad guys today.* Reacher is an olden-day hero. He is instinctively protective, especially when women are small, like Serena Rose Sanderson in *The Midnight Line*, and her equally diminutive twin sister Tiffany, known as Jane.

'I like your books,' one woman tweeted, 'but please stop sexist comments like: She was wearing no make-up. She was one of those women who absolutely don't need to.' (*Persuader*) 'I love the books,' tweeted another, 'but Lee Child has no sense of women's height:weight ratios. A 5'7" woman who weighs 120 lbs is described as "neither fat nor excessively thin". That sounds pretty thin to me and is NOWHERE near fat.' In the same book (*The Affair*) he describes a 5-foot-6-inch man weighing 140 pounds as 'lean and wiry', which was 'far more accurate'.

A likely response to such prosaic real-world objections might be that writing was wish-fulfilment for the writer, as much as the reader. He spent six months of every year living with his invented characters. His women would be *petite* and *gamine* and/or *lithe* without fail. *Neither fat nor thin* meant slim – while implying a self-avowed tendency on the part of the writer to judge (both self and others) on the basis of weight.

Lee consciously manufactured respect for women through his preferential use of the feminine pronoun: *she is burning her calories to read my book, it's her creative mind at work, we are making the book together.* It was suggestive of a private relationship, that intense one-on-one intimacy with his audience the one-time backstage guy had been looking for. But more than this – and far more than mere deference to his predominantly female readership – it was a clear political statement.

In her 2014 essay 'Grandmother Spider' (*Men Explain Things to Me*), Rebecca Solnit – citing both the patriarchal genealogy of the Gospel according to Matthew and Argentina's *desaparecidos* – calls out the erasure, exclusion, elimination and obliteration of women from personal and public record, tracking back through generations of mothers, grandmothers and great-grandmothers. In *The Hero* Lee restores the female lineage, telling the story of human history in ten thousand words by putting his own grandmother – and her ancestors – front and centre. 'A girl left the cave and met a sabre-toothed tiger, but she had her axe with her and she killed the tiger with a single blow'; 'probably she lived on a coast or a riverbank'; 'perhaps she lived in a fertile valley'; 'as it happens she went west'; 'she brought brains, language, reality-based planning, a ferocious will to live and a deep love of story'. It's stunningly simple, but transformative. And says nothing about appearance.

Women hold the mirror up to Reacher. It turns out the not-so-uncomplicated hero had a tragic flaw all along.

> The fundamental psychological tension inside Reacher is that he loves being alone, but also worries about being lonely. That's a very fine balance for him to manage. So I think that at some point his fear of loneliness will get the better of his love of solitude.

Lee had seen it coming as far back as *The Visitor*. Towards the end of the story Reacher speaks to Jodie on the phone. The next day she will make partner in her law firm.

Down the line Reacher heard 'a quiet, urgent siren. Probably right there on Broadway, he thought. Under her window. A lonely sound.'

'I've no idea what the members of my family are doing,' Lee once said when I asked after them. 'And the truth is that's just how I like it.' A 2008 anniversary card from Jane is dedicated to 'the other half of my nation of two', a metaphor as suggestive of separation as togetherness. She had never been a company wife, and like Jim, had grown used to flying solo. They had signed up to a club though (along with E. L.

Doctorow and his wife Helen; historian David Nasaw and Dinitia Smith, novelist; Victor Navasky, founder of *The Nation* magazine and Anne Navasky, Wall Street trader): a New York nation of eight known as the Lonely Writers' Club. 'All the guys except me were into boxing and went to Vegas for the fights.' Lee had never bought into 'that American ideal' of a group of five or six male buddies you went to the bar with; he would rather wander solo down to the Village to check out the live music.

In January 2019 Lee did a gig with Naked Blue at the Hamilton, in snowbound Washington DC. He liked seeing Scott and Jen and was sorry to say goodbye. But the following day he said to me as we were going our separate ways on Carmine Street: 'I think the theme of the biography should be that line from the song ['Alone']. "I was born alone. I have lived alone. I will die alone."'

The albatross would only ever briefly touch down on earth. He was only ever passing through.

'Who's in your tribe?' Abby asks Reacher in *Blue Moon*.

'Almost nobody,' Reacher said. 'I live a lonely life.'

40

Cloverleaf

He wasn't comfortable, but he guessed he was
happy enough where he was.
Die Trying, 1998

Lee knew what happiness sounded like: Beethoven's 'Für Elise' – the aural equivalent of reading Shakespeare's sonnet 'Shall I Compare Thee to a Summer's Day?' (*New York Times*). 'It's the deftest illustration I know of what it is to be human, to be happy, to have loved, to have been loved, to have known ecstasy. If you listen to it and get it, you know that the whole long strange trip has been worth it.'

Lee got it. He had a lovely daughter and a great (if often long-distance) relationship with his wife. The job had gone well and he had enough money for everything they needed, or wanted. It was all just about as good as it could be, or at least very hard to imagine how any of it could possibly be better.

He knew what it was to be human.

But, he said in January 2019, he would never describe himself as happy.

Much less contented. He hated 'contented'. Contented was too complacent. Too smug. Too satisfied. He would never be satisfied. He was 'a completely normal person in every possible way', 'a completely normal middlebrow person', but he could not, would not settle for satisfied. Satisfied had about it the whiff of mediocrity. 'As you know,' he said, 'if there's one thing I hate it's mediocrity.'

It was never a charge that would be levelled at Reacher. He wasn't 'normal', either. 'You're a hard man,' Alice says in *Echo Burning*.

> 'I think I'm a realistic man,' he said. 'And a decent enough guy, all told.'
>
> 'You may find normal people don't agree.'
>
> He nodded.
>
> 'A lot of you don't,' he said.

Reacher was willing to respect 'normal'. 'Open up the encyclopaedia to N for normal American family and you're going to see a picture of the Hobies, all three of them, staring right out at you,' he says of (the real, missing-in-action) Victor Hobie and his distraught parents. But not axiomatically or unthinkingly. Within the conventions of the genre it was always liable to be sinister:

> Chester Stone's day started out in the normal way. He drove to work at the usual time. The Benz was as soothing as ever. The sun was shining, like it should be in June. The drive into the city was normal. Normal traffic, no more, no less. The usual rose vendors and paper sellers in the toll plazas. The slackening congestion down the length of Manhattan, proving he'd timed it just right, like he usually did. He parked in his normal leased slot under his building and rode the elevator up to his offices. Then his day stopped being normal. (*Tripwire*)

Normal was the perfect camouflage for evil.

Reacher was wary of 'satisfaction' too. It was reasonable to feel satisfied after a trip to the diner, or after sex. After sex he might even feel briefly 'contented'. But these are not feelings he indulges for long.

Nine times out of ten satisfaction is expressed by the wrong people over the wrong things. Which makes it dangerous. Borken and Hook Hobie and Lamarr are all satisfied. But not for long. Not once Reacher shows up.

When were you happiest? the *New Statesman* asked in 2017. And because Lee had an answer to everything, because by then his job consisted mostly in answering questions, he said:

> Manjack Cay in the Bahamas, February 1993. We were broke, but my wife assembled offers and we had a holiday. The hotel had boats you could borrow to visit uninhabited islands. I remember standing on one and thinking how absurd it would have been to predict ever being there.

This *Swallows and Amazons* moment dates from a year and a half before he started writing *Killing Floor*. He was Jim Grant, not Lee Child; television technician, not multimillion-selling global superstar. Like the Beatles said, money can't buy you love.

Happy is OK, so long as you don't feel entitled to it or make a big deal of it.

'I'm always happy,' Reacher tells Jodie. 'Always was, always will be.'

It was the same with Lee. *I'm always well. I'm never ill. I'm always hungry.* He could deflect a cold just by facing it down; he was hungry however much he did or didn't eat. Conditions that were temporary, things that were supposed to go up and down on the graph, for him were steady states: he wasn't subject to them, he'd chosen them. This was who and what he was. Maybe he could add that to his business card: *Lee Child: Smoker and Hungry Man.*

Happy doing what? Jodie asks. Nothing much, Reacher says.

> I don't go round looking for involvement. [. . .] I was happy, living
> quiet down there.

'There' was Key West, 'way farther south than most of the Bahamas'.
Jim and Jane and Ruth had holidayed there in October 1996, so Ruth
could visit Universal Studios in nearby Orlando, just before Lee put
the finishing touches to *Die Trying* and started on *Tripwire*.

It isn't the jumping-up-and-down happiness Jodie experiences
when she makes partner in the law firm. It's a toned-down stripped-
back muted happiness, in the style of his prose or his manner of dress,
the kind of sober *not-unhappiness* that is all a sane man might rationally
accept.

The only time Reacher's happiness was seriously threatened was
when Jodie's father left him a house and car and garden.

> Now his nose was pressed right up against the border fence. He could
> see normality waiting for him on the other side. Suddenly it seemed
> insane to turn back and hike the impossible distance in the other
> direction. That would turn drifting into a conscious choice, and
> conscious choice would turn drifting into something else completely.
> The whole point of drifting was happy passive acceptance of no
> alternatives. Having alternatives ruined it.

Reacher is an absurdist hero. There is no B to get to, and therefore
dwell in, and to pretend otherwise would be to live a lie. Dambuster
Mickey Martin was his boyhood hero; Richard Dawkins – 'waging a
bitter battle of a different sort' (*New Statesman*) – was the intellectual
equivalent.

Lee said to me: 'I don't see how a thinking person can look out at
the world and be happy.'

He recalled a boy from King Edward's: a prodigy, but restless and angst-ridden with it. Around the time he left school he was involved in a traffic accident in which a number of passengers were killed, and had sustained severe brain trauma. When Jim saw him at a party some months later he was fully functioning, which was a miracle, but had been transformed from 'twitchy genius' into 'happy fool'. Sometimes – he knew it was a terrible thing to say but said it anyway because it was true – Lee had fantasised about being that guy.

For a guy whose brain was firing on all cylinders, happiness was not an appropriate response to being alive. This was not merely an existential problem, but a social one too. Happiness was not a personal good. It depended not simply on things being right for me; they had to be right for others too. Not just my family and friends, my tribe, my race or my species, but dogs and horses and roosters, trees and forests and oceans too, for every living thing. The prospects weren't great.

Lee had read Rachel Carson's *Silent Spring* back in the sixties and ever since had seen climate catastrophe as the elephant in the room.

He couldn't solve the world's problems. Nor could Reacher. The happiness he offered was only going to last the length of the World Series at best, then the reader was on her own again, like Roscoe or Turner or Chang. If he was lucky – wasn't he always? – then reading one of his books might be like watching a football match or a play in the theatre: ninety minutes on the clock, maybe even one hundred and twenty and penalties, but timeless in intensity. Eventually the lights would come up and the crowd would stream out of the stadium and the millions of readers close up their Reacher books, but for the duration all our fears would fall away. If he could work that magic, liberate each of us from the burden of our biographies, then yes, he would die lonely, but happy, too.

Lee didn't entirely like being a big man. There wasn't much he could do about his height, and he recognised it as one of his immense 'structural' advantages, but he didn't want to big himself up any further. Being big was a lie, an illusion. It might trick you into believing you were important, the centre of your own universe. He had always been thin and was getting thinner ('old age and loss of muscle mass, mainly') but he didn't mind that. Losing weight was OK. What he hated was putting it on. 'A normal person puts on a pound and they don't even notice, but I feel uncomfortably bulky around the middle.' It wasn't the first time I'd heard this. 'I feel it here,' he'd said the year before, pinching his hip like a nineties supermodel or prima ballerina.

His big brother Richard had always had 'what now would be called an eating disorder. He looks like a famine victim.' If you said *let's get food* it was like 'asking him to stick needles in his eyes'. Whereas James had eaten everything. He wasn't fussy. Like his father said, in this respect at least, he'd been a success from the word go. But the older he got the less he ate. Thanks to Audrey and the poverty of post-war British cuisine (in 1957 spaghetti was considered an exotic delicacy) his 'gratification pathways' had been set in a different direction (caffeine, nicotine, weed) before he ever discovered that food could be a form of pleasure.

He conscientiously sought out cakes and muffins with real butter, causing bemusement when he strayed into Whole Foods. Whenever we met at a diner he would order big and enthusiastically: silver-dollar pancakes with smoked bacon and two eggs over easy on the side. But he only ever ate half of it. Once when he pushed his plate aside I nudged it back towards him saying (like the mother I was): *You should eat more.* He nudged it away again, with a slight shake of the head.

He never left any strawberry milkshake though. 'I'm thinking of investigating those meal-replacement drinks,' he said once. It would take the work out of having to feed himself, like streamlining his wardrobe took the worry out of choosing which outfit to wear. But they would have to be pink.

'I hate eating,' he said at Bristol CrimeFest in 2018. 'I actively like the sensation of feeling hungry.'

'Consume' was a verb he used mostly of books.

He weighed himself every day. 'Not because I'm worried, just because I like numbers.' But it was the opposite of book sales. These were numbers he didn't like to go up. Six foot four and sixty-four, he was shocked one morning to weigh in at 138 pounds, rather than 135. (Reacher was six foot five and 250.) If he wasn't careful he'd be back up to 10 stone (140 pounds), which was what he weighed when he first met Jane.

One way he kept the weight down was by writing *lean and hungry*. It was like he was transferring all that muscle mass to his alter ego, enacting Oscar Wilde's *Dorian Gray* in reverse.

There were three main reasons Lee would never see a doctor. (Reacher won't either, just kneads his broken nose into shape and pinches it together with duct tape.) First, they would tell him to give up smoking (and put on weight, probably). Second, he would never do anything they told him to do, because it would be 'too boring'. And third: 'I don't share this obsession with longevity, with staying alive at all costs.'

There was no afterlife. We were all condemned by the cosmos. The physical deterioration of cells and neurones would get us all in the end. It was a case of when, not if. And frankly, in the great scheme of things, if you zoomed out and took the long view – as any thinking person must – 'when' didn't amount to a hill of beans. Each of us was no more than a speck, always already on the point of melting into thin air. 'Who in their right minds could think the presence of one single human being makes any difference either way?' This was true on both the macro and the micro scale, and he counted on those who loved him to grasp this nettle with both hands when his own infinitesimal spark of light snuffed out or a stiff wind blew him away.

He wasn't a cynic, just a realist. By keeping his weight to the minimum, by whittling himself down to the bone, he was simply facing facts. He was looking destiny straight in the eye. *We are such stuff / as dreams are made on; and our little life / is rounded with a sleep.*

Are we all doomed, the *New Statesman* asked?

> Of course we are. Evolutionary history shows we're a vicious bunch, clever but not clever enough. We'll be done soon, and the planet will recover. Call it fifty thousand years, from the invention of language to extinction. A tiny blip.

Perhaps there would be a tree on the cloverleaf, where he could shelter from the sun or the rain. But either way there was nothing to be done. So long as he had a good book to read, Lee Child was happy to wait for a lift out of town.

41

Blue Moon

Once in a blue moon things turn out just right.
Blue Moon, 2019

'It's totally time to stop,' Lee said to me over coffee in May 2019. *Blue Moon* had been easy enough to write. It had a certain fluency about it. He was pretty sure people would praise it as one of the good ones, especially when seen through the misty-eyed lens of nostalgia. But he felt like he was faking it.

'The minor characters were just machines to get me to the end of the book.'

I hadn't yet read it, then, but he'd sent me the final paragraph. It seemed the sun was about to set on Reacher after all. Had it been difficult, I asked, to write the ending, knowing it was THE END?

No, he said, looking faintly disappointed. 'I was close to tears when I finished *Killing Floor*. I'd been so absorbed in it. It felt unbearably poignant to be leaving all those characters behind.'

He wrote the ending to *Blue Moon* just like any other. No fuss, no fanfare. No big blockbuster season finale. More the opposite. Soothing, gentle, set to the lullaby rhythm of a bus out of town.

> Ten days later he was drifting north with the summer. By chance on a bus he found a copy of the *Washington Post*. There was a long feature

story inside. It said organized crime had been cleaned out of a certain notorious city. A longstanding problem, finally solved. Two rival gangs, both gone. No more extortion. Drugs gone, vice gone. No more random violence. No more reign of terror. The new police commissioner was taking all the credit. He called himself a new broom, with new ideas, and new energy. There was talk he might run for office one day. Mayor possibly, or maybe even governor. No reason why not. So far his record was sparkling.

Not even Lee could fault Reacher's housekeeping. He'd stomped on all the cockroaches, swept up the vermin, and left the place gleaming. The sky over Blue Moon Town was as clear as his conscience.

But the bell is tolling. The tone is elegiac. And Reacher is gone.

Like Reacher, Lee Child was putting his house in order.

On 26 August 2018, six days before he started work on *Blue Moon*, now with a view out over the high plains shading into the first foothills of the Rockies, Laramie distant in one direction, Colorado in the other, it was announced that he would donate his archive to the University of East Anglia. 'Felt weird that anyone was interested. Always does.'

On 31 March 2019 he finished writing *Blue Moon*: '7pm Mountain Time'. 'Last word: "sparkling".'

On 24 April he finished writing *The Hero*, also in Wyoming, 'my last paid word, on the day Shakespeare is thought to have died'.

On 13 May in London he was named Author of the Year at the British Book Awards: for being 'a person who people quite like, but above all sells a lot'. He wore a midnight-blue tie patterned in tiny silver stars.

On 8 June he was appointed Commander of the British Empire in the Birthday Honours list: 'Very pretty medal.' He didn't yet know the colours were claret and blue. He would probably buy a new suit. In the meantime he bought a small house on a 'sweet street' in Fort

Collins, Colorado, for (in no particular order) its 'more forgiving' microclimate, proximity to Ruth, and access to legal weed.

On 25 June he received a request from the Folio Society to publish a collector's edition of *Killing Floor*. He didn't yet know who the artist would be, or if they would ask to show Reacher's face.

Then life got messy again.

On 4 July his mother-in-law died. No funeral: she was the last of the four parents to go.

On 15 July the news leaked that Reacher's bus had let him out at Amazon Prime, where he would go on to star in his own TV show and some dodgy customers presumably needed sorting out. It was true that the bidding had been aggressive, Lee said, but Amazon were the most invested, had 'the most coherent and ambitious strategy, with the funding to back it up'.

On 10 August a rumour began circulating that Lee had been invited to judge the 2020 Booker Prize for literary fiction. The outsider was storming the establishment.

But all he really wanted was to get away from it all. That's why he'd bought Wyoming in the first place. He saw more people on a late-night shopping trip to Gristedes on Columbus than he did in three months at 'Mule Crossing'. Though ironically his six-foot-four frame stood out in the emptiness much more than in New York City, and should he ever happen to go to the supermarket it was an immediate news item on social media. All he really wanted was to be left alone, to finish building his wildflower rockery, or play his guitars. He'd bought at least two since he moved there: the first a vintage Martin, 'hopefully right for cowboy songs'; the most recent a Rob Allen 'Mouse' fretless bass in maple and mahogany, 'my most prized possession'. But the industry wasn't going to let go of the golden goose so easily.

The last time I'd looked in the *London Gazette* was in search of

Harry Dover Scrafton, listed in Promotions under 'Skilled Workmen' on 4 October 1929, just weeks before the Wall Street Crash.

But Harry's grandson made a bigger splash:

Civil Division
Central Chancery of the Orders of Knighthood
St James's Palace, London SW1

8 June 2019

THE QUEEN has been graciously pleased, on the occasion of the Celebration of Her Majesty's Birthday, to give orders for the following promotions in, and appointments to, the Most Excellent Order of the British Empire:
C.B.E.
To be Ordinary Commanders of the Civil Division of the said Most Excellent Order:

James Dover GRANT, (Lee Child)
Author
For services to Literature.

'I felt good about it,' he said, when I asked. He was anti-royal on principle, but the satisfaction was the same as he'd experienced at O level, when he won the foundation scholarship at King Edward's. 'I'd made the bastards give it to me.'

I complimented him on having skipped the interim ranks of 'Member' and 'Officer' and stepping straight up to 'Commander'. 'I would have declined anything less,' he joked, imperiously. But when it came to the investiture, no way was he going to retreat obsequiously without turning his back. He'd already figured out what to say if challenged, neatly turning the tables on whichever royal might be officiating: 'There was no refusal to bow. I didn't ask him to. Why would I? I think we're all equal.' If anything, he thought the royals should be bowing to him. They'd had it all on a plate. 'The people receiving the awards have busted their ass.'

The sentiment went back to his letter to the *Sunday Times* in March 1998:

> I was staggered by your front page last Sunday: apparently some woman I have never met is debating with her husband and her son whether or not I should be released from my obligation to bow to her. To expect any normal person in Britain in 1998 to feel an obligation to bow to any other person is at best pompous and at worst delusional.

The original letter ('Hello? *Hello??* Let me toss this into the debate') had been 'judiciously edited', with the adverbs 'stupefyingly' and 'massively' having been deleted along with the writer's judgement – 'w-a-a-y beyond absurd' – on the paper's sense of priorities. Lee Child of Kirkby Lonsdale, Cumbria, already felt no obligation towards the monarchy: 'Never have, never will.'

His parents would be proud of him, I said. But how had his brothers responded?

'Fantastic,' said Andrew, when he dropped by the day the news broke. He and his wife Tasha (Alexander) were already planning to buy Jim a ceremonial sword with the citation engraved on it.

David sent a message: 'Congratulations, James!' Underneath his email signature was a proud photograph of the Brecon Mountain Rescue Team vehicle against a background of valleys and lakes.

Richard said nothing.

The next time I googled 'Lee Child', it reverted straight to 'James

Dover Grant, CBE'. Reality was reclaiming fiction. He had finally grown into his name. And was growing out of his pseudonym.

On 14 May 2019 Lee had lunch in Covent Garden with the old Transworld crew. Larry Finlay (publisher), Marianne Velmans (editor) and Patsy Irwin (publicist): the ones who'd been with him from the beginning.

'I'm done,' he said. 'I've written my last Reacher book.'

The shock and horror were palpable. There were three dynamics of emotion, and Finlay cycled through all three of them within about ten short minutes.

First: Lee would come to his senses. He would change his mind. (He wouldn't.)

Second: What if Lee just wrote the books? No media, no touring. (They'd tried it before. It didn't work.)

Third . . . How about someone else doing it?

Child said nothing.

But he was already mulling it over.

A few weeks later he emailed Larry, in London, and Gina Centrello, in New York.

Gina was president of the Random House Publishing Group. Like Patsy and Marianne, she was worried about his welfare. Was he dying? No (or rather, yes, but we all were). That was good. Was he well? Yes, he felt good (spending more time outside and getting closer to nature). Even better. But he could do with a break, they could see that. He should look after himself. He'd put in the hours. He'd done his bit.

Lee wrote: How about my baby brother? How about Andrew Grant? After all, he was Reacher's oldest fan, had been living with him for a good twenty-five years, if not fifty-one. It would be the same but different.

Gina was enthusiastic. A dream from heaven, she said.

Larry was 'boisterous'. It could really work, he said, because Lee's style was 'quite easy to mimic'.

'Yeah,' said Lee drily. 'That's for sure.'

There was debate about when to go public. Lee wanted to be upfront with his readers. The publishers wanted to delay, right up to the publication of *Blue Moon* in paperback if they could. There was anecdotal evidence to suggest that people wouldn't buy the last book in a long-running series, because they didn't want to read it, because they were in denial, and didn't want to admit the love affair was over. They hated the last book. The last book was a slap in the face. Like they'd been rejected and shown the door.

So the publishers dreamed of a seamless transition. They wanted to preserve the illusion of immortality until the last possible moment, only pulling back the curtain when the marketing machine was oiled and ready to go, so that grief and anger might succumb immediately and ecstatically to anticipation and excitement.

In the meantime Andrew would take the gig seriously. He would sit down at his desk on 1 September 2019 and begin work on Reacher no. 25. No plot, no title. 'Lee Child's Jack Reacher', by Andrew Child. Or possibly 'with', or even 'and', for the sake of consumer confidence – though as Andrew himself told *Crimespree* magazine in 2012, he, like his big brother, was 'not the type who plays well with others'. No big deal. Lee's name would still be up there in lights. He would get a percentage for intellectual property rights. It was win–win all round.

It would be a huge challenge for Andrew. A huge risk too. The backlash could be worse than for Tom Cruise. But there was no way he could turn it down. It was like winning the lottery. Tasha would never have to work again.

'I feel good about it,' Lee said, when I asked. Andrew was his little brother. Not quite a twin soul, but 'sufficiently like me that the natural process will bring the Reacher out in him'. He had 'maybe 95 per cent' of Jim's appetite for books and his phenomenal memory. Perhaps more of a taste for the high life. His perfect day wasn't sitting reading in a deck chair, but 'Watching Aston Villa win the Champions' League final followed by *Richard III* at The Globe, dinner at The Ivy, and a night at Brown's Hotel in London' (*Crimespree*). But it would keep Reacher ticking over a little while longer while letting him, Lee Child, off the hook. Reacher had finally transcended his creator, like all the greatest mythical heroes, and now both were floating free.

Jane and Ruth felt good about it too. They weren't sentimental about Lee Child. Lee Child was a business proposition, nothing more. And it meant Jim wouldn't have to worry about Andrew, wouldn't have to feel responsible. He was weary of the role of patriarch. Now Andrew and his family would be provided for – if things went well, forever.

Good housekeeping all round.

His fellow writers responded sympathetically, as conveyed by Paraic O'Donnell in the *Irish Times* (January 2020). Two comments resonated with me, as I knew they would with Lee. It 'dismantles the fetishisation of the author in such a nimble way,' said Max John Porter. Like Reacher himself, he's 'living his life the way he chooses to,' said Eleanor Catton. It was no kind of a small deal, said O'Donnell, but he took comfort from these words. Lee liked them too: spot on, he said.

In *Blue Moon* Reacher rocks up in a city he's never been to before. But 'Reacher knew cities'. This one might have reminded him of that other city with no name, that he'd cleaned up so efficiently in *One Shot*. It had been mapped out perfectly for him, with an old stage manager's eye for balance and symmetry. The set up was skilfully choreographed. Perhaps the Shevicks reminded him of the Hobies from *Tripwire*, another old couple busting their ass for their only, beloved child. There were even echoes of *Killing Floor* and Margrave: Howlin' Wolf, a starring role for a 'muscular' luxury vehicle, and the weight and heft of a wad of cash, thumping and bouncing and fluttering.

It's like the writer is revisiting old haunts, taking leave of loyal friends and well-worn mantras, getting in a last round of drinks before riding off into the sunset. *How hard could it be? Not bad for an old guy. The same but different. The law moves slow.*

The body count is high. Very high. But so too is the level of compassion. The stealthy avenger – peak Reacher, 'steady, calm, amused, predatory, unhinged' – with his preternatural sense of hearing, his acute sense of smell and his quasi-divine peripheral vision, is as exacting as ever in executing those logical imperatives, both mental and physical, while at the same time being the kindest, most considerate man to walk the face of the earth.

'Who are you?' someone asks. Which means he gets to say, one last time (in his original incarnation): 'The 110th Special MP.' But deep in his soul, looking out from behind his eyes, is a lonely boy from Birmingham: Reacher's alter ego and constant companion, Lee Child. The guy who respects an old machinist like Aaron Shevick, 'cutting things by eye and feel to a thousandth of an inch'. The guy whose previous life had been highly regimented, whose work ethic was indomitable, and whose obsessive passion for semantics (and punctuation) informs so many of Reacher's most inspired insights.

In *Blue Moon*, Reacher is hanging with a bunch of musicians, just like Lee was while he was writing it. Reacher recruits them to his cause, just like Lee does. Towards the climax, Reacher finds himself looking out on the city from a high-rise hotel room, just like the little boy in that never-forgotten picture book at Elmwood Library, making sense of the mystery he has been charged with solving even while having a tear-jerking conversation about children, love and marriage. Turns out it all hinges on how you interpret the Ukrainian word for 'nest', or 'hive', or 'burrow'. Which leads him to 'penetrate the innermost lair' of his prey, which bears an uncanny resemblance to Granada's central control room.

Death was always going to come knocking in the middle of the movie. In *The Enemy*, the 'emotionally feminine' Lee Child chooses Josephine Reacher as his mouthpiece. In *Blue Moon*, he chooses theatre-loving Abby.

We'll go back to your place tonight, Reacher says. 'For how long?' Abby asks.

> He said, 'What would be your answer to that question?'
>
> She said, 'I guess not forever.'
>
> 'That's my answer too. Except my forever horizon is closer than most. Full disclosure.'
>
> 'How close?'
>
> He looked out the window, at the street, at the brick, at the afternoon shadows. He said, 'I already feel like I've been here forever.'

Abby doesn't want to go with him. Why not? Reacher asks.

> 'Seems to me I have a choice of two things. Either a good memory with a beginning and an end, or a long slow fizzle, where I get tired of motels and hitchhiking and walking. I choose the memory. Of a successful experiment. Much rarer than you think. We did good, Reacher.'

Lee wrote to me.

'I have Abby talking to Reacher. But really it's my own message to the world.'

Epilogue

On 27 January 2020 at 21:20 GMT, Lee sent me this message:

> As a final rumination, lately I have been thinking along these lines,
> which might be a kind of epitaph:

> 'People ask, am I happy now I have retired? The truth is, I retired
> because now I'm happy. The times I grew up in, and the place, and my
> family, all left me with an implacable horror of being mediocre.
> Finally, after all these years, I have grown to accept I escaped that fate.'

In his tidy, precise way, he had sent it neatly pre-packaged in quotation
marks.

The Man in the Mirror

Reacher could feel her gaze on his face in the mirror.
A Wanted Man, 2012

'I t feels weird,' he told me. 'Like my life should be over.'

It wasn't, thankfully. Although he was definitely looking death in the eye, not exactly rushing towards it, perhaps, but refusing to back down. Win or lose, there was no third option.

He was talking about the biography, not retirement. Retirement was still an aspiration. People – mostly less rational than Reacher – were struggling to let go, and COVID-19 had made a mockery of his dream of well-earned freedom. In a way, all our lives were over. At least as we knew them.

Things had changed for *The Reacher Guy* too. It was no longer a book in the making, but one that was being read and talked about, generating new conversations between the two of us, and new questions from Lee's interviewers.

Being 'biographed' was 'an interesting experience', he said. Had anyone come up to Jim Grant as a kid and told him that one day someone would write his life story, he 'would have called the men in white coats'. But it was different for Lee Child.

It's like when they interview the scorer of the winning goal on the pitch after the cup final and ask *did you ever think*, and he always says *no, never, it's outside of my wildest dreams*. But of course that's nonsense, that kid has scored that winning goal a thousand times in his back garden as a child, and he's thought about nothing else. So of course I imagined that I could one day be a number one bestseller and I could have newspapers and biographers writing about it, of course I imagined that. The question is, did I expect that and, just like the footballer, no I didn't expect it. Because if you do expect it, that's a deranged delusion, because the odds are so heavily stacked against it. Did I expect? No. Did I imagine? Yes.

Football was the stuff of dreams. But it was also, like theatre, 'an antidote to isolation and loneliness'. Whether on the pitch or backstage, football and theatre allowed the young Jim Grant to cooperate with others as part of a team and, even when he was only watching, to feel part of something larger than himself. The joy was shared but 'also somehow secret', because however many were involved, 'those were all the people that it was happening to at the time'. The highs were real but fleeting, the brief light they shed swiftly engulfed by the prevailing gloom. You could see it in his photographs, Lee said, the way the 'openness and optimism' had rapidly been scoured out of him and the 'beaming smile' replaced by a 'guarded look', as though he were wondering how he was 'going to be betrayed or disappointed next'. As a writer Lee Child surrendered to that existential loneliness, softened only by that secret indefinable something he shared with each of his millions of readers.

Listening to Lee interact with others I learned new details about his life story. That according to family legend Harry Scrafton's drawing talents had been discovered by a passing duchess on a state visit to his school during the First World War; that Harry had once carved and whittled a replica Bowie knife out of wood for his six-year-old grandson after they had admired one together in a shop window; that to have leather rather than plastic beach shoes was a talisman of respectability; that in Sheffield Jim had lived on seven pounds a week; that thirty-five years after leaving he'd returned to visit his brother, Andrew, only to find the same book-loving couple behind the counter at the Hunter's Bar chippie, but now reading *Killing Floor*; that the magical afternoon on which he'd seen Aston Villa for the first time and watched them thrash Leicester City 8–3 was only the start of a magical weekend, culminating in a confirmatory 5–1 thrashing of Nottingham Forest on Easter Monday.

Striking out on his own, aged seven, to walk the two miles from Handsworth Wood to Aston was emblematic of his pioneering spirit, the will to forge his own path. The first guy in the family to adopt a football club, as significant in evolutionary terms as the first to go to school. No role model to follow. No one to tell him what to expect or how it was done. No money in his pocket. No thought of having to pay to get in. He just hung around at the gates till some friendly soul slipped him under the turnstile. But he soon learned the steps in the dance.

Everyone arrived early in those days, to bag a prime position on the terraces, and, because everyone paid in coins, to allow for the couple of hours it took to get in. On the way, everyone bought a print newspaper, which everyone could afford, to while away the time when they got there, and then when they were done with it, to roll into a tube to direct the flow of piss to the earth underfoot. It was a man's world, but one in which any given adult male was as likely (or in this case, more likely) to look out for a boy as his (in this case absent) father, threading him through the throng to a privileged spot at the front.

'It was all much more tribal,' Lee said. Now that localised sense of belonging had been lost, but he could still remember how life-affirming it felt to be part of something bigger and warmer and more inclusive than the Grant family of 6 Underwood Road.

Lee was used to dealing with doubters. Going back to the chippie after thirty-five years to find someone reading his own first book was 'a beautiful thing, a very circular thing – if you put it in a movie, people would say come on, that's too crass, but it's true'. *The Times* review of *The Reacher Guy* opened with just such a challenge: 'In 2016, the year his 21st Jack Reacher novel was published, Lee Child made 90 cents a second. Almost $30 million. That's if you believe every word the author tells his biographer.' Lee laughed. 'He's right,' he said. 'I got that wrong. According to my tax lawyers, I seem to have *under*estimated that 2016 figure – truth is it was $1.04 per second.'

A tendency towards scepticism among those listening to his stories, whatever the subject, could largely be attributed to the Lee Child brand, which was synonymous with the ability to spin a good yarn. But in his view, those doubting his depiction of a rough-tough upbringing betrayed a lack of historical awareness. People had too easily forgotten, or had never known, how different life was back then: how parochial, regional and class-conscious Britain was; how epic the hundred and twenty-mile journey from Birmingham to Otley in an unreliable car with no ring roads, no bypasses and no motorways; how bold the notion of moving out of where you belonged, from the North East to Yorkshire, let alone from the Midlands to the south. It was perhaps this widespread failure of memory, or imagination, that accounted for his increasing weariness, his habit of prefacing his words by the admonition to remember. *I'm old*, he insisted (though eleven years younger than the forty-sixth president of the United States). *You've got to remember that I'm very old; you've got to remember what it was like.*

As I continued to investigate contemporary experiences of growing up in Birmingham in the fifties and sixties, such as those gathered by

Ian Francis for his Birmingham '68 retrospective *This Way to the Revolution*, for example, or documented in the photographs of Nick Hedges, Lee's recollections were more often corroborated than contested. 'Lee Child could have been in our book,' Francis said. The biography was Lee's way of calibrating his memories and leaving his individual eyewitness record, his own account, albeit mediated, of his own city: an industrial powerhouse with full employment, more prosperous than places further north, but subject to the financial structure of the country as a whole, which meant the profit was skimmed off to pay down war loans, and life for those who earned it was pinched, with zero margin for anything discretionary.

And what of Reacher? Had he happened to pass through town in those bleak boyhood years it seems certain he would have rescued the young Jim Grant from the 'dour, repressed cult of miserable middle-class respectability' by which he felt so painfully suffocated: 'Everything was grey, depressed, deferred. I was constantly knocking into things, not just in the family but in the real world as well, constantly being stonewalled. I felt like it crushed the happy-go-lucky spirit out of me and made me reserved, and very introverted.' As always he was quick to exonerate his parents, who had 'suffered very badly', who 'for two long, dour, miserable decades had lived hard, miserable lives, first of all the depression, then the Second World War, then rationing. From the age of thirteen to nineteen my mother never owned a new pair of shoes.'

'The most important thing about Reacher,' Lee concluded, 'is that whatever else you might say about him, he's not ordinary. That's what mattered most to me. I had a horror of the ordinary, of being trapped by it, of succumbing for life. Reacher saved me from that.'

I too had reached some conclusions about Reacher. In the books, he went around beating people up. He'd broken more than a few obnoxious noses, had put plenty of bad guys in hospital and as many in the morgue; he'd even shovelled some straight into the ground. It was messy. He'd spilt a lot of blood, especially other people's. Most of it justified. Always in the name of righting wrongs. In the books he had to destroy things in order to fix them. But beyond the books, through some peaceable alchemy wrought by reading, he was transformed into something else altogether, or more accurately, something the same but different. Beyond the books, in the real world – and how casually we accepted the evaporation of this boundary – he served as a cross between nurse and counsellor, patching things up, soothing and smoothing, dispensing comfort, consolation, companionship and courage. Lee knew all about this healing power, because readers regularly wrote to him about how Reacher helped them. Now I did too, because they were writing to me as well.

It was at Harrogate, a few miles north-east of Otley, that *The Reacher Guy* took root. So it was fitting that we should return there, for the 2020 (virtual) Raworth's Literary Festival, when it finally blossomed into a book. I asked Lee about one of the few photographs I had taken of him, which shows him reading in his Manhattan apartment, by reflection in a mirror. I reminded him of what he'd once told me, that it was his 'desire' to be shown 'with something between me and the viewer', and asked if the image could be seen as a metaphor of the biography itself. 'That's exactly right,' he said. 'I could never do an autobiography. I need it filtered through someone else.'

Mirrors proliferate in Lee's writing, their polished, mottled, spotted, streaked, fogged, smeared, steamed and misty symbolism undiminished by their functional role in the plot. Rear-view mirrors, motel mirrors, mirrored walls in diners, shop windows acting as mirrors, reflective steel surfaces all came in handy for surveillance and covert communication, and a lot of bad stuff (and some good) goes on in bathrooms. Reacher even uses them perfunctorily to check his appearance, which he mostly deemed acceptable, though he had no real opinion about it, and it was what it was and he couldn't change it.

Mirrors reproduce, multiply, distort, misdirect and reveal, limiting what can be seen while allowing it to be seen in new ways.

Lee spoke of an author photo that captured the exact relationship between the author and the book.

> The book is the thing that's in the marketplace, with the author at some distance behind it in the shadows. It's the book that's there for examination, not the author. I kept asking people to take the shot through a window, or partially obscured, because I think theoretically the author is partially obscured. I always wanted that distance in photographs and the one reflected in the mirror is exactly that – you're not looking directly at me. Maybe it's a shyness, too. I don't believe like a native tribe that it's in some way stealing my soul, but I do feel to be directly photographed is intrusive, and it's something I don't enjoy.

For the boy from Birmingham, all that mattered was the product. 'I'm glad if readers think that these are somehow organically occurring books that leap spontaneously out of Jack Reacher's head. That's how it should be. The book succeeds or it fails. The reader doesn't need to know about the author.'

And it didn't matter if the author was Lee Child or Marcel Proust, as he told the (virtual) Winter Hay Festival, causing further excitement in *The Times*, because it was the book that mattered, and the book existed only for the reader, and the reader had a whole marketplace to choose from, and all choices were equally valid and equally worthy of respect.

I had just written a whole book about the author. But Lee wasn't worried. 'If I'd been the kind of guy who wanted a biography,' he said, enjoying the circular logic, 'you wouldn't have wanted to do it.'

It's not as though he hadn't dreamed of it.

Bibliography

Lee Child (sole authorship only)
Novels
All published by Penguin Random House

Killing Floor, 1997

Die Trying, 1998

Tripwire, 1999

The Visitor/Running Blind, 2000

Echo Burning, 2001

Without Fail, 2002

Persuader, 2003

The Enemy, 2004

One Shot, 2005

The Hard Way, 2006

Bad Luck and Trouble, 2007

Nothing to Lose, 2008

Gone Tomorrow, 2009

61 Hours, 2010

Worth Dying For, 2010

The Affair, 2011

A Wanted Man, 2012

Never Go Back, 2013

Personal, 2014

Make Me, 2015

Night School, 2016

The Midnight Line, 2017

Past Tense, 2018

Blue Moon, 2019

Novellas and Short Stories

Featuring Jack Reacher:

Published by Penguin Random House

Second Son, 2011

Deep Down, 2012

High Heat, 2013

Not a Drill, 2014

Small Wars, 2015

No Middle Name: The Complete Collected Short Stories, 2017

The Fourth Man (Random House Australia), 2018

'James Penney's New Identity', *Fresh Blood*, ed. Mike Ripley and
    Maxim Jakubowski (Do-Not-Press, 1999)

'Guy Walks into a Bar', *New York Times* (6 June 2009)

'Everyone Talks', *Esquire* (June/July 2012)

'No Room at the Motel', *Stylist* (December 2014)

'The Picture of the Lonely Diner', *Manhattan Mayhem*,
    ed. Mary Higgins Clark (Quirk, 2015)

'Maybe They Have a Tradition', *Country Life* (December 2016)

'Too Much Time', *No Middle Name: The Complete Collected Short Stories*
    (Bantam, 2017)

'The Christmas Scorpion', *Mail on Sunday* (December 2017)

'Smile', *Invisible Blood*, ed. Maxim Jakubowski (Titan, 2019)

Other

'Ten Keys', *The Cocaine Chronicles*, ed. Gary Phillips and Jervey Tervalon (Akashic, 2005)

'The Greatest Trick of All', *Greatest Hits*, ed. Robert Randisi (Carroll & Graf, 2005)

'Safe Enough', *Death Do Us Part*, ed. Harlan Coben (Little, Brown/Back Bay Books, 2006)

'The .50 Solution', *Bloodlines*, ed. Jason Starr and Maggie Estep (Vintage, 2006)

'Public Transportation', *Phoenix Noir*, ed. Patrick Millikin (Akashic, 2009)

'Grit in My Eye', *Woman & Home* (April 2010)

'Me and Mr Rafferty', *The Dark End of the Street*, ed. Jonathan Santlofer and S. J. Rozan (Bloomsbury USA, 2010)

'Section 7 (a) (Operational)', *Agents of Treachery*, ed. Otto Penzler (Vintage, 2010)

'The Bodyguard', *First Thrills*, ed. Lee Child (Forge, 2010)

'Addicted to Sweetness', *The Rich and the Dead*, ed. Nelson DeMille (Grand Central, 2011)

'The Bone-Headed League', *A Study in Sherlock* (Bantam, 2011)

'The Hollywood I Remember', *Vengeance*, ed. Lee Child (Mulholland, 2012)

'I Heard a Romantic Story', *Love is Murder*, ed. Sandra Brown (Mira, 2013)

'My First Drug Trial', *The Marijuana Chronicles*, ed. Jonathan Santlofer (Akashic, 2013)

'Wet With Rain', *Belfast Noir*, ed. Adrian McKinty and Stuart Neville (Akashic, 2015)

'The Truth About What Happened', *In Sunlight or in Shadow*, ed. Lawrence Block (Pegasus, 2016)

'My Rules', *Speaking of Work* (Xerox, 2017)

'Pierre, Lucien & Me', *Alive in Shape and Color*, ed. Lawrence Block (Pegasus, 2017)

'New Blank Document', *It Occurs to Me that I am America*, ed. Jonathan Santlofer (Touchstone, 2018)

'Shorty and the Briefcase', *Ten Year Stretch*, ed. Martin Edwards and Adrian Muller (Poisoned Pen Press/No Exit Press, 2018)

'Normal In Every Way', *Deadly Anniversaries*, ed. Marcia Muller and Bill Pronzini (Hanover Square Press, 2020)

'Dying for a Cigarette', *The Nicotine Chronicles*, ed. Lee Child (Akashic, 2020)

Collected Fiction and Non-fiction
A Little Gold Book of Unconsidered Trifles (Borderlands Press, 2021)

Selected Non-fiction
'Jack Reacher', *The Lineup*, ed. Otto Penzler (Little, Brown/Back Bay Books, 2009)

'Living with Music: A Playlist', *New York Times* (20 May 2009)

'Theseus and the Minotaur', *Thrillers: 100 Must Reads*, ed. David Morrell and Hank Wagner (Oceanview Publishing, 2010)

'Why Anyone Can Write American', *Daily Mail* (30 January 2010)

'Speech Day 2010', *King Edward's Gazette* (2011)

'Ian Fleming: The Empire Strikes Back', *Daily Mail* (29 September 2012)

'So Real You Can Sense the Artifice', *Wall Street Journal* (5 October 2012)

'A Simple Way to Create Suspense', *New York Times* (8 December 2012)

'By the Book', *New York Times* (20 December 2012)

'Paul McCartney, Action Hero', *Wall Street Journal* (30 August 2013)

'Give Me Cowans Over Cruise', Aston Villa matchday programme (16 January 2016)

'The Frightening Power of Fiction', *New Yorker* (9 May 2016)

'No. 1 in America', *New York Times* (7 October 2016)

'We'll Be Done Soon, and the Planet Will Recover', *New Statesman* (12 June 2017)

'The Fortune Cookie', *Anatomy of Innocence: Testimonies of the Wrongfully Convicted* (Liveright, 2017)

'Lee Child on Birmingham', *Guardian* (8 September 2018)

The Hero (TLS Books, 2019)

'Lee Child', *Dear NHS: 100 Stories to Say Thank You*, ed. Adam Kay (Orion, 2020)

'Never Outline!', *How to Write a Mystery: A Handbook by Mystery Writers of America*, ed. Lee Child with Laurie R. King (Scribner, 2021)

Selected Secondary Literature
This biography is largely based on my many interviews with Lee Child and others, his own introductions to the collectors' editions of his novels produced to date by the Mysterious Bookshop, his introductions to the Transworld editions of the novels of John D. MacDonald (branded in the style of the Reacher

books), and on events at which I have heard him speak, in particular: New York's ThrillerFest 2016 and 2017, St Hilda's Mystery & Crime Conference 2016, Sheffield's Off the Shelf festival 2017, Harrogate's Theakston Old Peculier Crime Writing Festival 2017 and 2018, and Bristol's CrimeFest 2018. I have drawn extensively on his private archive, held at the University of East Anglia, on back numbers of the *Chronicle* and *Gazette* from the archive of King Edward's School, Birmingham, and on the blogs, reviews and interviews collected (and until 2020 accessible) on his official website: www.leechild.com.

Not all sources below are cited but all those that are have been listed, with the exception of podcasts and broadcast interviews, which are referenced in the text (and in numerous cases no longer accessible).

Barber, John, 'First Impressions: "A Midsummer Night's Dream", RSC, August 1970', *Independent* (1 February 2008; first published in the *Daily Telegraph*)

Barnes, Clive, 'Theater: Historic Staging of "Dream"', *New York Times* (28 August 1970)

Beahm, George, *The Jack Reacher Field Manual: An Unofficial Companion to Lee Child's Novels* (BenBella Books, 2016)

Beckett, Samuel, *Waiting for Godot* (Grove Press, 1954)

Bidinotto, Robert, 'An Interview with Lee Child: Parts 1, 2 & 3', *The Vigilante Author* (13, 14, 17 October 2011)

Bishop, Rob, *Euros & Villans* (E & T Publishing, 2018)

—, 'Reach for a Villa Thriller', AVFC Official (2011)

Borges, Jorge Luis, *Obras completas* (Emecé, 1976)

Brook, Peter, *The Empty Space* (Penguin, 2008; first published 1968)

Brown, Josie, 'Digging Up the Past', *The Big Thrill* (31 October 2018)

Clinton, Bill, 'By the Book', *New York Times* (13 June 2018)

Coe, Jonathan, *Middle England*, (Penguin, 2018)

—, *The Rotters' Club* (Viking, 2001)

Crampton, Robert, 'Lee Child Talks Jack Reacher, Tom Cruise and New Book *The Hero*', *The Times* (23 November 2019)

Darnford-Slater, John, *Commando: Memoirs of a Fighting Commando in World War Two* (Greenhill, 1991)

Dawber, Tony, 'A Spellbinding Thriller', *Lancaster Guardian* (4 July 1997)

Day, Peter, 'The Rise and Fall of Britain's Steel Industry', *BBC News* (22 May 2016)

Drabble, Margaret, 'Books that Made Me', *Guardian* (18 January 2019)

Ewing, Sarah, 'Lee Child: Me and My Motor', *Sunday Times* (15 July 2018)

Fitzwalter, Raymond, *The Dream that Died: The Rise and Fall of ITV* (Matador, 2008)

Gapper, John, 'Lunch with the FT: Lee Child', *Financial Times* (15 July 2011)

Gekoski, Rick, 'Why I Love Lee Child's Jack Reacher Novels', *Guardian* (24 August 2019)

Gladwell, Malcolm, 'The Lawless Pleasures of Lee Child's Jack Reacher Novels', *New Yorker* (9 September 2015)

Graham, Natalie, 'Writer Had Thrilling Escape from Debt', *Sunday Times* (26 May 2002)

Haythorne, Jodie, 'Lee Is Set to Make a Killing', *Lancaster Guardian* (2 May 1997)

Heathcote, Charlotte, 'Moral Code Behind Lee Child's Success', *Express* (30 October 2011)

Heisler, Todd, 'Lee Child and the Macho of Minimalism', *New York Times* (1 September 2013)

Higgins, Charlotte, 'Fearless, Free and Feminist: The Enduring Appeal of Jack Reacher', *Guardian* (18 October 2019)

Inglis, Simon, 'Last Rites for the Holy Trinity', *Guardian* (13 May 2000)

—, *Villa Park: 100 Years* (Sports Projects Ltd, 1997)

Jordan, Jon, 'Interview with Tasha Alexander and Andrew Grant', *Crimespree*, no. 48 (August/September 2012)

Karim, Ali, 'The Persuasive Lee Child', *January* (May 2003)

Keates, Nancy, 'Reacher's Minimalist Roost', *Wall Street Journal* (7 May 2010)

Lanchester, John, 'How Jack Reacher Was Built', *New Yorker* (7 November 2016)

Leith, Sam, 'Looking Up to Jack Reacher', *Times Literary Supplement* (13 July 2018)

Levin, Martin, 'Q&A: Lee Child', *Globe and Mail* (30 September 2011)

Lodge, David, *Nice Work* (Secker & Warburg, 1988)

Martin, Andy, 'Lee Child: Adventures of an Over-Reacher', *Independent* (3 December 2010)

—, 'Lee Child on Jack Reacher: How the Best-selling Author Writes His Mysteries', *Independent* (5 January 2015)

—, 'The Man with No Plot', *The Conversation* (27 November 2015)

---, '*Nothing to Lose* by Lee Child', *Independent* (2 April 2008)

—, 'The Professor on Lee Child's Shoulder', *New York Times* (22 November 2015)

—, *Reacher Said Nothing: Lee Child and the Making of* Make Me (Penguin Random House, 2015; Polity Press, 2020)

—, *With Child: Lee Child and the Readers of Jack Reacher* (Polity Press, 2019)

Maslin, Janet, 'Action Hero Travels Light and Often Takes the Bus', *New York Times* (9 June 2005)

—, 'Brothers in Crime Writing: The Tyro and the Veteran', *New York Times* (13 May 2009)

—, 'A Gentler Jack Reacher Emerges in Lee Child's Latest Novel', *New York Times* (8 November 2017)

—, 'Jack Reacher Is Still Restless: But His Creator Has Settled Down', *New York Times* (23 October 2019)

—, 'Tough Guy at the Border of Hope and Despair', *New York Times* (2 June 2008)

McGrath, Charles, 'Creating a Don Quixote of the Cheap Motel Circuit', *New York Times* (3 June 2008)

Mendelsohn, Daniel, *An Odyssey: A Father, A Son and An Epic* (William Collins, 2017)

Meyer, Mary, 'Crime Writer Gets a Kick from Renoir', *Sunday Times* (20 April 2008)

Monsarrat, Nicholas, *The White Rajah* (Cassel & Company Ltd, 1961)

Nash, Graham, *Wild Tales* (Crown Archetype, 2013)

Nelson, Victoria, 'The Non-attachment Virtue', *Times Literary Supplement* (7 December 2018)

Odell, Michael, 'This Pencil Changes Lives', *Esquire* (October 2012)

O'Donnell, Paraic, 'End of the Real Jack Reacher?', *Irish Times* (20 January 2020)

Oney, Steve, 'Lee Child', *Playboy* (October 2012)

Parker, James, 'Jack Reacher Still Won't Quit', *Atlantic* (December 2018)

Persaud, Joy, 'If I Ruled the World: Lee Child', *Reader's Digest* (July 2018)

Poole, Steven, 'Haruki Murakami', *Guardian* (13 September 2014)

—, 'Personal by Lee Child Review', *Guardian* (4 September 2014)

Rubinstein, Mark, 'The Emotional Contract of Jack Reacher, *CrimeReads* (30 April 2018)

Sanderson, Caroline, 'Lee Child on Jack Reacher', *Penguin* (27 November 2018)

Sexton, David, 'Clash of the Titans – Lee Child vs Ian McEwan', *Evening Standard* (31 March 2010)

Sheehan, Jacqueline, 'Lee Child and Paul Doiron', *Writer* (22 April 2019)

Sherez, Stav, 'Five Reasons Why the Jack Reacher Novels Are Brilliant', *Spectator* (19 October 2016)

Simpson, Dave, 'Made of Steel: How South Yorkshire Became the British Indie Heartland', *Guardian* (2 February 2018)

Smith, Emma, *This is Shakespeare* (Pelican, 2019)

Solnit, Rebecca, 'Flight', in *The Faraway Nearby* (Viking, 2013)

—, 'Grandmother Spider', in *Men Explain Things to Me* (Haymarket, 2014)

Standish, David, 'Kurt Vonnegut', *Playboy* (July 1973)

Stasio, Marilyn, 'Crime', *New York Times* (22 July 2001)

Styron, William, *Sophie's Choice* (Random House, 1979)

Sutherland, Amy, 'Lee Child Reads "Anything"', *Boston Globe* (29 August 2015)

Tayler, Christopher, 'I Just Hate the Big Guy', *London Review of Books* (4 February 2016)

Trott, Anthony, *No Place for Fop or Idler: The Story of King Edward's School, Birmingham* (James & James, 1992)

Upton, Chris, 'A Lost Masterpiece: Birmingham's Original King Edward's School', *Birmingham Post* (4 March 2011)

Vinjamuri, David, 'The Strongest Brand in Publishing Is . . .', *Forbes* (4 March 2014)

Weiner, Rex, 'Lee Child', *High Times* (22 November 2017)

Wouk, Herman, *War and Remembrance* (Little, Brown and Company 1978)

—, *The Winds of War* (Little, Brown and Company, 1971)

Wray, Daniel Dylan, 'Sheffield's Sound Map Helps Reveal the City's Aural Character', *Guardian* (25 October 2013)

Wright, Abbe, 'A Conversation with Andrew Grant and Lee Child', *Read It Forward* (2019)

Zephaniah, Benjamin, 'Seven Deadly Sins of Football: Villa Fans, Violence and Me' (*Guardian*, 17 May 2009)

Additional credits

The poem 'Canal-Side in Birmingham' by Andy Forbes is reproduced by kind permission of the author.

Quotations from Martin Bell, David Liddiment, Jude Kelly and Tony Brill are taken from Fitzwalter.

The song 'Nature Boy', first released in 1948 by Nat King Cole for Capitol Records, was written by eden ahbez [*sic*].

Acknowledgements

My heartfelt thanks are due to all the teachers, friends and colleagues of Jim Grant who so generously contributed to this biography, many of whom appear in the book; likewise to friends and colleagues of Lee Child. I am especially grateful for the early encouragement of Harold Bloom, Gillian Beer, Dan O'Hara and Carl Cederström; to the Graduate Center at CUNY for supporting a year of research in New York; and to Joy Connolly, Giancarlo Lombardi and Brian Peterson for hosting the 2018 Lee Child Seminars. The staff at King Edward's School in Birmingham and the British Archive for Contemporary Writing at the University of East Anglia – in particular archivist Justine Mann – have given unstintingly of their expertise, as has Tamsin Rosewell of Kenilworth Books. I am indebted to my agent Sarah Such, to my editors Andreas Campomar and Bernadette Marron, and to publicity and marketing duo Jess Gulliver and Aimee Kitson along with the rest of the terrific team at Little, Brown UK.

Lee's first readers were the members of his immediate family; the same is true for me, and their belief throughout has sustained me. But above all my lifelong thanks go to Lee himself, for his spellbinding stories, for giving so freely of his time and thoughts, and – despite his unwavering conviction that the writer remains subordinate to his characters – for agreeing to the idea in the first place.

Index